APPRECIATION AND HISTORY OF ART

APPRECIATION AND HISTORY OF ART

AIDAN O'SULLIVAN

'Still-life with a Mandolin', Pablo Picasso (National Gallery of Ireland, Dublin).

GILL & MACMILLAN

Gill & Macmillan Ltd
Hume Avenue, Park West
Dublin 12
with associated companies throughout the world
www.gillmacmillan.ie
© Aidan O'Sullivan 1998
0 7171 1666 2

Index compiled by Helen Litton
Design and print origination in Ireland by
Denis Baker, The Unlimited Design Company, Dublin
Colour repro by Ultragraphics, Dublin

The paper used in this book is made from the wood pulp of managed forests. For every tree felled, at least one tree is planted, thereby renewing natural resources.

CONTENTS

INTRODUCTION

1. APPRECIATION OF ART   3

2. APPRECIATION OF DESIGN   14

EUROPEAN ART

3. THE MEDIEVAL PERIOD: ROMANESQUE AND GOTHIC STYLES   27
   ROMANESQUE: ELEVENTH AND TWELFTH CENTURIES   27
   GOTHIC: MID-TWELFTH CENTURY TO FIFTEENTH CENTURY   36

4. FIFTEENTH AND SIXTEENTH CENTURIES   52
   FIFTEENTH CENTURY: EARLY RENAISSANCE   52
   SIXTEENTH CENTURY: HIGH RENAISSANCE AND MANNERISM   68

5. SEVENTEENTH AND EIGHTEENTH CENTURIES   92
   SEVENTEENTH CENTURY   92
   EIGHTEENTH CENTURY   110

6. NINETEENTH AND TWENTIETH CENTURIES   124
   NINETEENTH CENTURY   124
   TWENTIETH CENTURY   155

IRISH ART

7. PRE-CHRISTIAN IRELAND   189
   THE STONE AGE: 7000–2000 B.C.   189
   THE BRONZE AGE: 2000–500 B.C.   193
   THE IRON AGE: 500 B.C.–A.D. 400   197

8. THE CHRISTIAN CELTIC PERIOD   202
   EARLY CHRISTIAN IRELAND: FIFTH AND SIXTH CENTURIES   202
   HIGH CHRISTIAN IRELAND: SEVENTH AND EIGHTH CENTURIES   207
   THE VIKING INVASIONS: NINTH AND TENTH CENTURIES   215

9. THE MEDIEVAL PERIOD   225
   IRISH ROMANESQUE: ELEVENTH AND TWELFTH CENTURIES   225
   THE ANGLO-NORMAN PERIOD: 1169–C. 1600   233

10 SEVENTEENTH AND EIGHTEENTH CENTURIES   242
   SEVENTEENTH CENTURY   242
   EIGHTEENTH CENTURY: IRISH GEORGIAN PERIOD   244

11. NINETEENTH AND TWENTIETH CENTURIES   257
   NINETEENTH CENTURY   257
   TWENTIETH CENTURY   267

   INDEX   293

   ACKNOWLEDGMENTS   311

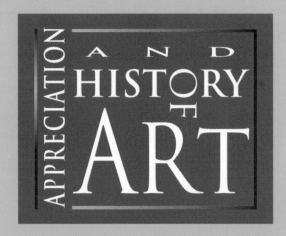

APPRECIATION AND HISTORY OF ART

INTRODUCTION

1

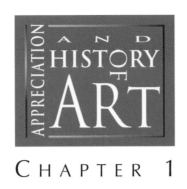

CHAPTER 1

APPRECIATION OF ART

There are so many ways to examine a work of art that even among experts there is no consensus as to the best way to come to an understanding of a piece. Worth is often confused with value when, in fact, the value of a work of art is a completely separate issue from its aesthetic qualities.

We should never allow ourselves to be distracted by the monetary value of one piece over another. It is important to remember that art dealing has more in common with the stock market than with the appreciation of art. Many issues beyond the strength and beauty of a particular work contribute to its monetary or collectable value, e.g. its rarity, age, size, the materials of which it is made; but although these considerations may have a bearing in assessing the market value of a work of art, they have none on our enjoyment of the work. [1,1]

Individual taste guides our preferences in art just as it does in music or fashion, and as our tastes in music and fashion change and develop so do our tastes in art. Different times and societies dictate taste in art. What is acceptable in one generation or society may be rejected by the next. Although art can be used by totalitarian governments to help control the thinking of their citizens, people are generally free to examine a work of art with an open mind and to accept or reject any aspects of historical or current art they choose. [1,2]

[1,1] Detail from 'A Still Life', 1651, by Pieter Claesz, oil on panel, 50 x 69 cm (National Gallery of Ireland, Dublin).
The amazing detail and finish in this valuable painting may not be to everyone's taste, though it is a masterpiece of genre painting.

Approaching art with an open mind is vitally important, although at times challenging and difficult. An understanding of the art of cultures that are distant in time or space from our own or of abstract art can require patience. Statements in the popular media may colour our views and make any kind of objective understanding more difficult. On the other hand, art is used more in popular culture than ever before, with past works

[1,2] 'Armstrong in the Cafe de Madrid, Madrid', c. 1900, by Walter Osborne, pencil on paper, 15 x 10.1 cm (National Gallery of Ireland, Dublin). A simple pencil sketch can sometimes have as much character and vitality as has much more elaborate work.

[1,3] Benetton poster.

or styles or newly commissioned pieces appearing in advertising campaigns. The controversial Benetton posters in the mid-1990s are an example of this type of work which is, supposedly, first a work of art and second an advertisement. [1,3]

For a proper appreciation, a work of art should be seen in the original. Images in books or on film or video have been translated through another medium, so the real colour, texture or size of an object may be lost. The pictures in this book are smaller in size, smoother in surface and distorted in colour through the printing process, in comparison with the original works of art they represent. It is important, therefore, to see some works firsthand so that the full range of artistic expression can be appreciated. Paintings and sculptures are often more loosely and ruggedly finished in reality than they appear in books, which can be encouraging for people who wish to make art themselves.

EXAMINING A WORK OF ART

In the same way that language and music change over the centuries, so do the visual language of the artist and the materials that are used. A medieval painting and a nineteenth-century painting are different in so many ways that we can only fully appreciate the work when we know a little about the society and technology from which it emerged. In the twentieth century styles and movements are closely interrelated, which makes it difficult to understand any work in isolation. [1,4]

A METHOD TO HELP WITH EXAMINING A WORK OF ART

The following is a method to help you examine a work of art. It is designed as a flexible plan to help gather the information you need to be able to discuss or write an account of a work of art. It is general enough to apply to painting, sculpture or other forms of art from any time or culture, whether seen in the original or in reproduction.

1. Begin with the name of the artist, the title and date of the work and any background information available to you. The background may include some biographical details on the artist, his/her training and his/her associations with movements

TECHNIQUE

[1,4] Composition sketches from different periods of art history.

A. Medieval paintings were decorative and symbolic.

B. Renaissance paintings created methods to show volume and space.

C. Baroque art was full of movement and drama in light and colour.

D. 20th-century painting sometimes combines elements from different cultures and phases of art.

and ideas of the time. The title or lack of it may point to issues of the artist's time or may simply describe the subject or idea behind the work.

2. Look carefully at the work. Make a small sketch of it, noting the size and proportions accurately. Give yourself some time to think about your reactions to it and make notes on your initial impressions. Making a sketch helps you pay closer attention to the work. Keep it simple. Note the basic composition and arrangement of line and tone. Do not concern yourself with details in your sketch.

3. Think about the subject of the work, the objects, ideas, style or influences that are addressed. Has the artist tried to express feelings or emotions or to arouse them in the viewer?

4. Try to determine whether the work is made of wood, stone, metal, canvas, plastics or a combination of materials. What has been done to the materials? For example, have they been carved, painted or assembled in some way?

5. Note the artist's handling of the materials. Materials and the artist's use of them change at various times in the history of art. Handling of materials can also be a mode of expression, particularly in nineteenth- and twentieth-century European art.

6. See how the formal elements of line, tone, colour, texture, form, pattern, shape, space, composition and structure were handled by the artist, how they were combined and which elements, if any, were emphasised and to what end.

7. Consider your own reactions to the work, your basic like or dislike of it, any thoughts or feelings it evoked in you. What do you think the artist was trying to achieve? For what audience was the work intended?

EXAMPLE

An example of how this method can be applied will help with your own explorations in the art world. We will use Paul Cézanne's 'Montagne Sainte-Victoire' as our example. [1,5]

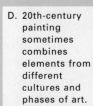

Most of what is written in the following example can be observed in the painting. The biographical detail can be found in your textbook. The structure is not meant as a formula for writing essays, but as a method to help with the examination of a work of art and to point out the sort of questions you might ask yourself so as to reach an understanding of a painting or sculpture.

• 'Paul Cézanne's painting "Montagne Sainte Victoire" was produced between 1885 and 1887 when he was working near his family home in Aix-en-Provence. He was trying to find a way to represent the landscape without using the conventions and academic clichés of his time. He wanted to make something more solid and permanent out of Impressionism. He had exhibited with the Impressionists in 1874 and 1877 and was a close friend of Pissarro, but he was not satisfied with their fugitive representations of light and tried to make a structural analysis of nature which can be seen in the colours and planes of the painting "Montagne Sainte-Victoire".'

Depending on what you are writing, or the question you have been asked, this biographical and contextual information can be extended by reference to exhibition catalogues in the case of contemporary work or textbooks in the case of historical pieces.

When making a sketch, first make a grid that joins the diagonals of the format and the centrepoint of each side of the format. A similar grid can be applied to a sculpture, possibly from a number of viewpoints if you are looking at the original. It is important to get the basic height and width proportions as accurate as possible, as otherwise the whole composition will be out of shape. [1,6]

Visualise this grid on the piece of art you are studying, using a pencil or ruler as a guide, and transfer the important elements of the composi-

[1,5] 'Montagne Sainte Victoire', c. 1887, by Paul Cézanne, oil on canvas, 66.6 x 91.7 cm (Courtauld Gallery, London).

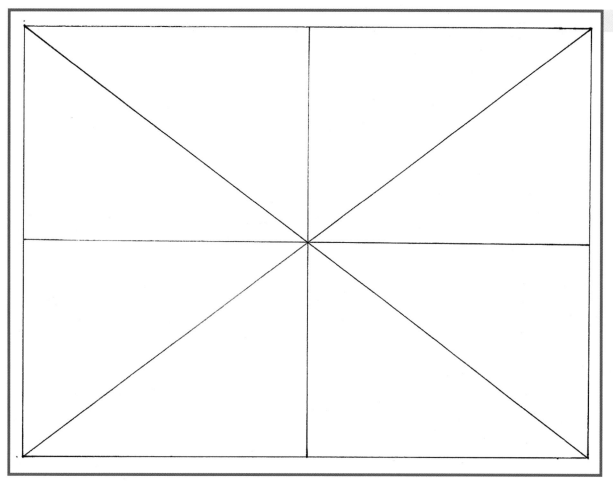

tion onto your sketch. The grid lines will often coincide with elements of the composition. In 'Montagne Sainte Victoire' they may help you notice the balance between areas of dark and light and the geometry of the receding lines in the farmland in the foreground. [1,7]

• 'The first things I noticed about the painting were the unusual use of colour and the underlying fragmented geometry.'

• 'At first glance the subject is an unremarkable piece of landscape framed by a pine tree but beneath the surface is a struggle to create a new structure using colour and geometry to express what Cézanne had learnt from prolonged close observation of the landscape. Elements of Impressionist brushwork and colour are still present but the emphasis on line and structure goes beyond Impressionism or academic drawing. The painting does not have a conventional perspective but relies on colour harmonies and line to hold the composition together.

This is not a "pretty" painting, Cézanne is not interested in conventional beauty, though that is not to say that his paintings are not attractive. It is the inner beauty and logic of nature that motivates him. His work is intellectual rather than emotional.'

• 'Montagne Sainte Victoire' is an oil painting on canvas. The brushwork is descriptive. Cézanne uses brush direction and various sizes of marks to help with the description of the landscape. The looser, more vigorous brushwork in the greenery of the pine tree suggests movement and creates a soft focus which diverts attention away to the more sharply painted mountain.'

Cézanne's use of line, tone, colour and the other formal elements breaks with tradition and would require a lot of space to discuss in any depth, so here we will only skim over the more obvious points which can be seen in this painting.

• 'Line is a very important element in this painting and is used in a number of ways. The

[1,7] Sketch of painting of Montagne Sainte Victoire on grid.

straight edges of fields and buildings are emphasised to direct our attention into the composition. The outlines of the major objects such as the tree and mountain are clearly drawn to help us focus on the important elements in the picture.

Tone and colour are used jointly to create depth and form. The warm dark greens and strong ochres give strength to the foreground; the softer tones and cooler colours of the receding landscape help create the illusion of space and the alternating ochres and purples describe the folds in the mountain. [1,8]

Texture was already looked at under the treatment of materials, and form is largely controlled by line and colour. Pattern is an important element in the painting, with shapes and colours alternating in a receding scale. Even the shapes used to describe the folds of the hills are repeated.

Cézanne's great contribution to the development of European art was his new convention for the description of shape and space which did not rely on traditional modelling and perspective. An examination of separate parts of the painting will reveal that the perspective in one area does not necessarily match that in another and that some parts are almost isolated from adjoining areas. Yet, the sense of space and volume is convincing. Cézanne tries to re-create the way we look at real landscape, noting one area, then another, getting a different view by moving our position. His paintings are more like a walk through the landscape than a 'view' from a single spot.

The composition and structure of the painting also break with convention. Traditional composition divided pictures into geometric shapes or movements, whereas Cézanne draws our attention back into space and then returns forward through his use of line, tone and colour.'

Looking at the painting, you should see the potential for a fuller description of any of the areas touched on above, depending on what you are trying to show in your writing.

• 'The longer I look at and the more I think about Cézanne's 'Montagne Sainte Victoire' the more I am drawn to it. It is a painting I did not immediately connect with because my expectations of a traditional landscape painting were not met. When I thought about what Cézanne had achieved and began to see it for myself, I could understand the excitement his work created in young artists of the late nineteenth century. He dared to isolate himself from his contemporaries and develop completely new theories and conventions in painting which he could accept and work with. He lived with the ridicule of even his friends in his search to find an honest means of expression for his art. His ability to create an alternative to the conventions of 300 years made him the father of modern painting.'

VISITING AN EXHIBITION

A gallery or museum is an environment designed to display artifacts to advantage so the visitor can appreciate and understand the work in a context which provides focus for the display. When museums and galleries were first constructed in the eighteenth and nineteenth centuries, large halls were filled with paintings, sculptures or display cases and work was often grouped simply by size or for some other arbitrary reason rather than by any plan. As time went on and collections grew larger, work was separated by style, date or country of origin, but remained tightly grouped and using natural light only. [1,9]

In the twentieth century the influence of display art has crept into museums and galleries, and much more thought and attention go into the arrangement of exhibits. With the advent of information technology, background and reference material is available on-screen in many public exhibitions.

The curator of a museum or gallery has an enormous influence on how the work in the collection is understood and appreciated by the public. The layout of the rooms can control the way the public moves through the exhibition, and the selection and grouping of pieces can add to the understanding of the work on display. The

[1,9] The Lord Lieutenant opening the National Gallery of Ireland, Dublin, January 1864. (Wood engraving from National Gallery of Ireland, Dublin.)

[1,11] Display in the Treasury, National Museum of Ireland, Dublin.

arrangement of space in the National Gallery of Ireland in Dublin is a good example of how trends in displaying art have changed over the years. [1,10]

The National Museum of Ireland houses examples of a number of different ways of displaying artifacts. Some of the old Victorian glass cases are still in use, with objects of similar date or style identified by little tags and grouped in large numbers. In another area Bronze Age gold is displayed with fewer pieces and more information. Careful lighting and background materials create an environment which shows the objects to greatest advantage. The Egyptian Room creates a walk-through history of ancient Egypt

with subdued lighting and carefully arranged material. The quiet darkened space cuts the visitor off from the distractions of the rest of the museum, allowing him/her to concentrate on the beautiful artifacts on display. [1,11]

Different kinds of exhibition demand different arrangements of layout, lighting and display material. The visitor should note these features and see how they affect access to and enjoyment of the material shown. [1,12]

[1,10] Interior view of National Gallery of Ireland, Dublin.

[1,12] People viewing an exhibition.

LENS ART: PHOTOGRAPHY, CINEMA, VIDEO

PHOTOGRAPHY

Photography is now a well-established art form, capable of a range of expression comparable to painting yet different from traditional painting and drawing in its materials and methods of creation. A photographic artist does not 'handle' his or her materials the way a traditional artist does, but modern technology allows the photographic artist a much greater level of intervention in the process than was formerly possible.

Photographs made as art can look very different from the photographs we are used to seeing as illustrations in newspapers, magazines or advertisements. Art photography may be abstract,

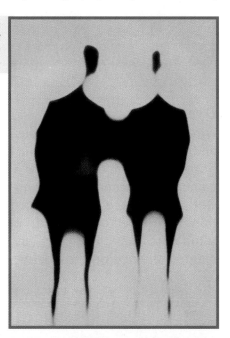

[1,13(a)] Two Men: Shadows on Yellow Background, Jason Beck.

[1,13(b)] Ban the Bomb sign, made up of arms, Ellen Carey.

surreal or expressionist depending on the intentions of the photographer. [1,13(a)] and [1,13(b)] Many of the criteria used to examine paintings can also be used in relation to photographs.

CINEMA

Cinema, the most powerful art medium in the twentieth century, is a relatively new art form. The combination of sound and vision makes it the most complete artistic experience available. It is also the most accessible, being available cheaply in public cinemas or at home on television or video. The power of cinema to tell a story or communicate an idea is unrivalled by other media.

When approaching cinema as art we should try to become aware of how the elements of sound, colour, lighting, camerawork, special effects, direction and editing affect our enjoyment of a film and how the art director uses make-up, costumes, settings and props to support the storyline and atmosphere of the film. [1,14]

SOUND

Sound can be a very important element in a film. The music of the soundtrack helps create atmosphere and a range of dramatic effects from joy to danger to sorrow, mirroring what is happening on-screen or reminding the audience of other times, places and atmospheres. The sound of the actor's or narrator's voice not only tells the story but creates atmosphere through accent or tone of voice. The incidental sounds of nature or man-made sounds again help in the creation of atmosphere and storyline. A darkened room with traffic sounds and sirens in the background places the viewer in a city; the sound

[1,14] Still from Irish film, Into the West.

11

of birds and running water creates a rural atmosphere. Sounds, voices and music can be very evocative and affect our reactions to any situation.

COLOUR AND LIGHTING

Colour and lighting have great significance in the appearance of a film. Dark colours and low lighting create an atmosphere of threat and danger, while bright colours and lighting have a lighter or more joyous effect. Some films may be colour co-ordinated to create a certain atmosphere with lighting, costumes and backgrounds chosen to complement the required effect. [1,15]

[1,15] Lighting can be used to create mood and atmosphere

CAMERAWORK

Camerawork can be a crucial element in the final appearance of a film. The framing of shots and the timing of close-ups and wide shots can change the effectiveness of a scene. A low camera angle can make a scene look dominating and threatening while the same scene viewed from high up may lose its menace.

Modern technology has made cameras smaller, lighter and easier to operate, allowing a new range of options for cinematographers. The steadycam is a specially balanced hand-held camera which allows smoother movements than were formerly possible without special rigs and machinery. In many respects the cameraman is one of the chief artists involved in film making. He/she frames the constantly changing image which we see in the cinema.

SPECIAL EFFECTS

Special effects are as old as cinema but the introduction of computer-generated images has created amazing possibilities, particularly in science fiction films. Photographed images can be merged with computer effects, and objects can be distorted and changed through computer programmes. As personal computers become more powerful, this technology is becoming more available to the general public. [1,16]

[1,16] Still from *Space Truckers*

DIRECTION

Directors are often as famous as the actors and actresses who appear in their films. The director brings a vision to the film. He/she decides on camera angles and the movements of the actors as well as the pace and style of the whole production. The director demands or encourages high standards from the actors and crew and has a major influence on the quality of the film. [1,17]

[1,17] Irish film director, Neil Jordan, checking the camera angles, with Ian Wilson, director of photography in *The Crying Game*.

EDITING

Editing takes place after the film is shot. The editor joins the scenes and soundtrack together, selecting from film taken by different cameras shooting the same scene from different viewpoints. Special effects and scenes shot in different times and places are all connected in a way that best tells the story of the film. The editor and director decide together on the final appearance of the film, reducing weeks or months of photography and acting to a film of less than a few hours' duration.

When we watch a good film the separate elements (direction, acting, lighting, camerawork, special effects, etc.) are not obvious. The storyline and atmosphere of the film are the focus of our attention. However, if we think about it afterwards or view it a second time we may be able to analyse the work. The enjoyment and critical analysis of any film we see are enhanced when we understand the film-making process.

VIDEO

Video making is a process closely related to film, but the differences in technology create their own problems and opportunities. Video is photographed for the television screen, which is smaller than the cinema screen and thus demands a more intimate but less detailed image.

Work videoed for television needs a constantly changing image to keep the attention of the audience who are in their own homes surrounded by alternative attractions and interests. This attention-getting imagery is at its most intense in advertisements which may only last thirty or forty seconds and have to tell a story or make a statement in that short time. It can be instructive to study advertisements and see how different ideas and concepts are delivered. Humour, drama, special effects, puzzles and borrowed images are all used to grab the attention of the viewer. Television advertising is often backed up by posters, newspaper and magazine advertising and point of sale display.

Videos made to promote music have become an art form in their own right. Images are photographed and combined with newly released music to produce music videos. A number of television stations specialise in showing music videos, most of which only last three or four minutes, so the challenge for the director is to provide images that will increase interest in the music. One of the simpler methods is to video the musicians performing in a number of settings and in different lighting conditions, using a variety of camera angles. These are then edited to follow the rhythm and lyrics in the music.

Some producers make mini-movies to enhance the music, with the full range of plot, camerawork and special effects that might be expected in a feature film. Viewing this type of pop video can be a good way to learn about the process of film making as they are short enough to replay and examine piece by piece as we try to work out why one angle or effect was chosen rather than another.

The study of film and video can provide a lifetime interest and enhance your enjoyment of film or video as art or simply entertainment.

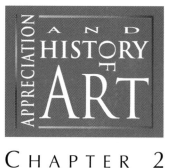
CHAPTER 2

APPRECIATION OF DESIGN

[2,1] Marking and cutting crystal, at Waterford crystal factory.

Design is a modern manifestation of man's need to control his environment. Designers are the people who plan the shape of our surroundings from motorways and cities to cutlery and shoes. In the past designers were also the potters, weavers and masons who made and sold their own products. Although some people still work in this way, it is now more common for designers simply to think, analyse, model or draw and make choices between materials or methods of manufacture, leaving others to carry out the practical work. [2,1] A good designer discusses the needs and the possibilities of the project with his/her client.

The basic requirements of good design are the same no matter what materials the designer is using. The product:

1. should suit the requirements of those for whom it was designed
2. should function properly and efficiently
3. should be made from suitable materials
4. should look well — be pleasing in shape, colour and texture.

ARCHITECTURE AND THE ENVIRONMENT

With the increase in world population man's impact on his environment has become even more important. The choices we make in Europe can have worldwide effects of which we are hardly aware. A building or manufacturing boom in Europe may have the effect of depleting forests and mineral resources in faraway places. Individually we may not be able to do much about the world situation, but if we are careful about buying renewable or recyclable products and take care with the disposal of wastes, we can play our part in the protection of the environment. [2,2]

[2,2] Polluted river.

[2,4]
Sculpture
on Earlsfort
Terrace,
Dublin.

On a smaller scale the environment is our surroundings — the urban or rural area in which we live. In recent years there have been general improvements in both rural and urban environments. Roadsides, parks, riverbanks and farms have been cleaned up and improved with greater thought to safety and visual appeal. The great sprawls of suburbs that surround our cities are now being built in smaller units with more green spaces and the centres of many towns and cities have been revitalised with new buildings and reconstructions of old ones. [2,3]

Sculpture is now included in many schemes. Roadside sculptures have been incorporated into the plans of new motorways and they also appear as part of urban and rural developments. [2,4]

Fitting large buildings into the rural environment is always a problem. The Office of Public Works have constructed a number of interpretative

centres in sensitive rural areas to help visitors interpret the landscape and places of historical and environmental interest. The Blasket Centre at Dunquin, Co. Kerry, is a large building containing an audio-visual theatre, exhibition and meeting rooms, a library, a bookshop and a restaurant. [2,5] It was designed to support the local community and to inform and entertain visitors. The outstanding element of the surrounding treeless landscape is the pattern of the field walls. The project architects for the Office of Public Works, Ciaran O'Connor and Gerard O'Sullivan, followed the orientation of the walls with the spine of the building and faced it in the same local stone from which the walls were built. The building is long and low and follows the slope of the landscape. Sculptures were commissioned as part of the project and are incorporated into the surroundings of the building.

[2,3] Urban sprawl, Crumlin, Dublin.

[2,5] Blasket Centre, Dunquin, County Kerry, by the Office of Public Works.

[2,6] Céide Fields Interpretative Centre, County Mayo, by the Office of Public Works. The stone, steel and glass pyramid protrudes from the landscape like a rock outcrop.

[2,7] The Green Building, Temple Bar, Dublin, by Murray O'Laoire Associates (completed 1994).

The Céide Fields Interpretative Centre in north Mayo is quite a different solution to a similar problem. [2,6] The building was designed to interpret the large Stone Age settlement that had been found under the blanket bog — the largest area of ancient stone walls discovered in Europe. Mary McKenna, the project architect for the Office of Public Works, designed a pyramid in stone, steel and glass which projects from the surface of the bog and makes a strong statement of man's presence in this otherwise empty coastal landscape.

Both projects have generated both controversy and praise, which demonstrates the kind of difficulty that is inherent in building in a sensitive landscape.

Building in an urban landscape is no less problematic. The architect still has to blend a new building into an existing environment. The choices of materials, height, size of doors and windows and the style of construction have to be judged against the function of the building and the needs of the client. This problem has been dealt with many times in Dublin's inner city where the Temple Bar and quays areas have been completely remodelled in the 1990s.

The architects Murray O'Laoire Associates designed the Green Building for Temple Bar Properties. [2,7] It was an attempt to make an environment- and people-friendly building in the heart of the city. Power comes from the renewable resources of wind and sunlight with back-up

from the ESB. Heat is taken from the bedrock and stored in an insulated water tank from where it can be pumped around the building. The roof of the central atrium can be opened in warm weather to allow heat and air to circulate and plants are used to oxygenate and humidify the air in winter. The building houses retail outlets, offices and apartments. The street front is largely a conventional modern design which harmonises with the scale and proportion of the surroundings. This building may simply be an experiment or it may point the way to a more environmentally responsible future.

Not far away from the Green Building, on Essex Quay, Temple Bar Properties have built Isolde's Tower Apartments, an apartment building with some office and public house space designed by the architects Gilroy McMahon. The new building adjoins Sunlight Chambers, an unusual construction in a Lombardo-Romanesque style which has a ceramic frieze running along its façade. The blue tile of the frieze is echoed in details of the new building and the roof line also follows through from the older building. The triple-glazed projecting bay windows which face the river acknowledge the noise and smell of the traffic on the quays. An open courtyard at the rear provides the air and light and an area to socialise in, away from the busy street. [2,8]

This building is not the standard red-brick, neo-Georgian solution to reconstruction which is seen all along the quays, yet it does manage to make itself an unobtrusive, if stylish, part of the streetscape.

[2,8] Isolde's Tower Apartments, Essex Quay, Dublin, by Gilroy McMahon Architects.

The wholesale destruction of older buildings which occurred in the 1970s and 1980s slowed down during the 1990s, and architects and planners began to reconstruct rather than demolish many fine stone and brick buildings. Examples of this type of renewal can be found in almost every town and city in Ireland.

Large-scale buildings which dominate their environment need to be looked at separately. Most university and college campuses have interesting structures which are designed to have their own impact. Shopping centres and large public or industrial buildings can also be designed to draw attention to themselves rather than blend into their surroundings.

Architects are required to work on a range of scales from small domestic buildings to huge industrial complexes. Their sensitivity to the surroundings of new buildings is as important a consideration as the building itself. [2,9]

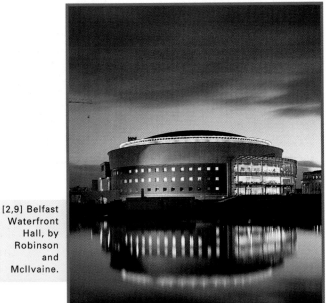

[2,9] Belfast Waterfront Hall, by Robinson and McIlvaine.

PRODUCT DESIGN

Industrial and product design has become an important part of the development of consumer products since the Second World War. The Bauhaus Design School in Germany during the 1920s and 1930s provided the groundwork for the connection between the designer and industry. The more affluent countries in Europe and America saw how good design could improve production and increase sales, and many large corporations developed their own design departments. Philips, [2,10] Braun and Olivetti developed company identities so that a link in shape and colour connected all their products and advertising. This kind of planning is common in almost every large business now.

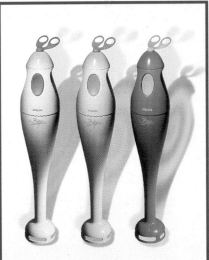

[2,10] Electrical products — Philips.

Designers are involved in such a range of products, from ships and aeroplanes to cutlery and pens, that it would be impossible to do anything more here than give some examples of the work of a designer.

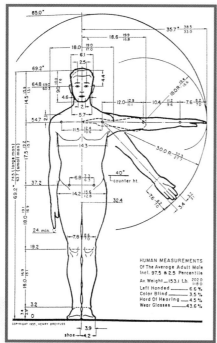

[2,11] Human measurement charts, by Henry Dreyfuss.

The American designer Henry Dreyfuss produced a book called *Designing for People* in 1955 and a series of charts on human measurement called *The Measure of Man* in 1960. [2,11] This literature helped form the basis of the study of 'ergonomics' which is the interaction between human beings and man-made objects. During the 1960s and 1970s furniture, hand tools and household machinery underwent a lot of revision in the light of ergonomic research.

Domestic objects like hairdryers, food mixers, electric drills and the whole range of cameras and video equipment have been intensely researched and their shape, colour and handling are aimed at different consumer groups. Personal stereos for teenagers look quite different from the equipment designed to suit their parents. [2,12] If you get

brochures or better still real equipment you can compare products in terms of colour and shape, placing of switches and buttons, how the equipment operates and handles. Use the basic requirements of good design outlined at the beginning of the chapter.

An outline of the development of telephones may help to show how changing materials and technology can affect the shape of a machine.

Early telephones worked through an operator. The caller lifted the telephone handset and told the operator who he/she wanted to call and the operator literally plugged a phone line into the line of the person being called. [2,13] As the number of users grew, this became very cumbersome, so automatic dialling was invented though this still required large mechanical switching systems. The introduction of digital technology allowed much larger numbers of calls to be processed and also increased reliability. Satellite communications made long-distance calls easier and quicker and microwave technology has produced the mobile phone.

[2,13] Changes in the design of telephones.

[2,12] Personal stereo.

Alongside all these changes in technology the shape of the telephone instrument was also changing. New materials were used in its construction and new ideas about handling and operation also influenced designs.

It can be interesting and instructive to trace the development of any man-made object from kettles to motor cars and note how changes in materials, technology and taste can affect their appearance and operation.

In the same way that artists and fashion designers can become well-known names and their signature can help sell products, some industrial designers, particularly in Italy, Scandinavia and Germany, have become symbols for style and increase the marketability of any product with which they are associated. Ferry Porsche, the designer of the Volkswagen Beetle, went on to design sportscars whose name became a status symbol.

[2,14] Otl Aicher's designs for the 1972 Munich Olympics.

GRAPHIC DESIGN

From simple beginnings in posters and advertising, graphic design has become an important element in twentieth-century culture. The symbols and images we are constantly bombarded with through the proliferation of old and new communication media are the work of the graphic designer.

A serious side of graphic design is the development of clear and easily understood signs and symbols to guide the public on motorways and in airports, hospitals and factories. The German designer Otl Aicher produced the pictograms which were used for the 1972 Munich Olympics. [2,14] Producing signs and images without words is an important element of the design brief for an international event. Aicher also designed symbols for logos of international companies like Lufthansa and Braun.

Company identity is an important consideration in a competitive world. Business people do not want their products or services to be mistaken for a competitor's, so the colour schemes, lettering and symbols they use need to be distinctive and capable of being used across their products, services, vehicles, communications and advertising. The investment this represents for a large company is considerable, so great care is taken with any choices or changes in logo, lettering and colour schemes. [2,15]

£122,042 /701·1·

In keeping with the need to be effective in an increasingly competitive and cluttered market place, Guinness, for example, seek to ensure that their brand identity is a consistent and high-quality expression of the company's identity.

The identity of Guinness consists of key visual elements associated with the brand — the Harp device, the holding device (gold lines), the Guinness wordmark and the Arthur Guinness signature.

There are two logo formats. The first format has been developed for on-trade communication, promotions, sponsorships, advertising and point of sale elements. The second has been developed for canned or bottled draught Guinness packaging (cans, bottles and packs) and off-trade

[2,15] Company identity.

[2,16] Roadside advertising.

refer to ideas and images from the history of art or cinema and which therefore would be difficult to understand for anyone who had grown up outside western culture. Sometimes a newspaper advertisement or poster can depend for its effect on the consumer being familiar with a television or cinema advertisement which in turn may convey its message by suggestion as much as by narrative.

The graphic designer is also responsible for the layout of books and magazines and packaging design. Many designers specialise in one area, such as magazine layout or the designing of CD covers and music-related promotions. [2,17] It can be interesting to compare books or magazines designed for different consumer groups and note the different layout pattern and use of colour and lettering that the designer chooses to aim the product at the target market.

[2,17] U2's 'Pop' CD cover.

communications. The single difference between these two logos is that the latter contains the word 'Draught' on the bottom part of the holding device (the bottom gold line).

Advertising design often links together a range of media — newspapers and magazines, television and cinema, and large roadside posters — in a sophisticated communication between designer and consumer. [2,16] A lot of modern advertising depends on humour or visual games which can

[2,18] Irish stamps.

Packaging design has become a very sophist-icated area of graphic design. With the growth of supermarket shopping in the second half of the twentieth century the consumer is faced with more choices of similar products sitting side-by-side on the shelf. The packaging designer uses colour, lettering, layout and images or symbols to give the consumer clues as to the nature and quality of the product and to try to influence him/her in the making of his/her choice at the point of sale.

The graphic designer works in many areas, but the design issues are similar whether a stamp [2,18] or an advertising campaign is being worked on. It is basically an exercise in visual communication in which the designer uses images, colours and words to put an idea to the public. The success or failure of the design depends on how readily it is understood by the viewer.

FASHION AND INTERIOR DESIGN

FASHION DESIGN

Most design is driven by changes in public taste. The challenge to the designer to anticipate and even to create new demands in consumer goods is at its most acute in the clothing industry. In the modern era, fashion designers and the models who show their clothes have become public icons and are given the same star treatment as actors and pop musicians. The fashions that are seen at the big seasonal shows of the top designers will

probably never appear on the streets of our towns or cities, at least not in their original forms. Many of the large fashion houses have a line of ready-made clothes which they sell through their own shops in the major cities of Europe and the USA. Fashion designers also lend their names to a range of accessories and perfumes they think will suit their designs. Many of these commercially driven goods with designer labels are a symbol of status in the consumer society.

The fashion business is highly technical with a huge range of possible materials and fabrics to choose from and with all the possibilities of cut and structure to consider. [2,19] Designers often 'quote' from styles of the past or from clothes of different cultures in their designs, which need to be fresh in colour, shape and fabric choice for each season. [2,20]

[2,19] Fashion design by Marc O'Neill for A Wear.

There have been enormous changes in the style, colour and fabrics used for sports and leisurewear. New technology has helped create fabrics which are waterproof and windproof but which still can breathe, allowing the wearer to remain comfortable even in extreme weather. Clothes in bright colours in these modern fabrics have also become fashion items, worn by all ages. The comfort and convenience of these clothes

[2,20] A Wear —
Marc O'Neill.

[2,21] Sports
or leisurewear.

[2,22] Casual clothes.

have brought them into everyday use from their beginnings in specialised sports and outdoor activities. [2,21]

Casual everyday wear is probably the largest market in the fashion business. As the twentieth century progressed the range of acceptable casual wear grew to the extent that now almost anything goes. The way we dress is often a statement of the social or economic group we feel we belong to or the sport or social activities in which we take part. [2,22]

In the world of work a dress code is often part of the environment. Uniforms of all kinds have become more common — staff in fast-food restaurants, shops and offices, workers in the

[2,23]
Uniform.

transport and other industries may all be required to wear special clothes. It can be interesting to look at a range of uniforms and work out the kind of statement different styles and colours make to the public. [2,23]

The fashion business is very complicated, with so many different levels and aspects to it. You might begin your study of this area of design by looking at the style of clothes you are interested in yourself and investigating the advantages and limitations of fabrics you like and how they can be made into clothes that you might like to wear.

INTERIOR DESIGN

Interior design has become a growth industry with increasing affluence in western society. Businesses, hotels and factories all take a greater interest in the working environment of their staff and customers, realising that pleasant surroundings can improve work rates and relations with customers. [2,24]

The areas of ergonomics (already looked at under product design), colour, materials and style are all considerations in interior design. The ambience created in pubs, restaurants and shops is a result of the combination of these considerations.

In the home the efficiency of a kitchen or workroom can be greatly affected by the layout of equipment, storage and work areas. Most domestic equipment and kitchen machinery has

[2,24] Office interior.

been designed to a range of standard heights and widths which have been worked out from measurements of men and women sitting, standing, reaching and bending. [2,25]

It can be an interesting exercise to draw up room plans, trying to arrange furniture and equipment efficiently to cut down on unnecessary movement for people using the space.

[2,25] Modern kitchen layout.

[2,26] Modern livingroom.

The arrangements of colours, textures, patterns and materials within the elements of a room design vary with changes in style from year to year. Styles in furnishing, fabrics, carpets and other flooring materials, wall coverings and painting techniques have to be chosen to suit the size and function of a room and the age and style of the building. [2,26]

As with most design choices, the decoration of a home is a very personal matter: the colours and furnishings that please one person will not necessarily suit someone else. What is good design in one generation may be bad taste in the next.

EUROPEAN ART

2

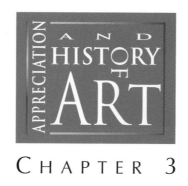

CHAPTER 3

THE MEDIEVAL PERIOD:
ROMANESQUE AND GOTHIC STYLES

ROMANESQUE: ELEVENTH AND TWELFTH CENTURIES

When the Roman Empire collapsed due to recurring barbarian invasions, art and learning in Europe almost disappeared. The warring tribes and petty kingdoms had little use for permanent art — small objects in precious metals, enamel and precious stones made up most of what was produced. [3,1]

The year 1000 was an important milestone in this period as it was prophesied that the end of the

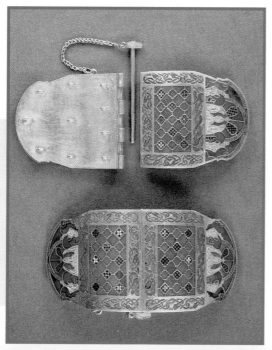

[3,1] Purse lid and shoulder straps from the Sutton Hoo ship burial c. 625 — gold, garnet, mosaic glass (British Museum, London).

world would occur on this date. When it passed without disaster, a strong impetus for renewal emerged throughout Western Europe. Considerable social change began to take place — kingdoms became larger, more prosperous and more stable. The Church also underwent change at this time — it began to reorganise itself through reforms and the creation of new monastic orders. In particular, the influential and powerful Benedictine order was reorganised and the Abbey Church at Cluny became the centre of a network of dependent monasteries located throughout France. This order, the Cluniac order, became quite powerful and acquired considerable wealth through donations from pilgrims and gifts of land.

The international Christian church was probably the single greatest influence on Romanesque art. The Crusades to Spain and the Holy Land brought back learning and technology from the Islamic and Byzantine cultures. Newly established monastic orders created centres of learning and culture, and became important patrons of the arts and architecture. Christian pilgrimages to religious sites and homes of relics [3,2] resulted in a need for large churches, in order to accommodate the number of pilgrims. The spread of Christianity also encouraged the building of churches in the newly converted lands of Scandinavia and Eastern Europe.

[3,2] Reliquary statue of St Foy at Conques in France, 10th century. The Relic of St Foy is housed in this little figure which is covered in gold leaf and decorated with crystals, precious stones and cameos donated by pilgrims, (Church of St Foy, Conques, France).

[3,3] Centre nave, S. Apollinare in Classe, Ravenna, mid-6th century, showing the basilica form.

Society in the Middle Ages was very different from our own — men saw themselves as the instruments of God's will, not as creative individuals, so most of the work was anonymous. Craftsmen were instructed on the subject, materials and methods to be used in their work and there were conventions for the portrayal of most subjects which they would have followed. The buildings, art and craftwork which remain today represent only a small fraction of what once existed. Most have been destroyed or built upon in the intervening 1,000 years.

ARCHITECTURE

There are many regional styles and local variations in Romanesque buildings but they all have common roots in the Roman basilica. [3,3] Common in Roman towns and cities as a market and meeting hall, Christians adapted the basilica to their own use when the Roman Empire was Christianised. A cruciform plan evolved to symbolise its function as a place of Christian worship. The round-headed or Roman arch was a characteristic feature of Romanesque buildings.

The earliest churches stayed very close to the Roman models on which they were based. The Cathedral at Pisa, [3,4] begun in 1063, is decorated inside with yellow, white and green coloured marble. The exterior is divided into arcades — rows of arches — which are separated by horizontal string courses. The vertical is emphasised by pilasters — flat pillars set against the walls. Under the eaves, corbel tables — rows of little arches projecting from the wall — can be found. There is a domed lantern tower over the crossing which allows light down into the chancel. The famous Leaning Tower, built between 1174 and 1372, is free-standing, unlike the towers on other churches in Northern Europe. There is also a separate baptistry. Only the aisles of Pisa Cathedral are vaulted; the nave and transepts have a wooden roof.

[3,4] Pisa Cathedral, begun in 1063 and enlarged in 1150–60; Leaning Tower, begun in 1174 and completed in 1372.

TECHNIQUE

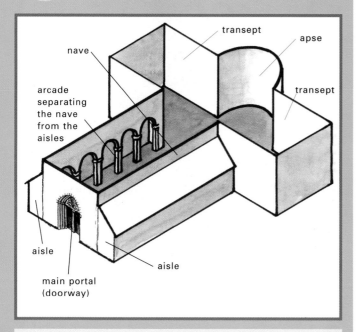

[3,5]
(a) Three-dimensional view of a Romanesque church.

(b) Romanesque vaulting.

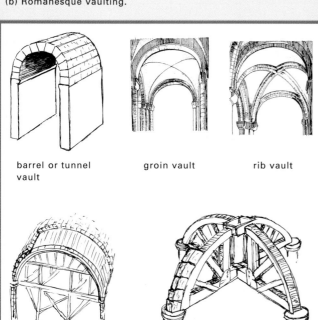

barrel or tunnel vault   groin vault   rib vault

Wooden 'centring' for a barrel vault. A large scaffolding had to be built up from the floor to support the section of vaulting under construction.

The 'centring' for a rib vault could rest on the pillars which would support the final vault, making construction quicker and cheaper.

Fires were a real hazard in early churches as roofs were wooden and church walls were hung with tapestries and wooden or fabric screens. Furthermore, candles or oil lamps were the only source of light. Stone-vaulted ceilings were devised specifically to overcome this hazard. The earliest examples of vaulting are found in Lombardy, northern Italy, and date back to the ninth century. The Lombard masons, expert at building in cut stone (ashlar), developed three types of vault: the barrel or tunnel vault, the groin vault and the rib vault. [3,5] These innovations revolutionised building design and were copied all over Europe. Heavy stone roofs required a lot of support and it was the struggle to cope with this weight that led to many of the developments in Romanesque architecture. The Basilica of San Ambrogio in Milan, begun in 940, is a good example of the Lombard style. It has rib vaulting dating from 1180.

Germany was politically connected to northern Italy at this time and, as a consequence, it borrowed heavily from the Lombard style of architecture, producing tall cathedrals with closely grouped towers and apses at both east and west ends. The Cathedral at Speyer [3,6] shows what a dramatic outline these German churches make.

[3,6] Speyer Cathedral, Rhineland Palatinate, Germany.

In France and Spain the popularity of pilgrimages created a need for large churches, where pilgrims could circulate to get a view of the relics of the saints to whom the church was dedicated. [3,7] Santiago de Compostella, in north-western Spain, was one of the most important centres of

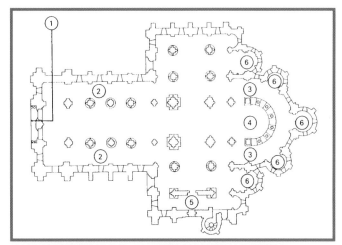

[3,7] Plan of Abbey of St Foy, Conques, France. Pilgrims entered by the west door (1) and went along the aisles (2) to the ambulatory (3) to view the principal shrine in the sanctuary (4). The monks entered the church by the transept (5) which was connected to the cloister. Other relics could be displayed in the minor chapels (6) around the apse.

[3,9] Abbey of St Foy, Conques, France — exterior, from the east.

pilgrimage, after Rome and the Holy Land. A large, richly decorated church was built there to house the relic of St James the Apostle. A similar church was built on each of the four major pilgrim routes to Santiago de Compostella — these were St Martin at Tours, St Martial at Limoges, St Serin at Toulouse and St Foy at Conques.

The Relic of St Foy is housed in the Abbey of St Foy which, although the smallest of these pilgrimage churches, is a fine example of Romanesque architecture. Inside, [3,8] we can see the heavy structure needed to support the barrel vault. The vault is divided into sections — called bays — by arches which are supported on pillars, which in turn take the weight to the ground. Light pouring down into the chancel, from the lantern tower over the crossing, brightens an otherwise dark interior. Outside, [3,9] the cruciform shape, heavy walls with buttresses and small windows are typical of the Romanesque style. The twin towers at the west end — called westworks — and the lantern tower emphasise the height of the building.

The most elaborate churches in France were built under the patronage of the Cluniac order. Abbot Hugh, who in 1088 commissioned Cluny III, [3,10] which was to be the largest church in Europe, also approved the plans of over 1,000 other churches. These churches were built to

[3,10] Model of Cluny III, 1088–c. 1121. The massive size of the building can be appreciated. Chapels and towers grouped around the crossing and the east end create a complex structure.

[3,8] Abbey of St Foy, Conques, France — interior looking east, showing vaulted ceiling, lantern at crossing and towers.

[3,11] Autun Cathedral, 1130 — interior. The pointed barrel vault is in the Clunaic style.

house the elaborate services of the Cluniac monks, who chanted psalms night and day. The church at Paray-le-Monial (built c. 1100) and Autun Cathedral (built 1130) [3,11] are in the style of the Abbey Church of Cluny itself, whereas other churches of the order, such as Vézelay (built c. 1120), had a slightly different structure. All the Cluniac churches had elaborate stone carvings over the main doorways and on the capitals of the pillars. The interiors were also richly painted, which can be easily forgotten as very little of this decoration has survived.

The Normans in the north of France and England were responsible for building the most technically advanced churches of this period. The

[3,12] Durham Cathedral, 1093–1130 — interior. The alternate composite and round pillars of the nave arcade support Romanesque arches, but the rib vaulting supporting the roof is pointed, ushering in the Gothic style.

Cathedral at Durham (built between 1093 and 1130) [3,12] has a comparatively bright interior due to the large clerestory windows which were made possible by the rib-vaulted roof. Here the arches are pointed, rather than semi-circular, marking the beginning of a development that led to Gothic arches. The decoration on Norman buildings was largely abstract and geometric, with figures appearing on capitals.

SCULPTURE

Sculpture was primarily a decorative feature on buildings during the Romanesque period and was generally regarded as a trade which fell within the realm of architecture. There were many regional styles of sculpture, but as sculptors moved about freely these do not always correspond to architectural styles. Sculptors seem to have travelled the pilgrim routes, from one building site to another, bringing their pattern books with them. Manuscripts were probably used as a source of inspiration for their designs — the tympanum at Mouissac, for example, closely resembles an illustration from a Spanish *Book of the Apocalypse*, a copy of which survives in the Bibliothèque Nationale in France. The similarity to manuscript designs would have been further emphasised by the brightly coloured paints originally used to decorate the sculptures. These works of art must have had an awe-inspiring effect on people who had little or no other experience of visual imagery. The vast majority of the population were illiterate and would never have seen pictures or images of any kind outside their church.

Pilgrim churches developed the most dramatic schemes of decoration. The main portal — doorway — at the western end, through which the pilgrims entered, was generally the most elaborately decorated area. The semi-circular space over the doorway — the tympanum — was usually carved with a scene which demonstrated the glory of God. The tympanum of the Church of St Pierre at Mouissac in France (c. 1120) [3,13] depicts the apocalyptic vision from St John's Gospel, with the crowned Christ enthroned at the centre surrounded by the symbols of the four Evangelists. An angel with a scroll stands on each side and the twenty-four crowned Elders sit in

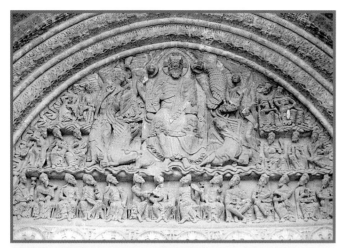

[3,13] Tympanum of the Church of St Pierre, c. 1120, Mouissac, France.

three rows separated by clouds. The Elders hold harps and scent bottles which represent the prayers of saints. The archivolts — rows of arches surrounding the tympanum — and the lintel are covered with leaf patterns. The linear style of the carving can be seen in the folds of the draperies. The varied movements of the Elders add a liveliness to the composition. This powerful sculpture represents the Languedoc regional style whose centre of influence was at Toulouse.

In Burgundy, the Abbey Church of Cluny was the central influence. Some capitals from the ambulatory survive; [3,14] subjects include the seasons, the virtues and the tones of Gregorian chant. Leaf and figure shapes are combined in a crisp and accomplished style. Sculptors who trained at Cluny then brought this style to the churches at Vézelay and Autun.

[3,14] Capital from the Abbey of Cluny.

Thousands of pilgrims visited the Abbey of Vézelay each year as it housed a relic of St Mary Magdalene, to whom the church was dedicated. The west portal tympanum [3,15] depicts Pentecost and the mission of the Apostles. The mandorla, the almond shape behind the Christ figure, represents the aura of the risen Christ. The fire of the Holy Spirit radiates out from his hands onto the heads of the Apostles, and surrounding them are scenes of the conversion of the pagan peoples of the world. The inner arch of the archivolts is made up of little medallions representing the signs of the zodiac and the labours of the months. The whole composition appears busy — all the figures seem caught in a moment of action, even the linear pattern on the robes appears to flow. This sense of compressed energy permeates Romanesque art, most noticeably in the pillar capitals which are carved with figure scenes.

[3,15] Western portal of the Abbey of Vézelay, c. 1150. The work of the Apostles is represented on the tympanum. John the Baptist is on the central pillar and the Apostles are on the pillars at the door jambs.

At Autun Cathedral some of the finest figure capitals [3,16] depicting highly dramatic biblical scenes can be found. The sculptor who carved them signed the tympanum under the feet of Christ — *Gislebertus Hoc Fecit*, Gislebertus made this. The style of the carving throughout the

[3,16] Nave capital, Autun Cathedral — Flight into Egypt. Note the combination of plant forms on a different scale to the figures.

[3,18] Scene (Christ before Pilate) from the bronze doors at Hildesheim Cathedral. Figures emerge from a plain background with only incidental foliage. The heads of the figures in particular are free of the surface.

church seems so unified that it is quite possible Gislebertus did it all himself. The Cathedral at Autun is dedicated to St Lazarus which explains the Last Judgment theme of the tympanum. [3,17] Christ, enthroned, is at the centre surrounded by four angels. At Christ's right hand, the Saved are being helped into Heaven by St Peter and the angels. At Christ's left hand, Archangel Michael weighs souls on a balance and the Condemned are thrown into hell. Below Christ's feet, an angel with a flaming sword separates people rising from their tombs into the good and wrongdoers. Priests, bishops and people who have done pilgrimage are those numbered among the good, while the bad include adulterers, misers and

thieves, all of whom are naked and cowering in fear. While the imagery may appear almost comic to twentieth-century eyes, these painted demons must have struck fear into the average medieval mind. These works were designed to instruct the illiterate on the meaning of the Bible.

Outside France other schools of sculpture were thriving. The Italians were working in a more Roman style, which was somewhat less dramatic than the French, while in England capitals with grotesque 'half-man, half-beast' figures were being carved. In Germany, the doors at Hildesheim Cathedral [3,18] are wonderful examples of sculpture cast in bronze. In Spain, a

[3,17] Tympanum of Autun Cathedral. The Last Judgment. This very individual work seems to glory in the artist's ability to shock the viewer. The suffering of sinners is graphically portrayed.

33

[3,19] West portal of Santiago de Compostella, 1168–c. 1200. This high-relief sculpture by Master Mateo shows Christ at the centre of the tympanum surrounded by angels and the Elders. Beneath his feet a figure of St James greets the pilgrims arriving at the church.

[3,21] 'Christ in Majesty' from the Bury Bible, c. 1135. The bright colour scheme and gold embellishment give us some indication of how sculpture and decoration might have looked when originally painted (Corpus Christi College Library, Cambridge).

PAINTING

Decoration was a very important and integral part of Romanesque churches. In Italy, marble and mosaics were frequently used to decorate church interiors. The closeness of the Byzantine Empire, with its rich tradition in mosaics, obviously had a strong influence. Wall paintings too were influenced by the Byzantine style. The Church of S. Angelo at Formis, near Capua, houses an almost complete series of wall paintings, showing various scenes from the life of Christ. [3,20] Blue and warm earth colours were used to paint this fresco, which has little background and uses formalised facial features and draperies. Most countries in Europe developed wall painting that was closely related in style to painted manuscripts.

By the twelfth century, the Byzantine influence within book painting had spread all over Europe, probably through books brought back from the Crusades. The Bury Bible (c. 1135), [3,21] which was painted by the lay artist, Master Hugo, for the Abbey of Bury St Edmunds, shows this influence

prolific school of sculptors decorated many beautiful churches which were largely based on the French style. The west portal of Santiago de Compostella (1168–c. 1200) [3,19] shows the apocalyptic vision in high relief. Figures on the central pillar under the tympanum and on the pillars of the door jambs give a foretaste of the Gothic doorways which were to come.

[3,20] The Last Supper and Christ Washing the Feet of the Apostles. A wall painting in the Church of S. Angelo in Formis near Capua, c. 1080. Two events from the story are shown simultaneously in the painting.

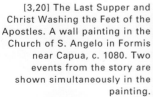

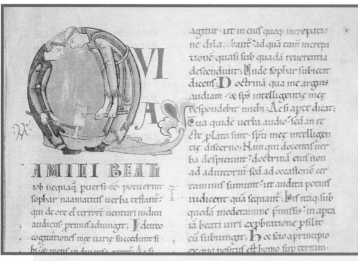

[3,22] 'Inhabited', initial from St Grégoire Le Grand, Moralia, 12th century (Bibliothèque Municipale, Dijon, France).

in its brightly coloured pages. The decorated initial letters [3,22] used in these books often have figures and plants entwined around them, which is somewhat reminiscent of the design of pillar capitals.

CRAFTS

Treasures of the church, including chalices, patens, book covers, reliquaries, crosses, boxes, crosiers, baptismal fonts, altar fronts, jewelled crowns and many other precious objects, were carefully crafted in lavish materials, as it was commonly believed that high-quality workmanship and materials were a prayer to God. The reliquary of St Foy, [3,2] which is covered in gold leaf and precious jewels, is a good example of this. The reliquary of St Valerie (c. 1120) [3,23] is a casket which illustrates her life in scenes enamelled in blue, red and turquoise on a rich gold background.

Other artifacts produced around this time from less precious materials also exhibit considerable artistic merit and refinement. The baptismal font (c. 1107–18) from the Church of St Barthélémy [3,24] in Liège, Belgium, was cast in bronze and

[3,24] Bronze baptismal font by Renier de Huy, c. 1107–18, Church of St Barthélémy, Liège, Belgium.

shows the Baptism of Christ in relief on the outside of a large basin supported on the backs of oxen. Little pieces of text explaining the scene are engraved into the background. Explanatory text also appears in the background of the Bayeux Tapestry (c. 1080) [3,25] which, in seventy-nine consecutive scenes, tells the story of Harold, Earl of Wessex, during the Norman invasion of England. The linen cloth, 0.52 m high and 70.3 m long, is embroidered in blue, green, yellow, red and grey woollen threads. The style is close to manuscript designs — lively, animated horses and soldiers move through the narrative which is framed in borders of fantastic animals and little figures.

The art of stained glass was closely related in style to wall painting and book illustration although little survives from before 1150. The oldest parts of Chartres Cathedral have some early glass in rich reds and blues. The beautiful Virgin and Child window dates from 1180. [3,26] The scale and harmony of the composition is remarkable considering its early date.

[3,23] 'The Life of St Valerie', patron saint of Limoges. Enamelled casket, c. 1120 (British Museum, London).

[3,25] Detail from Bayeux Tapestry, c. 1080 (Musée de la Tapisserie, Bayeux, France).

[3,26] Virgin and Child window from Chartres Cathedral, 1180.

CONCLUSION

The Romanesque period was a melting pot of styles from within Europe and beyond. The classical influence of Italy, the Celtic and Germanic styles of Northern Europe and the Byzantine influence from the East all finally amalgamated into the style which was later to become the 'International Gothic'. That is not to say that this time was merely a phase of experiment. Quite the contrary. Romanesque art can stand with any style in the world for strength and refinement.

GOTHIC: MID-TWELFTH CENTURY TO FIFTEENTH CENTURY

The Gothic era was a period of rapid development in Europe. In the 200 years between 1100 and 1300, the population tripled. New towns were founded and established towns and cities expanded dramatically. Through the use of new technology and improved farming techniques, trade flourished, creating a surplus which could be spent on luxuries.

Scholarship also made great advances during the Gothic era. The works of Aristotle and other Greek philosophers were translated into Latin for the first time. Arabic numbers replaced Roman numerals, making it easier for mathematicians to work on complex mathematical problems. Secular universities replaced monasteries as centres of learning and this brought about the conditions which led to the development of a new Humanist philosophy. Peter Abelard, Thomas Aquinas and Alighieri Dante, three of the greatest intellects in history, all came from this background.

The Church was no longer the only patron of the arts. Kings and nobles built palaces, commissioned works of art and collected books. City councils also commissioned buildings and works of art. A new merchant class had begun to develop and these people frequently made donations towards the building of churches — both as a symbol of their piety and to elevate their position in society. [3,27] Early in the Gothic era, works of art or buildings were considered to be 'by' the person who commis-

[3,27] 'Building of Twelve Churches' — 15th-century manuscript painted by Girant de Roussillon and his wife.

sioned or paid for them. It was only as the social standing of artists and architects increased that they began to be credited for their work.

Some of the subjects and images seen in Gothic art may seem obscure to a modern observer. This is probably because they are based on stories and ideas that are no longer commonplace. The ideas of chivalry and courtly love, which were popular in songs and stories of the time, may be foreign to us but at that time these concepts inspired great devotion to the Virgin Mary, who was seen as the epitome of purity and love. Many of the great French cathedrals are dedicated to Mary — the Cathedral of Notre Dame de Paris and Chartres Cathedral, to name but two. It was this desire to express spirituality that led to the huge, light-filled buildings which became typical of the Gothic period.

ARCHITECTURE
FRANCE

It has been estimated that eighty cathedrals and almost 500 abbeys were built between 1180 and 1270 in France, and these were built not by hundreds of labourers as had been the case during the Romanesque period, but by a small number of skilled craftsmen. Guilds were organised to train apprentices in specific trades and to protect standards of workmanship. Masons were the building specialists and they were classified into architects, carvers and assemblers.

The Abbey Church of St Denis (the Apostle of Gaul), just north of Paris, was extended and remodelled by Abbot Suger, friend and adviser to King Louis VI. An elaborate dedication ceremony in 1144 was attended by the king and queen as well as most of the nobles and senior clergy of northern France. The design of the new parts of the building so impressed those at the ceremony that cathedrals in this new style were built all over northern France in the subsequent fifty years. [3,28] The west front had twin towers, three carved portals and a rose window. This became the standard French Gothic façade. Inside, the apse was opened up through the use of pointed rib vaults resting only on pillars. This design allowed large windows to light up the whole interior, creating a unified space. The windows of the apse were the first large-scale series of stained glass windows ever seen. The Abbey Church of St Denis, being the burial place of the kings of France, was severely damaged during the French Revolution, and so we have to look elsewhere to see the full effect of the early Gothic style.

TRANSITIONAL AND EARLY GOTHIC (1150–1200)

Chartres Cathedral [3,29] shows the same features as the Abbey Church of St Denis on its west façade. [3,30] Though the openings are larger, the north tower was finished in the 'flamboyant' style some 300 years after the north tower. The tendency to add pieces in later styles was quite common in the Gothic period. The other parts of Chartres — nave, transepts and choir — are almost unique in this respect as they were finished in the same style and have remained unaltered down through the years. A fire in 1194 destroyed the original wooden-roofed basilica and only the more recent west front survived. The most precious relic of Chartres, a tunic worn by the Virgin Mary, survived the fire and this miracle provided the impetus to build a large cathedral exclusively dedicated to her.

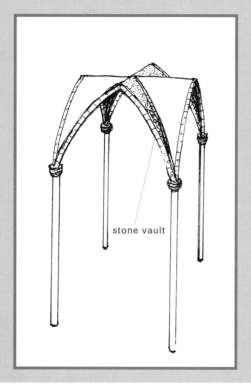

stone vault

[3,28] Gothic structure.
(a) Gothic rib vaulting bay. A constant ceiling height could be maintained over different-sized openings due to the flexibility of the pointed arch. The entire weight of the stone vault is gathered at four points which can be supported by pillars alone.

(b) The steepness of the pointed arch helped deflect weight downwards. The flying buttresses are connected to the pillars between windows at the points of greatest stress.

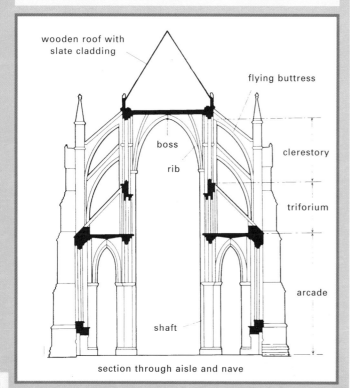

wooden roof with slate cladding

flying buttress

boss

rib

clerestory

triforium

arcade

shaft

section through aisle and nave

[3,29] Chartres Cathedral from the north-west. Here we can see the cruciform plan of the cathedral. The flying buttresses reach over the roof of the aisles to support the weight of the roof bearing on the pillars between the windows. Only two of the seven towers originally planned are completed; the towers on the transepts have only reached eaves level. The façade of the north transept, with its large rose window and deep porch, can also be noted.

[3,30] Chartres Cathedral — west front.

The whole emphasis in the interior of Chartres is on height and light. [3,31] The lines of the ribs of the four-part vaults are carried directly to the ground through the multiple shafts. The coloured light from the large clerestory windows infuses the interior with a mystic atmosphere. These large windows were made possible by transferring the weight of the stone roof outside the building to supporting buttresses called flying buttresses. In

[3,31] Interior of Chartres Cathedral — nave wall, completed 1230. The nave elevation is in three parts: the nave arcade, triforium gallery (used for access and maintenance) and clerestory windows (here each bay has two lancets with a small rose window above). The nave is 36.5 m tall.

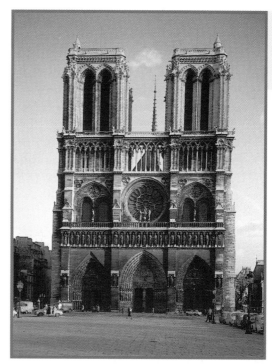

[3,32] The Cathedral of Notre Dame, Paris — west front.

HIGH GOTHIC (1200–1300) — 'RAYONNANT' STYLE

The Cathedrals of Amiens and Reims are good examples of the High Gothic period of development. The differences from earlier architectural styles can be seen most readily in the building façades. At Reims, [3,33] which was begun c. 1229, the portals are deeply set in porches and are topped by carved triangular open-work pinnacles. The central one of these depicts the crowning of the Virgin. The space over the door, which would normally have had a

the Gothic style of architecture, it is the structure of the building which is immediately striking. Inside, the arches, pillars and ribs combine in a network of lines which lead the eye to heaven. Outside, the towers and flying buttresses create an intricate and complicated outline against the sky. Chartres was the first building to have all these features.

The Cathedral of Notre Dame de Paris [3,32] is another early example of Gothic architecture. Its west front is of a later date than that at Chartres and is more completely Gothic. The portals spread across the whole façade, and over these, the king's gallery creates a horizontal balance. The rose window framework is lighter than that at Chartres. The grand gallery over the rose window creates another horizontal contrast. The spires of the twin towers were never completed but, despite this, their tall openings and vertical emphasis lead the eye heavenward.

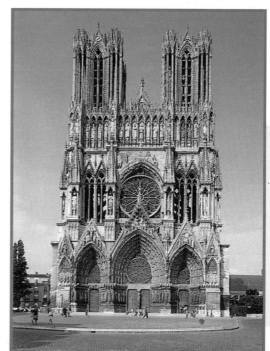

[3,33] Reims Cathedral — west front. The west façade at Reims (late 13th century) shows the fully developed Gothic style.

39

carved tympanum, is filled by a rose window. The stone ribs, which form the framework of the large rose window, make a flower-like pattern of radiating lines and it is this feature which led to the name 'rayonnant' being applied to this style. The towers at Reims are open-work — the buttresses of the nave can be seen through the tower at the level of the rose window. A gallery of huge figures, many times life size, provides almost the only relief to the vertical thrust of the pillars and openings that make up the façade.

LATE GOTHIC (1300–1550) — 'FLAMBOYANT' STYLE

The tendency to lighten structure and add decorative elements, which had already been established during the first two periods of French Gothic architecture, was taken to extremes during the Late Gothic period. The façade at Rouen Cathedral [3,34] shows how surfaces took on an organic, encrusted appearance where everything was decorated. Note how complex the framework of the rose window has become. It is this flame-like tracery and extravagant decoration which led to this style being called 'flamboyant'.

[3,34] The flamboyant style can be seen on the west façade of Rouen Cathedral (early 16th century).

GOTHIC ARCHITECTURE OUTSIDE FRANCE

Gothic architecture in Germany followed the French style quite closely. Cologne Cathedral, for example, is similar in style to Amiens. It was unfinished until 1842 when the original plans were discovered. Some later German churches have beautiful open-work towers and spires.

SPAIN

Spanish architecture had smaller windows and the roofs were less steep than those in Northern European buildings. Window surrounds tended to be elaborately carved. Burgos Cathedral is a good example of the vital Spanish style which continued well into the sixteenth century.

ENGLAND

In England, a style different in many ways to the French developed. English cathedrals were often located in rural areas rather than in towns and cities, as was the case in France and Germany. Salisbury Cathedral, begun in 1220, the same year as Amiens, is small by comparison. It has a screen façade rather than twin towers and a large crossing tower dominates its outline. The east end is finished square, without an apse. Heavier walls and smaller window openings made flying buttresses unnecessary. Later in the Gothic era, an interest in creating decorative effects using vaulting ribs led to fan vaulting — good examples of this can be seen at King's College Chapel, Cambridge, which was finished in 1515, and in the remarkable roof of Henry VII's Chapel in Westminster Abbey, London. [3,35]

ITALY

Italian architecture was least affected by the Gothic style. It retained a classical base to which some Gothic detail was added. In Florence Cathedral, [3,36] for example, pointed arches and rib vaults are the only obvious Gothic elements. Outside, the building is panelled in white, pink and green marble. The campanile, designed by Giotto in 1334, shows a rhythmic progression in the sizes of the openings as they rise. The huge Cathedral at Milan borrows heavily from French and German styles. It is the most Gothic and least Italian church of medieval Italy.

[3,35] Roof vault of Henry VII's Chapel, Westminster Abbey, London. The roof of Henry VII's Chapel at Westminster Abbey shows how late fan vaulting could appear almost frothy. Stone pendants appear to hang from the roof.

[3,37] The Doge's Palace, Venice.

CONCLUSION

The greater stability and prosperity of the later Middle Ages became evident in civic and domestic architecture. Town halls like the Palazzo Pubblico in Siena (1298), the City Hall in Münster, and the Town Hall in Bruges (c. 1376) were demonstrations of civic pride. Wealthy merchants also built impressive houses — Jacques

Coeur's house in Bourges, central France (1442–53), is a wonderful example of a large private town house. Some Italian city palaces also survive — the Doge's Palace in Venice is a wonderful reminder of how cultivated and refined the lives of the wealthy had become by the end of the Gothic era. [3,37]

SCULPTURE

The range of work undertaken by sculptors increased during the Gothic period. Decorative sculpture as part of architecture was still of primary importance, but the carving of other objects like rood screens, tabernacles, pulpits and tombs also occupied sculptors of talent. [3,38] On a smaller scale, wood and ivory carvings were created in great numbers for private devotions of princes of Church and state. Carvings in stone, wood and ivory continued to be painted as they had been since Romanesque times. [3,39]

The subject-matter for most sculpture was still dictated by patrons, particularly in church work. Sculptors did, however, have more freedom in the decorative details of their work, such as capitals [3,40] and gargoyles — carved waterspouts designed to throw rainwater from roofs, away from building walls where it might cause damp or damage. [3,41] The dramatic scenes of judgment and damnation found on Romanesque doorways were replaced by more benign and welcoming scenes portrayed in a calmer and more realistic style of carving.

[3,36] Florence Cathedral — nave.

TECHNIQUE

TRACERY

plate
late 12th and
early 13th
century

bar
mid–13th
century
onwards

Y-tracery
late 13th and
early 14th
century

geometrical
mid–13th and
early 14th
century
(and later)

intersecting
late 13th and early
14th century

reticulated
early and mid–14th
century

curvilinear
early 14th century
(England)
later 14th century
(France)

flamboyant
15th century
(France)

[3,38] These drawings show the development of tracery during the Gothic period.

[3,40] Gothic capital showing foliage design (Naumberg Cathedral).

[3,41] A gargoyle (Paris Cathedral, Notre Dame).

The figure of Christ at the south portal of Chartres Cathedral is that of Christ the Teacher. Book in hand, he greets the faithful as they come in to hear his words. At Notre Dame de Paris, the Virgin Mother and Child greet those who enter the north transept. These are not the awesome judgmental figures of Romanesque sculpture; they are more human and compassionate.

The west or royal portal at Chartres was completed c. 1150, [3,42] less than twenty years after Autun Cathedral, but is totally different in style. The pillar-like figures on the jambs of the doors are calm and remote, their delicately carved draperies hanging in parallel patterns over their slender static bodies. Naturalism is attempted only in the faces. The tympanum over the main door represents Christ in majesty, surrounded by the symbols of the Evangelists. Angels and the twenty-four Elders of the Apocalypse fill the archivolts and the Apostles are carved on the lintel. The tympanum over the north doorway of the west front shows the Ascension of Christ, while the tympanum over the southern doorway is dedicated to the Virgin Mary. The labours of the months and the signs of the Zodiac appear in the archivolts of these doorways. The quality of the carving is uneven, suggesting it is the work of several sculptors, but the figures of the kings and queens of the Old Testament on the pillar of the main door represent twelfth-century sculpture at its best.

The porches of the transepts at Chartres were carved during its reconstruction after the fire of 1194 and contain some fine examples of the next phase of Gothic development. Figures show

[3,39] The Meilander Madonna (Madonna di Milano), 1320–30, Cologne Cathedral. Statues in painted wood were common in the Gothic period. This one from Cologne Cathedral is thought to be by the same sculptor who worked on some of the figures in the choir.

[3,42] Western portal, Chartres Cathedral. The northern tympanum, left of picture, shows the Ascension of Christ; the central tympanum represents the Apocalyptic Vision; and the southern one is dedicated to Our Lady. Scenes from the life of Christ are on the capitals, and the figures on the pillars beside the doors represent the Old Testament kings and queens, ancestors of Christ.

greater movement and expression and the draperies are more realistic. The figure of St Modeste [3,43] on the north porch is almost completely free-standing. Her shoulders and face turn naturally, though there is still some stiffness in the stance. The variety of carved figures found

[3,43] Figure of St Modeste from the porch of the north transept at Chartres Cathedral shows the greater movement and naturalism achieved by the 13th century.

[3,44] Visitation Group, Reims Cathedral, Virgin's portal, west front. The classical influence, probably from Roman sarcophagi in the area, can be seen, particularly in the drapery of the 'Visitation Group' at Reims from about 1230.

here, representing the Life of the Virgin, the Final Coming, the Apostles, saints, martyrs and lesser themes, are of remarkably high quality and indicate that a number of talented sculptors were working at Chartres in the thirteenth century.

A classical influence can be seen in the figures on the west portal at Reims. The Visitation Group could almost be Roman. [3,44] The figures gesture and turn and their weight is carried on one foot, creating a graceful movement.

By the mid-thirteenth century, technical mastery had also been achieved in Germany. The 'Wise and Foolish Virgins' [3,45] in the portal of Strasbourg Cathedral show how the expression of emotion was now possible. Similarly, the figures representing the 'Founders' of Naumberg Cathedral [3,46] possess a portrait-like, individual quality. Large-scale, free-standing sculpture also began to appear at this time in Germany. The Bamberg Rider (King Stephen) was a forerunner of the equestrian statue of Otto II [3,47] at Magdeburg, the latter sculpted between 1240 and 1250. The Emperor sits astride his horse. A great naturalism has been attained in this piece, particularly in the facial expression and in the flow of the garments.

[3,45] 'Wise and Foolish Virgins', Strasbourg Cathedral portal. Emotional expression has been achieved in these figures. Note also the animated movement.

[3,47] Equestrian statue of Otto II, Magdeburg Cathedral, 1240–50. This completely free-standing figure sculpture group is one of the earliest surviving civic monuments.

[3,46] Herman and Regelindes, 'Founders Group', Naumberg Cathedral.

[3,48] 'Well of Moses' by Claus Sluter. Sluter's work represents the finest achievement of Northern European Gothic sculpture. Emotional expression and realism are combined with technical achievement in carving.

CLAUS SLUTER (C. 1350–1405)

Claus Sluter was the most outstanding late Gothic sculptor in Northern Europe. Born in the Netherlands, he worked mostly in Dijon under the patronage of Philip the Bold, Duke of Burgundy. The group of six figures which surround the 'Well of Moses' [3,48] represents the culmination of the search for realism and emotional expression which motivated many Gothic sculptors. The wrinkled and expressive faces, the flowing hair and the deeply folded robes possess a wonderful energy. Sluter's style quickly spread throughout Europe to Spain, Portugal, Germany and France.

THE PISANO FAMILY

Italian sculpture of the Gothic period was dominated by the Pisano family — father Nicola (c. 1225–1284) and son Giovanni (c. 1250–1320). Nicola Pisano worked in a style strongly influenced by classical sculpture. A fine hexagonal pulpit designed for the Baptistry in Pisa is mounted on Gothic arches and has a bold relief on each of its six sides. In a superbly balanced composition, the Birth of Christ panel shows Mary as a Roman matron surrounded by smaller figures in tightly grouped composition. [3,49] Nicola also carved a more complex pulpit for Siena Cathedral. Giovanni Pisano carved the figures for

[3,49] 'Birth of Christ'. Nicola Pisano's ability in composition and figure carving is clearly visible in this panel from the pulpit in Pisa Baptistry.

[3,51] Pulpit from the Baptistry at Pisa by Nicola Pisano.

[3,50] Figures by Giovanni Pisano from the façade of Siena Cathedral (left, Plato; right, Eritrean Sibyl).

the exterior of the Pisa Baptistry as well as those for the façade of Siena Cathedral, [3,50] the most richly decorated Gothic façade in Italy. The statuary there has a remarkable inner life and energy. The figure scenes designed by Giovanni for the pulpits of S. Andrea, Pistoia and Pisa Cathedral demonstrate his ability to express emotion through his sculpture. [3,51]

CONCLUSION

By the end of the Middle Ages, European sculpture had changed dramatically. From its humble beginnings as decoration on architecture, it had become an art form in its own right. Great

technical feats had been achieved to the point where almost any desired effect could be created. The work of Claus Sluter and the Pisano family created a standard which would not easily be surpassed.

PAINTING

Many changes in painting styles and techniques evolved during the Gothic period. Early work was full of conventions, some of which were carried on through the International Gothic style (see below) well into Renaissance times. Figure sizes depended on their importance. In 'Madonna in Maestà' by Cimabue (Cenni di Peppi, c. 1240–1302), [3,52] for example, the Virgin is the largest figure, with angels and saints shrinking in size as their significance decreased. The turn and angle of their heads and their simplified features — long noses and small mouths — were considered elegant and graceful. Precious materials, such as the gold leaf used in the background and the blue made from the semi-precious stone lapis lazuli used in the robes, made the work more valuable and therefore more pleasing to God. Colour was often used for decorative effect rather than for representation, as can be seen in the angels' wings. Even this work, which looks very stylised to modern eyes, attempted greater realism than earlier icons. The perspective in the throne and the soft drapery of the robes heralded the changes that were to come in Gothic painting.

[3,52] 'Madonna in Maestà' by Cimabue, 386 x 225 cm (Uffizi Gallery, Florence). 'Maesta' means majesty and usually refers to the Madonna and Child enthroned, surrounded by angels. Cimabue worked mainly in Florence.

[3,53] 'Holy Women at the Sepulchre' by Duccio di Buoninsegna, tempera on wood (Museo dell'Opera Metropolitana, Siena).

expressions to great effect. The perspective of the tomb and the representation of the mountain go beyond symbolism towards realism. Duccio's drawing skills and his story-telling abilities, as seen in this work, elevate him above his contemporaries.

ARTISTS

GIOTTO DI BONDONE (C. 1266–1337)

Giotto, the painter mentioned in Dante's *Divine Comedy* as having surpassed his master, Cimabue, is often considered to be the father of modern painting. This Florentine artist seems to have used contemporary sculpture — the work of the Pisanos — rather than painting as the model on which to base his work. A sense of weight and volume is only part of the strength of his painting; in his series of frescoes in the Arena Chapel in Padua, [3,54] for example, it is the expressive actions and faces of the figures which stand out, like dramatic scenes from a play frozen in time. The fresco on 'The Deposition of Christ' [3,55] illustrates much of what is important in the work of Giotto. The Christ figure is the focal point and

[3,54] Interior of the Arena Chapel in Padua. The Arena Chapel in Padua was paid for by Enrico Scrovegni in 1303 to atone for the sins of his father, a notorious usurer. This chapel contains Giotto's finest frescoes representing scenes from the Life of the Virgin and the Passion of Christ. The end wall has a Last Judgment and there is an Annunciation over the chancel arch.

In Siena, 9 June 1333 was declared a public holiday to celebrate the installation of a new altarpiece. Painted by the local artist, Duccio di Buoninsegna (active 1278–1318/19), it comprised ninety-two panels in all. A 'maesta' was the centrepiece of the front of the altarpiece while the back was made up of panels illustrating the life of Christ. In the 'Holy Women at the Sepulchre' panel at the back of the altarpiece, [3,53] we can see how Duccio tells the story using body movements, gestures and facial

[3,55] 'The Deposition of Christ' by Giotto, fresco, 230 x 200 cm (Arena Chapel, Padua).

all faces are turned towards him. His mother holds him in her arms, Mary Magdalene holds his feet and St John flings his arms wide; the difficult perspective of the far hand is almost correct. The little figures of the mourning angels are like a series of exercises in figure perspective. Though the figures are beautifully modelled in light and shadow, there are no cast shadows. The landscape setting is no more than a shallow stage. Greater than all the small faults a modern eye might notice is the sense of drama created here, the clarity of the story portrayed in the scene.

Giotto's contemporaries considered his work a miracle of naturalism. No other artist at the time had the talent to follow his lead, and it was almost 100 years before the Florentine painter, Masaccio, took up and developed Giotto's innovations.

SIMONE MARTINI (C. 1284–1344)

Simone Martini was a pupil of Duccio. Following the Byzantine-based tradition of his master, he developed the decorative linear quality and graceful gestures of the Gothic style. His work seems like a step backwards compared to Giotto's, but it was the preferred fashion of the time. Simone Martini worked for the Anjou court in Naples and for the Pope at Avignon, where his style became a major influence on International Gothic painting and book illumination. His 'Annunciation' [3,56] is considered to be the

TECHNIQUE

[3,56] 'The Annunciation' altarpiece, 1333, by Simone Martini (c. 1284–1344), 275 x 305 cm, tempera on wood (Uffizi Gallery, Florence).

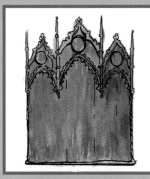

Panel painting technique based on Martini's 'Annunciation'
1. The elaborate wooden panel was supplied by a member of the carpenters' guild. The wood was prepared with a layer of linen and up to eight coats of gesso — a chalk-white pigment mixed with size.

2. The gesso surface was polished smooth and the design painted on. Outlines and major folds in drapery were incised into the surface. Gold leaf was applied over several coats of red bole bound in egg white. The gold was burnished and designs were punched or incised into it.

3. Drapery was painted before the flesh. All flesh areas were underpainted in green earth and lead white. The green earth could be left uncovered in the shadows. Flesh colours were finally painted and details reinforced in black or sinoper. Gold lines were applied to garments using a sticky oil.

[3,57] Wilton Diptych (National Gallery, London).

epitome of his style. It is a blend of grace and sentiment and is an outstanding work of craftsmanship.

INTERNATIONAL GOTHIC STYLE

The International Gothic style was a fusion of Italian and Northern European styles which had evolved by the end of the fourteenth century. The Wilton Diptych [3,57] is a good example of this, as it cannot be attributed to any one country or artist. The diptych is made up of two painted panels which are hinged together in the centre. The left panel shows King Richard II of England with St Edmund, St Edward the Confessor (with the ring) and St John the Baptist, all worshipping the infant Jesus in the right panel, who is held in the arms of his mother and surrounded by angels. The work exhibits great delicacy and refinement, and has a calm, graceful quality that is typical of the International Gothic style.

PAINTED MANUSCRIPTS

Numerous painted manuscripts were produced throughout Europe during the Gothic period, including the Psalter and Breviary and the *Book of Hours*. It was the nobility and the more educated and wealthy merchant classes who created a demand for these books. *Les Très Riches Heures* was produced by the Limbourg brothers for the Duc de Berry, younger brother of Charles V of France. It is a book of prayers suitable for various times of the day and for different seasons. It contains a beautifully illustrated calendar with a picture for each month. [3,58] *Les Très Riches Heures* represents the high point of the Inter-

[3,58] Picture depicting the month of August, from *Les Très Riches Heures du Duc de Berry*, 1413–16, 29 x 20 cm (Musée Condé, Chantilly).

national Gothic style in book illumination. The style combines beautifully observed details from nature with an attempt at rendering space which was very advanced for fifteenth-century France.

CRAFTS

With the increased wealth of the Gothic period, the quality, quantity and variety of craftwork produced during this time increased considerably. Abbot Suger of the Abbey Church of St Denis kept records of all the work the Abbey commissioned during his time in office. He focused much more on craftwork in gold and jewels than he did on architecture, although he is more renowned for the latter. A chalice from St Denis (c. 1140) gives some idea of the work being produced under his patronage. [3,59]

RELIQUARIES

Reliquaries in the shape of houses and churches were also quite common and in the later Gothic period these became even more elaborate. The 'Little Gold Horse' tabernacle, dedicated to the Virgin and Child, was given to Charles VI of France (a nephew of the Duc de Berry) by his wife. It is a remarkable work which was made using gold, enamels, pearls and jewels. [3,60]

TAPESTRIES

Tapestries were produced in large numbers and were generally hung in castles and large houses where they had a practical function in keeping the building warm. The six French tapestries of the 'Lady with the Unicorn' series, [3,61] made c.

[3,60] 'Little Gold Horse' altar tabernacle, c. 1404 (Treasury of Altötting).

1500 for the Le Viste family, are exquisitely woven. Their rich colours and elegant figures are typically Gothic in style, despite the late date.

STAINED GLASS

Stained glass reached the high point of its development during the Gothic era. Building styles were modified to get the best effect from coloured glass. The ideal of the glass 'lantern' church was achieved at Sainte Chapelle in Paris [3,62] as early as 1240, where the overall effect of coloured light was more important than the individual scenes of the scheme.

[3,59] Chalice of Abbot Suger of St Denis, c. 1140, agate with silver gilt, 19 cm tall (National Gallery of Art, Washington DC).

[3,61] 'À mon Seul Désir' from the 'Lady with the Unicorn' series of tapestries made around 1500 in France (Musée de Cluny, Paris).

[3,62] La Sainte Chapelle, Paris — interior. La Sainte Chapelle was built to house the relic of the Crown of Thorns and as a private chapel for St Louis. The stained glass combined with the gilded and enamelled interior creates the impression of a gilded casket.

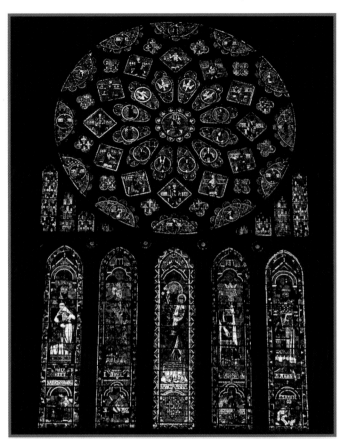

[3,64] North transept rose window, Chartres Cathedral, c. 1230. In the centre is the Virgin and Child, surrounding her are doves and angels, next are squares containing the twelve kings of Judea and at the perimeter are twelve semi-circles showing the twelve minor prophets. Below the rose are five lancets containing Old Testament figures.

[3,63] 'Death of the Virgin', a scene from one of the multi-scene windows in Chartres Cathedral. We can see the similarity in style between this and manuscript illumination. The richness of the colour scheme with the predominance of blue and red can be noted.

With a total of 120 windows, Chartres Cathedral has one of the most complete series of stained glass windows in Europe. The oldest glass dates from the twelfth century and can be found in the west façade. In the aisles, ambulatory and chapels there are multi-scene windows. [3,63] Higher up, the clerestory windows mostly depict single-figure scenes of saints, kings, prophets and bishops, all of which can be seen clearly from ground level. In the aisle and ambulatory windows, donor scenes can be found in the lower panels. The Queen of France, Blanche of Castile, donated the glass for the rose and lancets in the north transept façade [3,64] and the Dreux family, the most important local nobles, donated the glass for the south rose. These windows represent the finest collection of medieval glass.

Stained glass continued to be a feature of the decoration of churches throughout the Gothic period. The kaleidoscopic effect of coloured light and pattern was an important element in the mystic atmosphere of Gothic cathedrals. [3,65]

CONCLUSION

Gothic art was unique primarily because it was the only style which was not classically based. Architecture and stained glass worked on two levels. Firstly, there was the initial impact of the work — the upward thrust of the buildings and the coloured light from the glass. Secondly, there was the carved detail on the buildings and the figure scenes in the windows. In a sense, all Gothic art has this quality whereby the more you look, the more you see. The final phase of Gothic architecture led to some of the greatest excesses in size and decoration ever achieved by man.

In Gothic painting and sculpture, the movement towards realism was well under way and the idea of the artist as a person of ideas as well as a skilled craftsman was evolving. Works of art were being viewed as an end in themselves and not just as decorations on buildings.

The Gothic period did not end abruptly at the beginning of the fifteenth century. As we have seen, in some areas the Gothic style continued on well into the sixteenth century, more than 100 years after the Renaissance had begun in Florence.

TECHNIQUE

[3,65] Making a stained glass window.

1. The same basic method has been in use since medieval times. The artist makes a coloured design on a small scale. A full-size drawing called a cartoon which emphasises the leading (see No. 3 below) is made on paper. In medieval times a whitewashed board or table was used for the cartoon. Pieces of glass, white or coloured, are cut to shape and laid on the cartoon.

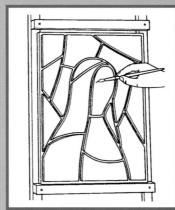

2. Black or dark brown enamel paint is used to paint details and textures. The glass is then fired in a muffle kiln to fix the painting.

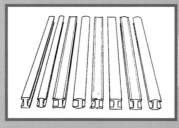

3. Leading in a variety of cross-sections is very flexible.

4. The painted glass is laid back on the cartoon and the leading is fitted around it and cut to size.

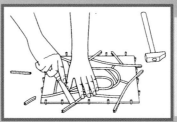

5. In larger windows iron bars are set in the frames and wired onto the leading to provide additional strength and support against wind pressure.

6. Joints in the leading are soldered.

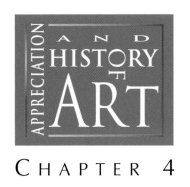

CHAPTER 4

FIFTEENTH AND SIXTEENTH CENTURIES

FIFTEENTH CENTURY: EARLY RENAISSANCE

The idea that the Renaissance was a 'rebirth' of creative thought and learning after the dark Middle Ages no longer holds true. The Renaissance emerged from the continuation in the study of the Greek and Roman past begun by medieval scholars. From this study the Humanist thinking evolved; this put man at the centre of God's creation, made in God's own image and therefore full of unlimited potential.

A new realism and self-reliance were in the air. The Black Death and continuous warfare had decimated Europe. Those who survived wanted to get on with life. The lands of the Duke of Burgundy in north-eastern France, Belgium and southern Holland and the northern states of Italy were comparatively stable. Consequently, it was in these areas that the new developments in art and learning took root.

The sense of competition which was driving the first great advances in industry and commerce spilled over into the arts, where individualism and pride in one's own achievements spurred on new ideas and techniques. Wealthy merchants and civic bodies vied with each other for the latest innovations or most magnificent works, joining with the Church as patrons of the arts.

The spread of ideas was greatly facilitated by the printing press. Texts by Roman scholars on painting and architecture were translated and printed, and the first contemporary art histories were written. In 1550 Vasari wrote his *Lives of the Artists*, the most influential book on the subject for generations. Engravings and woodcuts by artists or copies in print of their work were distributed throughout Europe. Many artists collected prints.

THE QUATTROCENTO

Quattrocento, literally meaning 400, generally refers to Italy in the 1400s, a time when the country as we now know it was divided into separate small city states, duchies and kingdoms who vied with each other for power and glory. [4,1] Among these states, Florence prided itself on its culture, with the flourishing of the arts and letters. A new class of wealthy and scholarly patron emerged who expected the artist to be a man of intellect as well as artistic ability. The Medici and Strozzi families and other wealthy merchants and bankers created a hothouse in which men of amazing ability such as Brunelleschi, Alberti, Donatello and Masaccio fulfilled their extraordinary talent and as friends exchanged ideas, thus forging the new

[4,1] Map of France and Italy showing territories of the Duke of Burgundy and the Italian city states and kingdoms in the 15th century.

1. Republic of Florence
2. Republic of Siena
3. Papal States
4. Kingdom of Naples
5. Kingdom of Sicily
6. Republic of Venice
7. Duchy of Milan
8. Republic of Genoa
9. Duchy of Savoy
10. Duchy of Burgundy

[4,2] Palazzo Rucellai, Florence, 1446–51. Alberti's design may seem ordinary because this type of street palace became the model for so many urban buildings right up to the 20th century.

Renaissance style. Brunelleschi was not only an architect but a goldsmith, sculptor and engineer. Alberti, also an architect, was a theorist, athlete, playwright and musician.

ARCHITECTURE

The contrast between Gothic and Renaissance architecture could hardly be greater. The vertical pointed emphasis of Gothic is the least classical of all architectural styles. The simple geometry of the Renaissance style, with emphasis on proportion and three-dimensional space, creates a more expansive impression. The architects of the early Renaissance succeeded in combining elements of classical design with the local Italian tradition which was largely Romanesque.

While the Gothic style of the Middle Ages was dedicated almost exclusively to church building, the Renaissance style found its greatest expression in secular architecture. These were still troubled times, with plots and treachery abounding. Thus the city palaces built for the important Florentine and Venetian families [4,2] and the ducal palace at Urbino [4,3] all present strong fortress-like exteriors, with small, barred windows on the ground floor. In contrast, the rooms inside faced onto a pleasant courtyard, a mixture of medieval cloister and Roman villa.

In medieval times a book of instruction on architecture by Vitruvius, a Roman engineer of the first century B.C., had been discovered. Titled *De Architectura*, this book became the bible of Renaissance architects. It provided instructions on the siting and construction of buildings and examined how different situations demanded a different order of decoration. However, there were no illustrations with the manuscript and the instructions were often vague or obscure, which

left much to the judgment of the architects themselves. This allowed for a lot of individual interpretation and the use of original designs rather than direct copies of Roman designs.

Greek and Roman philosophers considered the circle to be the perfect shape. This idea was given Christian expression in the phrase 'God is the centre of the universe and yet encompasses it'. If

[4,3] Main courtyard of the Palace at Urbino, 1464–6, designed by Luciano da Laurana. The courtyards were open and light in contrast with the severe exteriors of Renaissance urban palaces. Corinthian columns support round arches on the ground floor arcade and pilasters with Corinthian capitals divide the wall space on the first floor.

man was made in God's image then he also must be perfectly proportioned. [4,4] These ideas merged into an ideal of proportion which was common from the early Renaissance. Thus the complicated geometry of the Gothic era was abandoned in favour of a geometry of elegant proportions and classical detail.

FILIPPO BRUNELLESCHI (1377–1446)

Florentine sculptor, architect and goldsmith, Brunelleschi is best known for his amazing feat of engineering in enclosing the great octagonal opening of Florence Cathedral with a dome. [4,5] Nineteen other architects competed unsuccessfully with him to design this, the largest dome since the Pantheon in Rome. Begun in 1420, it took sixteen years to complete the double-skinned structure. The octagonal wall of the drum is 5 metres thick. Brunelleschi designed a system of construction which was self-supporting, thus avoiding the need for a wooden centring. A stone rib rises from each corner of the octagon and the spaces between are filled with a herringbone pattern of brick which is strong and light. The structure is bound at intervals internally with chains of wood and iron, which became the norm for Renaissance cupolas.

During the same period Brunelleschi was also involved in the design and construction of the Ospedale degli Innocenti (Foundling Hospital), which is considered to be the first real

[4,5] Santa Maria del Fiore, Florence Cathedral. Notice the scale of the surrounding buildings compared to the Cathedral. The lantern on the dome is as large as a two-storey house.

Renaissance building. [4,6] The arch-on-column motif which he uses in the external colonnade and the internal courtyard is constructed according to carefully reasoned proportions. The Corinthian capitals which Brunelleschi designed for the hospital are his own invention and are not copied from the Roman buildings he had studied and measured with Donatello with the aim of increasing their knowledge of classical architecture and design.

The design of the small Pazzi Chapel built inside the cloisters of Santa Croce is, however, based on Roman temples, with the entrance porch outside inspired by the Roman triumphal arch. To contrast with the white walls, green/grey 'pietra serena' stone is used for the orders and mouldings in the carefully proportioned interior. [4,7]

[4,4] Study of the Proportion of the Human Body by Leonardo da Vinci, c. 1500 (Galleria dell' Accademia, Venice). The notion of ideal proportions based on classical models was an important element in art and architecture during the Renaissance.

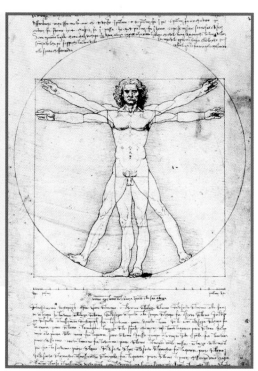

[4,6] Ospedale degli Innocenti, Courtyard, Florence. Brunelleschi's design of 1419 uses the local pietra serena stone to contrast with the white stucco walls. The use of simple geometry is clearly seen in the design.

[4,7] Pazzi Chapel, Santa Croce, c. 1430, Florence, designed by Brunelleschi.

[4,8] Façade of Santa Maria Novella, 1458–60. Alberti's new façade for the old basilica is based on simple geometry, mainly the circle and the square.

Brunelleschi's interests and achievements extended beyond architecture. He entered a panel in the competition for the new bronze doors for the Baptistry in Florence. He is also credited with having invented single-point perspective, in which all receding lines meet at one point on the horizon (eye level), an innovation which was an important element in the development of Renaissance art. This interest in three-dimensional space is seen in Brunelleschi's buildings, where grace combined with strength is the hallmark of his work.

LEON BATTISTA ALBERTI (1404–72)

A Florentine who spent a number of years in Rome, Leon Battista Alberti was one of the leading theorists of the Renaissance. The books he wrote on painting, sculpture and architecture were very influential in his own time and after. His theories found practical expression in a number of buildings, including the Palazzo Rucellai [4,2] in which he used classical orders on pilasters (flat pillars raised only a few centimetres from the surface) — Doric on the ground floor, Ionic on the second and Corinthian on the upper storey. These pilasters, set in the wall between the windows, help to break up the surface of the large building. The façade Alberti designed for Santa Maria Novella [4,8] became the standard for Renaissance basilicas. He uses a temple front for the upper part and a triumphal arch for the entrance. The two levels are connected by volutes (scroll-shaped ornaments). Alberti's reinterpretation of Roman models for modern buildings was a very important development in Renaissance architecture.

SCULPTURE

During the fifteenth century the nature of sculpture changed considerably. From being a decorative feature of architecture, sculpture evolved into an independent art form, particularly in Italy. The human figure, free-standing and capable of expressing emotion, became the focus of the sculptor's work. Life-size nudes and equestrian statues appear for the first time since the Roman era. Though the sculptors of the time did make studies of classical sculpture, their own work was more lively and emotional than the older models.

The important changes in style and subject-matter that characterise the sculpture of the early Renaissance originated in Florence. The efforts to complete the Cathedral of Santa Maria del Fiore, which had been under construction for a hundred years, created work for a huge number of craftsmen and artists. In 1401 a competition to design a set of gilt bronze doors for the north side of the Baptistry was organised by the merchant guild. These doors were to match a pair, based on the life of John the Baptist, designed in the previous century by Andrea Pisano for the south

[4,9] The competition reliefs by Brunelleschi (left) and Ghiberti (right, 1402) (Museo dell' Opera del Duomo, Florence). We can see the contrasting styles of the two panels. Brunelleschi's is full of movement and drama in the Gothic style, while Ghiberti's is calmer. Note the more classical robes and the anatomy of Isaac's figure in Ghiberti's work.

[4,10] The north and east doors of the Baptistry in Florence by Ghiberti, 1425 and 1452.

side. The artists in the final selection were given a sum of money and a year to produce a quatrefoil plaque on the 'Sacrifice of Isaac'. Brunelleschi's and Ghiberti's entries [4,9] survive and are housed in the Museo dell'Opera del Duomo in Florence.

LORENZO GHIBERTI (1378–1455)

Winner of the competition to design the Baptistry doors, Lorenzo Ghiberti spent the next twenty-three years working on, designing and casting twenty scenes from the life of Christ and eight figures of saints for the door panels. The style of these scenes relates closely to his original competition-winning design, and while physically maintaining a strong Gothic influence the sense of composition and observation of anatomy is more classical.

In 1426, a year after he had finished the first doors, Ghiberti was commissioned to make doors for the east side of the Baptistry. [4,10] In that year his whole concept for these doors had changed. He designed ten larger panels which were much more advanced in their composition and demonstrate a use of relief which was closer to painting than sculpture. In the Jacob and Esau panel [4,11] very clear single-point perspective has been used and the movement of the figures is different to anything we have seen before. Note the twisting movement of the woman with her back to us in the group on the left. These doors continued to be a great influence on painters and

sculptors into the High Renaissance. Michel-angelo remarked that they were fit to be the 'Gates of Paradise', and they have been known by that name ever since. The second set of doors was not completed until 1452, fifty years after Ghiberti began the first commission. During this time a large workshop was needed to carry out this and other works. Donatello, Uccello and many others received part of their training there.

DONATELLO (DONATO DI NICCOLO) (C. 1386–1466)

Donatello, considered to be the greatest European sculptor of the fifteenth century, was a master in all aspects of sculpture. His 'St George', [4,12] carved for the armourers' guild, makes a striking figure. Standing alert and tense, head held defiantly, he manages to give the impression of a figure ready for action. This life-like quality had not been achieved in stone or any other material before. The bronze 'David', [4,13] which is famous as the first free-standing nude figure since

[4,11] The Jacob and Esau panel from the 'Gates of Paradise', 1452, eastern door, Baptistry, Florence. Ghiberti's knowledge of perspective can be seen in the receding figure sizes, the lines of the tiles on the floor and the geometry of the buildings in the background.

[4,12] 'St George' by Donatello, 208 cm tall, 1417 (Fratelli Fabri, Milan). One of a series of figures that Donatello carved for Florence Cathedral and Orsanmichele, where the St George originally stood in a niche specially built for it.

[4,13] 'David' by Donatello, 158 cm tall (Bargello, Florence). The bronze figure of David is a mixture of classical and non-classical features.

From 1443 to 1453 Donatello lived in Padua, where he carried out a commission to create an equestrian monument to the 'Condottiere', Erasmo da Narni. The bronze has been given the nickname 'Gattamelata' (honeyed cat) — a tribute to the perfection or slickness of the work. [4,14] The figure on horseback, in the style of a Roman general, is 3 metres tall, the first large-scale bronze equestrian sculpture since antiquity.

Donatello created a huge range of work, from marble and bronze reliefs to terracotta, stone, bronze and wood sculpture in the round. His late wood carving of Mary Magdalene shows a tragic, ragged, emaciated figure, carved in a rugged style. Donatello was the master craftsman, brilliant in every aspect of his art, but much more than that he was the master of expression in sculpture.

CONCLUSION

Other distinguished sculptors worked in Florence in the fifteenth century. Antonio Pollaiuolo (c. 1432–98) and Andrea del Verrocchio (1435–88) worked in bronze as well as painting. Verrocchio is remembered as Leonardo da Vinci's master, but he was a fine sculptor in his own right, producing a David [4,15] and an equestrian statue to rival Donatello's.

Fifteenth-century sculpture was the most advanced art form of the time. It achieved a confidence and technical excellence which did not emerge for another hundred years in painting and architecture. Restrained elegance rather than showy skill is the mark of Quattrocento sculpture.

[4,14] 'Gattamelata', 1443–1453, by Donatello, 300 cm tall.

antiquity, stands dressed only in his shepherd's hat, holding a sword which seems too big for him. His left foot rests on Goliath's helmeted head. The base is a laurel wreath, symbol of victory. David appears thoughtful or sad rather than triumphant, as if to express the idea that we are all diminished by any violent death. The vulnerability of the figure is thought to express the Christian sentiment of our powerlessness without God's help. The figure is beautifully modelled in a graceful turning pose.

[4,15] 'David' by Andrea del Verrocchio (Bargello, Florence). Verrocchio's training as a goldsmith comes out in his love of detail and fine finish which can be noted in the borders of the garment.

[4,16] A Dissection, woodcut, by unknown artist for 'Fascicolo di Medicina' by J. de Ketham, Venice, 1493 (University of Bologna Collection). The professor lectures students while the cadaver is dissected. Artists as well as medical students attended such lectures and even dissected corpses themselves to study muscle and bone structures.

PAINTING

The new realism in painting achieved during the fifteenth century attempted to portray three-dimensional space on a two-dimensional surface. In Florence and in Italy generally this was based on Brunelleschi's theories on perspective and an idealised realism based on the geometric proportions of the human form. In the Flemish region the interest was in observed reality and accuracy of detail.

Both traditions were interested in light and shadow and in softening contours to create a smoother modelling of forms. The Italians took a formal analytical interest in anatomy [4,16] and colour theory, while north of the Alps there was greater emphasis on the observation of natural light and its effects. The Florentines considered fresco to be the greatest test of an artist's skill, [4,17] with tempera on wooden panels being suitable for smaller or portable work. In Northern Europe the climate was less suited to fresco, though it was commonly practised, and tempera painting gave way to oil painting on prepared wooden panels and later on canvas. Oils were introduced to Italy later in the fifteenth century through the northern states, particularly Venice, where Giovanni Bellini was one of the early masters of the technique.

Religious and public works were still the main sources of commissions for artists, though portrait painting was becoming more popular due to the interest of lay patrons. Subject-matter was still dictated by the patron, but the artist had greater freedom of interpretation. Intellect and originality were considered virtues among the new Humanist intelligentsia.

Painting styles began to develop and in local schools like the Florentine, Venetian and Flemish schools these were passed from master to pupil. Throughout Europe a number of styles of painting evolved. The International Gothic or court style, with its gold frames and backgrounds and elegant lines, was most popular in the princely courts of Europe. A monumental style, which developed mainly in Florence, placed heroic figures in impressive settings; Masaccio and Mantegna were exponents of this style. Scientific interests became the focus of some artists' work, like Uccello with his fascination with linear perspective. Devotional paintings remained important and several monk-artists, including Fra Filippo Lippi, produced works with a spiritual emphasis.

Drawing was considered to be the foundation of all good art, and masters produced sketchbooks of figure types and compositions which they used as resources for their own work and for instructing pupils. [4,18] Paper making had been introduced to Europe, making drawing experi-

TECHNIQUE

[4,17] Fresco-painting technique.

1. The bare masonry was first covered in a thick layer of lime and sand plaster called the 'arriccio'.

2. A composition drawing in red earth pigment called the 'sinopia' was made on the plaster.

3. The painter applied as much smooth plaster, the 'intonaco', as he could paint in one day, quickly putting in outline and modelling in earth colours while the plaster was still fresh. This is called 'fresco' technique. The artist usually started in the top left and worked across and down.

4. The blue areas were added later over the modelling which was in reds and earth colours. Blue azurite pigment was mixed with size and egg yolk and applied in a technique called 'secco fresco'. This is prone to flaking off over the years.

[4,18] Silverpoint drawing from the sketchbook of Jacopo Bellini, father of Giovanni (Louvre, Paris). The Bellinis were one of the most successful families of painters in the Renaissance. Jacopo's sketchbooks were the inspiration for many of Giovanni's paintings.

ments and practice more feasible than on expensive vellum. Pen and ink, charcoal and chalk were frequently used, with metalpoint being used for smaller line work on a specially prepared surface.

Many of the artists of the Quattrocento are known by nicknames or shortened versions of their own names. This seems to have been a practice of the time which was recorded by Vasari in his *Lives of the Artists*.

FLORENTINE QUATTROCENTO
MASACCIO (TOMMASO DI SER GIOVANNI DI MONE) (1401–28)

In his short life Masaccio managed to bring about a complete change in the direction of painting, not only in Florence but in Europe. His work represents the introduction of Renaissance ideas into painting. After Giotto's death in 1337 there had been little development in Florentine painting. The International Gothic style prevailed. But a new era dawned with Masaccio's frescoes in the Brancacci Chapel.

The scenes from the life of St Peter which make up part of the fresco cycle, particularly the 'Tribute Money' scene, [4,19] demonstrate Masaccio's grasp of perspective and three-dimensional modelling. The scene is brightened by light coming from a single source on the upper

[4,19] 'The Tribute Money', c. 1427, by Masaccio, fresco (Brancacci Family Chapel, S. Maria del Carmine, Florence). Masaccio's use of perspective and modelling can clearly be seen in this fresco. His knowledge of colour perspective can be observed in his use of strong reds for the foreground figures set against cooler and paler colours as the space recedes.

right. The shadows are soft, gradually blended down from the lit areas, each figure casting its own shadow. This treatment creates fully rounded figures which occupy space almost as sculptures. The simple hilly landscape and buildings which form the background are in one continuous linear perspective, creating a sense of open receding space. The placing of the feet and the shadows cast by the foreground groups fit perfectly with this scheme. Masaccio manages to express realistic facial expressions and natural body movements and gestures.

There are three scenes in the picture. In the centre the tax collector in the short red garment with his back to us is demanding taxes from Christ and his apostles. Christ and St Peter gesture to the left of the picture where we see St Peter in the distance taking money from a fish's mouth, as he was instructed to by Christ. On the right Peter pays over the money to the tax collector.

Another fresco in Santa Maria Novella in Florence represents 'The Holy Trinity'. [4,20] Here Masaccio uses a very strong perspective to create the impression that the viewer is looking up into a Renaissance arch which is enclosing the figure group. These two frescoes, though not fully appreciated by contemporary artists, were much admired and studied by artists of the following generation.

PAOLO UCCELLO (PAOLO DI DONO) (1396–1475)

Uccello's style is a paradox of medieval decoration and Renaissance perspective. His brightly coloured compositions cling to a strong

[4,20] 'The Holy Trinity', c. 1427, by Masaccio, fresco (S. Maria Novella, Florence). The strong illusionist perspective Masaccio uses in this fresco is designed to match the real eye level of the viewer. The figures of the Trinity, Mary and St John are within the arch. The donors, Lorenzo Cardoni and his wife, are placed outside at a lower level, though still in the same scale. Formerly donors were shown in reduced size. The skeleton in the tomb below represents Everyman.

underlying linear perspective scheme with horses, figures and lances pointing towards a vanishing point. Uccello's painstaking experiments in perspective [4,21] are expressed in the rounded figures and animals he drew in his panel paintings of the 'Battle of San Romano' [4,22] for the Medici family. The stylised prancing horses look almost inflated in their roundness. The lances, shields and figures on the ground are used to accentuate the linear perspective. Indeed, the armoured figure lying under the white horse's tail is known as the man who died for perspective, since he is such a deliberate exercise in perspective. Nevertheless, the background does not flow into the foreground as the scale and angle change. Uccello was, however, more successful in achieving a continuous perspective

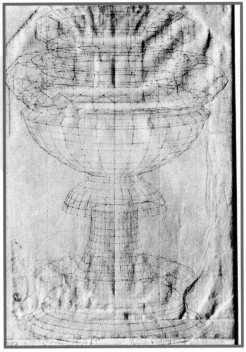

[4,21] Perspective drawing of a chalice by Paolo Uccello, pen and ink on paper (Uffizi Gallery, Florence).

[4,23] 'The Annunciation' by Fra Angelico, fresco (upper corridor, S. Marco, Florence). The devotional style of Fra Angelico's work sometimes masks his achievements in colour, perspective and rendering of light and form.

in his later work, 'The Hunt in the Forest', where the foreground recedes into the darkened woods. Uccello was also very conscious of colour perspective, even painting pink horses to accentuate this effect.

FRA ANGELICO (GUIDO DI PIETRO) (c. 1400–55)

A Dominican friar, Fra Angelico began his career as a manuscript illuminator; but despite life as an enclosed monk he managed to stay in touch with the great advances in Florentine art. The murals he painted in S. Marco in Florence (1438–45) are miracles of innovation in composition, colour, perspective, portraiture and landscape. An example of this work is the beautiful 'Annunciation' [4,23] which takes place in an arcaded space, as accurate in perspective as

anything by Masaccio. The delineation of the figures is more refined and the colouring, particularly of the angel's wings, has a simple beauty. The devotional nature of Fra Angelico's work and the refinement of his style sometimes hide the revolutionary impact of his achievements. The National Gallery in Dublin has a tempera panel of 'The Attempted Martyrdom of Saints Cosmos and Damian' [4,24] which was part of a large altarpiece painted for S. Marco in

[4,24] 'The Attempted Martyrdom of Saints Cosmos and Damian', 1438–40, by Fra Angelico, 36 x 46 cm, tempera on panel (National Gallery of Ireland, Dublin). The subtlety of Fra Angelico's composition can be seen in his use of the foreground figures to frame the scene and lead the eye into the central figures. These foreground figures are also in quite difficult perspectives.

[4,22] 'Battle of San Romano' c. 1455, by Paolo Uccello, tempera on wooden panel (National Gallery, London). This is one of three battle scenes Uccello painted for the Medici family. His keen interest in perspective shows in all his work.

1438–40. The strong colours, subtle composition and perspective are used to tell the story and to focus the viewer on the saints grouped in the centre of the panel. It is interesting to compare the style and technique used by Fra Angelico in the tempera painting to those he used in fresco. The detail and strong colour of the tempera painting are not possible to achieve in the more technically challenging fresco technique, which demands a broader treatment.

SANDRO BOTTICELLI (ALESSANDRO FILIPEPI) (1444–1510)

By the late Quattrocento Florentine taste had tired enough of the new innovations to make Botticelli's style fashionable, a style that was linear and decorative in the Gothic tradition. Botticelli's work was neither old-fashioned nor unskilled; rather he made use of many of the innovations of fifteenth-century art while allowing elegance, grace and decoration to predominate. His two most famous paintings, 'Primavera' (allegory of spring) and 'The Birth of Venus', are full of symbolism and mystery, a manifestation of the new, more secular philosophy current in Florence. These paintings, commissioned by a member of the Medici family to decorate his home, are the first large-scale secular works to survive from the Early Renaissance.

Botticelli's female types are similar to traditional renderings of the Virgin Mary, probably a deliberate device to emphasise spiritual and other-worldly qualities in his goddesses. 'Primavera' [4,25] combines a number of scenes into a landscape of spring flowers and ripening trees. On the right Zephyr, the warm breeze of spring, embraces Chloris who metamorphoses into Flora, goddess of Spring, dressed in and strewing flowers. Venus is at the centre with a blindfolded Cupid over her head shooting arrows at the three graces, while Mercury, messenger of the gods, picks fruit on the left-hand side. There are many theories about the meaning of this work, but no conclusive one.

'Primavera' is a tempera painting on a wooden panel, but Botticelli's other allegorical painting,

[4,25] 'Primavera', c. 1478, by Sandro Botticelli, tempera on wood panel, 315 x 205 cm (Uffizi Gallery, Florence). The complicated composition of figures is carried off with deceptive simplicity and grace by Botticelli, whose use of line and pattern separates him from the innovators of the Quattrocento.

'The Birth of Venus', [4,26] is on canvas — an early survivor of a technique that was to become the standard method, since it was less expensive and easier to prepare than wood panels. The meaning of 'The Birth of Venus' is simpler. Zephyr and Chloris blow Venus, in her shell, ashore, where she is met by a nymph who brings her a robe embroidered in spring flowers. The elegant turning figure of Venus and the patterning of surfaces are typical of Botticelli's style.

FIFTEENTH-CENTURY ITALIAN PAINTING OUTSIDE FLORENCE

While Florence led the way, many of the other states of Italy were not long in joining the Renaissance. The courts of Urbino and Mantua and the city state of Venice were soon providing patrons for artists working in the new style.

[4,26] 'The Birth of Venus', c. 1484, by Sandro Botticelli, tempera on canvas, 175 x 280 cm (Uffizi Gallery, Florence). Botticelli's work was much admired in the 19th century by the Pre-Raphaelites and later Art Nouveau artists.

[4,27] 'The Baptism of Christ' by Piero della Francesca, tempera on panel, 168 x 117 cm (National Gallery, London). Piero's use of light and colour and his interest in landscape can be appreciated in this work.

[4,28] 'The Resurrection of Christ' by Piero della Francesca, fresco, 225 x 205 cm (Pinacoteca, San Sepolcro, Umbria). The underlying geometry of Piero's compositions can be seen in this mural from his native town.

PIERO DELLA FRANCESCA (PIERO DE' FRANCESCHI) (C. 1420–92)

Rediscovered in the nineteenth century, Piero della Francesca is now considered to be one of the most important painters of the fifteenth century. Many influences merged in his style — Florentine perspective and modelling, Sienese colour and Flemish interest in observed landscape. Most of his work was carried out in his native Umbria in his home town of Borgo San Sepolcro and in Arezzo. He also worked for the court in Urbino.

His panel painting of 'The Baptism of Christ', [4,27] originally part of a triptych, demonstrates his calm, almost still, rendering of a scene. The pale Christ figure is bathed in light; a brightly coloured group of angels stand behind the overarching tree. The hilly landscape in the background has a more natural look than many we have seen before. The underlying geometry, which was an important part of Piero's studies, is less obvious in this panel than it is in much of his other work.

'The Resurrection of Christ', [4,28] which he painted in his home town of San Sepolcro, is a composition clearly built on triangles. The soldiers' armour is based on studies he made of antique art on a visit to Rome. Piero's very direct frontal views of his main figures is in contrast with contemporary Florentine style which liked to portray movement.

While in Urbino Piero painted portraits of the Duke and Duchess. He also painted a 'flagellation' which makes dramatic use of perspective and is an unusual composition with three large figures in the right foreground and the scourged Christ in the distance on the left. Piero wrote a treatise on perspective while in Urbino and spent the later years of his life studying mathematics.

ANDREA MANTEGNA (1431–1506)

Andrea Mantegna was a native of Padua and studied there under his adoptive father, Francesco Squarcione, who had a large collection of antique sculpture. Giotto's frescoes in the Arena Chapel, Padua, must have been an influence. As a boy he would also have witnessed the creation of Donatello's 'Santo Altar' and 'Gattamelata'. Uccello also carried out work in Padua, which may have helped Mantegna's mastery of perspective. Mantegna developed his sculptured figure style and use of the illusion of perspective early in his life and quickly came to the attention of Duke Lodovico Gonzaga who appointed him court painter in Mantua in 1460.

The fresco decoration of the 'Camera degli Sposi' (Bridal Chamber) in the Ducal Palace at Mantua is probably Mantegna's most famous work. Red curtains originally hung on two walls of the room and in his fresco Mantegna painted matching curtains drawn back to reveal scenes from the Gonzaga court. On one wall the Duke, sitting in

[4,29] The Duke greeting his son the Cardinal from the 'Camera degli Sposi', c. 1474, by Andrea Mantegna, fresco, Palazzo Ducale, Mantua. The figure group set in the Mantuan landscape shows Mantegna's clarity of drawing and strength of modelling in his figure painting. This is part of a room decoration designed to create the illusion of space and perspective which became a model for Renaissance and Baroque artists.

court with his wife and family, receives a message. On another the Duke greets his son, the newly appointed Cardinal, in the countryside near Mantua, which Mantegna decorates with Roman ruins to suggest a connection between the ruling family and the Roman past. [4,29] The ceiling of the room is painted with false architectural detail, including a central opening to the sky in which putti fly about. This mural was the model for many illusionist works of the later Renaissance and beyond.

Mantegna's love of sculpture and illusion come together in a tempera painting which now hangs in the National Gallery of Ireland. 'Judith with the Head of Holofernes' [4,30] is painted in monochrome in imitation of a stone relief sculpture. The technique is called 'Grisaille' and was used for decoration rather than painting proper. Mantegna's sharply outlined forms and sculptural treatment of modelling were not appreciated by the Florentines but were widely admired and copied elsewhere. Dürer, on a visit to Italy, admired the way Mantegna seemed to make classical art understandable to fifteenth-century eyes.

VENICE

GIOVANNI BELLINI (C. 1430/40–1516)

Giovanni Bellini was the youngest member of a distinguished family of artists. He married Mantegna's sister. He was the founder of the Venetian school of painting. Although Bellini focused on colour and atmosphere rather than on structure, he did use and understand geometric composition which he may have learnt from Mantegna. There is evidence to show that the two artists sometimes worked together, using sketches and compositions drawn by Giovanni's father, Jacopo Bellini (c. 1400–70/71). They both produced paintings of the 'Agony in the Garden' around 1460 based on the same elements but quite different in style and mood.

Bellini was one of the early masters of oil painting, displaying the technique to its best advantage in effective use of light and colour. In his portrait of 'The Doge Leonardo Loredan' [4,31] Bellini demonstrates the Venetian trend for observed realism, showing accurate use of colour and texture, influenced by Northern European artists whose work was known in Venice.

Bellini painted portraits and scenes from mythology, but he is best known for his religious paintings. His 'Madonna of the Meadow' [4,32] uses a simple pyramid composition and an elegant balance of warm and cool colours. The whole scene is brightly but gently lit. The Madonna prays over her sleeping son in a landscape contemporary with Bellini's Venice. In the left middle distance a raven, harbinger of

[4,30] 'Judith with the Head of Holofernes' by Andrea Mantegna, tempera on linen, 48 x 37 cm (National Gallery of Ireland, Dublin). Mantegna displays his skills at creating illusions in paint in this Grisaille (a painting which imitates the colour and texture of stone, in shades of grey). It also emphasises the training he received in drawing from sculptures in his master's workshop.

[4,31] Portrait of 'The Doge Leonardo Loredan' by Giovanni Bellini, oil on wood panel, 61.5 x 45 cm (Accademia Carrara, Bergamo). The rendering of rich fabrics and carefully observed light and colour mark a trend in Venetian painting separate from Florentine tradition.

[4,32] 'Madonna of the Meadow' c.1500, by Giovanni Bellini, 67 x 86 cm, oil painting (National Gallery, London). Bellini's paintings of the Madonna and Child theme were rarely surpassed in the Renaissance.

death, and a battle between an egret and a snake, representing good and evil, symbolise the difficulties awaiting the sleeping Christ child in his adult life.

The rich colouring and brightly lit compositions of Bellini were a crucial influence on Giorgione and Titian who trained in his workshop, and on the generations of Venetian artists that followed.

FIFTEENTH-CENTURY PAINTING OUTSIDE ITALY

The International Gothic style flourished in Europe from Paris to Prague during the fifteenth century, except in the regions of Burgundy and Flanders which were under the patronage of the Duke of Burgundy and his court. Whereas in the fourteenth century the Dukes of Burgundy commissioned works in the Gothic style from the best artists, by 1426 they were commissioning paintings in a style different to both the Italian and Gothic.

The Humanist influence current in Europe, which we have already noted in Italian art, inspired Flemish artists to create a realistic, contemporary look in their work. They abandoned the gold backgrounds and linear decoration of the Gothic for observed realism in landscape, interior background and figures. The new technique of oil painting, which allowed greater detail and richer colours, helped form the new style.

JAN VAN EYCK (D. 1441)

Little is known of van Eyck's early life. He may have begun as a book illuminator. His first known work is the magnificent 'Ghent Altarpiece', a polyptych (made of many parts) of twenty panels which he painted in collaboration with his brother, Hubert. The central panel is 'The Adoration of the Lamb' [4,33] set in a green landscape sprinkled with spring flowers, with the heavenly city in the distance. Four processions converge on the altar of the Lamb. The fountain of life is in the foreground, symbolising redemption. The procession continues in the panels on either

[4,33] 'The Adoration of the Lamb' (Ghent Altarpiece), 1434, by Hubert and Jan van Eyck, tempera and oil on panel, 375 x 517 cm open (St Bavo Cathedral, Ghent). This is the first great masterpiece of the Flemish school. The scenes in the lower panels show virtuous people arriving from the four corners of the world to adore the 'Lamb of God'. The detail in the painting is remarkable. The faces of even the smallest figures are carefully painted and the flowers and plants in the landscape are recognisable. The larger figures in the upper panels include nudes of Adam and Eve in an unidealised style.

side of the lower row. The figures in the upper row are larger. God the Father is at the centre, with the Virgin and John the Baptist on either side. Angels playing music take up the next panels, with Adam and Eve in the narrow outer panels. Closed, the altarpiece shows portraits of the donors, Josse Vijdt and his wife, in colour, while the remaining sections are in Grisaille and represent the Annunciation. This, the greatest of the early Flemish masterpieces, hangs in the Cathedral of St Bavo in Ghent, for which it was originally made.

Van Eyck's rendering of realistic light and detail is seen in the 'Arnolfini Wedding' portrait [4,34] which was painted for Giovanni Arnolfini, an Italian banker working in Bruges. The bride and groom stand in their richly decorated room, surrounded by symbols of their faith and their commitment to each other. Van Eyck's rendering of materials immediately stands out — the weight and surface of fabrics and furs can almost be felt. The shine on the brass chandelier, with its single lighted candle representing faith, is picked up in the little convex mirror which reflects the whole scene and acts as a compositional centre around which the picture is focused. Van Eyck's elaborate signature and his image in the mirror bear witness to his presence at the ceremony. The rich colour scheme and carefully observed perspective are characteristic of van Eyck's work and can be seen

again in 'The Virgin of Chancellor Rolin' which combines figures in an elaborately decorated interior with a view of a Flemish town and countryside seen from a balcony. Van Eyck's sheer precision discouraged imitation, but his work was much admired throughout Europe.

ROBERT CAMPIN (MASTER OF FLÉMALLE) (C. 1375–1444)

Robert Campin was from Tournai in Belgium and was one of the masters of early Flemish art. His style was harder than van Eyck's, with more remnants of Gothic detail in some of his work. His 'Nativity' [4,35] combines figures in a ruined stable with a Flemish landscape. It is interesting to compare this painting with Masaccio's 'Tribute Money' which is contemporary and see the very different approach to figures and landscape north and south of the Alps.

ROGIER VAN DER WEYDEN (1400–64)

Rogier van der Weyden, a pupil in Robert Campin's workshop, became the leading Flemish painter of his day. His mature style combines features of Campin's and van Eyck's, but there is an emotional element in his work which is unique. His 'Deposition' (descent from the cross) [4,36] is considered to be his great masterpiece. The group is set in a shallow architectural space, rather than a landscape. The rich colouring and careful detail of the clothes almost go unnoticed, in contrast with the emotional impact of the work.

[4,34] 'The Arnolfini Wedding', 1434, by Jan van Eyck, oil on wooden panel, 82 x 59 cm (National Gallery, London). Many of the objects in this wedding portrait of Giovanni Arnolfini and Giovanna Cenami are symbols of good wishes for the marriage. The single candle in the chandelier is the light of faith, the mirror a symbol of purity, the dog a symbol of fidelity. The figure on the carved chair, back beside the bride's head, is St Margaret, patron of childbirth. Other details follow this theme.

[4,35] 'Nativity', c. 1425, by Robert Campin, 85 x 71 cm (Musée des Beaux Arts, Dijon). Gothic details like the small angels and the inscribed ribbons are counteracted by the realism and sense of space created in the rest of the painting.

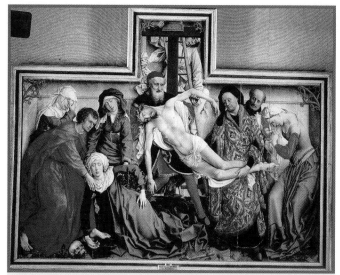

[4,36] 'Deposition', c. 1435, by Rogier van Der Weyden, 220 x 260 cm, oil paint on wood panel (Museo del Prado, Madrid). Rogier van der Weyden's emotional rendering of religious themes was popular all over Europe. His work was exported to France, Germany, Italy and this one to Spain.

[4,37] 'The Portinari Altarpiece', c. 1476, by Hugo van der Goes, each wing 254 x 140 cm, central panel 254 x 305 cm (Uffizi Gallery, Florence). When this triptych arrived in Florence it created a lot of interest among the local artists. Florentine eyes were unused to the realistic backgrounds and oil painting techniques.

The slumped figures of Christ and his mother are supported by apostles and saints who display a range of emotions from suppressed grief to open anguish. There is a great range of facial types among the carefully grouped figures.

The fame of Rogier van der Weyden spread throughout Europe and he ran a large and prosperous workshop, creating sculpture and banners as well as religious and secular paintings and portraits. His work was exported to Spain, France, Germany and Italy, including two paintings for the Medici family.

HUGO VAN DER GOES (C. 1436–82)

Work by van der Goes was influential in the second half of the fifteenth century. His 'Portinari Altarpiece' [4,37], a triptych commissioned by Tommaso Portinari, a Medici agent in Bruges, for the Hospital of Santa Maria Nuova in Florence, is a large work with near life-size figures. The colour scheme and oil painting technique were carefully noted by contemporary Florentine painters. Van der Goes's modelling and sense of space and realism in the landscape were also influential.

HANS MEMLING (C. 1440–94)

Popular and wealthy in his own lifetime, Memling did not achieve the emotional expression of his master, Rogier van der Weyden. His work was conservative, but his portraits tend to be more original and lively than his religious works. [4,38]

CONCLUSION

By the end of the fifteenth century all the elements needed for realistic, three-dimensional representation in painting had been assembled, though not yet in the work of any one artist. The Italians had developed formal perspective and accurate human proportions and anatomy, while the Northern European artists had focused on observation of nature and the development of oil painting. Both traditions had developed composition and the representation of space through colour, light and shadow. A grammar of visual expression had been found that formed the basis of western art for the next 300 years.

[4,38] 'Portrait of Martin van Nieuwenhove', 1487, by Hans Memling, oil on panel, 44 x 33 cm (Hospital of St John, Bruges). Like many Flemish artists before him Memling was a master at rendering textures. Note the detail in the windows as well as in the hair and the fabrics of the sitter's clothes.

SIXTEENTH CENTURY: HIGH RENAISSANCE AND MANNERISM

The sixteenth century was a period of great change in Europe. America had been discovered, bringing increased wealth and power to those countries which had colonies there. Africa had been circumnavigated, opening up alternative trade routes to the Far East.

The development of publishing houses led to an easier dissemination of knowledge throughout Europe at a time when the Reformation was offering a challenge to traditional beliefs and practices in Church and society.

At this time Italy, in particular, was suffering from internal conflicts and external invasion. It is surprising then that one of the most brilliant phases in world art took place in Italy in the first twenty years of the sixteenth century. The High Renaissance style developed in Florence and Rome, which were then enjoying comparative peace and prosperity. However, the sacking of Rome in 1527 ended this phase and scattered the great artists all over Europe, where they spread the Mannerist Renaissance style.

MANNERISM

Vasari, in his second edition of the *Lives of the Artists* published in 1568, uses the word 'Mannera', meaning style or stylishness, to signify graceful, well-executed, sophisticated work. The term Mannerism also refers to Renaissance art after 1520 which depends for its effect on some quirk of style such as elongation of figures or a dramatic posture that allows the artist to flaunt his skill. At best it is self-conscious elegance or skill; at worst, soulless virtuosity.

The status of the artist slowly changed from tradesman to gentleman. The artist could now choose his own subjects and could accept or refuse commissions. Patrons would accept any work from the hand of a great master. Michelangelo was able to argue with the Pope as an equal; Raphael had a large, princely retinue and lived in a palace. Artists thought not only about subject and style of execution, but about the creative process itself — the artist became a creator, an intellectual.

ARCHITECTURE

Rome had fallen into decay over the centuries and its rebuilding was undertaken by a series of popes, most energetically under Julius II (Pope 1503–13) who wished to create a modern Rome to rival the Imperial City. He made Bramante his chief architect and together they planned the reconstruction of not only the Vatican palaces and St Peter's, but much of the city.

DONATO BRAMANTE (C. 1444–1514)

Buildings designed by Bramante in Rome in his later life embrace much of what is considered to be the High Renaissance style of architecture. His Tempietto [4,39] at S. Pietro in Montorio, Rome, on what is traditionally believed to be the site of St Peter's crucifixion, is considered the first truly High Renaissance building. Its influence on the course of architecture is much greater than its small size would suggest. The plain Doric columns support a straight entablature rather than an arcade which was common in the Early Renaissance. Likewise, the windows and niches deeply set in the drum of the dome break with classical models. The Tempietto's interest, however, lies not in any structural innovation but in its harmonious proportion and in the simplicity of its design and circular plan.

[4,39] The Tempietto, 1502, by Bramante (S. Pietro, Montorio, Rome). Bramante intended the building to be surrounded by a cloister. In spite of an internal diameter of only 4.5 m, this beautifully proportioned little building has a monumental quality.

A plan based on the circle and square was an ideal in Renaissance architecture and was proposed by Bramante for a new St Peter's Basilica, but by the time of his death only the piers to support the dome had been built. [4,40] The palaces designed by Bramante within the Vatican and in the city of Rome continued to influence city architecture up to the nineteenth century. Bramante spent a number of years in Milan before he went to Rome where he became friends with Leonardo da Vinci. They may well have discussed centrally planned churches, for which Leonardo made a number of sketches in his notebooks.

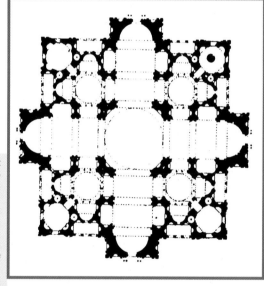

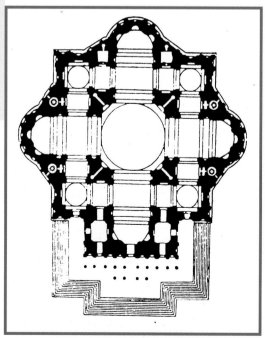

[4,40] Plans of St Peter's in Rome by Bramante and Michelangelo. Bramante's plan for St Peter's in Rome (1505/6) (top) was a complex web of walls and pillars. Michelangelo's plan (c.1546) (below) was greatly simplified, using massive walls and only four huge piers to support the giant structure.

MICHELANGELO BUONARROTI (1475–1564)

(SEE ALSO UNDER SCULPTURE AND PAINTING)
Michelangelo dedicated a large part of his later life to architecture. With Pope Leo X (Giovanni de Medici) as patron, he was given a number of commissions in Florence. The Laurentian library and the Medici chapel of San Lorenzo, although never completed, were influential works. The Medici chapel, designed to complement Brunelleschi's sacristy on the other side of the church, uses the same materials — dark stone framing white walls. Only two of the originally planned four tombs were completed, those of Giuliano and Lorenzo de Medici. Complicated niches and friezes crowd the lower part of the square building, providing a setting for the sculpture. The upper parts become progressively simpler and brighter, culminating in the cupola. This expressed the Humanist idea of greater purity and light as thoughts rose to heaven away from the busy world. In light of the questions posed by Reformation thinking, Michelangelo had some doubts about Christian image making, so it suited him to concentrate on architecture for a time.

In 1534 Michelangelo went to Rome, where he spent the final thirty years of his life working mainly as an architect. He reorganised the buildings on the Capitoline Hill into the Campidoglio, [4,41] a beautifully planned square approached by ramped steps which are flanked at the top by huge Roman statues of Castor and Pollux, protectors of Rome. An enormous bronze equestrian statue of Marcus Aurelius, salvaged from old Rome, is placed at the centre of the oval decoration of the paved square. The three palazzos which enclose the space have giant Corinthian pilasters passing through two storeys of each building. All the buildings facing the square are topped by balustrades and figure sculptures.

An important part of Michelangelo's design for St Peter's, [4,42] which had not been worked on since Bramante's time, was the use of giant orders. [4,43] Michelangelo simplified and strengthened the design and in his lifetime it was built up to the drum of the dome. Although building was completed and altered after

[4,41] 'Campidoglio', Rome, begun 1539, by Michelangelo and others. Michelangelo's use of a giant order of pilasters unites the buildings in this group. The smaller columns flanking the openings on the two facing buildings produce a more human scale. The Palace of the Senator at the back of the square is elevated on a basement to dominate the other buildings and to lift it into the view of people ascending the steps. The massive sculptures at the top of the steps are of Roman origin.

[4,43] The Roman orders.
a. Doric
b. Ionic capital
c. Corinthian capital
d. Composite capital
e. Tuscan capital

[4,42] St Peter's, the Vatican, Rome, begun 1546. Pairs of giant Corinthian pilasters separate deeply recessed windows and niches. The plain attic storey leads the eye up to the massive dome.

Michelangelo's death, his remains the greatest contribution to this most important Christian monument.

SPREAD OF RENAISSANCE STYLE
The Renaissance style spread throughout the cities of Italy and then further afield. In Venice Jacopo Sansovino (1486–1570) designed a number of buildings. The library of St Mark's, though quite different in style, matches the scale and sculptural niches of the Doge's Palace which is opposite it.

ANDREA PALLADIO (1508–80)
Andrea Palladio designed the Church of S. Giorgio Maggiore [4,44] on an island facing St Mark's and the Doge's Palace. In his design he echoed the shapes of the dome and the bell tower of St Mark's. The façade is based on classical temple fronts, combining half-columns with pilasters which are also used inside the building.

[4,44] Church of S. Giorgio Maggiore, Venice, begun 1565, by Andrea Palladio, view from the water showing dome and bell tower. The classical façade is backed by the dome and bell tower which mirror the outline of St Mark's across the water.

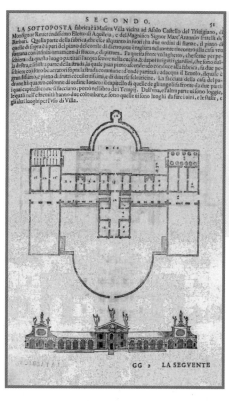

[4,46] Plan and elevation of the Villa Barbaro, c. 1549, from Book 2 of the *Four Books of Architecture* by Andrea Palladio. The numbers in the rooms on the plan relate to each other harmonically. This idea of using musical harmonies to create mathematical proportions was not uncommon in the Renaissance.

Palladio is probably best known for his country villas which were copied for centuries, particularly in England. His *Four Books of Architecture* set out plans for a variety of buildings. In Book 2 the design for the Villa Barbaro [4,45] combines a country retreat with a working farm. To ensure the harmony of the design the sizes of the rooms are related to each other as parts of a musical octave. [4,46] The master's house forms the centre. It has four Ionic columns supporting a carved pediment. A loggia on each side ends in a dovecote, under which are stables and places for winemaking and other farmwork. This combination of work and leisure in one structure suited generations of country gentlemen.

ARCHITECTURE OUTSIDE ITALY

The Renaissance style was only gradually assimilated north of the Alps, where the Gothic style persisted well into the sixteenth century. In France the court employed Italian artists and masons to build and decorate their châteaux. The design of Chambord [4,47] demonstrates how classical pilasters and mouldings were added to what were basically medieval structures. The Italian architects Rosso and Primaticcio were employed by François I at Fontainebleau, where their long gallery [4,48] became the model for much interior decoration in France, Flanders and England. Stucco, painting and carving combine into an overall unified scheme.

[4,45] Villa Barbaro, Maser, Italy, 1558, by Andrea Palladio. The master's house at centre is flanked by two loggie which house farm buildings.

[4,47] Château of Chambord, Loir-et-Cher, France, begun 1519. Built as a hunting lodge for François I, Chambord still has the tall roofs and chimneys of the Gothic style, though the proportions and articulation of the three storeys are Renaissance. The decoration is mostly classical.

[4,48] Galerie François I, Fontainebleau, 1533–7, by Rosso and Primaticcio. The stucco work designed mainly by Rosso includes the first example of strapwork — geometric scrolls which imitate leather or parchment — which became a very popular element in North European decoration. The stucco work, painting and wood panelling were designed as a unified whole.

Sixteenth-century English architecture is known as 'Elizabethan'. Although classical elements are to be found, the Renaissance sense of proportion was common. At Longleat House [4,49] pilasters flank the windows and strong horizontal bands separate the storeys; but the comparatively flat walls and large windows are typically English.

Renaissance decoration was common throughout Europe long before its architectural style. Italianate furniture, painting and plasterwork were in demand before any true Renaissance-style buildings were constructed. The Italian style of town planning, with spacious streets and squares, gradually spread, however, as did the idea of relating country houses to their gardens and landscape.

[4,49] Longleat House, Sir John Thynne and Robert Smythson. Longleat is the first Elizabethan house to show the full French and Italian influence.

SCULPTURE

The artistic and technical achievements of the sculptors of the fifteenth century were not easily surpassed, but the sheer power of expression and vigorous technique of one man created a new standard in the sixteenth century.

MICHELANGELO BUONARROTI (1475–1564)

(SEE ALSO UNDER ARCHITECTURE AND PAINTING)
A heroic figure in the history of art, Michelangelo worked and lived on a larger than life scale. We have witnessed the breadth of his thinking in architecture and will now see how this proud man applied himself to sculpture, which was his great passion in life.

Apprenticed to Domenico Ghirlandaio at thirteen years of age, he learnt the basics of the fresco technique and made drawings from the work of Giotto and Masaccio. He then went on to learn sculpture from Bertoldo di Giovanni who ran a school in the Medici gardens. After a short time in Bologna he went to Rome in 1496, where he studied classical sculpture. His first large commission was the Pietà, now in St Peter's in Rome, which immediately established him as the greatest living sculptor. The flawless carving and polished finish, as well as the sheer beauty and emotion of the piece, still impress today. [4,50]

[4,50] 'Pietà', 1498–9, by Michelangelo Buonarroti (St Peter's, Rome). One of the masterpieces of Christian art, the pyramidal composition was an unusual solution for this subject, which was more commonly a theme for North European artists.

[4,51] 'David', 1501–4, by Michelangelo Buonarroti, 450 cm tall, marble (Galleria dell'Accademia, Florence). Originally meant to top a buttress of the Cathedral, the David was placed in the Palazzo della Signoria, near the entrance to the Palace of Government, where it stood as a symbol of Florence's defiance of her enemies.

[4,52] Unfinished sculpture by Michelangelo Buonarroti, marble. This incomplete sculpture gives an insight into how Michelangelo worked. Able to carve faster than any mason, he felt he was literally releasing the figure from the marble.

On his return to Florence Michelangelo accepted the commission for the now famous 'David'. [4,51] Standing 4.5 metres tall, this figure is a completely different concept to Donatello's 'David'. Michelangelo's figure expresses the moment *before* the conflict. Slingshot on his shoulder, David looks towards the enemy, leaning slightly back, weight on one leg. This small movement creates a life-like quality and emotional intensity which put this sculpture beyond the Greek and Roman models that Michelangelo had studied. Michelangelo's carving of the huge block of marble from which David emerged is flawless; his rendering of flesh and muscle almost makes one forget that what we are looking at is stone.

This was a particularly productive period in Michelangelo's life. [4,52] He finished a few small pieces in painting and sculpture and was commissioned to undertake larger projects; these included a series of the Twelve Apostles, of which only St Matthew was ever started, and a mural which only reached cartoon stage.

In 1505 Pope Julius II summoned Michelangelo to Rome to make a tomb for him. Originally conceived as a vast affair, 6 metres by 9 metres, with roughly forty figures, it was more than any man could carve in a lifetime. Only two slave figures and a seated Moses, which forms the centrepiece of the final wall-mounted tomb, were

ever completed. Moses, larger than life size, is a powerful and fierce-looking figure and may express some of the anger and frustration Michelangelo felt at Julius's insistence on the painting of the Sistine Chapel, thus preventing Michelangelo from working on the tomb.

After Julius's death Pope Leo X, a Medici, gave Michelangelo several commissions, the most important of which was the Medici tomb in Florence. [4,53] The figures of night and day, dawn and dusk, and the idealised portraits of Giuliano and Lorenzo de Medici go beyond realism in an attempt to express the abstract ideas of the active and contemplative life.

[4,53] Tomb of Lorenzo de Medici, 1520–34, Michelangelo, marble (New Sacristy, San Lorenzo, Florence). The portrait and the tomb figures are idealised and designed to portray the idea of contemplation rather than any physical reality.

Michelangelo returned to Rome in 1534 where he remained for the last thirty years of his life. He worked on murals, architecture and a few sculptures which he carved for himself. Two unfinished Pietàs mark the final phase of his sculpture; their emotional and spiritual qualities seem almost Gothic, with very little of the pride and anger of his early work.

Other sixteenth-century work pales in comparison with Michelangelo's achievement, but there were some fine sculptors in Italy, France and Germany who should be noted.

JACOPO SANSOVINO (JACOPO TATTI) (1486–1570)

Jacopo Sansovino, architect and sculptor, worked mainly in Venice. His colossal figures of Mars [4,54] and Neptune on the staircase of the Doge's Palace highlight his knowledge of antique sculpture, though they have a vitality which goes beyond mere imitation of classical forms. Many of the buildings he designed are richly decorated with sculpture.

BENVENUTO CELLINI (1500–71)

A Florentine goldsmith, metalworker and sculptor, Benvenuto Cellini worked for a time for François I at Fontainebleau, mainly as a goldsmith. His bronze 'Perseus' [4,55] in Florence is considered one of the masterpieces of Mannerist sculpture. The sometimes fussy detail in his work shows that the transfer from very fine goldsmithery to large-scale sculpture was not always easy.

GIAMBOLOGNA (JEAN DE BOULOGNE) (1529–1608)

Flemish born, Florentine sculptor Giambologna was considered second only to Michelangelo in the sixteenth century. 'Rape of the Sabine', [4,56] a showy piece in the Mannerist style, uses, in a dramatic way, the turning pose first developed by Michelangelo and combines young and old, male and female figures in a demonstration of virtuosity. Giambologna's small bronze figures continued to be cast up to the nineteenth century and helped spread his fame and Italian Renaissance style throughout Europe.

[4,54] 'Mars', 1550, by Jacopo Sansovino, marble (Palazzo Ducale, Venice). Sansovino designed a whole scheme of buildings and sculptures that created the impressive centre of Venice we see today. This massive sculpture is part of the scheme of improvements, very classical but also lively.

[4,55] 'Perseus', 1554, by Benvenuto Cellini, bronze (Loggia dei Lanzi). Considered to be one of the masterpieces of Mannerism, Cellini's 'Perseus' has the sense of style and attention to detail that is characteristic of late 16th-century sculpture in Italy.

[4,56] 'Rape of the Sabine', 1582, by Giambologna, 410 cm, marble (Loggia dei Lanzi, Florence). This Mannerist sculpture was originally carved as a demonstration of skill and only titled after it was finished.

SCULPTURE OUTSIDE ITALY

Italian artists and craftsmen who were brought in by François I to work at Fontainebleau greatly influenced native artists.

JEAN GOUJON (1510–65)

Possibly influenced by Cellini when the latter worked in Fontainebleau, Goujon's masterpiece is considered to be the six relief panels for the 'Fontaine des Innocents'. [4,57] In the panels, nymphs fill the narrow spaces with rippling decorative draperies, their turning figures beautifully carved in the Mannerist style.

GERMAIN PILON (1537–90)

Germain Pilon was influenced in his early years by the school of Fontainebleau. The 'Three Graces' [4,58] are similar to Goujon's figures but are more still and realistic, though the fabrics flow in fanciful sweeps around the figures in the Mannerist style.

[4,58] 'Three Graces', 1560–3, marble, 150 cm tall (Louvre, Paris). Monument to the heart of King Henry II of France.

PIETER FLÖTNER (1495–1546)

In Germany Pieter Flötner was a sculptor and engraver who worked mainly in Nuremberg. Following visits to Italy he produced the 'Apollo Fountain', [4,59] a graceful Mannerist creation which was very advanced in design even by Italian standards.

[4,57] 'Fontaine des Innocents', 1547–9, by Jean Goujon, marble (Musée des Monuments Français, Paris). The turn of the figures and the flowing robes show the Italian influence on these relief panels.

[4,59] The 'Apollo Fountain', 1534, by Pieter Flötner (Nuremberg Town Hall). The figure is about half life-size. The pyramidal design of the fountain seems to pre-date similar Italian examples.

75

CONCLUSION

By the end of the sixteenth century, sculpture had moved beyond realism to emotional expression and decorative individualism in design. Michelangelo had pushed standards of sculpture and expression to a point where his contemporaries thought there was no more to be achieved. All that remained was to find an individual style or mode of expression that would make their work stand out.

PAINTING

The outstanding talents of Leonardo da Vinci, Michelangelo and Raphael quickly brought painting to the forefront of the Renaissance arts. In the first twenty years of the sixteenth century they created a new standard in art known as the 'grand manner', which surpassed all previous generations and made painting the equal of sculpture in realism and expressive power. Artists studied classical art, made drawings from the works of earlier masters, studied nature and human anatomy and learnt techniques and theories of art from their masters.

Those who followed these three great artists felt that perfection had been achieved and that they could only make variations of technique, style or subject to draw attention to their work. This led to the Mannerist period of sixteenth-century art.

LEONARDO DA VINCI (1452–1519)

Leonardo was a painter, sculptor, architect and engineer, but most of all he was a man with an insatiable curiosity about the workings of nature in all its aspects. His notebooks and drawings reveal studies of human and animal anatomy; [4,60] the workings of weather and water; the study of plants; and preparatory sketches for paintings, sculptures, architecture, machinery and engineering works. Very little was ever finished. Only fifteen paintings survive and many of these are damaged or incomplete. No sculpture or architecture remains that we can definitely attribute to him. In spite of what appears to be a list of failures, Leonardo was in many ways *the* Renaissance man — well educated, an accomplished musician, a gentleman in dress and behaviour, an addition to any princely court.

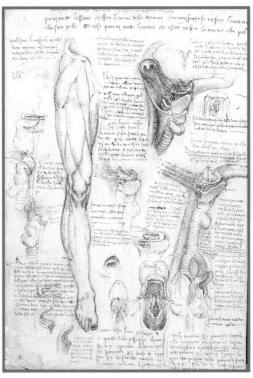

[4,60] Anatomical Studies (larynx and leg), 1510, by Leonardo da Vinci (Windsor Castle, Royal Library). Leonardo's scientific curiosity led to studies beyond his needs as an artist. His notes were written right to left and can only be read with a mirror, partly for secrecy, partly because he was left-handed.

Apprenticed to Andrea del Verrocchio in Florence, Leonardo learnt the skills of painting and sculpture from his master. He painted one of the angels in Verrocchio's 'Baptism of Christ' after which Verrocchio is reputed to have given up painting to concentrate on sculpture. Leonardo may have taken over painting for the workshop as he remained there for four years after he was made a master artist. While his contemporaries copied paintings and drawings, Leonardo's early painting shows that he worked from direct observation. The angel's wings on his 'Annunciation' are from studies of birds' wings and the drapery is also drawn from life.

A series of Madonnas and portraits in the 1470s led to commissions for two altarpieces, only one of which, the 'Adoration of the Magi', survives unfinished. [4,61] The 'Adoration' is, in fact, only an underpainting in shades of brown, which gives us an insight into the painstaking method Leonardo used when painting with oils. A complete tonal sketch was developed with all the detail included and then glazes of transparent colour were applied. White lead paint was used for the highlights and flesh tones. This method suited Leonardo's interest in light and shadow. He uses 'chiaroscuro', a strong contrast of light and dark, to focus the viewer's attention on faces and hands so that the gesture and expression tell the story of the painting.

[4,61] 'Adoration of the Magi', c. 1481, by Leonardo da Vinci, oil on wood, 243 x 246 cm (Uffizi Gallery, Florence). The pyramidal composition and organisation of the large number of figures into inner order and outer confusion was a landmark in picture design.

Leonardo moved to Milan in 1482. His letter of introduction to Lodovico Sforza, Duke of Milan, outlining all his abilities, concentrates on military engineering and only mentions painting as an afterthought.

While in Milan he painted the 'Virgin of the Rocks' which now hangs in the Louvre. [4,62] A later version of the same composition is in the National Gallery in London. This is a good example of the pyramid composition which Leonardo frequently used. The flowers in the foreground are based on his botanical studies and the fantastic rock formations which make the grotto highlight his knowledge of geology. The 'sfumato' (smoked) technique is also used, with edges softened so that tones gently blur into each other — a technique also later employed to create the so-called mystic smile on the 'Mona Lisa'. The beautiful portrait of Cecilia Gallerani, 'Lady with an Ermine', mistress of the Duke, was also painted around this time.

'The Last Supper', [4,63] painted on a wall of the refectory of S. Maria delle Grazie in Milan, is considered by many to be the first High Renaissance painting. It manages to convey the dramatic moment when Christ declares, 'One of you will betray me.' Through gesture and expression each apostle shows his reaction. Only Judas sits still, stunned by Jesus's words. The composition is revolutionary, with the groups of figures arranged so that our first focus is on Christ, silhouetted against the window behind him. We then follow the movement and gesture to each end of the table and back. Leonardo tried an oil painting method for this mural because he did not like fresco which required broad technique and quick work, neither of which suited him. Unfortunately, his experimental technique did not work and the mural began falling apart even in his own lifetime.

After Milan fell to the French in 1499 Leonardo moved back to Florence where he painted the 'Madonna, Child and St Anne' and a number of paintings which are now lost. He was commis-

[4,62] 'Virgin of the Rocks', c. 1483, by Leonardo da Vinci, oil on wood (Louvre, Paris). The studies of botany and geology that Leonardo made are used in this and other paintings. His development of subtlety in modelling light and shadow advanced oil painting technique.

[4,63] 'The Last Supper', 1495–7, Leonardo da Vinci, oil tempera, 420 x 910 cm (Convent of S. Maria delle Grazie, Milan). The revolutionary composition of Leonardo's 'Last Supper' makes it the first true High Renaissance painting.

sioned to paint the 'Battle of Anghiari' in the Grand Council hall of the Palazzo Vecchio, but did not get very far. Sketches and copies of his cartoons greatly influenced younger artists and many later battle scenes are based on his designs. The young Michelangelo was commissioned to paint a battle scene on the opposite wall of the Grand Council at the same time, but he was called to Rome before any painting began.

'St John the Baptist' and the 'Mona Lisa' [4,64] are among Leonardo's later works. In these paintings, although the subjects look directly at the viewer, inviting communication, it is difficult to get beyond the ambiguous expression of cool reserve.

Much of his later life was spent in the study of science and mathematics as he wandered from Florence to Milan and to Rome and finally to France, where he died. His influence on Raphael, Bramante and Giorgione was decisive in the development of sixteenth-century art and continued in the generations of artists that followed.

MICHELANGELO BUONARROTI (1475–1564)
(SEE ALSO UNDER ARCHITECTURE AND SCULPTURE)
We have already seen much of Michelangelo's life and works under the headings of architecture and sculpture. He painted only reluctantly, but even so he created probably the most influential fresco cycle in the history of art, the Sistine Chapel Ceiling.

While Leonardo had an insatiable appetite for science, nature and the arts, Michelangelo had a single obsession — the human figure. Its physical beauty and its power to express emotion and ideas consumed him. He believed his ideas could best be expressed in the beauty and purity of the nude figure. The early 'Holy Family' (Doni Tondo) [4,65] has almost no other elements but the human figure. Even the background is composed of nude male figures. Michelangelo's interest in the work seems to have been the complicated figure perspective involved in Mary handing the Christ child to Joseph.

His cartoon for the Battle of Cascina, which was being made for the Signoria of Florence at the same time as Leonardo's battle scene, also

[4,64] 'Mona Lisa', 1503, by Leonardo da Vinci, 77 x 53 cm, oil on wood (Louvre, Paris). All the refinements of technique and composition that Leonardo had developed are included in this unidentified portrait.

influenced younger artists greatly, particularly Raphael. The Mannerist preoccupation with nude figures in action stems from this work.

However, before he could start work on this fresco, Pope Julius II called Michelangelo to Rome initially to design his tomb and then to paint the Sistine Chapel ceiling, [4,66] possibly the most influential work in the history of art. Commissioned on 10 May 1508 it was completed on 31 October 1512, a feat of physical endurance undertaken almost unaided in extremely uncomfortable conditions. The meaning of some of the figures is still the subject of debate, but the main panels represent scenes from Genesis, from the Creation to the drunkenness of Noah. Christ's ancestors are above the windows and the huge

[4,65] 'Holy Family' (Doni Tondo), 1503, by Michelangelo Buonarroti, 120 cm diameter (Uffizi Gallery, Florence). This Holy Family has none of the prettiness of contemporary Madonna and Child paintings. The physical strength of the figures seems to dominate.

[4,66] Sistine Chapel Ceiling, 1508–12, by Michelangelo Buonarroti, full ceiling, fresco. The painted architecture of the barrel vault of the Sistine Chapel frames over 300, mostly nude, human figures, depicting characters and scenes from creation up to the law of Moses.

[4,67] 'The Creation of Adam', 1512, by Michelangelo Buonarroti (from Sistine Chapel Ceiling), fresco. The power of this image of the transfer of the spirit of God to man has captured the imagination of generations.

[4,68] 'Study for the Libyan Sybil', by Michelangelo Buonarroti (Metropolitan Museum of Art, New York). Michelangelo made studies from life in preparation for all his work. Details were reworked and retried to get the correct effect.

Sibyls and prophets fill the remaining space at each side of the building. The painted architecture and nude figures between the scenes seem to stand forward in relief.

For his most dramatic scene Michelangelo chose the moment when God gave the spark of life and soul to Adam. Adam raises himself from a rock on one elbow and reaches a languid hand towards a powerful god figure who sweeps in, surrounded by angels. [4,67] The dramatic poses and perfect anatomy were developed in hundreds of preparatory drawings, with no detail overlooked in the creation of this masterpiece. [4,68] The vibrant colours of the clothes of the prophets and Sibyls were lost in the smoke and dirt of generations, only to be revealed in cleaning completed in the 1990s.

The effect of this work on the artists of the time and following generations is hard to imagine. They saw perfection revealed in anatomy and figure composition, in dramatic scenes of larger than life beings and events.

The 'Last Judgment', [4,69] commissioned in 1534, painted on the end wall of the Sistine Chapel is quite different in mood. A powerful Christ figure rises from his throne, arm raised as if about to smite the wicked who rise from their graves at the bottom of the mural. The judgmental spirit of the Counter-Reformation seems to have influenced this image of the Last Day. Michelangelo painted little after this, devoting his later years to architecture and sculpture.

RAPHAEL (RAFFAELLO) SANZIO [SANTI] (1483–1520)

Born in Urbino, the son of a local artist, Raphael was an independent artist by the age of seventeen. He worked with Perugino for a while and then came under the influence of both Leonardo da Vinci and Michelangelo when he was in Florence from 1504 to 1508. It was Raphael's ability to absorb the ideas and techniques of other artists that led to his advanced style. From Leonardo he learnt the importance of developing ideas and composition through sketches; from Michelangelo he learnt grand figure compositions; and from antique Roman sculpture he learnt poise and meaningful gesture. He was not yet famous enough for large

[4,69] The 'Last Judgment', 1536–41, by Michelangelo Buonarroti, fresco, 1,463 x 1,341 cm (Sistine Chapel, Rome). The darker atmosphere and imagery of this vision of the Day of Judgment may result from Counter-Reformation beliefs in the sinful nature of man.

commissions in Florence, so he concentrated on portraits and religious paintings, particularly Madonna and Child compositions for which he is rightly famous. [4,70]

In 1508, when Raphael was only twenty-five, Pope Julius II summoned him to Rome, where he

[4,70] 'Madonna of the Meadow', 1505, by Raphael, oil on panel, 113 x 87 cm (Kunsthistorisches Museum, Vienna). The influence of Leonardo can be seen in this early Madonna and Child painting of which Raphael made many in his lifetime.

was put to work decorating rooms in the Vatican. The walls of the Stanza della Segnatura are designed with large frescoes symbolising the themes of literature, theology, philosophy, poetry and law.

In the fresco the 'School of Athens' [4,71] Raphael creates an ideal world, with Plato and Aristotle engaged in discussion with groups of philosophers. Noble and graceful figures, arranged in perfectly balanced groups and linked together by glances and gestures, people the huge architectural setting. In the colour and detail of his frescoes Raphael approached the richness of oil painting.

From this time on commissions poured in and Raphael answered the demand by taking on a large number of assistants. He continued to carry out what he considered to be the most important works — designs for tapestries for the Sistine Chapel, portraits of important patrons, the 'Galatea' fresco in the Villa Farnesina. The composition, lighting and colour of a portrait of 'Baldassare Castiglione' [4,72] highlight

[4,71] 'School of Athens', 1510–11, by Raphael, 772 cm wide at base, fresco (Vatican, Rome). Raphael's open and elegant figure compositions created the standards by which artists judged their own work in succeeding generations.

[4,72] Portrait of 'Baldassare Castiglione', 1515, by Raphael, oil on canvas, 82 x 67 cm (Louvre, Paris). Raphael's late portraits combined realism with elegant composition and colour harmony.

Raphael's mastery of portraiture and oil painting as he appears to catch the sitter in a passing moment. There is nothing static or posed in the sitter's glance. Of his architectural work none, however, survives as he designed it.

Raphael's gentle and harmonious style made him the artist most admired by the following generations. His work established a pictorial convention for almost 300 years, which is all the more remarkable when we consider his short life.

MANNERISM IN ITALY

Few artists could match the talent of the three great painters of the sixteenth century, but many produced work of quality in their own distinctive style. Jacopo Carucci (1494–1556), called Pontormo, [4,73] had a highly individual style. His use of dramatic colours and flowing forms creates a fantasy world in his religious paintings. He also painted lively and interesting portraits. His pupil and adopted son, Agnolo Bronzino (1503–72), developed a darker and stiffer court style of portraiture for the Medici in Florence.

In Parma Antonio Allegri da Correggio (1489–1534) developed a romantic style in which everything appears charming and attractive. His work, with its perfect finish and warm and natural colouring, was popular and much copied in the eighteenth century. A younger artist from Parma,

[4,74] 'Madonna with the Long Neck', 1534–40, by Parmigianino, oil on wooden panel, 216 x 132 cm (Uffizi Gallery, Florence). The elongated figures and surreal background in this painting, along with the restrained movement and subdued colours, create a tense elegance.

Francesco Mazzola (1503–40), called Parmigianino, [4,74] painted in a style remarkable for its exaggerated elegance. The restrained movement and elongated limbs of his figures are a good example of the Mannerist style.

THE HIGH RENAISSANCE IN VENICE

The Venetian painters managed to stay aloof from much of what was happening in the rest of Italy. Beginning with Bellini's students, they developed a style more preoccupied with colour, texture, the qualities of paint and mood than with the dramatic effects of composition and perspective that characterised the Florentine school.

GIORGIONE (GIORGIO BARBARELLI) (c. 1478–1511)

Although very few works remain from Giorgione's short working life, his ideas and style had great influence. He is one of the earliest artists to make smaller paintings for private collections rather than for public or ecclesiastical patrons. Giorgione developed a style of painting known as 'Poesia' (poetry) in which subject is less important than mood. His contemporaries did not understand these paintings without a clear story or meaning.

[4,73] 'Deposition', 1525–8, by Pontormo, oil on wooden panel, 312 x 190 cm (Church of S. Felicità, Florence). The colour, movement and expression of Pontormo's style create an emotional drama which was a common attribute of Mannerist work.

[4,75] 'The Tempest', 1505–10, by Giorgione, oil on canvas, 82 x 73 cm (Accademia, Venice). As much a landscape as a figure painting, 'The Tempest' marks a new departure in Italian painting in which the mood or atmosphere is more important than the story.

[4,76] 'The Assumption of the Virgin', 1516–18, by Titian, oil on panel, 690 x 360 cm (S. Maria Gloriosa dei Frani, Venice). 'The Assumption' is a masterpiece of colour and figure composition.

In his painting 'The Tempest' [4,75] figures and landscape are combined in a harmonious composition without a clear focal point. The eye is free to move from the town in the distance to the mother feeding her baby to the soldier and round again. The 'sfumato' technique which softened edges owes something to Leonardo da Vinci who visited Venice in 1500 and again in 1503. Titian may also have worked on later paintings such as the 'Sleeping Venus' and the 'Concert Champêtre'. These created the nude in landscape type of painting which was popular up to the time of Manet who also painted a version of it.

TITIAN (TIZIANO VECELLIO) (1488–1576)

In his long working life Titian painted and mastered all the current themes — religious, mythological and portrait — and developed a freedom in oil painting which was unmatched in his generation. 'The Assumption of the Virgin' [4,76] is a masterpiece comparable with the paintings of Michelangelo in the Sistine Chapel and Raphael's 'School of Athens'. The Virgin, lifted on a cloud by cherubs, is met by God the Father who is materialising overhead. The apostles at the foot of the painting reach up, amazed to see her ascend. The complicated composition of figures remains clear, with the intervals of groups and spaces masterfully handled. The warmth of colour and dramatic lighting create a wonderful atmosphere.

Dramatic lighting forms a part of the 'Danae', [4,77] a mythological painting made for Philip II of Spain who was an important patron. Painted thirty years after the 'Assumption', this picture attempts to incorporate something of Michelangelo's style of figure composition. The painting has become much looser, applied in dashing strokes which render the textures of flesh and fabric beautifully. Titian referred to these mythological paintings as 'Poesia', developed from Giorgione's ideas.

[4,77] 'Danae', 1545–6, by Titian, oil on canvas, 129 x 180 cm (Museo di Capodimonte, Naples). The rendering of flesh tones and fabrics is beautifully handled. Titian's sketchy brushwork was ideal for creating atmospheric effects.

[4,78] Portrait of 'Pope Paul III', 1546, by Titian, oil (Museo di Capodimonte, Naples). Titian was capable of a 'speaking likeness' in portraits. The personality of the sitter seems to come across in this portrait of Paul III: clever, defensive, yet spiritual.

TINTORETTO (JACOPO ROBUSTI) (1518–94)

A painter of imaginative compositions, Tintoretto reputedly set himself the task of combining Michelangelo's drawing with Titian's colour. His mature work emphasises sharp, sometimes distorted, perspectives, quite unlike either of the older masters. His 'Last Supper', [4,79] the final version of a series made during his life, is lit as much by the spiritual light from Christ as by the rush lamp. The dramatic perspective of the table sweeps the viewer into the composition. The grouped figures and gestures lead the eye around to the almost transparent angels who hover overhead. Tintoretto spent most of his life in Venice, where many of his paintings still hang in the places for which they were designed. He had a huge studio where his sons Domenico and Marco and daughter Maria also worked, producing a range of work which was very influential in Venice and beyond. Examples of his work hang in the National Gallery of Ireland.

PAOLO VERONESE (PAOLO CALIARI) (C. 1528–88)

Born in Verona (hence the nickname), Veronese worked in Venice where he produced a large body of decorative work. His paintings of huge feasts from the Bible are among his most famous works. He loved to render splendid scenes with pillars and beautiful costumes painted in blues, oranges, yellows and silvery whites. 'The Feast in

Titian portraits were also of the highest quality. His rendering of textures in paint and his composition created a new standard in portraiture. He did not flatter the sitter but tried to express the character of the subject in the work. The portrait of 'Pope Paul III' [4,78] is considered to be one of Titian's finest.

In his later life Titian's work became darker and looser, with shimmering light picking out the focal points in the painting. His last work, 'Pietà', was in this style, painted as much with the fingers as with the brush.

[4,79] 'Last Supper', 1592–4, by Tintoretto, oil on canvas, 366 x 569 cm (Chapel of S. Giorgio Maggiore, Venice). The dramatic perspective and mystical light show Tintoretto's leaning towards Mannerism.

[4,80] 'The Feast in the House of Levi', 1573, by Paolo Veronese, oil on canvas, 556 x 1,280 cm (Accademia, Venice). The illusionistic architecture and flamboyant costumes were a feature of Veronese's biblical feasts. His ceilings became the models for much architectural decoration in the following centuries.

the House of Levi', [4,80] with its wonderful illusionist architecture, was originally a painting of the Last Supper. However, the title was changed due to objections by the Inquisition. Veronese's frescoed ceilings were influential, particularly in the eighteenth century when Venice again had a Golden Age.

CONCLUSION

The sixteenth century was a Golden Age in Italian painting. Some of the most influential figures in the history of art changed the course of painting for ever, creating new ways of studying and working in art. Drawing became an integral part of developing ideas and compositions, and oil paint on canvas made larger, bolder works possible. Subject-matter and style were also changed, with myths and legends becoming as popular as religious and historical themes. Portraits were more life-like and sophisticated. Landscape was no longer merely a background, but a subject in its own right.

GERMANY

ALBRECHT DÜRER (1471–1528)

Due to his skill as a printmaker Dürer was an artist of great influence throughout Europe. Copies of his work were used by artists and craftsmen as a basis for their own work. He visited Italy twice where he was well known for his prints. He was strongly influenced by the work of Mantegna and Bellini. The status of artists in Italy greatly impressed him. In his 'Self-Portrait' [4,81] of 1491 he portrays himself as a fashionable gentleman rather than a craftsman.

[4,81] 'Self-Portrait', 1491, by Albrecht Dürer, 52 x 41 cm, oil on vellum fixed to canvas. Dürer's vanity comes across in this self-portrait. His fashionable Italian clothes portray him as a gentleman, above manual work. The style is a mixture of Northern European and Italian influences.

Dürer published editions of his own prints, even a book of the 'Apocalypse' where full-page woodcuts illustrate the text. 'The Four Horsemen of the Apocalypse' [4,82] represents the best woodcutting technique and design of the time and spread Dürer's fame in Germany and Italy.

Dürer also worked in engraving and etching. His engraving of 'St Jerome in his Study' [4,83] represents some of the finest work ever achieved in this medium. Throughout his life Dürer made sketches and notes on his thoughts and what he saw. He produced drawings in a variety of media

[4,82] 'The Four Horsemen of the Apocalypse', 1498, by Albrecht Dürer, woodcut, print on paper (British Museum, London). Dürer brought the woodcut to a new level, creating tone and form with his use of line and hatching. Note the bold monogram signature in the bottom centre of the print.

and watercolours of nature for his own amusement. He produced two books on measurement and proportion and was the first North European artist to theorise on the art process. He presented his paintings of the 'Four Apostles' to Nuremberg Town Council. The inscriptions from Luther's translations of the writings of the apostles on the foot of each panel confirm his conversion to Protestantism at the end of his life.

LUCAS CRANACH (1472–1553)

Court painter to Frederic III, Elector of Saxony, who was Martin Luther's protector, Cranach painted mythological scenes, religious subjects and portraits, including a number of Luther. 'The Rest on the Flight into Egypt' [4,84] is an early work which highlights the influence of the Danube landscape school. Cranach's work shows a rejection of Renaissance ideas in preference for a more traditional, linear style.

MATHIS GRÜNEWALD (C. 1470/80–1528)

Almost an exact contemporary of Dürer, Grünewald painted in an expressive, painterly style, more related to Gothic than Renaissance. Neglected for many years, his work became fully appreciated in the 1920s in light of Expressionist thinking.

[4,83] 'St Jerome in his Study', 1514, by Albrecht Dürer, 25 x 19 cm engraving, print on paper (Dresden: Kupfer Stichkabinett). The very closely worked cross-hatched lines in Dürer's engravings produce a refinement of light, tone and texture previously only possible in paint.

[4,84] 'The Rest on the Flight into Egypt', 1504, by Lucas Cranach, oil on wooden panel, 69 x 51 cm (Gemaldgalerie). The German landscape background and linear treatment show Cranach's rejection of much of Renaissance thinking.

[4,85] 'Crucifixion' from the 'Isenheim Altarpiece', 1515–16, by Mathis Grünewald, oil on wooden panel, 269 x 307 cm (Unterlinden Museum, Colmar). The large altarpiece is one of the most expressive works in North European art.

The 'Isenheim Altarpiece' is a polyptych which folds out in three stages. Its centrepiece is the 'Crucifixion' [4,85] which shows a grotesquely contorted Christ, his body scarred from scourging, nailed to the cross. The figures of the mourners are painted smaller, in the medieval tradition, to emphasise the importance of Christ. The risen Christ appears in another scene on the altarpiece in an aura of supernatural light, which creates a wonderful colour scheme in the surrounding robes and figures. Some of Grünewald's work demonstrates that although he understands the Renaissance use of light, shade and perspective, he chooses to suppress them in favour of dramatic expression and colour.

HANS HOLBEIN (1497/8–1543)
Born into a family of artists in Augsburg, Holbein became one of the leading painters in Germany. His work includes a number of designs for printers, the 'Dance of Death' series of woodcuts, portraits and religious works. 'The Madonna of Burgomeister Meyer' [4,86] shows an Italian influence in the idealised beauty and soft modelling of the Virgin, but the Meyer family are portrayed with the Northern European interest in detail.

[4,86] 'The Madonna of Burgomeister Meyer', 1526, by Hans Holbein, oil on wooden panel, 142.5 x 101.8 cm (Schlosmuseum, Darmstadt). One of the last of Holbein's religious paintings, the soft modelling of the Madonna shows Italian influence.

The disturbances surrounding the Reformation encouraged Holbein to seek employment in England, where he painted several portraits of the English aristocracy and a number of merchants and diplomats in London. He returned to Germany, but was back in England in 1532 when

[4,87] 'The Ambassadors', 1533, by Hans Holbein, oil on wooden panel, 207 x 210 cm (National Gallery, London). Jean de Dinteville, Ambassador to London, and George de Selve, Bishop, later Ambassador to Venice, are portrayed with their achievements displayed on the shelves between them — the study of the heavens on the upper shelf, learned worldly pursuits below. The shape between the men's feet is a distorted skull, a reminder of mortality amid all the splendour. Holbein's rendering of fabrics and background detail is remarkable.

he became court painter to Henry VIII. His court portraits are more formalised than his private work which is among the best portraiture in the world. [4,87]

[4,88] 'The Garden of Earthly Delights', c. 1500, by Hieronymus Bosch, centre panel 220 x 195 cm, wings 219.7 x 96.6 cm (Museo del Prado, Madrid). Bosch's imagery and colour make him unique. His painting style was fluid and accomplished.

THE NETHERLANDS
HIERONYMUS BOSCH (C. 1450–1516)

Bosch had a unique style of painting, basing his themes and images on folktales, proverbs and medieval poetry and sermons. He held a pessimistic view of the world, seeing temptation and depravity everywhere. In his triptych, 'The Garden of Earthly Delights', [4,88] although the creation in the left panel and hell in the right are conventional subjects, they are treated with great imagination. The central panel displays all kinds of strange sexual behaviour, with changes in scale and mixtures of human, animal and man-made creatures in a prettily coloured landscape. The strange imagery seems to have been approved and understood by the Catholic Church of the time, since Bosch enjoyed Church patronage and his work was collected by Philip II, Catholic King of Spain. Bosch painted a series of parables — 'Death and the Miser', 'The Ship of Fools', 'The Path of Life' — and other triptychs, all in a richly coloured and fluid painting style. He was popular in the sixteenth century. Artists made prints and copies of his work to the end of the century.

PIETER BRUEGHEL THE ELDER (C. 1525–69)

A strong moralist, Brueghel was influenced by the work of Bosch. He travelled to France and Italy, but was unimpressed by the Renaissance style. His landscapes and moral tales show an acute observation of the real world and of man's frailty.

[4,89] 'Hunters in the Snow', c. 1565, by Pieter Brueghel the Elder, oil on canvas, 117 x 162 cm (Kunsthistorisches Museum, Vienna). Brueghel's paintings of peasants and landscape were a strong influence on the genre painters of the following centuries.

The series of the months made for an Antwerp banker, of which five survive, are among his finest works. 'Hunters in the Snow' [4,89] probably depicts January, beautifully composed by diagonal lines. The pattern of the dark figures against the snow recedes to the jagged peaks in the distance. The sense of weather atmosphere achieved in the series is unique. Brueghel's moral tales and parables peopled with peasants were very popular. His family continued the style for three generations. In the National Gallery in Dublin the 'Country Wedding' by Pieter the Younger shows how faithfully the style was continued. Brueghel left many drawings from observation, as well as his paintings, and was the major influence on painting in the Netherlands in the following generations.

SPAIN

EL GRECO (DOMENIKOS THEOTOCOPOULOS) (1541–1614)

Born in Crete and trained in Venice under the ageing Titian, El Greco was influenced particularly by Tintoretto and also by Michelangelo and Raphael. In 1577 he moved to Toledo in Spain to paint the 'Assumption of the Virgin', an altarpiece for the Church of S. Domingo el Antiguo. He never left Toledo again, spending the rest of his life working on large altarpieces, portraits and devotional works in a very individual Mannerist style.

[4,90] 'Burial of Count Orgaz', 1586, by El Greco, oil on canvas, 487.5 x 360 cm (Church of S. Tome, Toledo). The visionary quality of El Greco's style is seen particularly in the heavenly upper part of the painting. The sweeping stylised clouds and changing perspectives, the Christ figure glowing with internal light, the jagged meeting of dark and light, all emphasise the supernatural quality of the event we are witnessing. The small heads and long limbs of the figures were designed to be graceful and elegant.

The 'Burial of Count Orgaz', [4,90] painted in 1586, demonstrates his mature style. St Augustine and St Stephen miraculously appear to put the armour-clad Count into his sepulchre (which was originally painted on a mural below, now missing). Nobles and clerics crowd the ground level. An angel in the middle lifts the insubstantial soul, in the form of a child, into the opening heaven, with the Virgin and John the Baptist assisting the soul. A distant, brightly lit Christ oversees all. The insubstantial space, strangely elongated figures and dramatic splashes of colour are typical of El Greco's strange and mystic style. The flame-like movement and disregard for perspective accentuate the other-worldly atmosphere in his work.

[4,91] 'St Francis Receiving the Stigmata' by El Greco, oil on canvas (Private collection, Madrid). Muted colours and minimal background create a soft, floating atmosphere in which the saint is transported. This painting is very close in design to 'St Francis in Ecstasy' in the National Gallery of Ireland, Dublin.

The 'St Francis Receiving the Stigmata' [4,91] is a smaller work in cool colours composed on the diagonals of the canvas, a design often used by El Greco in his later work. Light, colour and movement combine with great expressive power, more fully appreciated in the twentieth century than in the generations following his lifetime. Although El Greco was appreciated by fellow artists there were no real followers of his individual style.

CONCLUSION

The Renaissance was the most influential period in the history of art. Local styles and traditions were superseded by a universal style which was, with variations, the accepted formula for creating works of art and design for over 300 years. Perspective was recognised as the 'correct' way to represent space in two dimensions. Drawing was based on observation of nature and an understanding of classical art. Painting was generally in oils, with methods recommended for preparing canvas and developing a painting. Work was expected to conform to what had been achieved by the great masters.

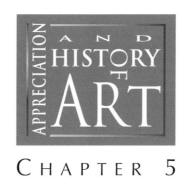

CHAPTER 5

SEVENTEENTH AND EIGHTEENTH CENTURIES

SEVENTEENTH CENTURY

The seventeenth century confirmed Rome's emergence as the centre of taste and culture in Europe at the end of the previous century. Most serious artists visited Rome to study the art of the antique world and of the Renaissance. The intellectualism and virtuosity of the Mannerists were rejected in favour of an art that could reach out to the ordinary citizen and involve him or her in the experience. Raphael was seen as the ideal artist, though the symmetry and clarity of his work were dropped in favour of more dynamic and dramatic composition.

The conflicts of the Reformation continued in much of Northern Europe, but peace and prosperity came to Flanders, an area now known as the Netherlands. Having made a treaty with the King of Spain, their overlord, the Dutch were free to develop a Protestant democracy which had no use for the old forms of religious art. Group portraits, landscape, still life and illustrations of moral tales became the stuff of Dutch art. With the disappearance of the Roman Catholic Church and royalty as patrons, artists had to rely on private sales or dealers to make a living. These fundamental changes heralded a new era for artists.

BAROQUE ART

The term Baroque, originally meaning 'misshapen' or 'oddly formed', was used by eighteenth-century critics of seventeenth-century work. More recently the term is used to refer to a style, created in Italy, which depended on balance and wholeness for its effect. Following the Council of Trent, the Catholic Church decided to commission work that was more accessible to the ordinary citizen. Artists, therefore, began to create colourful, dramatic work which had an emotional rather than an intellectual appeal, and architects designed elaborate, awe-inspiring buildings. The Baroque style attempted to draw the spectator into the event. Rather than being seen simply as a place in which to live or pray, whole rooms and churches were designed and decorated as an experience. [5,1]

ARCHITECTURE

Most Baroque architecture was commissioned by the Church, princes or kings to provide a splendid setting for ceremony and court. The design of the Gesù in Rome [5,2] became the standard for many later churches. The large open nave is flanked by chapels for private devotion, the transepts are small and the crossing is crowned with a dome. The façade contains many classical elements, but they are arranged differently from those of Renaissance buildings. The focus is on the entrance, which is flanked by a double frame

[5,1] 'Triumph at the Name of Jesus', 1674–9, by Baciccio. Painted 100 years after the building of the church this fresco on the ceiling of the Gesù, Rome, is an illusionist piece that combines painting and plaster relief to create the impression of a roof open to heaven with figures moving in and out of the opening. The theme of salvation and damnation is carefully worked out in the writhing figures. The Gesù was the first church of the Jesuit order, which was so influential in the Counter-Reformation.

[5,2] The Gesù, Rome, 1568–75, by Vignola and della Porta. The huge size of this church is partly masked by the large scale of the giant pilasters and the massing of pediments, pillars and arches at the centre of the building to emphasise the entrance.

GIAN LORENZO BERNINI (1598–1680)
(SEE ALSO UNDER SCULPTURE)

Architect, sculptor and painter, Bernini liked to combine all the arts in illusionist works of great intensity. In fountains, sculptures and buildings, Bernini has probably made a greater impression on the appearance of Rome than any other artist. As architect to several popes, he created the great colonnade around the Piazza of St Peter's in Rome. [5,3] He applied coloured marble inside the Cathedral and designed the bronze

[5,3] The Piazza of St Peter's, Rome. Colonnade by Bernini, 1656. The rows of simple Tuscan columns reach out like arms welcoming pilgrims to the Cathedral.

of columns and pilasters. Attention is drawn to the centre of the building by sculptures over the main entrance and two smaller doorways. There is less repetition than in High Renaissance buildings. The scrolled volutes used to join the two storeys are not classical; rather they are curved in section which is a Baroque design trait. The mixing of elements and the unity of design is what makes this building different from Renaissance designs.

baldaccino (canopy) over the tomb of St Peter as well as St Peter's Chair over the High Altar. [5,4] These works have a strong impact on the interior of St Peter's, crossing the boundaries between sculpture and architecture.

Bernini worked for the powerful Barberini and Borghese papal families. He designed part of the Barberini Palace and the Scala Regia stairway in the Vatican, which reduces in height and width as it ascends to increase the illusion of size. He designed the church of S. Andrea al Quirinale on an oval plan and populated the lower dome with sculptured figures that represent the ascension of St Andrew the Apostle into heaven.

Bernini was a very religious man and highly regarded in his own time. He received most of the important commissions in Rome, much to the annoyance of his rivals.

[5,4] Baldaccino and St Peter's Chair, St Peter's, Rome, by Bernini, 1624–33. St Peter's Chair seen behind the baldaccino combines coloured glass, brass rods and stone carving, creating a focal point over the high altar. The twisted bronze columns of the baldaccino create a frame for ceremonies in the cathedral.

[5,5] Façade of S. Carlo alle Quattro Fontane, Rome, by Borromini, 1667. The sculpted and curved surfaces of Borromini's buildings contrast strongly with the regularity and simplicity of Renaissance architecture.

FRANCESCO BARROMINI (1599–1667)

Borromini's training as a mason can be seen in his interest in the sculptural qualities of architecture. His little church of S. Carlo alle Quattro Fontane in Rome [5,5] is built on a complicated oval plan, with niches flowing into each other. Outside, concave and convex curves create an undulating surface which is punctuated with pillars, sculptures and medallions. The complex decorative surfaces were less popular in Rome during the seventeenth century than they became in Austria and Germany in the next century.

FRANCE

The curves and strong contrasts of Italian Baroque were not to the taste of the French. Bernini, invited to France to design a wing of the Louvre, could not make a design that pleased Louis XIV and the French architects Perrault and Le Vau produced the classical east front.

The work of Louis Le Vau (1612–70) and Jules Hardouin Mansart (1646–1708) best illustrate

[5,6] West or garden façade, garden front, Versailles, by Louis Le Vau and Jules Hardouin Mansart. The huge scale and elaborate setting of Versailles demonstrate the power of the French court. The formality and classical detail of the architecture are typical of the period.

seventeenth-century French architecture. Between them they created the palace at Versailles. [5,6] The scale of the finished building almost swallows the detail of projecting colonnades, skyline balustrades and sculptures. The great glory of Versailles is its setting in a huge pleasure garden designed by Le Nôtre. Canals, woods, ponds, steps, sculptures, fountains, flower gardens and avenues all combine in a layout that became a model for later town planning.

Le Vau, who was influenced by Italian design, created many other buildings including Vaux-le-Vicomte in 1657, one of the great houses of the century. The main rooms are oval in plan, and the whole house is set in a false moat and formal garden. Jules Hardouin-Mansart designed the huge Church of St Louis, Hôtel des Invalides in Paris, which now houses the remains of the Emperor Napoleon. It has a classical façade and a tall Baroque dome.

French interiors are far more decorative than the classical exteriors of their buildings. The Galerie des Glaces (Gallery of Mirrors), [5,7] with its green marble, mirrors and panels painted by Lebrun, is an example of the style and colour of many seventeenth-century interiors.

ENGLAND
INIGO JONES (1573–1652)

Inigo Jones introduced classical architecture in the style of Vitruvius and Palladio into England. Jones had been to Italy twice before being appointed as surveyor to the King's works (King's chief architect). He had clear theories on design, saying, 'Architecture should be disciplined, masculine and unaffected' — thus ruling out much of Baroque design.

The Queen's House, Greenwich, is almost shockingly plain and simple in comparison with Italian Baroque. A rusticated ground floor with plain first floor walls is broken by a colonnade, while at roof level there is a simple balustrade without sculpture or decoration.

The Banqueting House at Whitehall, London, [5,8] is less severely plain. The two-tier façade is articulated by columns and pilasters, stronger mouldings on the windows and a band of carved decoration on the upper floor. The building inside, however, consists of one large room and not two floors as suggested by the façade. A painted ceiling by Rubens decorates the interior.

[5,7] The Galerie des Glaces at Versailles, 1680. French 17th-century interiors are sophisticated confections of colour and form combining a range of arts and crafts for their effect.

[5,8] The Banqueting House at Whitehall, London, 1619–22, by Inigo Jones. This carefully proportioned building has a single hall inside, although the façade is in two tiers. The use of columns and pilasters to divide the rusticated stonework creates interest in the surface. The mouldings around the windows and the band of carved decoration on the upper floor complete the strongly defined decorative scheme.

[5,9] St Paul's Cathedral, London, 1675–1711, by Sir Christopher Wren. The tall Baroque dome of St Paul's is one of the finest in Europe.

Several churches and houses are attributed to Jones, the finest of which is Wilton House. Its simple exterior belies an interior that contains some of the most richly decorated rooms in England.

SIR CHRISTOPHER WREN (1632–1723)

Christopher Wren started out as a professor of astronomy at Oxford. He was also keenly interested in geometry. Following a visit to Paris, where he met Bernini who was working on designs for the Louvre, he returned with books and sketches and a great enthusiasm for architecture. The fire of London in 1666 destroyed 13,200 houses and eighty-seven churches in nine days. Within two weeks Wren had submitted a plan for the rebuilding of the city, which was accepted. However, the citizens would not co-operate with the building of the planned city and rebuilt on the old foundations.

Wren, however, remained responsible for the rebuilding of many parish churches, of which St Mary-le-Bow and St Bride's, Fleet Street, survive. His churches were simple brick-and-stone halls with some good plaster ceilings and woodcarving. The towers and spires were more complex above roof height so that an interesting skyline would be created for the city.

St Paul's Cathedral [5,9] was to be the centrepiece of Wren's plan. It was a compromise between Gothic-style nave, aisles and transepts which the clergy wanted and the centrally planned church that Wren wanted. Despite the compromise the Cathedral, particularly the dome, remains impressive.

The twin domes and long colonnades of paired columns give the Royal Hospital at Greenwich [5,10] the appearance of a Baroque monument. Among the architects who worked on the project with Wren were his assistant Hawksmoor and Sir John Vanbrugh.

[5,10] Royal Hospital, Greenwich, 1696, by Sir Christopher Wren and others. Past the twin domes and colonnades of Wren's Royal Hospital, Inigo Jones's Queen's House of 1616–35 can be seen, contrasting 60 years of development in English architecture.

SIR JOHN VANBRUGH (1664–1726)

English architecture of the period came closest to European Baroque in the work of Vanbrugh. In his design for Castle Howard in Yorkshire, curved colonnades link a domed central block to kitchen and stable courts, thereby adding to the huge scale of the house. [5,11] The entrance hall is considered the finest Baroque interior in England. His use of skyline sculpture in his design of Blenheim Palace in Oxfordshire, a gift from the people of England to the victorious Duke of Marlborough, creates the impression of a decorated castle.

CONCLUSION

Baroque design continued into the eighteenth century, particularly in Spain and Germany, where it became more elaborate and decorative, leading on to the Rococo style.

SCULPTURE

Baroque sculpture was more vigorous and more complicated in shape and form than Renaissance work and relied for its effect on light, shadow and overall impact rather than on clarity. Italian, Spanish and German sculptors, working mainly on religious themes, used colour and light to create illusion and dramatic effect. Some work is close to painting in its conception. In France, sculpture for royal courts and gardens, and for memorials, almost always had some classical reference, though the work was often dramatic and emotional.

[5,11] Castle Howard, Yorkshire, 1699, by Sir John Vanbrugh. This country mansion is the closest English equivalent to an Italian palazzo or a French château.

ITALY

GIAN LORENZO BERNINI (1598–1680)
(SEE ALSO UNDER ARCHITECTURE)

Son of a sculptor, Bernini learnt his trade at a young age and was introduced to influential patrons by his father. Even his early work is accomplished. The 'David' he carved when he was only twenty-five represents a new naturalism and sense of movement in sculpture.

Bernini's 'Ecstasy of St Teresa' [5,12] is a departure in illusionist sculpture. The saint falls back on a cloud while an angel prepares to pierce her heart with a dart. Everything is in a flutter — fabrics, clouds, hair — with no sense of the group as part of a block of stone. The coloured light pouring down from a concealed window above is reflected on brass rods which represent rays of light from heaven. Reliefs, representing members of the Cornaro family who were the donors, are in shallow panels on the side walls of the chapel, like spectators in theatre boxes. In fact the whole scene is theatrical — a moment from a drama.

The 'Fountain of the Four Rivers' in the Piazza Navona in Rome is a large-scale, boldly carved piece and is the most celebrated of his fountains. Bernini could also work on a small scale. His bronze portrait bust of 'Louis XIV of France', the carved marble portrait of his mistress 'Costanza

[5,12] 'Ecstasy of St Teresa', 1645–8, by Gianlorenzo Bernini, marble, S. Maria della Vittoria, Rome. St Theresa's vision, in which her heart is pierced by an angel with a dart, is a multi-media spectacular designed to make the viewer share the moment.

[5,13] 'Costanza Buonarelli', c. 1635, by Gianlorenzo Bernini (Bargello, Florence). Bernini's portraits manage a 'speaking likeness' of the sitter. His subtle handling of textures in marble created a new standard.

[5,14] 'Milo of Crotona Attacked by a Lion', 1683, by Pierre Puget, 270 cm tall, marble (Louvre, Paris). This figure from Greek legend shows the expressive energy that Puget liked to portray in his work. Milo, an athlete from 6th century B.C., is caught in a tree that he is trying to destroy and is devoured by a wild beast. Some features of the Milo figure are borrowed from the 'Lacoon Group', a late classical piece.

Buonarelli' [5,13] and several portraits of prominent churchmen highlight his ability to capture a fleeting moment, when the sitter apparently turns to speak to the artist. This lively realism is a hallmark of Bernini's work.

Like so many men of genius, Bernini was multi-talented. John Evelyn, an English diarist, records attending an opera by Bernini 'wherein he painted the scenes, cut the statues, invented the engines, composed the music, wrote the comedy and built the theatre'. This tremendous output was made possible by a large workshop of assistants, which was common among artists favoured with papal or court patronage.

FRANCE

In the seventeenth century the French court was the outstanding patron. The sheer scale and number of the schemes to glorify the monarchy kept teams of artists busy. To replace the guilds Louis XIV founded the Académie Royale de Peinture et de Sculpture in 1648. Colbert and Lebrun, two powerful courtiers, controlled the arts in France from 1661, when they were made Vice-Protector and Director of the Académie. Artists who failed to get their work exhibited at the academy had little hope of a successful career.

PIERRE PUGET (1620–94)

Originally a ship carver, Puget trained as a sculptor under Cortona in Rome. His style was too emotional and Italian to gain court patronage, but his 'Milo of Crotona' [5,14] was bought for the palace at Versailles. Technically his work was of a very high standard and was popular in Italy as well as in his home town, Marseilles. He carved a pair of Atlas figures for the entrance to the Town Hall in Toulon.

ANTOINE COYSEVOX (1640–1720)

Born in Lyons, Coysevox studied at the Académie in Paris and was appointed royal sculptor in 1666. He produced works for Versailles and other state properties. He was especially skilled at portraiture and made busts of most of the leading public figures of the time. He also made portraits of friends and fellow artists, beginning a tradition which was a special feature of French sculpture.

Coysevox epitomises the restrained style preferred by Louis XIV. He carved a marble 'Portrait Bust of Louis XIV' [5,15] in 1686 which demonstrates his skill in rendering textures as well as life-like expression. The statues of 'Mercury' and 'Fame' which stand at the entrance to the Tuileries Gardens in Paris are probably his best-known works.

[5,15] 'Portrait Bust of Louis XIV', 1686, by Antoine Coysevox, marble, 89 x 80 cm (Musée des Beaux Arts, Dijon). Coysevox was famed as a portraitist. He combined life-like features with carefully handled hair and fabrics — an elegant combination of textures and suggested movement.

[5,16] 'Venus and Anchises, Vault of the Galleria Farnese', 1597–1601, by Annibale Carracci (Palazzo Farnese, Rome). Carracci used false architecture and nude sculpture to divide the ceiling into scenes from the 'Loves of the Gods'. This large-scale 'Pagan' piece was highly influential in the 17th century. The classical figures, strong gestures and bright colours were copied by Baroque and history painters.

PAINTING

The Italian dominance of the arts was finally broken in the seventeenth century. While Rome remained the important cultural capital, Italian artists began to be influenced by French, Spanish, Flemish and Dutch artists.

The guilds that had controlled the training and development of artists were being replaced by academies which were more like colleges of art than the old apprentice system. Through this academic system, methods and techniques of drawing, painting and sculpture became almost standardised throughout Europe.

Classical art was still the ideal, but artists of all cultures were trying to make their work more realistic. Whether this involved real emotional expression or visual reality, it was a preoccupation of the time.

ITALY

ANNIBALE CARRACCI (1560–1609)

Annibale Carracci was the most talented member of a family of artists from Bologna. They ran one of the first teaching academies which emphasised carefully developed drawing skills. Carracci was called to Rome in 1595 by Cardinal Odoardo Farnese to decorate rooms in the Palazzo Farnese. [5,16] He first completed a small room, the Camerino, with scenes from the life of Hercules.

He then took on the ceiling of the much larger gallery on which he painted the fresco 'The Loves of the Gods'. His style and composition were heavily influenced by Michelangelo and Raphael and were a return to classical Renaissance style, breaking away from Mannerism which was the current style in Rome. This ceiling was ranked with the Sistine Chapel as a model for seventeenth-century artists.

Carracci's method of making numerous preparatory drawings became the norm for large history paintings. His language of gesture and expression and his representations of gods and goddesses were also much copied.

Carracci's late easel paintings were also highly influential. His 'Domine Quo Vadis' (Christ appearing to St Peter on the Appian Way) [5,17] and the 'Pietà', now in the Louvre, were an important influence on history painters. Their clarity of form and gesture and their colouring in the Venetian manner had great appeal in the seventeenth century. The classical landscape may also have been an invention of Carracci. His 'Flight into Egypt' is the forerunner of a line of classical or biblical figures in landscape paintings that remained popular in later years.

The Carracci family gained many followers, partly through their academy but more especially through the work of Annibale, who combined classical and Renaissance figures with Venetian painting and colour.

CARAVAGGIO (MICHELANGELO MERISI DA) (1573–1610)

Nicknamed after his birthplace in Lombardy, 'Caravaggio' was a very different artist from Annibale Carracci. He painted directly onto canvas from observation; but he was criticised for his use of the ordinary people of the streets as his live models, as they were considered inelegant and unsuitable as biblical figures. His direct style of painting and use of strong colour came from the influence of the Venetian masters. In 1592 he moved to Rome where he eventually won church commissions to paint altarpieces.

Caravaggio created dramatic scenes in oils on canvas. Beginning on a dark ground, he gradually built up to the lighter colours. The paint is smoothly applied, without a lot of visible brushwork. Great care and accuracy went into the painting of textures like hair, skin, fabrics and metal.

[5,17] 'Domine Quo Vadis', (Christ appearing to St Peter on the Appian Way), 1601–2, by Annibale Carracci, 76 x 53 cm, oil on wood (National Gallery, London). Carracci's later oil paintings were much admired by the next generation of artists. The classical-looking figures, the expressive gestures and expressions, the bright colour and the clear composition were imitated by many.

[5,18] 'The Taking of Christ', c. 1602, by Caravaggio, oil on canvas (National Gallery of Ireland, Dublin). The tightly framed composition and dramatic action are typical of Caravaggio's later work. Because he worked directly onto the canvas without preparatory drawings, some corrections were seen when the work was cleaned and x-rayed

For almost 200 years 'The Taking of Christ' [5,18] was thought to be lost until it was rediscovered in 1994. Capturing the moment when Judas betrays Christ with a kiss, it highlights many of the characteristics of Caravaggio's painting. Set in a shallow, dark space, the group is tightly composed, with parts of figures cut off at the edge of the canvas. A disciple exits in alarm at the left, while those following Judas crowd in at the right. The dark chiaroscuro or tenebrism picks out the most important areas in the light of the lantern hidden behind the head of the armour-clad soldier. A great sense of movement and drama is created by the gestures and expressions of the figures. Caravaggio uses props such as the armour of the soldier or the red cloak to add interest to the colour and texture of the work. The soldiers are not those of his own or Christ's time, but an invention of his own.

In 'The Supper at Emmaus' [5,19] Caravaggio makes a dramatic use of perspective, with figures reaching out of the canvas towards the viewer. Again we have the theatrical moment of truth, when Christ is revealed in the breaking of bread.

Caravaggio led a short, eventful life. His quarrelsome nature involved him in many fights and court cases. Powerful patrons could not protect him when he killed a man in a quarrel over a bet. He spent his last few years on the run and died alone of a fever in 1610. He was only thirty-six years old.

[5,19] 'The Supper at Emmaus', c. 1598, by Caravaggio, oil on canvas, 139 x 195 cm (National Gallery, London). Caravaggio's work often has the look of a photograph, a moment frozen in time; but there is nothing casual or haphazard about the arrangement, shape, colour, light and dark — all are carefully calculated for dramatic effect.

[5,20] 'Et in Arcadia Ego', 1638–40, by Nicolas Poussin, 85 x 121 cm, oil on canvas (Louvre, Paris). The shepherds reading the inscription on the tomb realise that death exists even in their ideal world. The figure on the right is a classical idea, closely related to antique sculpture.

FRANCE

As in architecture there was a preference for a more classical style of painting among French artists. The two major French painters of the century, Poussin and Claude Lorrain, lived and worked in Rome where they absorbed the classical and Renaissance past and transformed it into works of harmony and order.

NICOLAS POUSSIN (1594–1665)

Born in Normandy, Poussin trained and worked in Paris until 1623. He went to Venice and then to Rome where he settled for most of the remainder of his life. His early work was in the Mannerist style, but he was influenced by Titian and particularly Raphael's late paintings which transformed his work into a reasoned, classical style.

Poussin put a lot of time and effort into developing a scheme of composition, colour, expression and subject-matter that would allow him to create paintings governed by reason and control. This was in stark contrast with the emotionalism of the Baroque style which was current in much of Europe.

The almost formulaic approach to painting can be seen in Poussin's 'Et in Arcadia Ego' (Shepherds of Arcadia). [5,20] There is a calm logic, unusual in the seventeenth century, to the clear geometry of the composition, with the formal gestures and expressions of the shepherds and the use of classical figures and robes set in an ideal landscape.

[5,21] 'Acis and Galatea' by Nicolas Poussin, c. 1630, 98 x 137 cm, oil on canvas (National Gallery of Ireland, Dublin). The formally grouped figures and carefully arranged light and shadow are typical of Poussin's thoughtful approach, even to a scene of revelry like this.

Poussin was an intellectual who tried to portray in his work the world he found in the classical texts he studied. He made drawings from classical sculpture and tried to develop a figure type for all the gods and goddesses. He drew gestures and expressions which conveyed emotions and ideas, and used these as reference for his paintings. His use of colour followed the Venetian style. 'Acis and Galatea' [5,21] is one of these imaginary classical scenes which had great influence on the following generation of French painters.

101

[5,22] 'Juno Confiding Io to the Care of Argus', 1660, by Claude Lorrain, 60 x 75 cm, oil on canvas (National Gallery of Ireland, Dublin). Claude's spacious landscapes with golden light were based on classical poetry and legend and managed to create a poetic vision of the ancient world.

CLAUDE LORRAIN (CLAUDE GELÉE) (1600-82)

Claude attached Lorrain to his name in memory of his home town in France. He painted 'ideal landscapes' in the tradition of Giorgione, Titian and Carracci. The scenery around the Bay of Naples and the Roman Campagna provided the inspiration for his landscapes. Claude's painting of 'Juno Confiding Io to the Care of Argus' [5,22] combines trees, water and distant, low-lying landscape as a backdrop to the small figure group. In fact the figures are often a small element in compositions which depend for their effect on lighting and the textures of large trees. Romantic, golden light and atmosphere are predominant elements in a painting by Claude. The 'picturesque' quality of his work was very influential in the seventeenth and eighteenth centuries, with landscape architects in England trying to create nature in imitation of Claude.

OTHER ARTISTS

The Le Nain brothers and Georges de la Tour (1593-1652) were provincial French artists who painted scenes from everyday life and religious subjects. Unappreciated in their own time because of their lack of classical knowledge, their work is now enjoyed for its insight into seventeenth-century life and its spiritual simplicity. De la Tour's 'The Cheat with the Ace of Diamonds' [5,23] is influenced by Caravaggio, with forms simplified and stylised.

[5,23] 'The Cheat with the Ace of Diamonds', c. 1635, by Georges de la Tour, oil on canvas (Louvre, Paris). The simplified forms and strong contrasts of de la Tour's work show an influence of Caravaggio.

SPAIN AND FLANDERS

Flanders remained a province of Spain, connected by trade and religion, after the Protestant Netherlands had gained independence.

PETER PAUL RUBENS (1577-1640)

The greatest of the Baroque painters, Rubens received his early training in Antwerp but the decisive influence on him was the eight years he spent in Italy in the service of the Duke of Mantua. There he studied the art of the great masters in Venice and Rome and worked with contemporary Italians.

On his return to Antwerp his work was in immediate demand. He was appointed court painter to the Spanish regents, the Infanta Isabella and Archduke Albert. Many of the commissions he received at this time were large-scale and he needed a workshop of assistants with which to complete them. Rubens made drawings and colour sketches of his designs. His pupils carried out the work according to his sketches and he then made adjustments and refinements to the finished pieces. The price reflected the degree of involvement by Rubens in the work.

The 'Mystic Marriage of St Catherine' [5,24] is a large Baroque composition from the height of Rubens's career. The spiralling composition of moving figures draws the eye up to the point where the enthroned figure of the Madonna is the only stillness in all the movement. The richness of colour and texture and the fluent brushwork demonstrate mastery of all aspects of painting.

[5,24] 'Mystic Marriage of St Catherine', 1627–8, by Peter Paul Rubens, oil on canvas, 565 x 401 cm (Staatliche Gemalde-Galerie, Berlin). This large composition is a masterpiece of balance and control over so much movement, light and colour. Rubens wrote of himself in 1621, 'My talents are such that I have never lacked courage to undertake any design, however vast in size or diversified in subject.'

[5,25] 'Chapeau de Paille', Portrait of Suzanne Fourment, 1620–5, by Peter Paul Rubens, 79 x 55 cm, wooden panel (National Gallery, London). The balance of warm and cool colours and dark and light areas focuses our attention on the beautifully painted skin tones.

Rubens painted on all themes, from large religious and allegorical pieces to intimate portraits and landscape. He also designed tapestries, book illustrations and decorations for pageants, and produced designs for architects, stone carvers and metalworkers.

Apart from all this artistic activity Rubens was a diplomat with great influence in European affairs. His status as the most important artist of his time made him welcome in all the courts of Europe where his work was eagerly sought.

Rubens painted a series of twenty-five enormous paintings on the life of Maria de Medici, widow of Henri IV of France and mother of Louis XIII. He also painted a series of canvases representing the reign of James I of England, for his son, Charles I, and this hangs on the ceiling of Inigo Jones's Banqueting House in Whitehall, London. He began a series of more than 100 mythological paintings for Philip IV of Spain, but these were destroyed in the eighteenth century. Much of Rubens's talent was used to glorify kings and beautify churches, the two most powerful forces in seventeenth-century, Catholic Europe.

However, there was also a more intimate side to Rubens's work which is evident in numerous family portraits and small landscapes of the Flemish countryside. The 'Chapeau de Paille' (feathered hat), [5,25] a portrait of his sister-in-law, demonstrates his feeling for rich fabrics and skin tones. Brown underpainting shows through to create warm tones in the background and even in some areas of flesh and fabric. This more sketchy technique helps account for the great volume of work produced by Rubens and his workshop.

ANTHONY VAN DYCK (1599–1641)

Born and trained in Antwerp, van Dyck worked with Rubens for a number of years and was strongly influenced by him. On a trip to Italy he made many copies of Titian's work, which was also an influence. His main contribution to painting was in the area of portraiture. His paintings of the royals and nobles of Europe created a new form of elegant and austere portrait which became the ideal for nearly 200 years.

The portrait of 'Charles I of England out Hunting' [5,26] standing in his fine silks in the company of horse and servants reveals the relaxed arrogance of a man of power without all the trappings of royalty. Van Dyck's silvery colouring contrasted with areas of warm tones was much copied by English portrait artists in particular. Van Dyck and Rubens were both knighted by Charles I.

[5,26] 'Charles I of England out Hunting', 1635–8, by Anthony Van Dyck, 266 x 207 cm, oil on canvas (Louvre, Paris). The elegant stance and rustic background in this portrait were much copied by English portrait painters in the following centuries.

[5,27] 'The Surrender of Breda', 1634–5, by Diego Velázquez, 307 x 367 cm, oil on canvas (Prado, Madrid). Velázquez manages to create a human event instead of a glorious one. The figure groups are carefully composed to create a focus on the victorious Spanish army with its lifted faces and colourful banners.

DIEGO VELÁZQUEZ (1599–1660)

The greatest painter of the Spanish school, Velázquez was born and studied in Seville. His early works were on religious themes and scenes from everyday life and were painted with great accuracy and realism in a style reminiscent of Caravaggio. By the age of twenty-four he was appointed painter to King Philip IV who regarded him so highly that he gave him several other court appointments also. This career as a courtier, though socially important to Velázquez, reduced his output as an artist.

Rubens's diplomatic visit to the Spanish court encouraged Velázquez to go to Italy, where he was influenced particularly by the work of Titian. On his return to Spain his brushwork became looser and his colour more adventurous. 'The Surrender of Breda', [5,27] painted to commemorate a Spanish victory in the Netherlands, is classical rather than Baroque in form. The defeated Justin of Nassau hands over the key of the town to Ambrogio Spinola, the Spanish commander. The scene is more like a meeting of gentlemen than a triumph. The subtle symbols of upright lances and raised faces on the Spanish side contrast with the disorganised, downcast group from the Netherlands.

While on a second trip to Rome, Velázquez painted Pope Innocent X, a painting considered to be one of the great masterpieces of portraiture. The rich colours and fine robes create a sumptuous setting for the penetrating glance of the Pope.

The painting entitled 'Las Meninas' (The Maids of Honour) [5,28] is a complex work. The Infanta Margarita is the central figure, attended by her maids and by dwarfs. Reflected in a mirror over her head is the royal couple. Velázquez stands in front of his canvas at the left, looking at the viewer. The scene may represent a moment when the Infanta interrupted a portrait painting session with the King and Queen. Whatever the occasion,

[5,28] 'Las Meninas', 1656, by Diego Velázquez, oil on canvas, 318 x 276 cm (Prado, Madrid). From a distance Velázquez's work looks sharp and precisely finished, but on close inspection it is loosely painted, a collection of brushmarks and smudges which turn into shining fabrics when the viewer steps back.

[5,29] 'Kitchen Maid with Supper at Emmaus', c. 1618, by Diego Velázquez, 55 x 118 cm, oil on canvas (National Gallery of Ireland). This early Velázquez is in his sharply observed early style, the still-life objects and the figure being treated with equal care. The supper at Emmaus is seen through the opening at the left.

[5,30] 'St Rufina', by Francisco de Zurbarán, oil on canvas, 176 x 107.5 cm (National Gallery of Ireland, Dublin). The simple forms and strong contrasts in light and dark combined with the stillness of the figure create a contemplative mood in this work by Zurbarán.

the work is a masterpiece of composition and space. The two paintings on the back wall, showing the downfall of humans who challenge the gods in the arts, are by Rubens.

Velázquez was little known outside Spain until after the Napoleonic Wars. The technical freedom of his work was much admired by progressive artists in the nineteenth century. Manet considered him to be the greatest of all artists. [5,29]

OTHER ARTISTS

A number of Spanish artists specialised in themes or genres as Velázquez had done in his early work. Francisco de Zurbarán (1598–1664) painted religious themes and still lifes. In his painting 'St Rufina' [5,30] the saint stands in stark contrast against the dark background. The stillness of the figure and the interest in the domestic utensils is typical of his work. Bartolomé Esteban Murillo (1617–82) lived and worked in Seville. He painted religious scenes in a soft, sentimental style. His genre paintings of street urchins were very popular in the nineteenth century. The handling of paint and colour and the gentleness of the scene in 'The Prodigal Son Feasting', [5,31] part of a series of six canvases, are typical of Murillo's work.

THE NETHERLANDS

When the Protestant United Provinces won their independence from Spain, they created one of the first states since ancient times that was not run by nobility. The Dutch soon became a prosperous, progressive nation, with advanced technology and a generally tolerant attitude to politics and religion.

These events had a dramatic effect on the artistic life of the nation. Gone were the clerical and aristocratic patrons. Artists had to sell their work on the open market. This affected the size of paintings and the subject-matter. Religious themes became unfashionable and the tradition of detailed realism, dating back to van Eyck, emerged as the dominant style. Landscapes and still lifes as well as group portraits and interior scenes were developed in a way unseen before. Many of the roots of modern painting can be traced back to the Dutch school.

[5,31] 'The Prodigal Son Feasting', c. 1670, by Bartolomé Esteban Murillo, oil on canvas, 104.5 x 135.5 cm (National Gallery of Ireland, Dublin). In this third painting in a series of six on the prodigal son, the gentle romantic air is typical of much of Murillo's work. The rich clothes and colours show a Venetian influence.

GENRE PAINTING

Paintings of domestic matter and everyday life are called *genre* paintings. The term is also used in a broader sense to refer to a particular branch of painting. Landscape, portrait and still life are all genres of painting. We have already seen the emergence of genre painting in the French and Spanish schools, and to a lesser extent in Italy, but the Dutch have the strongest group of genre painters.

REMBRANDT VAN RIJN (1606–69)

As a painter, draughtsman and etcher, Rembrandt has rarely been surpassed. Born in Leiden, he studied in Amsterdam and became a successful portrait painter there during the 1630s and 1640s. 'A Portrait of a Young Lady' [5,32] is from this period, displaying the wonderfully life-like quality that was a mark of Rembrandt's portraits. The handling of paint is very refined, though touches in the fabrics point to his later luscious painting style.

The famous 'Night Watch' [5,33] comes from the end of the most commercially successful period of his life. The large group portrait shows the gathering of the local militia under Captain Frans Banning Cocq, in black, in preparation for parade. The richness of light, colour and

[5,32] 'A Portrait of a Young Lady', c.1636, by Rembrandt van Rijn, oil on canvas, 72 x 62 cm (National Gallery of Ireland, Dublin). This beautifully lit portrait is from the time when Rembrandt was in greatest demand as a portrait artist.

movement and the complexity of the composition create a scene full of humour, incident and humanity, so different from previous group portraits.

Following the death of his wife in 1642, Rembrandt spent more time painting Bible scenes. He neglected the business side of his life and by 1656 he was bankrupt. He never recovered financially. All through this personal trauma he painted and drew incessantly, producing some of his best masterpieces. Rembrandt also left a remarkable series of self-portraits from the beginning of his career through

[5,33] 'The Night Watch', 1642, by Rembrandt van Rijn, oil on canvas, 363 x 437 cm (Rijksmuseum, Amsterdam). This group portrait was paid for by contributions from members of the militia whose faces appear in it. Rembrandt added the colourful detail of antique helmets and lances and the more light-hearted elements to enliven what might have been a boring scene.

[5,34] 'The Jewish Bride', 1665, by Rembrandt van Rijn, oil on canvas, 122 x 168 cm (Rijksmuseum, Amsterdam). One of Rembrandt's beautifully painted late works, the encrusted paint has an almost metallic glow. The warm colours and simple composition help express the tenderness of the couple.

[5,35] 'Christ Preaching the Forgiveness of Sins', by Rembrandt van Rijn, etching (British Museum, London). In this beautiful print Rembrandt describes a group of real people. Young and old, rich and poor, attentive and bored, all group around a human and accessible Christ.

to wrinkled old age. The portrait of 1661–2 shows him looking confident and relaxed with brushes and palette in hand.

The biblical scenes of Rembrandt's later life are in rich reds and golds, with the paint applied heavily with palette knife in places. 'The Jewish Bride' [5,34] is an example of this style. The obvious tenderness in the faces of the couple highlights Rembrandt's ability to express humanity in his work. This warmth of colouring and gentleness of expression seems almost at odds with the tragedies and disappointments in Rembrandt's personal life. Only one of his children survived him.

Many of Rembrandt's drawings and etchings were made as works in their own right and not merely as preparation for or records of paintings. He drew from nature, both landscape and the ordinary folk of Amsterdam. His etching of 'Christ Preaching the Forgiveness of Sins' [5,35] demonstrates his fluent drawing style and technical mastery of the medium. The etching demonstrates the same balance of light and dark and compositional skill as characterise his paintings.

Rembrandt's handling of paint and his mastery of light and shade have made him one of the most highly regarded artists in the history of art, especially among painters. Delacroix rated him more highly than Raphael, which was high praise from one so steeped in academic tradition.

FRANS HALS (C. 1580–1666)

An older artist than Rembrandt but nonetheless influenced by him, Hals spent his working life in Haarlem. He painted genre scenes, but mainly portraits. The 'Young Fisherboy of Schevenigen' [5,36] is a genre piece, but almost a portrait as well. The looser brushwork and brighter colours are typical of his earlier and genre paintings. His mature portraits are darker in colour and tonality and more 'polished' in their appearance. 'The Laughing Cavalier' (Isaac Massa) [5,37] is typical of his lively portrait style, which often shows the sitter laughing or talking. The quick expressive brushwork is seen more in the rich clothes than in the face.

[5,36] 'A Young Fisherboy of Schevenigen', 1620, by Frans Hals, oil on canvas, 72 x 58 cm (National Gallery of Ireland, Dublin). This genre painting shows the free brushwork and lively expression of Hals's earlier work.

107

[5,37] 'The Laughing Cavalier', 1624, by Frans Hals, oil on canvas, 86 x 69 cm (Wallace Collection, London). Hals's ability to capture an expression in a fleeting moment, a twinkle in the eye, made him the most popular portrait painter of his day.

[5,38] 'Lady Writing a Letter', c. 1670, by Jan Vermeer, oil on canvas, 71.1 x 60.5 cm (National Gallery of Ireland, Dublin). The cool colours and soft light in Vermeer's paintings create a restful atmosphere. There are always clues to a story in the incidental details. The crest in the window, the objects on the floor, the painting of the 'Finding of Moses' make us wonder: who is she writing to and why? who is the second woman?

Throughout his life Hals was in financial trouble and ended up living on charity. His group portraits of the 'Regents' and the 'Regentesses of the Old Men's Alms House' are two of the most highly regarded group portraits in the world. Hals had a large family, many of whom were artists, and he trained a number of Dutch artists, but his work was largely forgotten until the 1850s when it came back into fashion. 'The Laughing Cavalier' fetched 51,000 francs in 1865, an enormous sum for the time.

JAN VERMEER (1632–75)

Vermeer lived and worked all his life in Delft. Although little known as a painter in his own time, he is now regarded as one of the great masters of Dutch art. The inn and art-dealing business he inherited from his father freed him from a dependence on painting for a living.

Most of Vermeer's work is of domestic interiors, with one or two figures calmly going about their work or leisure activities. 'Lady Writing a Letter' [5,38] is typically lit from the left, with the woman at the table highlighted by the light coming through the window. The composition is constructed of rectangles — window, picture-frame, table, chair — which creates a calmness that pervades all Vermeer's work. The impact of the work belies the small size of most of his paintings.

There are no known drawings by Vermeer and little is known of his working methods, but it seems likely that he adopted the use of the 'camera obscura', a device involving the use of lenses to project images onto paper. The images were then drawn by the artist. This technique is similar in principle to the photographic camera. Some of Vermeer's interiors have the exaggerated perspective of that produced by a lens.

Vermeer produced fewer than forty paintings in his lifetime and there are no records of his having sold any. His work was forgotten for years but rediscovered in the last century. In photographs Vermeer's work can look very smooth, but in reality it is quite richly painted. [5,39]

[5,39] 'Maid Pouring Milk', 1658, by Jan Vermeer, oil on canvas, 45 x 41 cm (Rijksmuseum, Amsterdam). Vermeer's mastery of light is well known and we can see his wonderful handling of textures and colour in this painting.

[5,40] 'Cardplayers in a Sunlit Room', 1658, by Pieter de Hooch, oil on canvas, 76 x 66 cm (Royal Collection, Windsor Castle). De Hooch specialised in scenes in and around taverns when he worked in Delft, contrasting interior and exterior light.

[5,42] 'The Village School' by Jan Steen, oil on canvas, 109 x 81 cm (National Gallery of Ireland, Dublin). Steen deliberately chooses dull colours to create the atmosphere in this painting. His tavern scenes are often brightly coloured, demonstrating a variety of personality types.

PIETER DE HOOCH (C. 1629–84)

A contemporary of Vermeer, Pieter de Hooch also worked in Delft, painting mainly tavern scenes. His 'Cardplayers in a Sunlit Room' [5,40] has much of the tranquillity of a Vermeer, with the receding exterior spaces creating a lovely effect. The composition has an almost abstract geometry of related rectangles, disturbed only by the card players.

PIETER CLAESZ (C. 1597–1661)

Master of the genre of still-life painting, Pieter Claesz worked in Haarlem and produced paintings of food and drink which were sometimes known as breakfast pieces. Colour was subdued in favour of effects of light and texture in the contrasting surfaces of the objects he chose for his still-life groups. [5,41]

JAN STEEN (1626–79)

Steen studied the human condition in his paintings of everyday life. In 'The Village School' [5,42] he renders the dull interior in great detail. But it is in contemplating the contrasting emotions of the three main characters that we are asked whether what we see makes us laugh or become annoyed. By creating a variety of characters in his paintings Steen often asked this kind of question. As an artist he had the full range of abilities to work in any genre.

JACOB VAN RUISDAEL (1628/9–82)

The most accomplished of all the Dutch landscape painters, Jacob van Ruisdael painted a variety of subjects from woodlands and rivers to beaches and seascapes. 'The Castle of Bentheim', [5,43] an early work, shows Ruisdael's gift for creating atmosphere with woodland and sky. The castle, which Ruisdael painted a number of times, is not in reality on a rocky outcrop, but the artist created one for dramatic effect. The sophistication of the work in its range of texture and light effects is surprising when we realise that this is one of the earliest pure landscapes with no human figures or story to tell.

[5,41] 'Detail of Still Life', 1637, by Pieter Claesz, oil on panel, 38 x 57 cm (National Gallery of Ireland, Dublin). Claesz chose objects with contrasting surfaces and colours as the basis for his meticulously painted still-life groups.

109

[5,43] 'The Castle of Bentheim', 1653, by Jacob van Ruisdael, oil on canvas, 110.5 x 144 cm (National Gallery of Ireland, Dublin). The dramatic skyline view of the castle is beautifully contrasted by the foreground elements of rocky outcrop and felled oak tree. The stream forms a middle ground space and the village among the trees connects the parts — a sophisticated piece of composition and atmosphere.

CONCLUSION

Although it may seem that Italian and North European art were at odds in the seventeenth century, they had, in fact, much in common. Greater realism and expression were sought in both traditions. Some Baroque artists were branching out into the new genres of landscape and still life and some Dutch artists liked Baroque composition and drama. The interest in painterly effects was universal, though the scale of work could be quite different. It could be said that Gothic and Renaissance elements were reconciled in Baroque and Dutch painting. The Gothic expression of the supernatural and interest in detail and the Renaissance interest in classical forms were combined in all the arts.

EIGHTEENTH CENTURY

The increased nationalism that led to the formation of new states like Holland in the seventeenth century brought about the American and French Revolutions at the end of the eighteenth century. Political and scientific thought preoccupied the age, leaving the visual arts in a less prominent position than they had been. Opera and ballet were new popular art forms and with music they became a focus for patrons of culture.

Eighteenth-century art differed from previous styles in that it was not promoting religious or political beliefs, nor was it breaking new technical ground. There were two main strands of development, the decorative Rococo style and a realist style which followed from Dutch genre paintings. Towards the end of the century a new classical style developed out of a renewed, more scientific, interest in the ancient world, particularly Greece. Increased freedom of trade and travel made the art of India, Asia and the Americas more accessible. The art and design of ancient cultures began to fascinate late eighteenth- and nineteenth-century Europe.

ROCOCO ART

Born from the Baroque style, Rococo is characterised by lightness, grace, playfulness and intimacy. Architecture and particularly interiors are decorative and colourful; white and gold often predominate. It was generally a court and church style, culminating in the fantastic Austrian and German palaces and church interiors which dazzle the visitor with their gilded and painted decoration.

ARCHITECTURE

Both decorative and classical designs were popular in the eighteenth century. In France classical exteriors sometimes hid Rococo interiors. Georgian architecture in the Palladian manner predominated in England, while in Italy, Spain, Austria, Germany and the Central European principalities the Rococo style was common, producing some elegant designs and incredible confections.

FRANCE

The court of Louis XV led the way in Rococo interior design. The 'Cabinet de la Pendule' in Versailles (Château de Versailles, France), [5,44] with its gilded plasterwork, white walls, mirrors and paintings, is typical of the French Rococo style. French aristocrats built a number of 'Hôtels' (town palaces) in Paris during the eighteenth century, with plain and classical exteriors enclosing Rococo interiors. The oval 'Salon of the Princess' [5,45] in the Hôtel de Soubise, Paris, is a beautiful example. The gilded plasterwork is in high relief. Eight canvases by Natoire depicting

[5,44] 'Cabinet de la Pendule' (The Clock Room), 1738, Palace of Versailles (Château de Versailles, France). The Louis XV style of Rococo can be seen in the gilt plasterwork and furniture which create brighter interiors than earlier design at Versailles.

[5,45] The oval 'Salon of the Princess', Hôtel de Soubise, Paris, 1735, decorated by G.G. Buffrand. The gilt stucco used to frame doors, windows and paintings dominates this salon interior.

[5,46] The Panthéon, Paris, 1755–92. Soufflot created one of the earliest examples of neo-classical design with the large temple front and dome on this otherwise plain building.

[5,47] The Abbey Church of Vierzehnheilígen (14 saints), near Langheim on River Main, Germany, 1743–72. Sited on a hilltop overlooking the River Main, Vierzehnheilígen Pilgrimage Church is externally modelled on medieval churches, though the details are Rococo.

the story of Psyche fill the spaces between the tops of the windows. The architecture is swamped and softened by the decoration that seems to grow over everything.

In contrast with this decorative style, the Panthéon, [5,46] originally built as the Church of St Genevieve but renamed after the French Revolution, was designed by Jacques Germain Soufflot (1713–80) who was trained in Italy. It combines a dome in the style of St Paul's, London, with a huge temple front, creating a starkly classical building. A series of domes on piers and columns creates a beautifully lit interior, a suitable resting place for French notables.

GERMANY
BALTHASAR NEUMANN (1687–1753)
Balthasar Neumann was one of the great architects of German Rococo. He designed the Abbey Church of Vierzehnheiligen (fourteen saints) [5,47] on a hillside overlooking the River Main. Built to replace a small pilgrim chapel, the twin-towered façade is constructed of honey-coloured stone. Its shape echoes medieval churches. Inside Neumann divided the nave into three intersecting oval vaults which were decorated by German and Italian decorative artists. [5,48] Neumann's structure and the Rococo decoration make this one of the most impressive interiors in Europe.

111

[5,48] Vierzehnheiligen Abbey, 1743–72. View of the nave looking east. Neumann's design of three oval vaults divides the church into quite separate areas. The painted ceilings and gilt stucco emphasise these divisions.

[5,49] Chiswick House, London, c. 1725, by Lord Burlington and William Kent. Based on Palladio's design of the Villa Rotunda at Vicenza in Italy, Chiswick House was the model for many of the Palladian mansions set in the English countryside.

Neumann also designed the residence for Prince Archbishop Johann Franz von Schönborna of Würzburg. Giambattista Tiepolo (1696–1770), the finest fresco painter of the century, painted the ceilings in the main reception rooms with a work entitled 'The Four Parts of the Earth' in homage to the Archbishop of Würzburg. Neumann's portrait is included as part of the decoration on the huge ceiling over the staircase. Large palaces in imitation of Versailles were built by several European aristocrats.

ENGLAND

In the eighteenth century, or 'Georgian' period, in England, English country gentlemen with vast lands and wealth wanted to redesign their homes and gardens in the style of paintings by Claude Lorrain. Their admiration of the classical past led them to imitate the designs of the Renaissance architect Palladio. Chiswick House in London, [5,49] designed by Lord Burlington and the architect William Kent, was an imitation of the Palladian Villa Rotunda at Vicenza in Italy. Lord Burlington had seen the villa when on the grand tour (European aristocracy toured the great cities and landscapes of Europe to broaden their education). Kent went on to design a number of country mansions.

Town planning was also spreading to English towns and cities. The Wood family designed streets, squares and crescents for the aristocracy in Bath, which was the most fashionable watering place in the eighteenth century. The Royal Crescent was built in the grand Palladian style. [5,50]

ROBERT ADAM (1728–92)

Robert Adam, a Scottish architect and designer, became famous for his classically based interior designs. The interior of Syon House, Middlesex, [5,51] is considered to be one of his finest. He was one of the first architects who attempted to create a unified style and proportion in exterior, interior and furnishings. The 'Adam style' went on to influence all branches of furnishing and design in England.

[5,50] Royal Crescent, Bath, 1764–74, by John Wood the Younger. One of the most impressive pieces of urban domestic architecture anywhere. The Royal Crescent at Bath was the basis for many planned streets in Britain.

[5,51] Syon House, Middlesex, 1762, by Robert Adam. The Red Room. Adam remodelled the interior of Syon House for the Duke of Northumberland. He based his designs on a free adaptation of Roman palaces. The strong colours are typical of his work.

[5,52] 'Cupid and Psyche', 1783–95, by Antonio Canova, marble, 46 x 58 x 43 cm. This small sculpture shows the refinement of Canova's style and his range of sculpting skills in rendering texture.

SCULPTURE

Although many talented artists were involved in sculpture based on classical themes and portraiture, the eighteenth century produced no sculptor of huge international stature. Rome was still the cultural capital and most sculptors spent time studying and working there. Workshops were generally open to the public and connoisseurs could call in to see work in progress and talk to the artists. People on the grand tour, admiring the Roman and Renaissance past, could commission work from the many European sculptors working in the city who were familiar with the classical style.

ITALY

ANTONIO CANOVA (1757–1822)

Canova was the most highly regarded sculptor of the late eighteenth century. He had a busy workshop in Rome and his work was commissioned by kings and heads of state all over Europe. His many assistants carried out the bulk of the work from his designs and models, and he added finishing touches.

Canova's sculptures are in the neo-classical style with clear form and outline, designed to be viewed from any side. The 'Cupid and Psyche' [5,52] gives an idea of the range of his carving skills. The polished surface of the figures contrasts with the refined textures of rock and fabric and the delicate treatment of feathers in Cupid's wings.

Canova also designed monuments and portraits. His sculpture of Pauline Bonaparte as Venus, [5,53] calm, elegant and life-like, controlled yet sensual, is considered one of the finest neo-classical sculptures.

FRANCE

JEAN BAPTISTE PIGALLE (1714–85)

Pigalle suffered great hardship as a student when he walked to Rome from Paris to study at his own expense. Later, having been a success at the Academy, he became a favourite at court. He

[5,53] 'Paolina Borghese as Venus', 1805–7, by Antonio Canova, marble, 87 x 185 x 67 cm (Galleria Borghese, Rome). This marble portrait of Napoleon Bonaparte's sister as Venus was much admired in neo-classical circles. The very stillness, which we may find strange, was admired. Canova's carving of fabrics and his polished finish were not often equalled.

[5,54] Monument to the Maréchal de Saxe, 1753–76, by Jean Baptiste Pigalle, marble (St Thomas's Church, Strasbourg). The lions on one side and Cupid on the other symbolise the courageous and loving nature of Maréchal de Saxe. The figure of France tries to hold back Death who crouches over the open tomb at the bottom.

[5,55] 'Voltaire', by Jean-Antoine Houdon, bronze. This bronze by Houdon shows his ability to produce life-like and animated portraits, which made him the most sought after portrait sculptor of his time.

moved in intellectual circles and made a startling nude portrait of his friend Voltaire which was a scandal at the time. Pigalle did small genre pieces, portraits and large monuments in inventive designs. The quality of his carving and design can be seen in the monument to the Maréchal de Saxe [5,54] which is somewhere between Baroque and neo-classical in design.

JEAN-ANTOINE HOUDON (1741–1828)

A pupil of Pigalle, Houdon won a scholarship to Rome. His work, based on classical art, brought him fame and an international reputation; but it is as a portrait sculptor that he is best known. His portrait bust of Voltaire captures such humanity and intelligence that the figure seems alive. [5,55] Houdon made portraits of the aristocrats of Europe, the statesmen of France and the leaders of Republican America. His portrait of George Washington stands in the Capitol in Richmond.

REST OF EUROPE

The Rococo style drew sculptors into participating in decorative schemes where sculpture did not exist as a separate entity. The Asam brothers from Bavaria were architects, painters and sculptors who produced some of the finest work in Germany. Egid Quirin Asam, the younger brother, designed the 'Assumption of the Virgin' [5,56] for the Abbey Church of Rohr, an extraordinarily illusionist piece in which the Virgin appears to fly up out of the tomb.

In England, the French influence was strong, following the work of Roubiliac who lived and worked most of his life in England. English sculptors such as Banks and Flaxman worked in a neo-classical style on monuments, portraits and other pieces based on classical art.

[5,56] 'The Assumption of the Virgin', 1722, by Egid Quirin Asam, Church of Rohr, paint on stucco (plaster). This group creates the illusion of the Virgin being lifted by angels rising from the tomb. Asam was trained in Italy where he was influenced by Bernini's work.

PAINTING

The decorative and realist styles in painting existed side by side in the eighteenth century. In Italy the large-scale fresco tradition continued with a revival of the arts in Venice. Though Italian artists painted Rococo interiors all over Europe, they retained a more classical style than did fresco painters in the rest of Europe. French Rococo painting, on a smaller scale, was mainly of landscapes with a classical element in the tradition of Poussin and Claude, but more decorative and artificial.

The realist style in genre painting continued in almost every country, progressing into a neo-classical style by the end of the century due to a more accurate study of the ancient world and a reaction against the frivolity of the Rococo style.

ITALY

Throughout the eighteenth century, Italian artists continued to paint religious themes and picturesque views of the famous cities and places on the grand tour. Many artists of quality were involved in this market which stunted artistic growth in Italy for a time.

GIAMBATTISTA TIEPOLO (1696–1770)

Probably the greatest large-scale painter of the eighteenth century, Tiepolo's work marks the end of the Italian fresco tradition. He revived the glories of Venetian painting in a style influenced by Veronese. His large illusionist schemes include false architecture painted by assistants. [5,57] He painted the entire space of the Gran Salone in the Palazzo Labia in Venice, between 1741 and 1750. The scenes from the life of Cleopatra in this series are justly famous.

Tiepolo's ceiling frescoes made for the residence of the Prince Archbishop of Würzburg in Germany are considered to be his greatest work. [5,58] Light in colour and vigorous in style, they harmonise beautifully with the architectural setting. The theme of the four continents on the ceiling of the stairway covers the vast space with an amazing array of exotic people and animals. Portraits of important court figures, including Balthasar Neumann who designed the building, are included in the fresco.

[5,57] 'An Allegory of the Incarnation', by Giambattista Tiepolo, painted on paper, 58 x 44 cm (National Gallery of Ireland, Dublin). The light colouring and vigorous composition of Tiepolo's work can be seen in this study.

[5,58] Ceiling of the residence of the Prince Archbishop of Würzburg, 1750–5, fresco by Giambattista Tiepolo. A portrait of Balthasar Neumann, architect of the building, can be seen in the foreground of this section of the ceiling, over the stairway.

Tiepolo also painted in oils and made drawings and etchings which were influential in his time. Towards the end of his life his style became unfashionable. He died in Spain working on a commission for the King.

CANALETTO (ANTONIO CANAL) (1697–1768)

Canaletto began as a scene painter for the theatre in his father's workshop in Venice and later became the most famous view painter of the eighteenth century. His clients were mainly

English visitors to Venice. When the Austrian War of Succession made travel difficult, Canaletto went to London where he painted views of the city around the Thames and some country houses. Years later he returned to Venice where he continued to paint and draw views of the city.

[5,59] 'Venice: The Stonemason's Yard', by Canaletto, oil on canvas, 125.8 x 102.9 cm (National Gallery, London). Expressive brushwork and beautiful lighting effects characterise Canaletto's earlier work.

Canaletto's early work is painterly with varied effects of surface and texture. 'The Stonemason's Yard' [5,59] is in this style, a picturesque scene of everyday Venice where the famous buildings form a backdrop to the activity in the foreground. Canaletto made many detailed, annotated drawings in preparation for his work and used the camera obscura device to increase accuracy. He also made drawings as collector's pieces, for which there was a strong demand.

Canaletto's later paintings of important or picturesque parts of the city were more detailed. He also painted scenes of pageantry and state occasions. The 'View of the Piazza San Marco', [5,60] an accurate wide-angle view in the style popular with English collectors, is from this period.

FRANCE
JEAN ANTOINE WATTEAU (1684–1721)
The outstanding painter of French Rococo, Watteau was born in Valenciennes, a Flemish town newly ceded to France. He was trained in Paris but his fellow Fleming, Rubens, was a great influence on him. Watteau invented a new genre,

[5,60] 'A View of the Piazza San Marco', by Canaletto, oil on canvas, 46 x 77 cm (National Gallery of Ireland, Dublin). The public demand for greater detail and more accurate representations of famous views of Venice made Canaletto refine his painting style to a harder, smoother finish.

[5,61] 'Les Fêtes Venitiennes', c. 1718–19, by Jean Antoine Watteau, oil on canvas, 56 x 46 cm (National Gallery of Scotland, Edinburgh). The apparently light-hearted or frivolous scenes painted by Watteau often have an underlying sadness or moral.

the 'Fête Galante' — parkland scenes with beautifully dressed young men and women engaged in games and romance. 'Les Fêtes Vénitiennes' [5,61] is of this type, with costumes and nature painted with great delicacy. Watteau invented a technique of placing flecks of colour side by side to enhance texture, and this technique was used by other artists as late as the post-Impressionists.

Watteau also painted scenes from the Commedia dell'Arte, an Italian troupe of performers famous for their fast-moving and irreverent pantomimes. The characters of Harlequin, Colombine and Pierrot come from this tradition. The figure of Giles, a French adaptation of Pierrot, painted towards the end of his life, shows a sadness which underlies much of Watteau's painting.

[5,62] 'Two Gentlemen and a Lady', c. 1710, by Jean Antoine Watteau, red chalk on paper, 15 x 16.5 cm (National Gallery of Ireland, Dublin). Watteau's beautiful drawings from life were used as references for his paintings.

[5,63] 'Diana Getting out of her Bath', 1742, by François Boucher, oil on canvas, 57 x 73 cm (Louvre, Paris). Boucher picks the moment just before Actaeon finds the goddess, Diana, bathing after the hunt, and is turned into a stag and devoured by his dogs as punishment for looking at her naked.

Drawing from observation was the basis for much of Watteau's work. He collected these drawings into large bound volumes which he used as references for his paintings. Figures often appear in more than one painting. [5,62]

Watteau suffered from poor health and a difficult temperament due to tuberculosis. His achievements, particularly as a colourist, maintained his reputation, and his paintings were collected even after the French Revolution, when his work might have been considered part of frivolous court society.

FRANÇOIS BOUCHER (1703–70)

Born and trained in Paris, Boucher began his career as an illustrator and engraver. He engraved a series of Watteau's paintings, which influenced his style. He won a scholarship to Rome, where he was influenced by the lighter colouring of Italian Rococo. Back in France, he designed tapestries and made paintings and engravings in a style which became fashionable with the French court. Madame de Pompadour, favourite mistress of Louis XV, became his patroness. He painted a number of portraits of her and made paintings for her château, as well as giving her art lessons.

'Diana Getting out of her Bath' [5,63] shows Boucher's idealised view of the world. Diana sits on a blue fabric, as do many of Boucher's nudes, at the edge of the stream with her attendant nymph. The background landscape is lightened and tamed. The birds she has shot and the alert hounds are painted with as much care as the beautiful figures.

Boucher's decorative, sensual style went out of fashion towards the end of his life when the morally serious, neo-classical movement frowned on such frivolity.

JEAN HONORÉ FRAGONARD (1732–1806)

A pupil of Boucher, Fragonard was the most decorative of the Rococo painters. His often erotic paintings are beautifully finished. 'The Swing', [5,64] a sort of smutty joke, shows Fragonard's beautiful use of colour and decorative texture. Everything seems frilly and light-hearted. The French Revolution in 1789 ended Fragonard's career, though his style was becoming unfashionable even before then.

JEAN BAPTISTE CHARDIN (1699–1779)

Chardin was a painter of still-life and genre pieces but was different in style from the Rococo court painters. His simple studies followed a Dutch realist tradition but avoided humorous or dramatic subjects. His colours were muted, mainly earth tones with pinks, blues and greys. He painted with deliberate brushwork, using an impasto technique. The middle-class subject-matter of his still-life and genre pieces reflected his clientele. Engravings of his paintings were very popular with the general public. 'The Governess' [5,65] is typical of his figure painting,

117

[5,64] 'The Swing', 1767, by Jean Honoré Fragonard, oil on canvas, 81 x 67 cm (Wallace Collection, London). Fragonard's work is often criticised for its frivolous nature, but this is to miss the drawing and painting skills he undoubtedly had.

[5,65] 'The Governess', by Jean Baptiste Chardin, oil on canvas, 62 x 73 cm (National Gallery of Ireland, Dublin). One of a number of versions of this domestic scene by Chardin. The strong, simple composition and muted colour are characteristic of his style.

a domestic scene from everyday middle-class life which promotes education and domestic harmony, ideals of the French bourgeoisie.

In Chardin's still-life paintings simple arrangements of food and drink are often set on a stone shelf, or nice pieces of glass or china point to the taste of his clients. In his later years, with weakening eyesight, he turned to portraits in

pastels and produced few genre pieces. Chardin's strong, simple compositions and realism have ensured that his work has remained popular and his influence continues into the twentieth century.

JACQUES LOUIS DAVID (1748–1825)

The most influential painter of the eighteenth century, David was born in Paris and trained for a short time with Boucher who was a relative of his. He moved to the studio of Vien, who was more interested in the classical past and Poussin. David won the 'Prix de Rome' which gave him a four-year scholarship at the Académie de France in Rome. This time in Rome was the strongest influence on his style. The theorists of the classical revival introduced him to the beauty and 'correctness' of Greek and Roman art. Back in Paris, David became involved in revolutionary politics and used his art to promote nationalism and self-sacrifice.

'The Oath of the Horatii' [5,66] shows three brothers swearing loyalty to Rome and receiving their swords from their father, while the women and children shrink back helplessly. The taut, muscular figures are set in an austere classical background without a hint of decoration, so different from the Rococo court paintings.

[5,66] 'The Oath of the Horatii', 1784–5, by Jacques Louis David, oil on canvas, 335 x 427 cm (Louvre, Paris). One of the most influential neo-classical paintings, it embodies the 'noble' simplicity and calm grandeur favoured by Winckelmann, the neo-classical theorist.

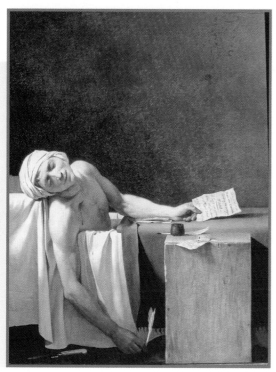

[5,67] 'The Death of Marat', 1793, by Jacques Louis David, oil on canvas, 160 x 125 cm (Musées Royaux des Beaux Arts de Belgique, Brussels). This is less a portrait of Marat than a propaganda piece about martyrdom for the cause. The beautifully painted detail and the abstract simplicity of the composition characterise David's smaller work.

[5,68] 'The Rake in Bedlam' from 'The Rake's Progress', 1733, by William Hogarth, oil on canvas, 63 x 76 cm (Sir John Soane's Museum, London). From the series of 8 paintings in 'The Rake's Progress'. Hogarth shows decline and fall due to a life of vice. The groups within the painting are skilfully arranged in the classical tradition.

David was a deputy in the National Assembly and voted for the death of King Louis XVI. He was *the* painter of the French Revolution and recorded some of the events in commemorative paintings. 'The Death of Marat', [5,67] a painting of a man murdered for his ideals, is again a moral statement. The neo-classical style of David's paintings emphasises clarity of line and form, which suits the seriousness and formality of his subjects.

David managed to work his way into favour when Napoleon came to power and became his official painter, creating works that glorified the exploits of the Emperor, including the enormous 'Coronation of Napoleon'. He had to change his style to suit these large paintings, so he studied the work of Rubens before commencing work on them. When the Royalists regained power in France David went into exile in Belgium, where he continued to paint portraits and historical pieces. He kept up a correspondence with many of his pupils including Gérard, Gros and Ingres, all famous in their own right.

ENGLAND

WILLIAM HOGARTH (1697–1764)

Hogarth, an important figure in English painting, was born, trained and worked all his life in London. He broke the dependence on foreign painters and helped create an English style and mode of expression. Initially, he trained as an engraver and then at the St Martin's Lane Academy run by Sir James Thornhill, whose daughter he married in 1729. Hogarth had early success while painting scenes like 'The Beggar's Opera' from the theatre. He then invented his own genre — sequences of pictures on moral or satirical themes. 'A Harlot's Progress' was followed by 'A Rake's Progress', [5,68] which in eight scenes describes in a melodramatic style the punishment for vice.

The engraved prints Hogarth made of his own series of paintings were very popular. The Copyright Act of 1735 was passed to prevent unlicensed copies from being sold. Portraits were also in his repertoire. In a Baroque style, and more often of the middle classes than of the aristocracy, they are vigorous and lively paintings of family groups and individuals. [5,69] Hogarth considered his portrait of 'Captain Coram', founder of the Foundling Hospital, to be his best.

In 1753 Hogarth published *The Analysis of Beauty*, the first treatise on aesthetic theory by an English painter. He opened his own academy which was a forerunner of the Royal Academy and was an important influence in the establishment of an independent English school of painting.

[5,69] 'The Mackinnon Children', by William Hogarth, oil on canvas, 180 x 143 cm (National Gallery of Ireland, Dublin). Hogarth's ability to animate his portraits can be seen in this charming portrait. His painting ability, which is sometimes forgotten, is evident in the fabrics in particular.

[5,70] 'Mary, Countess Howe', 1763–4, by Thomas Gainsborough, oil on canvas, 244 x 152.4 cm (Kenwood House, London). The sophistication of Gainsborough's style is seen in the colour and texture of this elegant portrait of a society lady in a pretty landscape setting.

THOMAS GAINSBOROUGH (1727–88)

Born in Sudbury in Suffolk, Gainsborough trained under the French engraver Gravelot in London. He set up as a portrait painter and engraver in Ipswich, painting country gentlemen and their families and the local landscape. Moving to Bath in about 1760, he quickly became a society portrait painter, taking on something of the style of van Dyck in the freedom of his handling of paint. He always achieved a good likeness and his landscape backgrounds have the lightness of Watteau's park scenes. The full-length portrait of 'Mary, Countess Howe' [5,70] highlights Gainsborough's free and elegant style of painting, which he carried out largely unassisted.

Gainsborough's greatest influence on English painting was through his landscapes and genre pieces which he painted for pleasure. 'The Watering Place' is one of his finest landscapes, much admired in his own day and of a quality to make Gainsborough one of the finest artists of the century. He was a founder member of the Royal Academy, but exhibited on his own after falling out with the Academy.

JOSHUA REYNOLDS (1723–92)

The leading figure in eighteenth-century art in England, Reynolds was the first president of the Royal Academy. He painted portraits in the grand manner, posing sitters in imitation of antique and Renaissance works. Born in Plymouth in Devonshire, son of a scholarly clergyman, Reynolds went to London to study under Hudson, a portrait painter. He spent two years in Italy where he was strongly influenced by classical and Renaissance art and the work of Carracci.

Reynolds regarded history painting as the highest form of art, so he tried to introduce an element of history into his portraits. The elaborate portrait of 'Charles Coote, 1st Earl of Bellamont' [5,71] is in this formal style. The popularity of his portraits led Reynolds to employ assistants as drapery painters. He produced as many as 150 portraits in 1758. In spite of this huge output Reynolds had a

[5,71] 'Charles Coote, 1st Earl of Bellamont', by Joshua Reynolds, oil on canvas, 245 x 162 cm (National Gallery of Ireland, Dublin). The elaborate setting and robes of this portrait fit in with Reynolds's theories of symbolism and gesture in the classical manner.

gift for finding the individuality in each sitter. Ruskin pronounced him 'The Prince of Portrait Painters'.

A good courtier, Reynolds raised the status of artists in England, making them acceptable at a social level they had not reached before. As president of the Royal Academy he gave fifteen 'Discourses' to the students between 1768 and 1790, and these remained the expression of the Academy's doctrine for years after his death.

GEORGE STUBBS (1724–1806)

More than a painter of horse portraits and sporting scenes, Stubbs, a self-taught artist from Liverpool, was interested in nature on a scientific level. His *Anatomy of the Horse,* published in 1766 and one of the greatest achievements in eighteenth-century natural history, is illustrated with his own engravings based on dissections he himself made of horses.

Stubbs first supported himself by portrait painting, but it is his animal paintings for which he is most celebrated. His 'Mares and Foals in a River Landscape' of 1763–8 [5,72] is a beautiful painting, remarkably accurate in anatomy and texture. His later series of a horse being attacked by a lion anticipates the romantic paintings of Delacroix in the next century.

JOSEPH WRIGHT 'OF DERBY' (1734–97)

The first major English artist to have a career outside London, Wright painted genre pieces with unusual lighting effects. The 'Experiment with an

[5,72] 'Mares and Foals in a River Landscape', 1763–8, by George Stubbs, oil on canvas, 100 x 190 cm (Tate Gallery, London). The lovely setting and careful arrangement are like a contemporary portrait painting. In fact many of Stubbs's paintings are portraits of racehorses and their owners, jockeys and stablelads.

[5,73] 'Experiment with an Air Pump', 1768, by Joseph Wright 'of Derby', oil on canvas, 182 x 243 cm (National Gallery, London). The dramatic lighting and study in emotions make Wright's a memorable painting.

Air Pump' [5,73] highlights his interest in current scientific experiments which were a major preoccupation in the eighteenth century. The range of expressions and ages of the group watching the bird struggle in the vacuum is a deliberate device to induce thought in the viewer. While in Italy Wright witnessed an eruption of Vesuvius and a fireworks display in Rome. It was these dramatic lighting effects that he painted rather than the classical models that interested other artists.

SPAIN

FRANCISCO DE GOYA (1746–1828)

Born in the small town of Fuendetodos near Saragosa where he first trained, Goya worked for the court painter, Bayeu, in Madrid and married Bayeu's sister on returning from a trip to Italy. Goya's mature style was slow to develop and his early church work, portraits and tapestry designs show a move from a decorative style to a more realist approach. He was strongly influenced by a commission to make aquatint etchings of the Velázquez paintings in the royal collection. His work for important aristocratic and political patrons kept Goya in contact with the court. When Charles IV succeeded to the throne in 1789 he was appointed court painter.

Goya's painting of 'Charles IV and his Family' [5,74] demonstrates his uncanny ability to show something of the personality of the sitter through the portrait. The royal family is not portrayed as

[5,74] 'Charles IV and his Family', 1800, by Francisco de Goya, oil on canvas, 280 x 336 cm (Prado, Madrid). The beautiful costumes and the wonderfully fluent painting of Goya do not hide the strained atmosphere in the Spanish royal family. Goya's treatment of precious materials in flicks of bright colour on the dark ground makes the painting shine with gem-like quality.

[5,75] 'Tooth Hunting', 1799, by Francisco de Goya, etching with aquatint, print on paper, 18 x 10 cm (British Museum, London). Goya's etching style was influenced by Rembrandt. The aquatint provides the grey tones. Goya is considered to be one of the best printmakers of all time.

attractive, despite the beautiful clothes. The domineering Queen controls the disorganised group; the King and prince look dull and isolated. This increased perceptiveness and imagination seem to have followed an illness in 1792 in which Goya lost his hearing. A series of eighty-two etchings, 'Los Caprichos' (Caprices), features satirical attacks on social customs and abuses of the Church. They reveal an increasingly dark side to Goya's imagination.

The 'Tooth Hunting' print [5,75] shows a woman pulling a tooth from a hanged man, for a witch's brew. Her superstitious belief is more powerful than the dangers and horrors she endures. There is a nightmarish quality in many of the prints, much more harsh than Hogarth's moral scenes earlier in the century.

Goya was to witness real horrors during the years of war that followed the French takeover of Spain in 1808. 'The Second of May 1808' (Rising of Madrid People against Napoleon's Army) [5,76] is the first of a pair of paintings that describe the attack on Napoleon's North African cavalry by the people of Madrid and the executions by the Napoleonic soldiers in retaliation on the third of May. Goya simplifies forms and colour to help the

viewer focus on the violent action. A series of thirty-five etchings on 'The Disasters of War' further develops the theme of man's inhumanity to man.

Fourteen large murals sometimes called 'The Black Paintings', which Goya painted for his own house, depict nightmarish scenes painted in a fluent, sketchy style on a black background. The meaning of 'The Colossus' (or 'Panic'), [5,77] part of this series, is difficult to decipher. The back of a huge figure appears over the horizon in the process of turning towards the viewer. The people

[5,76] 'The Second of May 1808', 1814, by Francisco de Goya, oil on canvas, 266 x 345 cm (Museo del Prado, Madrid). Goya does nothing to glorify the rising. It is a scene of confusion and death.

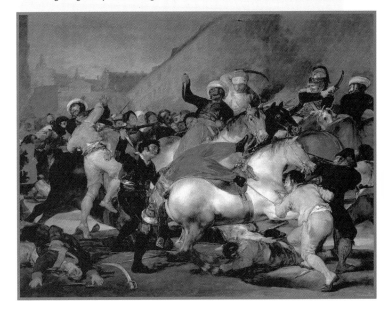

[5,77] 'The Colossus', 1810–12, by Francisco de Goya, oil on canvas, 115 x 105 cm (Museo del Prado, Madrid). The sometimes mysterious subjects of Goya's 'Black Paintings' are disturbing images from Goya's imagination, often focusing on human fears and cruelty.

and animals scatter for safety. This series marks the final phase of his painting before his retirement to Bordeaux in France to escape the intrigues of Spanish politics.

Goya completed a huge body of work, including 500 oil paintings and murals, 300 etchings and lithographs and hundreds of drawings. His versatile range of subjects and techniques brought much admiration in nineteenth-century France. Delacroix and Manet were both influenced by his work.

CONCLUSION

The great social change brought about by the liberal and democratic movement had an enormous effect on the arts. The Church and royal courts were no longer the guiding influences they had been. Artists became independent thinkers, producing work for their own satisfaction rather than to please a patron. The other side of independence was the need to make a living and find buyers for their work. This created the new categories of art dealers and connoisseurs who were the middlemen and creators of taste.

A new middle class of businessmen and professionals — doctors, lawyers, engineers, etc. — created a market for smaller paintings and sculptures suitable for town houses. New streets of gentlemen's houses were built in all the cities of Europe during the eighteenth century.

The style and content of all art and particularly of painting changed completely at this time. The decorative work of earlier in the century gave way to art of greater honesty and forcefulness by 1800. In comparing the work of Goya to Watteau, the stark reality and power of Goya's painting is in sharp contrast with the unreality of Watteau's fashion-conscious aristocrats painted in artificial landscapes.

Academies became the normal method of training artists, rather than apprenticeships, though most spent some time working as assistants to established artists. The social status of artists also changed. They were no longer considered as tradesmen, but moved in intellectual circles, mixing with the new middle class.

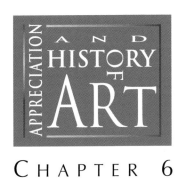

APPRECIATION AND HISTORY OF ART

CHAPTER 6

NINETEENTH AND TWENTIETH CENTURIES

NINETEENTH CENTURY

The political change brought about by the French Revolution in the eighteenth century was matched by the social and economic change created by the Industrial Revolution in the nineteenth. The appalling living and working conditions of the poor, labouring classes in the rapidly expanding industrial cities are recorded in the novels of Dickens, but surprisingly few artists dealt in any critical way with the social ills of the time.

The results of the Industrial Revolution — expanded urban populations, rapid transport by rail, increased scientific knowledge and more leisure time for the middle classes — did have an effect on the arts. A romantic view of the countryside and rural life grew out of the harsh realities of the industrialised cities. Greater freedom of movement brought ideas from all over the world to the masses. New technology created opportunities for designers to challenge traditional approaches to design. Increased leisure time for the middle classes led to the creation of new holiday resorts and other forms of entertainment which became the subject-matter of artists in the later part of the century.

The state of political turmoil in nineteenth-century France was not conducive to art. The fall of Napoleon Bonaparte and the First French Empire brought about a return of royal power under Louis-Philippe. This, however, was followed by a series of revolutions and then by the Franco-Prussian War of 1870–1. It may have been this enormous social upheaval that dictated the great changes in French art. While artists found it difficult to make a living, they were now more free to choose their own subject-matter and methods of working.

THE ROMANTIC MOVEMENT

In the early part of the nineteenth century Romanticism was the principal movement in the arts, particularly in music and literature. In architecture it is represented by the Gothic revival; in painting it had a number of sometimes contradictory manifestations. The emotional or dramatic subject-matter of the Romantic movement differed greatly from the reason and order of classicism. Ancient heroic tales and exotic settings were often portrayed by figure painters. 'The Death of Sardanapalus' by Eugène Delacroix, [6,1] with its chaotic composition and gory events so different from neo-classical simplicity and morality, is a dramatic fantasy which must have horrified the followers of Jacques Louis David.

[6,1] 'The Death of Sardanapalus', 1827, by Eugène Delacroix, oil on canvas, 391 x 496 cm (Louvre, Paris). Based on a poem by Byron, this scene of destruction of the women, horses and valuables of the legendary dictator is almost glossed over by Delacroix's attention to the colour and movement within the composition.

German and English landscape painting expresses the gentler aspects of the Romantic movement in moods and atmospheres that symbolise human emotions. Caspar David Friedrich's 'The Cross in the Mountains' [6,2] depicts the impact of Christianity on the world and the gifts of faith and hope.

The Romantic movement embraces artists as different as Goya, Blake, Delacroix and Turner. The common threads throughout their work were an individual, 'poetic' style of expression and a love of dramatic events whether in nature or history. The medieval idea of man's insignificance in the face of God and nature and his struggle to overcome events was popular with the Romantics. Paintings of shipwrecks by Turner and Géricault express this idea.

ARCHITECTURE

As a result of the expansion and prosperity which followed the Industrial Revolution there was a huge building boom in the nineteenth century. Ironically this did not lead to the creation of tasteful architecture, but to the 'collapse of taste'. At a time that saw the emergence of the first professionally qualified architects, as opposed to the amateur, gentlemen architects of the eighteenth century, those engaged in architecture failed utterly to explore the possibilities of the new materials of iron, glass and factory-made brick. The new, professional architects graduated from the universities with a knowledge of all the historical styles. This led to a 'battle of the styles' in which Gothic or Classical designs were often proposed and chosen for literary or intellectual reasons rather than practical ones. The idea of designing buildings to suit their function and materials only emerged towards the end of the century.

Patronage was at an end and most commissions now took the form of public buildings. Museums, libraries, universities, court houses and government buildings were constructed in huge numbers. Private speculators also built many of the streets and squares of houses and apartments which are a feature of so many European cities. Local variations on the Renaissance style were the most popular solution to the design of city streetscapes in the nineteenth century.

ENGLAND

As the leader in the Industrial Revolution, England was to the fore in the new technology involved in the cast-iron construction which was first used to build railway bridges, stations and factories. More often it was engineers rather than architects who designed the buildings using the new materials: Thomas Telford designed the Menai Suspension Bridge; Joseph Paxton, the Crystal Palace in London; and Isambard Kingdom Brunel, the Clifton Suspension Bridge near Bristol. [6,3] Iron and steel allowed larger spaces to be spanned and structures lightened, but architects usually hid iron and steel structures under masonry or stucco.

[6,2] 'The Cross in the Mountains', 1808, Caspar David Friedrich, altarpiece (Gemaldegalerie). German Romantic landscapes often used moments of natural drama to express feelings and ideas of a spiritual nature.

[6,3] Clifton Suspension Bridge, near Bristol, 1830–59, by Isambard Kingdom Brunel.

[6,4] University Museum of Natural History, Oxford, 1855–60, by Deane and Woodward. Above: West front. Left: Vaulted roof of glazed exhibition court. The plain Gothic exterior gives no hint of the wonderful glass-roofed interior of the museum. The cast Gothic decoration on the iron framework harmonises with the detail on the stonework.

The architects Deane and Woodward designed the University Museum at Oxford [6,4] in a Gothic style, but used an iron structure to support a glass roof which lights the building beautifully. The cast-iron capitals of the interior display Gothic motifs and the decorated iron structure harmonises well with the Gothic stonework of the walls. This open use of iron was unusual in architecture, with most designers preferring more traditional appearances.

[6,5] Houses of Parliament, London, 1834, by Charles Barry and Augustus Pugin. The symmetrical waterfront of the parliament building is given a random Gothic look by the irregular placing of the towers. The building was influential in establishing Gothic revival architecture.

In 1834, when the Houses of Parliament were destroyed by fire, Charles Barry (1795–1860) designed a new building in the Gothic style which was considered appropriate to the dignity and antiquity of the Parliament. [6,5] Augustus Pugin (1812–52), Barry's assistant, designed most of the Gothic detail inside and out in the perpendicular style. The building was a major influence in the revival of the Gothic style in England.

The art critic John Ruskin (1819–1900) strongly supported the Gothic revival, while opposing the mass production and effects of the Industrial Revolution. Although he helped with the design and sculpture of the Oxford Museum he did not approve of the glass roof.

William Morris (1834–96) took the ideas of Pugin and Ruskin further in founding the 'arts and crafts movement' which was connected to the pre-Raphaelite painters in England and the Art Nouveau movement in Europe. Morris and his associates produced designs for and manu-factured furniture, fabrics, stained glass, carpets and much more. Many of Morris's designs are still in production.

Philip Webb designed the Red House, Bexley Heath, [6,6] for Morris in a style related to medieval country houses combined with some more modern elements. The notion of the modern craftsperson producing handmade work in his or her own studio/workshop originates in the arts and crafts movement.

[6,6] Red House, Bexley Heath, Kent, England, 1859, by Philip Webb. Built for the designer William Morris, the Red House combines medieval with later elements. The interior has many features which became important in the arts and crafts movement.

Many of the large public and private buildings that occupy dominant sites in English cities date from Victorian times. Although they are often impressive they are rarely beautiful or refined. They are buildings that reflect the time — a time of great industrial and imperial power.

FRANCE

Napoleon Bonaparte's reorganisation of the French state led to much redevelopment in Paris. During the Second Empire Napoleon III commissioned Baron Haussmann (1809–91) to demolish and reconstruct a large part of this city. With the Arc de Triomphe as a focus, Haussmann built twelve radiating boulevards. The main boulevard, the Champs-Elysées, provided a vista down through the Tuileries Gardens to the Louvre Palace. The tree-lined boulevards were flanked by grand town houses in a neo-Renaissance style.

Of the many architects who collaborated in the plan the most important contribution was made by Charles Garnier (1825–98) who designed not only the Paris Opéra but many of the luxury apartments. These well-planned apartments with their elegantly proportioned rooms became the norm in many European cities.

The Paris Opéra, [6,7] built at the conjunction of three streets, has a façade on each side, constructed in a highly decorative neo-Baroque style. It is rich in architectural detail and exotic materials. The great staircase inside the building creates a sense of occasion, and there are long foyers and promenades decorated with rich marbles and hung with chandeliers. The Opéra and the boulevards of Paris were imitated throughout Europe.

[6,7] The Paris Opéra, 1861–75, by Charles Garnier. This festive building became a model for theatres in many European cities. The elaborate neo-Baroque façade and sculptures create one of the most harmonious 19th-century buildings.

The interest in new materials, first seen in England, is evident in the imaginative use of iron construction in the Eiffel Tower and huge railway stations such as the Gare du Nord in Paris. Iron and glass construction were also used by Labrouste in the library of St Genevieve and the French National Library. The ironwork is highly decorative in a neo-classical style.

ART NOUVEAU

A deliberately modern style based on the English arts and crafts movement developed late in the nineteenth century. It was consciously anti-classical and historical, basing its decoration on sinuous plant forms. Some of the earliest designs in this form can be attributed to Victor Horta (1861–1947), the Belgian architect. In the Tassel House (1892–3) in Brussels he uses iron, both structurally and decoratively, in a revolutionary design in which spaces flow into one another in an organised way. The Maison des Peuples [6,8] and the Innovation Shop (1901), also in Brussels, both use iron and glass in a manner which only became common in the twentieth century.

The Art Nouveau style spread rapidly throughout Europe. In Spain, Antoni Gaudí (1852–1926) developed a unique, organic style which can be seen in the Casa Battlo in Barcelona. [6,9] The forms applied to the building and surrounding the windows seem to move before our eyes. Even the roof seems to defy any convention. The

[6,8] Maison des Peuples, Brussels (now the Victor Horta House Museum), 1896–9, by Victor Horta. The iron structure is clearly seen as part of the façade of the building. Iron also forms the decorative elements of the balconies and the skyline.

[6,10] Glasgow School of Art, 1897–1909, by Charles Rennie Mackintosh. Many aspects of Mackintosh's design anticipate 20th-century architecture, though the decorative detail is Art Nouveau.

unfinished Sagrada Familia Church in Barcelona, begun in 1883, is an amazing structure which, although based on Gothic design, evolved into something unique.

In Glasgow, Charles Rennie Mackintosh (1868–1928) designed the School of Art [6,10] in a style that goes beyond Art Nouveau into the beginnings of Modernism. Mackintosh's furniture and interior design was influential throughout Europe.

[6,9] Casa Battlo, Barcelona, 1907, by Antoni Gaudí. The extraordinary surface development of this apartment building is almost beyond 'style'. Whether ugly or beautiful, it is certainly unique in architecture.

Art Nouveau buildings and interiors can be found in Vienna, Paris, Prague and Rome. However, the style ended with the First World War almost as suddenly as it started.

SCULPTURE

The classical academic approach to sculpture which was stifling innovation and creativity in the eighteenth century continued in the nineteenth. European cities are full of skilful, realistic monuments and sculptures that lack any originality or charm.

The Romantic movement had little effect on sculpture. Only a few sculptors broke from the classical mode.

FRANÇOIS RUDE (1784–1855)
François Rude was a great admirer of Napoleon. His most famous work, the 'Departure of the Volunteers in 1792', [6,11] popularly called 'La Marseillaise', is a relief on the Arc de Triomphe. The romantic vigour and drama of the group make it one of the best-loved monuments in France.

ANTOINE-LOUIS BARYE (1796–1875)
Antoine-Louis Barye was noted for his spirited rendering of wild animals, based on drawings made at the zoo in Paris. His 'Tiger Devouring a Gazelle' [6,12] highlights his interest in the moments of violence or tension so much admired by the Romantics. Delacroix's paintings of wild animals influenced his work.

[6,11] 'Departure of the Volunteers in 1792', 1833–6, by François Rude, stone (Arc de Triomphe, Paris). The dramatic group and range of expressions make Rude's carving one of the more original and dramatic monuments of the 19th century.

[6,12] 'Tiger Devouring a Gazelle', c. 1850, by Antoine-Louis Barye, bronze, 32.5 x 31.5 x 12 cm (National Gallery of Ireland, Dublin). The Romantic interest in exotic creatures and moments of drama is captured in Barye's sculptures of wild animals.

JEAN-BAPTISTE CARPEAUX (1827–75)

A student of Rude's at the École des Beaux Arts, Jean-Baptiste Carpeaux won the Prix de Rome in 1854 and spent eight years studying in Rome where his work was popular with the French community. Back in Paris he won favour at the

[6,13] 'La Danse', 1869, by Jean-Baptiste Carpeaux, stone (Musée d'Orsay, Paris). The joyous dancing figures of this rhythmical work are not the serious nymphs and satyrs of classical sculpture. This frankness and reality caused a scandal when the work was first seen.

court of Napoleon III and got many commissions for portrait busts, including a portrait of the Empress Eugénie. His most famous sculpture, 'La Danse', [6,13] was commissioned for the decoration of the Paris Opéra building. The uninhibited, nude dancing figures were considered immoral when they were first exhibited in 1869. Carpeaux continued to paint and sculpt with considerable success and is considered to be the major sculptor of his time.

AUGUSTE RODIN (1840–1917)

Born in Paris of a poor family, Rodin suffered years of rejection by the Academy and the Salon (see below under 'France and the Salon') before his first sculpture, 'The Age of Bronze', [6,14] was accepted in the Salon of 1878. There was controversy over the naturalism of the work and Rodin was accused of casting it from a live model. At the age of forty, with the submission of his second figure, the striding 'John the Baptist' at the 1880 Salon, his reputation was finally made. He received a state commission, a set of bronze doors for a proposed Musée des Arts Décoratifs. He never produced a definitive version, but the figures and images he developed for it provided the basis for many of his works, 'The Thinker' and 'The Kiss' [6,15] among them.

An early trip to Italy inspired Rodin. 'Michelangelo freed me from academism,' he wrote to a friend, and references to Michelangelo

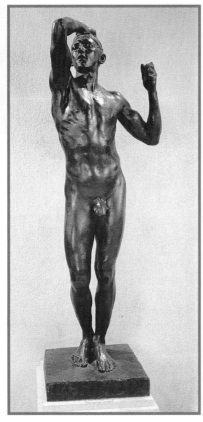

[6,14] 'The Age of Bronze', 1878, by Auguste Rodin, bronze (Louvre, Paris). The free-modelling style Rodin used gave a more life-like texture to flesh. He was accused of casting this sculpture from the live model.

[6,16] 'Balzac', 1898, by Auguste Rodin (Musée d'Orsay, Paris). Plaster and bronze version. This figure represents more the spirit of Balzac than his physical appearance, a concept difficult to understand in the 19th century. This may be the most original piece of public sculpture of the age.

can often be found in his work. The design for the bronze doors, the so-called 'Gates of Hell', was influenced by the 'Last Judgment' fresco in the Sistine Chapel. Rodin preferred to model in clay because of the freedom it allowed him. He engaged other artists to carry out marble carving to his design, which explains the various versions of his work, sometimes in different sizes.

Controversy seemed to follow all his large commissions. 'The Burghers of Calais', a group of six hostage figures expressing different responses to their fate, was not unveiled for years because it was not the sort of heroic monument the citizens of Calais had expected. The figure of 'Balzac', [6,16] which Rodin described as 'The sum of my whole life', was not put in place for more than twenty years after his death.

Rodin's influence on the development of modern sculpture was immense. After years of stagnation in this branch of art, he made sculpture a mode of personal expression.

PAINTING

The pace of change in the art world increased with the social changes of the nineteenth century. New movements and ideas quickly spread and different ideologies created conflicting approaches to art. The popularity of the photograph as a method of creating portraits and views led painters to seek alternative modes of expression. The development of portable materials later in the century allowed artists to paint in oils out of doors.

THE ROMANTICS IN ENGLAND
WILLIAM BLAKE (1757–1827)

William Blake, artist, philosopher, poet and visionary, created a unique personal style to express the imagery of his writings. He preferred engraving and watercolour to oil painting and

[6,15] 'The Kiss', 1886, by Auguste Rodin, marble (Musée Rodin, Paris). Many of Rodin's sculptures have deliberately unfinished areas. There is a sense of 'a work in progress' similar to Impressionist painting.

[6,17] 'The Good and Evil Angels', 1795, by William Blake, colour-printed monotype, finished with pen and watercolour, 45 x 59 cm (Tate Gallery, London). Blake's visionary world goes beyond reality in an effort to express the mystical.

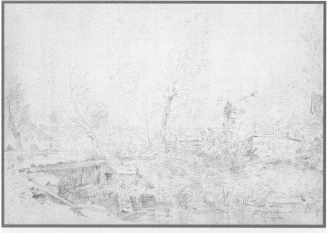

[6,18] 'Flatford Lock and Cottage Bridge, Suffolk', dated 5 October 1827, by John Constable, pencil on paper, 22.1 x 32.9 cm (National Gallery of Ireland, Dublin). Constable constantly sketched scenes which he later used to develop finished paintings in studio.

developed a method of colour printing which he used for some of his work. He printed illuminated books in which he combined text and illustration. 'The Good and Evil Angels' [6,17] shows the strong influence of Michelangelo in his work, and also his efforts to re-create his own visions in images. Blake was largely ignored in his own time but he had a following among younger artists and among the pre-Raphaelites at the end of the century.

JOHN CONSTABLE (1776–1837)

The son of a well-to-do Suffolk miller, John Constable painted from childhood. He went to college in his twenties and slowly developed his mature style. He painted and drew his native countryside continuously and was initially influenced by Claude Lorrain and the eighteenth-century Dutch painters. The imitation of old masters was not for Constable. He wanted to express the moving sky and changing light which was so much part of his native landscape. He painted oil sketches out of doors, including notes on the time of day and the weather. [6,18] These loosely painted works are often more admired than his large, finished exhibition pieces, the 'Six Footers' as he called them.

'The Haywain' [6,19] was probably Constable's most influential work. It won a gold medal in the Paris Salon of 1824 and was greatly admired by Delacroix who imitated his loose brushwork, use of broken colour and points of highlight.

[6,19] 'The Haywain', 1821, by John Constable, oil on canvas, 130 x 185 cm (National Gallery, London). Constable painted over a warm-coloured (earthy pink) ground, building up his painting in layers and gradually adding more detail and making corrections. In the later stages he used a palette knife to build texture and used points of highlight which create the sparkle we often see in his work.

131

[6,20] 'Cloud Study', by John Constable, oil on cardboard, (Hugh Lane Municipal Gallery of Modern Art, Dublin). Constable's direct studies from nature are sometimes considered more exciting than his finished work. He made many observations of changing weather and sky.

[6,22] 'A Ship Against the Mew-Stone at the Entrance to Plymouth Sound', c. 1814, by J.M.W. Turner, watercolour on paper, 15.6 x 23.7 cm (National Gallery of Ireland, Dublin). This painting was made as an illustration to Cooke's picturesque views of the southern coast of England printed in 1816. It shows Turner's interest in dramatic weather and its effects on man which was a recurring theme throughout his life.

Surprisingly, Constable's approach to landscape painting did not have a following in England and it is mainly in France that his influence was felt, immediately with the Romantics, later with the Barbizon School of plein-air painters and ultimately with the Impressionists. [6,20]

JOSEPH MALLORD WILLIAM TURNER (1775–1851)

Turner was the most original landscape painter of the nineteenth century. His later works are creations of light and atmosphere. A precocious artist, he was admitted to the school of the Royal Academy at the age of fourteen and exhibited his first watercolour in the Academy a year later. He had a very successful academic career and was appointed deputy president of the Academy in 1845.

Turner developed his interest in light and atmosphere early in his career and this is often reflected in the title of the paintings. By 1791 he had begun his practice of sketching tours, first in Britain, later in Europe, from which he made watercolours or engravings. He did not exhibit oil paintings until the late 1790s.

'Snow Storm: Hannibal Crossing the Alps' was made after one of his trips to Europe. [6,21] In this painting the Romantic interest in Hannibal is combined with an expression of the force of nature.

Turner developed most of his finished work from imagination and memory. Sketches were used as an aid to memory and did not restrict his intuitive approach to his work. [6,22]

[6,21] 'Snow Storm: Hannibal Crossing the Alps', 1812, by J.M.W. Turner, oil on canvas, 145 x 236 cm (Tate Gallery, London). The swirling storm is a feature of many of Turner's paintings. The vigorous, almost violent brushwork in a sky in which shape and form are lost contrasts with the rocks and figures in the foreground.

[6,23] 'S. Giorgio Maggiore, Venice', 1840, by J.M.W. Turner, pencil and watercolour on paper, 22.5 x 29 cm (National Gallery of Ireland, Dublin). The absolute stillness created by the misty image of Venice is another aspect of Turner's interest in atmosphere.

themselves into a secret society. They felt that vibrancy and honesty had been lost in art after Raphael and they wanted to return to the idealism of earlier times. John Everett Millais (1829–96), William Holman Hunt (1827–1910) and Dante Gabriel Rossetti (1828–82), were the first artists in the Pre-Raphaelite Brotherhood. They sought the expression of genuine ideas, the close study of nature, the valuing of direct and serious art and the rejection of conventional and second-hand work.

The pre-Raphaelites painted largely from literary sources — the Bible, Dante, Shakespeare and the contemporary poets, Keats and Tennyson. Rossetti was also a poet in his own right. The critic John Ruskin first opposed and then defended the group. William Morris, the designer, was closely associated with the Brotherhood. Their influence continued in the Art Nouveau movement on the continent.

Millais took the ideals most seriously in his work. He made careful, painstaking studies of plants and figures which he combined into finished paintings such as 'Ophelia' [6,25] from Shakespeare or 'The Carpenter's Shop', an imaginary biblical scene. The studied details and poses often create a posed look, which is ironic when one looks at the ideals of the Brotherhood.

Hunt also painted literary and religious scenes in sharp colour and minute detail. 'The Light of the World' [6,26] is one of his best-known paintings.

In his later years Turner's experience of Mediterranean light and the new colour theories of Goethe led to a style which is almost abstract, though the subject is always important to him as it was in all early nineteenth-century work. [6,23] 'Rain, Steam and Speed — The Great Western Railway', [6,24] a celebration of the achievements of the Industrial Revolution, is from this late phase, when earth, sky and man's inventions merge in a passing moment. In this work Turner seems to have gone beyond the achievements of the Impressionists even before they began.

THE PRE-RAPHAELITE BROTHERHOOD

The rebellion against academic tradition took an unusual turn in England in 1848 when a group of students at the Royal Academy, dismayed at what they saw as the stagnation of art, organised

[6,24] 'Rain, Steam and Speed — The Great Western Railway', 1846, by J.M.W. Turner, oil on canvas, 90 x 121 cm (Tate Gallery, London). In Turner's later works form is almost dissolved in atmosphere. Many of the critics of the day ridiculed his later work, implying that he had lost his mind. He did have his supporters, including Ruskin.

[6,25] 'Ophelia', 1851–2, by Sir John Everett Millais, oil on canvas, 75 x 112 cm (Tate Gallery, London). Millais spent four months painting the background on location and got the model to lie in a bath of water to achieve accuracy. The flowers in the water have symbolic meanings — death, innocence, etc.

[6,26] 'The Light of the World', 1853, by William Holman Hunt, oil on canvas, 138 x 308 cm (Manchester City Art Galleries). Cold nights spent in an orchard and careful observation of jewels and fabrics must have seemed a waste of time when the Scottish writer Thomas Carlyle described this painting, in front of the artist, as 'empty make-believe'.

[6,27] 'Day Dream', 1880, by Dante Gabriel Rossetti, oil on canvas, 160 x 92 cm (Victoria and Albert Museum, London). The languid, dreamy figures associated with the pre-Raphaelites and the Art Nouveau movement are an invention of Rossetti's, based on the tragic figure of his wife, Elizabeth Siddal.

Rossetti continued to paint in a decorative style removed from the Brotherhood's ideals after the group disbanded in 1853. He influenced a group of followers who continued to paint medieval compositions into the twentieth century. [6,27]

GERMANY
CASPAR DAVID FRIEDRICH (1774–1840)
Friedrich was one of the most original painters of the Romantic movement. His landscapes portray spiritual meanings. His 'The Cross in the Mountains', [6,2] an early oil painting, was not well received because a landscape was not considered suitable as an altarpiece. Like Blake's, his work was visionary. 'Close your bodily eye, so that you may see your picture first with your spiritual eye,' he advised. His later landscapes often include figures, usually with their back to the viewer. 'The Stages of Life' [6,28] highlights his beautiful, imaginative use of colour and the way in which his paintings pose questions.

Friedrich was forgotten in his later life but was rediscovered and popularised by the Symbolists at the end of the century.

FRANCE AND THE SALON
The exhibitions of the French Royal Academy of Painting and Sculpture began in 1667 and were held in the Salon d'Apollo in the Louvre, from

[6,28] 'The Stages of Life', 1836, by Caspar David Friedrich, oil on canvas, 73 x 94 cm (Museum der Bildenden Kunst, Leipzig). Friedrich's paintings were designed for contemplation, so the viewer was invited to think about what the images might mean.

which the name 'Salon' derives. [6,29] In the nineteenth century an exhibition of work selected by a jury was held annually. This was, until the mid-century, the only public exhibition held in Paris. Artists whose work was selected had a monopoly on publicity and a hope of sales to galleries and museums sponsored by the state.

JEAN AUGUSTE DOMINIQUE INGRES (1780–1867)
A pupil of David, Ingres was a neo-classical artist who experienced considerable success in the French academic system. He was an opponent of

[6,29] Preparing the Paris Salon, 1876. The dense hanging of paintings is a testament to the demand for space at the exhibition. An artist could not gain public recognition until his/her work was exhibited at the Salon.

[6,31] 'The Raft of the Medusa', 1819, by Théodore Géricault, oil on canvas, 490 x 716 cm (Louvre, Paris). In spite of winning a medal at the Salon, the controversial subject-matter and lack of a hero brought condemnation on Géricault's portrayal of the fifteen survivors of a contemporary shipwreck.

Delacroix and the Romantic movement, believing that line was more important than colour in painting. Line is the most striking element in Ingres's work. He uses it not only to define his shapes but in a decorative way. Some of his early work was criticised as being 'Gothic', too detailed and linear. His later bathers and harem scenes, however, are sensual, with line emphasising the contours of the body and the carefully arranged drapery. Ingres's interest in beautiful fabrics and jewellery comes across in much of his work. [6,30]

[6,30] 'The Turkish Bath', 1802, by Dominique Ingres, oil on canvas, 146 x 98 cm (Louvre, Paris). The cool lighting and smooth finish of Ingres's work emphasise the linear quality of the body contours and the fabrics. He considered himself a neo-classical painter, in spite of his interest in exotic settings and fabrics.

The history paintings and large canvases which made his public reputation are not as highly regarded by modern critics as are his portraits and smaller works. Ingres was very influential in his day and had a busy studio with many pupils. Renoir, Degas and Picasso were influenced by his draughtsmanship.

THÉODORE GÉRICAULT (1791–1824)

Although Géricault trained in the studios of an animal painter and a history painter, it was more his own studies of the masters in the Louvre, particularly Rubens, that were the formative elements in his style. He also visited Rome, where he was influenced by Michelangelo and the Baroque artists. On his return to Paris he painted the huge canvas of 'The Raft of the Medusa', [6,31] a scene of a contemporary shipwreck. He chose the moment when the rescue ship was first seen on the horizon and despair, represented by the group on the bottom left, was turned to hope, seen in the diagonally opposite group waving the rag. The pyramidal composition and the portrayal of a contemporary dramatic event did not bring the recognition Géricault had hoped for, so he took the painting to England on a touring exhibition.

While in England he painted racing pictures, including the 'Epsom Downs Derby', and made a series of lithographs of the lives of the poor in London. Later, in France, he painted portraits of the insane patients of a doctor friend, which were among the first sympathetic portrayals of insanity.

135

Géricault was an unconventional figure. His love of action and drama in his own life as in painting brought about his early death after a riding accident. He was the first of the French Romantics. His energetic handling of paint and love of dramatic subject-matter became important features of the movement.

EUGÈNE DELACROIX (1798–1863)

A fellow student of Géricault in the studio of the history painter Guerin, Delacroix also spent time studying the old masters, particularly Rubens and the Venetians. His use of colour, vigorous brushwork and dramatic compositions distracted from his sometimes gruesome subject-matter. 'The Massacre at Chios' (1824) and 'The Death of Sardanapalus' [6,1] are paintings of great beauty, full of colour and exotic detail in spite of the horrible events described.

A trip to Morocco in 1832 with a diplomatic mission allowed Delacroix to fill sketchbooks with drawings of the local people and customs and heightened his sense of colour. The experience provided him with subject-matter of a non-classical nature, but removed from everyday French life. He produced a series of paintings of the 'Lion Hunt' in which Arab horses and riders are locked in combat with ferocious lions. To get authentic detail he made drawings of the lions at feeding time in the Paris zoo. The colour, movement and drama of these scenes have rarely been surpassed. [6,32]

[6,33] 'Study for The Death of Sardanapalus', 1827, by Eugène Delacroix, pastel and crayon on paper, 45 x 59 cm (Louvre, Paris). Delacroix made many sketches in line, tone and colour before he moved on to final compositions.

Delacroix was well connected politically and he got large commissions from the state. His huge mural paintings include decorations on the Chambres des Députies, Palais Bourbon and the Luxembourg Palace. He also made large religious murals for the Chapelle des Anges of St Sulpice in Paris. The 'Jacob and the Angel' scene from this series is among his finest work, demonstrating his mastery of colour and composition.

Delacroix produced a huge body of work. He left more than 9,000 paintings, pastels and drawings in his studio on his death. He worked quickly, making many preparatory drawings and colour sketches before he produced a final composition. [6,33] His influence was strong, particularly in the area of colour. He inspired Renoir, Seurat and van Gogh.

THE REALISTS

The term 'realism' has different meanings in different contexts, but in nineteenth-century France it referred to a group of artists who rejected mythical, historical and religious subject-matter in favour of scenes of everyday life. Unidealised landscapes and scenes of peasant life characterise the work of the realists.

THE BARBIZON SCHOOL

A group of artists settled on the edge of the Forest of Fontainebleau near Paris in the middle of the century. They formed a small colony of 'plein air' painters and became known as the Barbizon

[6,32] 'Lion Hunt in Morocco', 1854, by Eugène Delacroix, oil on canvas (Hermitage, St Petersburg). The fluid brushwork and dramatic colour of Delacroix's painting help to create the movement and drama in his work.

School. They painted out of doors, capturing the real light and colour of nature, but their exhibition pieces were made in studio. The group included Théodore Rousseau (1812–67), Charles Daubigny (1817–78), Narcisse Virgile Diaz de la Peña (1807/8–76), Jules Dupré (1811–98), Charles-Emile Jacque (1813–94) and Constant Troyon (1810–65). Corot and Millet worked and lived in the area for a time, but were not strictly members of the group. They were influenced by the work of Constable and the Dutch eighteenth-century landscape artists and in turn they influenced the Impressionists. [6,34]

JEAN BAPTISTE CAMILLE COROT (1796–1875)

One of the most influential French landscape artists of his time, Corot only took up painting full-time at the age of twenty-six. He travelled the French countryside making sketches and paintings to develop into compositions in his studio. He also visited the Low Countries (Holland and Belgium), England, Switzerland and Italy. Corot's work is never controversial. He painted calm views of his native countryside from direct observation, in a loosely brushed, impasto style. His later work is more romantic with wispy trees and nymphs, somewhat in the style of Claude. [6,35]

Corot also painted portraits and figure studies, though he was not well known for these in his own time. He was well regarded by his fellow artists and he was generous, supporting Millet's widow and the aged Daumier.

[6,35] 'Ville d'Avray', c. 1867–70, by Jean Baptiste Camille Corot, oil on linen, 49 x 65 cm (National Gallery of Art, Washington).

HONORÉ DAUMIER (1808–79)

A caricaturist and painter, Daumier made his living by satirising political and social mores in the newspapers *La Caricature* and *Le Charivari*. [6,36] He was even imprisoned for six months for criticising the government in his cartoon 'Gargantua', which shows Louis-Philippe swallowing bags of gold extorted from the people.

Daumier's paintings were hardly seen in public in his own lifetime, but the simple forms and colours and sketchy brushwork have gained a substantial following since his death. Scenes of everyday life, the theatre, clowns and a series on Don Quixote make up the majority of his paintings. Daumier was a dedicated democrat and many of the 4,000 lithographs he produced highlight social

[6,34] 'Cattle on a Riverbank', 1876, by C. Daubigny, oil on panel, 44 x 69 cm (National Gallery of Ireland, Dublin). The artists of the Barbizon School painted 'en plein air', though exhibition pieces were developed in studio. The time of day and weather conditions are often significant in their work. Direct painting and strong brushwork are a feature of the group's style.

[6,36] 'Nadar Elevating Photography to the Height of Art', 1862, by Honoré Daumier, lithograph first published in *Le Boulevard,* 25 May 1862 (Victoria and Albert Museum, London). This caricature satirises the popularity of photography in Paris. Nadar, a friend of Daumier, took the first aerial photographs of Paris. The first Impressionist exhibition in 1874 was held in Nadar's studio.

[6,37] 'The Third Class Carriage', 1803–5, by Honoré Daumier, oil on canvas, 67 x 92 cm (Private collection). Daumier's simplified forms give a monumental quality to his everyday scenes.

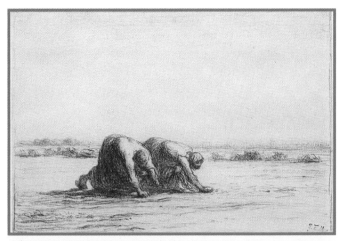

[6,38] 'The Gleaners', c. 1857, by Jean François Millet, charcoal drawing on paper (Hugh Lane Municipal Gallery of Modern Art, Dublin). This drawing from life was used as preparation for the oil painting of the same title. The assured handling and strength of drawing were admired by contemporary artists.

injustice. He never made a commercial success of his art, but was appreciated by his artistic contemporaries including Delacroix and Corot. [6,37]

JEAN FRANÇOIS MILLET (1814–75)

Millet was born of farming stock in Normandy. He trained locally in Cherbourg before moving to the studio of Paul Delaroche (1797–1856) in Paris in 1837. His early work was traditional portraiture, with scenes from mythology and genre scenes painted in a Rococo style. However, with the 'Winnower' exhibited at the Salon of 1848 his interests changed to scenes of peasant life. He moved to the town of Barbizon in the following year and spent most of the remainder of his life there.

His painting of 'The Angelus' in 1859 became the most widely reproduced nineteenth-century work of art, creating the false impression that his work was pious and sentimental. Millet's drawings and paintings have simplicity and strength. They depict rural tasks without any romantic overtones. He said he wanted 'to make the trivial serve to express the sublime', and to a great extent he did. [6,38]

In 'Going to Work' [6,39] we see Millet's use of earth colours and a limited palette on a white ground. The landscape is reduced to a minimum and does not represent any real place. He sketched out of doors, but painted in the studio and his compositions were based on memory, imagination and drawings from life.

[6,39] 'Going to Work', 1857, by Jean François Millet, oil on canvas, 55.5 x 46 cm. (Glasgow Museum) Following the revolution of 1848 Millet's scenes of peasant toil were thought to be socialist, but they were more probably simple records of the unremitting labour of rural living.

Millet was poor for most of his life but had some success in the 1860s. Van Gogh and Pissarro were both influenced by his work, particularly by his drawing.

GUSTAVE COURBET (1819–77)

Born at Ornans in eastern France of a well-to-do farming family, Courbet trained with a number of minor artists and at the Atelier Suisse. However, he owes his style to the time he spent copying old masters in the Louvre. His early work was Romantic and includes many self-portraits, but his individualism and strong personality soon led to a more revolutionary style.

[6,40] 'Burial at Ornans', 1850, by Gustave Courbet, oil on canvas, 314 x 663 cm (Louvre, Paris). This large canvas painted in heavy impasto in places broke conventions of subject-matter, composition and technique. It was fiercely criticised by the academics and praised by the realists and socialists.

His painting 'After Dinner at Ornans' won a second-class medal at the Salon of 1849 and was bought by the state. This encouraged Courbet and he returned the following year with 'Burial at Ornans', [6,40] a huge canvas over 3 metres tall and nearly 7 metres wide, which depicted forty-five citizens of Ornans standing by an open grave.

The composition is almost frieze-like, with the plain people of his home town standing in rows. None of the social niceties is observed. No particular deference is paid to the priest, no one is flattered by his or her portrait. The technique also is unusual for the time, with paint applied thickly by brush and palette knife in an act that Courbet seemed to enjoy — applying paint, building up texture in sweeping strokes — very different to the smooth finish of the Academy artists.

The 'Burial' met with huge opposition not only for its unconventional composition and technique, but because Courbet, by painting them on a huge canvas in an epic manner, had given ordinary folk the same importance that traditional artists gave to gods and history subjects. This elevation of the common people was also politically significant as Courbet was a revolutionary socialist and sometimes used his art to that end.

At the Universal Exhibition of 1855 Courbet did not get the recognition he felt he deserved, so he put up a temporary pavilion of his own outside the gate and exhibited his work there. He wrote a manifesto on the exhibition called 'Le Réalisme'.

One of the works he included was 'The Painter's Studio' which he subtitled 'a real allegory summing up seven years in my artistic life'. He portrays himself in the centre painting a landscape. Beside him is a nude model who may represent the muse of truth; on the right are his supporters, patrons and friends including the poet Charles Baudelaire and the anarchist philosopher Pierre Joseph Proudhon; on the left of the painting he placed the people who formed the subject-matter of his work, country people and the unwanted of society.

Throughout his career Courbet painted landscapes, places in his home region, waterfalls, crags and simple scenes from nature in an unidealised fashion. It was important to him to paint 'real and existing things' only, a cry which was to be taken up by the Impressionists. [6,41]

[6,41] 'Stream in a Ravine' by Gustave Courbet, oil on canvas, 94 x 131 cm (Musée d'Orsay, Paris). Simple scenes from the hills and vales of his home region in eastern France were the subjects of Courbet's landscapes. Painted freely with brush and palette knife, they often have strong contrasts in light and dark.

ÉDOUARD MANET (1832–83)

The son of a senior civil servant, Manet was an independently wealthy man about town, enjoying the fashionable café life of Paris. Though considered a rebel artist, he was keen to achieve public approval and recognition, and consequently produced large exhibition pieces for the Salon rather than smaller work for private sale.

He trained in the studio of Thomas Couture (1815–79) for six years from 1850 and copied the old masters in the Louvre where Velázquez's work impressed him. He visited many European galleries, sketching and copying the paintings of others, and later used this work as reference for his own paintings. He had mixed success at the Salon and in 1863 his 'Déjeuner sur l'Herbe' was rejected. [6,42]

The Salon des Refusés was established by Emperor Napoleon III to allow artists who were not in favour with the Academy to show their work and Manet exhibited with this group. 'Déjeuner sur l'Herbe' was severely criticised on moral as well as artistic grounds. The nude, unidealised woman sitting with men in contemporary dress, looking frankly at the viewer, posed too many questions and unsettled critics and public alike. Nudes were acceptable as goddesses or nymphs of ancient times or harem girls in far-off places, but not as ordinary people here and now.

[6,42] 'Déjeuner sur l'Herbe', 1863, by Édouard Manet, oil on canvas, 206 x 265 cm (Musée d'Orsay, Paris). Based on a design of Raphael's and the 'Concert Champêtre' by Giorgione, the contemporary setting and loose painting style caused controversy when it was exhibited at the Salon des Refusés in 1863.

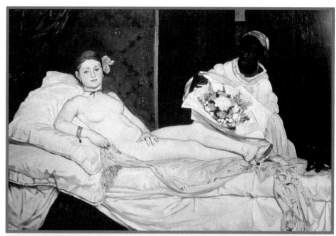

[6,43] 'Olympia', 1865, by Édouard Manet, oil on canvas, 130 x 190 cm (Musée d'Orsay). The influence of Oriental prints can be seen in the simplified linear style and the lack of depth portrayed in the painting.

The 'Olympia', [6,43] which he exhibited two years later, caused even greater outrage — 'this was not a goddess but a prostitute' — even though it was based on Titian's 'Venus of Urbino' which Manet had copied on a visit to Florence ten years earlier. The free handling of paint and the strong frontal lighting which eliminated intermediate shadows gave the image an added starkness. Manet focused equally on fabrics and background patterns which created a flatter, more two-dimensional effect.

Manet's painting appears spontaneous and immediate, but he erased and corrected until an area looked right. He was influenced by Japanese prints which have no tradition of perspective or depth of field. This explains the apparent flatness of many of his paintings. Though not a revolutionary by nature, he became a leader of the avant-garde and was admired by the young Impressionists. He was a friend of Degas, who had a similar background, and a brother-in-law of Berthe Morisot, who was his pupil and model for a time. His friends, the writers Baudelaire and Émile Zola, both supported his ideal of creating art from the world around them.

The influence of the Impressionists encouraged Manet to paint out of doors and to lighten his palette. When he became ill in the late 1870s he began to work more frequently in pastels which required less physical effort. His last oil painting, 'A Bar at the Folies-Bergère', [6,44] is one of the masterpieces of nineteenth-century painting.

[6,44] 'A Bar at the Folies-Bergère', 1882, by Édouard Manet, oil on canvas, 97 x 130 cm (Courtauld Institute Galleries, University of London). Manet's last masterpiece, painted a year before his death, spotlights a scene from fashionable Parisian society. The mirror behind the barmaid reflects the smoky scene in the bar. Beautifully painted and brightly lit by the new electric light, it is one of the most Impressionist of Manet's works.

ORIENTAL ART

When Oriental art was first seen in Europe at the end of the eighteenth century it was regarded as a curiosity, but artists gradually discovered that an ancient and vibrant culture had simply reached a different conclusion about artistic representation than Europeans had. The alternative method of representing space and the emphasis on line and flat areas of colour were just some of the more obvious differences. 'Sudden Shower at Ohashi Bridge at Ataka' [6,45] is one of the coloured woodblock prints which were so influential among the Impressionists and later artists. Van Gogh made a copy of this design in 1887 having seen a print at the Paris exhibition. Degas's composition was influenced by the alternative sense of balance and tension he had seen in Japanese prints.

The Art Nouveau style was strongly influenced by the Oriental love of flowing line and pattern based on nature. [6,46] The renewed interest in craftsmanship was also influenced by the disciplined Japanese approach to printmaking and ceramics.

[6,45] 'Sudden Shower at Ohashi Bridge at Ataka', 1857, by Ando Hiroshige (1797–1858), woodblock print in colour, 37 x 25 cm (Fitzwilliam Museum, University of Cambridge). The Japanese alternative forms of composition and representation of space impressed European artists who tried to incorporate these changes into their own work.

Oriental art was one of the key influences in late nineteenth-century art and design from the choice of subject-matter to alternative methods of drawing and painting.

[6,46] 'Bird Diving over an Iris', c. 1902, by Ando Hiroshige, woodblock print in colour, 37 x 16.5 cm (Victoria and Albert Museum, London). The use of line in Oriental art influenced graphic designers in particular, as well as Toulouse-Lautrec's posters, Beardsley's illustrations and Art Nouveau design in general.

[6,47] 'Bathers at La Grenouillère', 1869, by Claude Monet, oil on canvas, 75 x 100 cm (National Gallery, London). Monet's broad brushwork turns the water into swipes of colour. The figures on the little island in the centre are very simply treated as patches of colour.

[6,48] 'La Grenouillère', 1869, by Pierre Auguste Renoir, oil on canvas, 66 x 81 cm (Private collection). Renoir's painting is lighter than Monet's; the brushmarks are smaller and there is more colour detail.

IMPRESSIONISM

The Impressionists were a group of artists who came together in the 1860s in the Paris region. They often met at the Café Geurbois to discuss art and air their opinions. Monet, [6,47] Renoir, [6,48] Sisley and Frédéric Bazille (1841–71) were students at the same time in the studio of Charles Gleyre (1806–74) and continued working together after it closed. Monet had met Pissarro earlier and Cézanne joined the group in 1863. In the 1860s they all submitted work to the Salon without much success. They met Manet and through him Degas through the Salon des Refusés.

Together, in various small groups, these artists often painted open-air scenes on the banks of the Seine and in the parks and recreation places of the middle classes around Paris. The bathing place and floating restaurant at La Grenouillère provided the location for a number of sketching trips for Monet and Renoir. It is interesting to see how the two artists worked with different styles on the same subject. The group looked on these paintings as sketches, producing larger, more finished pieces for the Salon. It was not until they began to hold their own exhibitions independent of the Salon that they presented as finished paintings works made directly from nature.

There was nothing as formal as a manifesto or even an agreed programme among the Impressionists. They all were individual artists working in their own way, developing their own style and subject-matter. They were, however, agreed in a general way on a number of points. Their work should be modern, observed with detachment, and not historical or emotional. Brushwork should be free and descriptive, with pure, spectrum colours applied directly rather than mixed. Much of this was a result of their outdoor painting method, when work had to be carried out quickly to capture the changing light and colour.

[6,49] 'Impression of Morning Sunrise', 1872, by Claude Monet, oil on canvas, 48 x 63 cm (Musée Marmottan, Paris). Monet said he called this painting 'Impression' because it was not developed enough to call it 'A View of Le Havre'. It is significant that Monet should pick a working industrial port as a modern subject, instead of traditional picturesque scenes.

[6,50] 'Women in the Garden', 1866–9, by Claude Monet, oil on canvas, 255 x 205 cm (Musée d'Orsay, Paris). Monet's interest in the effects of sunlight and shade is quite clear in this early, large exhibition piece. The bold brushwork which is always a feature of his work is already there.

The group dispersed during the Franco-Prussian War of 1870–1. Some joined the army — Bazille was killed in the front lines; some moved to the countryside. Pissarro, Sisley and Monet went to London.

Back in Paris after the war, the group re-formed and held their first group exhibition in the gallery of the photographer, Nadar, in 1874. Monet's painting 'Impression of Morning Sunrise' [6,49] became the focus of negative reaction to the collection and the journalist Louis Leroy dubbed the whole group 'Impressionists' in derision. The group kept the title for all their exhibitions, eight in total. Their final group exhibition was in 1886, after which they all went their own way artistically.

In their years together the Impressionists changed a number of things. The power of the Salon was broken and artists held group and individual exhibitions, usually through art dealers like Durand-Ruel who was the first promoter of Impressionist painting. The academies were no longer the only way for artists to get an education. Modern subjects and simple scenes of no historical or emotional importance were acceptable as fine art. The Impressionists were both an end and a beginning. They were, at the same time, the last expression of realism and the development that began with the Renaissance and the first step towards modern painting where the two-dimensional surface is of primary importance.

CLAUDE MONET (1840–1926)

Monet was in many ways *the* Impressionist, attempting for most of his working life to 'render my impressions in front of the most fleeting effects'. He grew up in Le Havre where in his teenage years he became known as a cartoonist. The artist Eugène Boudin (1824–98) encouraged him to take up landscape painting and to study in Paris. He attended the Atelier Suisse, which had a less formal regime than many studios, where he met and befriended Pissarro. A spell of military service in Algeria was followed by a return to Le Havre where he met the Dutch landscape artist Johan Barthold Jongkind (1819–91), to whom Monet said he owed 'the definitive education of my eye'.

In 1862 Monet returned to Paris where he worked in the studio of Gleyre and began his acquaintance with the group of artists that became the Impressionists. Monet produced larger works painted out of doors for the Salon. A seascape he painted was accepted in 1865 but little thereafter. 'Women in the Garden' [6,50] is one of these exhibition pieces that Monet painted out of doors. He had to dig a trench so that the painting could be raised and lowered in order for him to reach it. Courbet, who visited him while he was working on it, said Monet would not even paint a leaf in the background if the light was not right.

[6,51] 'Le Pont d'Argenteuil', 1874, by Claude Monet, oil on canvas, 60 x 80 cm (Musée d'Orsay, Paris). The boats and bridge at Argenteuil turn up in a number of paintings from this time. Monet's use of complementary colours to express light and shadow is a feature of many of the Impressionists' work.

During the Franco-Prussian War Monet went to London where he saw the work of Constable and Turner, though there is no obvious influence of their style in his work from that time. Monet loved the effect the fog had on the city and painted Waterloo Bridge and the Houses of Parliament a number of times in later years. On his return to France he lived at Argenteuil, a village downriver from Paris, where middle-class people came for boating and swimming. Some of the best-loved Impressionists' work comes from this time, from Monet [6,51] and his visitors, Manet, Renoir and Sisley. As time went by Monet moved further away from Paris, finally settling at Giverny forty miles outside the city.

By the 1880s Monet was having moderate success and there was a demand from art dealers for his work. He travelled a lot, looking for dramatic natural subjects and extremes of light and weather. The painting of a 'Storm on Belle-Isle' on the Brittany coast shows the change in Monet's brushwork. Marks are more even in size and they contour around forms in a way that anticipates van Gogh's style, though not as sharply defined.

In the next decade Monet produced his series of paintings of haystacks and Rouen Cathedral. [6,52] He believed that these had to be seen together for full effect. They describe changes in light and atmosphere that go beyond direct

[6,52] 'Cathedral at Rouen: Harmony in Blue and Gold, Full Sunlight 1894', by Claude Monet, oil on canvas 100 x 66 cm (Musée d'Orsay, Paris). The shimmering heat and light that emanate from this painting are the result of carefully selected colour harmonies and a build-up of texture on the painted surface. It was part of a series of paintings which were designed to be seen together. Five are in the Musée d'Orsay in Paris.

observation. Monet finished most of the paintings in the studio where he could work on the colour harmonies and the surface pattern of the painting, based on moments of observation too short to paint on location.

In his final years Monet retired almost completely to Giverny where he had built a beautiful water garden. Painting the lilies and the effects of light on the water occupied most of his time. [6,53] He even painted a continuous decoration for a circular room which is housed in the Orangerie in Paris. About 2 metres tall and based on outdoor sketches, it was painted in studio in large calligraphic brushmarks with greens and blues predominating. It is a continuous water surface without horizon, broken by lily pads and the reflection of trees and sky. After almost fifty years of painting Monet was still making 'impressions' of 'fleeting effects'.

[6,53] 'Water-lilies', c. 1910, by Claude Monet, oil on canvas (J.W. and P. Guillaume Collection, Paris). Many of Monet's water lily paintings have an almost abstract quality due to the angle of view and the gestural brushwork.

[6,54] 'L'absinthe', 1876–7, by Edgar Degas, oil on canvas, 92 x 68 cm (Louvre, Paris). Degas's early work was not Impressionist in colour, but it was certainly modern in subject and composition and in the freedom of painting technique.

EDGAR DEGAS (1834–1917)

Son of a wealthy banker, Degas was originally educated as a lawyer, but entered the École des Beaux Arts in 1855 where he was trained in the classical tradition. The drawing skills he developed in college and by copying old masters separate him from the other Impressionists whom he met through Manet. Manet gradually persuaded him to change his style and subject-matter from the classical tradition and to paint modern subjects in a freer style. Degas did not like landscape. He said, 'The study of nature is of no significance, for painting is a conventional art', so he chose subjects from everyday Parisian life — the theatre, horse races, domestic scenes, anywhere he could observe formal or practised movement.

In 'L'absinthe', [6,54] thought to be a scene from the Café Geurbois, the actress Ellen André and the engraver Marcel Desboutin are sitting, lost in their own thoughts. The composition is very modern. The man, partly cut off by the edge of the format, and the large geometric shapes of the table tops create a tension within the composition. This type of off-balance composition is deliberately used by Degas to create a feeling of interrupted movement and spontaneity, though the work was carefully planned and prepared.

Degas liked to experiment with media and enjoyed working in pastels, particularly later in life when his eyesight began to fail. His many drawings of dancers and bathers were given a

freedom that would not be possible in paint. [6,55] Poor eyesight led Degas to make wax models of horses and nude female figures. He only exhibited one, the 'Young Dancer 14 Years Old', made of wax and dressed in a real tutu and ballet shoes.

Degas was highly regarded by his contemporaries. Pissarro believed him to be the greatest artist of the epoch. He certainly created new ways of composing pictures, influenced by Oriental prints, and had wonderful drawing and painting skills.

[6,55] 'Two Ballet Dancers in a Dressing Room', 1880, by Edgar Degas, pastel on paper, 48.5 x 64 cm (National Gallery of Ireland, Dublin). Degas often provides an unusual angle of view in his paintings and foreground objects to help create a sense of space. Accuracy of drawing is always a feature in his work.

145

PIERRE AUGUSTE RENOIR (1841–1919)

Renoir was a close friend of Monet and their styles were similar for a while, but Renoir's joy in painting pretty women and children led him away from landscape. Born in Liège, he began work as a painter in a porcelain factory in Paris. The decorative style he learnt there and from eighteenth-century French paintings in the Louvre carried over into his Impressionist painting when he joined the group at the studio of Gleyre. His scenes of Parisian life in the 1820s have immediate appeal in their warm colours and attractive subjects. 'Le Moulin de la Galette' [6,56] shows a scene of open-air dancing in Montmartre, a complicated composition of light and movement which is beautifully handled in his Impressionist style.

Renoir was having some success as a portrait painter in the 1880s and became dissatisfied with Impressionism. 'Les Parapluies' shows sharper definition and more blended brushwork than does the Impressionist style, although the two little girls in the bottom right are still in this older style.

Later in his life Renoir developed a softer handling and less-defined subjects, as in 'In the Meadow' [6,57] which is not specific to time or place. He also painted numerous nudes and mythological subjects. Rheumatism made him seek the warmer climate of the Mediterranean where he ended his days.

CAMILLE PISSARRO (1830–1903)

A kind of father figure among the Impressionists, Pissarro worked with most of them and was instrumental in organising their exhibitions. He was the only member to exhibit in all eight group shows.

Born in the West Indies, he came to France in 1855 and studied under Corot. He met Monet and Cézanne in 1860–1 when he was painting simple landscapes in muted colours in the style of the Barbizon School.

By the 1870s Pissarro's style had changed to smaller, more colourful canvases. His 'Hoar-Frost', [6,58] which was exhibited in the first Impressionist show, is typical of his style — simple landscapes and simple people. The colour harmony of this painting was a feature of his art even when he tried pointillism for a few years under the influence of Seurat. His painting style in later years was evenly marked in parallel brush or palette knife marks to create a unity of surface. He shared this technique with Cézanne, who worked with him for a number of years.

[6,56] 'Le Moulin de la Galette', 1876, by Pierre Auguste Renoir, oil on canvas, 131 x 175 cm (Louvre, Paris). Renoir's beautifully pure colouring and gestural brushwork create a wonderful sense of light and colour in this scene of outdoor dancing with friends of the artist.

[6,57] 'In the Meadow', c. 1895, by Pierre Auguste Renoir, oil on canvas, 81.3 x 65.4 cm (Metropolitan Museum of Art, New York). The lighter, more romantic style of Renoir's later work originates in studies of old masters, particularly Fragonard.

[6,58] 'Hoar-Frost', 1873, by Camille Pissarro, oil on canvas, 65 x 93 cm (Musée d'Orsay, Paris). Landscape in different lights and weathers with the people of the countryside at work was Pissarro's subject-matter for most of his life. He liked to harmonise his colours and his brushwork to create an evenness in the work.

[6,60] 'Le Corsage Noir', by Berthe Morisot, oil on canvas, 73 x 65 cm (National Gallery of Ireland, Dublin). The loose brush technique learnt from Manet is evident in this charming portrait of a young woman.

ALFRED SISLEY (1839–99)

Born of English parents, Sisley lived and worked most of his life in the countryside near Paris. He painted only landscapes, with carefully selected colours and beautifully handled brushwork. He was the least appreciated of the Impressionists, probably because of the simplicity and harmony of his work.

'Flood at Port Marly' [6,59] highlights Sisley's clever use of blues for shadows and the descriptive brushwork he used in the 1870s. His work was exhibited in the first three Impressionist exhibitions. He spent time painting with Monet and the others from Gleyre's studio where he had studied.

[6,59] 'Flood at Port Marly', 1876, by Alfred Sisley, oil on canvas, 60 x 81 cm (Fitzwilliam Museum, University of Cambridge). One of a series of paintings made of the flood at Marly. Sisley, like Monet, did a number of series, painted in the Impressionist technique.

BERTHE MORISOT (1841–95)

A granddaughter of the painter Fragonard and a pupil of Corot, Morisot's greatest influence was Manet, whose brother she married in 1874. Her oil paintings and watercolours display the influence of Manet's freely brushed style. She took up the Impressionist rainbow colour scheme in the 1870s and introduced it to Manet. She exhibited in all but one of the Impressionist group's exhibitions and had some success at the Salon. Her subjects were mainly domestic scenes and seascapes, which she painted with a light touch. 'Le Corsage Noir' [6,60] shows the influence of Manet's style in the soft colour and careful drawing which is retained in her later work.

POST-IMPRESSIONISM

The post-Impressionists were not an organised group but the artists who followed on from Impressionism, developing from it or in reaction to it. They were aware of each other's work — van Gogh and Gauguin even shared ideas and worked together for a time. Otherwise much of their work is unrelated and the title is used merely to cover the artists working in new styles from about 1880 to the end of the century.

NEO-IMPRESSIONISM

In a letter to his dealer Durand-Ruel in 1886, Pissarro attempted to explain the changes in his style by describing them as 'a modern synthesis by methods based on science, that is, based on the theory of colours developed by Chevreul, to substitute optical mixture for the mixture of pigments'. Also called 'divisionism' or 'pointillism', the new technique employed dots of pure colour side by side, which the viewer mixed in the mind's eye, creating secondary and tertiary colours. A number of neo-Impressionist paintings were shown in the final Impressionist exhibition of 1886. Pissarro, Seurat and Paul Signac (1863–1935) all exhibited work in the new style.

GEORGES SEURAT (1859–91)

Georges Seurat was the most significant of the neo-Impressionist artists. Born in Paris, he trained at the École des Beaux Arts where he studied classical sculptures and the Renaissance masters. He immersed himself in aesthetic and colour theory and developed a formalised process to create paintings from composition to finish. Seurat was a very skilled draughtsman and produced a large number of subtle tone sketches on textured paper.

Seurat's last painting 'The Circus' [6,61] demonstrates many of his theories. The warm colours and upward curving lines represent happiness. The unconventional use of space and scale in the ring contrast with the formalised rows of spectators behind. The simplified outlines and flowing patterns of coloured dots go beyond realism, creating an expressive style which was rarely attained by any other painter in the neo-Impressionist group.

PAUL CÉZANNE (1839–1906)

A difficult and reclusive man, Cézanne had little critical acclaim except in the final years of his life. Born at Aix-en-Provence of a well-to-do family, he was reluctantly supported by his father until he inherited the family estates in 1886. He took up painting with the encouragement of his friend Émile Zola, the writer, and studied at the Atelier Suisse in 1861 where he met Pissarro, an important influence on his work for many years.

Cézanne had a difficult early career. His clumsy painting style did not suit the classical themes he was attempting. He studied in the museums and galleries and was particularly impressed by the work of Delacroix and Poussin. In 1872 he moved from Paris to Auvers-sur-Oise, where he worked directly from the landscape in the company of Pissarro. His style changed and developed,

[6,61] 'The Circus', 1891, by Georges Seurat, oil on canvas, 185.5 x 152.5 cm (Musée d'Orsay, Paris). Seurat's formalised painting method was developed from theories on colour and aesthetics. Cubists and abstract artists of the next century were influenced by him.

though he was not interested in the Impressionist effects of catching a fleeting moment. The weather or time of day never seems to be of importance in his work; it is the underlying structure he tried to represent, even in his early landscapes.

'The House of the Hanged Man', [6,62] which Cézanne exhibited and sold in the first Impressionist exhibition in 1874, demonstrates this interest in structure. It is made up of planes and solid forms. The receding landscape is hardly visible and the brushwork contours around the surfaces. The feeling of weight in the painting is different from Impressionist work which emphasises light. Cézanne took part in one further Impressionist exhibition in 1877, in which he exhibited sixteen paintings.

[6,62] 'The House of the Hanged Man', 1873, by Paul Cézanne, oil on canvas, 55.5 x 66.3 cm (Musée d'Orsay, Paris). Even when he painted with the Impressionists Cézanne's interest in form and structure was developing. The Impressionist use of spectrum colours was vital in his studies of nature.

[6,63] 'Rocky Landscape near Aix', 1886, by Paul Cézanne, oil on canvas, 65 x 81 cm (National Gallery, London). Cézanne studied the landscape of his childhood near Aix-en-Provence and found a means to describe his understanding of it through colour rather than conventional perspective.

In an effort to make of Impressionism 'something solid and enduring like the art of the museums', Cézanne had to follow his own path. He returned to Aix where he spent most of the remainder of his life developing his methods. Before beginning work on a painting he studied his subject intently, taking time to get to the essence of the landscape, still life or person. He was not interested in *how things looked* but in *how they really were*. What was the nature, structure, form of his subject? The 'Rocky Landscape near Aix' [6,63] shows how he tried to describe the landscape without using conventional perspective. Carefully balanced colours suggest distance and structure. The warm and cool tones describe the forms rather than simply showing how they look on a certain day at a certain time.

[6,64] 'Still Life with Basket', 1890, by Paul Cézanne, oil on canvas, 65.5 x 81 cm (Musée d'Orsay, Paris). The multiple viewpoints and use of colour to describe form created a new method for constructing paintings which was quickly realised by the younger generation of artists who saw Cézanne's work.

Cézanne's still lifes can sometimes show more clearly what he was trying to achieve in his art. The 'Still Life with Basket' [6,64] offers a number of different viewpoints within the same picture. In comparing the two sides of the table, we have a higher angle of view of the left side than of the right. The bowl and the basket at the back of the group are on quite different planes. There is no continuous perspective throughout the picture. Again it is colour rather than light and shade that is used to describe forms; there is no consistent lighting in the painting.

Cézanne had come to the realisation that a painting was not a representation of a piece of nature but a thing in itself, a composition of colour and shape, separate from the real world, i.e. a human invention.

In 1895 Cézanne was given a one-man show in Paris by the dealer Vollard. The young artists who saw it were very excited by what he had achieved and he became greatly respected in his final years. His work was exhibited in a number of countries. Cézanne is regarded as the father of modern painting, having broken the chain of development that began with the invention of perspective and modelling in the Early Renaissance. His work had a powerful effect on young artists at the turn of the century, with many styles and movements including Cubism developing from his ideas.

PAUL GAUGUIN (1848–1903)

Born of a French father and Peruvian mother, Gauguin spent much of his childhood in Lima in beautiful surroundings. He returned to France and, having spent a number of years at sea, became a stockbroker. He took night classes in art and began to exhibit his work. Through Pissarro he met the Impressionists and began to collect their work, particularly that of Pissarro and Cézanne. He exhibited with the Impressionists in their last four shows. He became a full-time artist in 1883 and abandoned his wife and children in 1886, moving to Pont-Aven in Brittany where he was the main figure in a group of avant-garde artists. He spent five years in Brittany, broken by visits to Panama and Martinique in 1887 and two months with van Gogh in Arles which ended in an argument and van Gogh's first nervous breakdown.

[6,65] 'The Vision after the Sermon', 1888, by Paul Gauguin, oil on canvas, 73 x 92 cm (National Gallery of Scotland, Edinburgh). Jacob wrestles with the angel in the imagination of these praying people, Gauguin wrote in a letter to van Gogh, which explains the unreal colour and perspective of the composition.

[6,66] 'Women of Tahiti on the Beach', 1891, by Paul Gauguin, oil on canvas, 68.5 x 90 cm (Musée d'Orsay, Paris). Gauguin's Tahitian paintings are full of the colour and pattern of the Tropics.

Gradually Gauguin's painting style progressed from the style of Pissarro and Cézanne to a more abstract, symbolic style which can be seen in 'The Vision after the Sermon': [6,65] In this painting colour and shape are used for emotional and symbolic effect rather than the expression of visual reality. Gauguin's contact with the Symbolist poets such as Stéphane Mallarmé and painters Émile Bernard (1868–1941) and Aurier influenced his work, as did Japanese prints and Indonesian and Japanese art he saw at the Paris World Fair of 1889.

A search for a more primitive and innocent way of life encouraged Gauguin to sell all his work in Paris in 1891 to finance a trip to Tahiti, where he found a French colony rather than the primitive life and religion he sought. Gauguin still painted some of his finest work in Tahiti, with vibrant colours and simplified drawing.

The 'Women of Tahiti on the Beach' [6,66] shows how he abandoned linear and aerial perspective and applied his colour in flat areas without modelling. Areas of pattern in clothes and background are given equal importance as figures. Gauguin's work avoids becoming mere decoration by its suggestive power; mysteries are always created in the images.

Gauguin also worked as a potter, woodcarver and woodblock printer. In fact he claimed to be the main mover in the revival of the woodcut as an art form. He was never in doubt about the importance of his own work, in spite of a life of poverty and comparative obscurity. Having returned to Paris for two years, he spent his final years in Tahiti and the Marquesas Islands where he painted and sculpted to the end. [6,67]

VINCENT VAN GOGH (1853–90)

The facts and myths of van Gogh's life sometimes overshadow his artistic achievements. Those around him found it difficult to cope with his great intensity of feeling. His early attempts to become a minister of the church were rejected because he threw himself into helping and supporting the poor and disadvantaged with such

[6,67] 'L'enlèvement d'Europe', a woodcut by Paul Gauguin (Victoria and Albert Museum, London). Gauguin's block prints create the primitive effect he was after through a simplicity of technique and stark contrasts.

wholeheartedness that the Church authorities thought it unseemly and beneath his dignity as a minister of the Church. He was also deeply affected by similar rejections in his love life. His 'madness' may have been a form of epilepsy which can have similar symptoms to schizophrenia.

Despite his problems adjusting to the constraints and conservatism of nineteenth-century society, he was an extraordinarily productive artist, painting over 200 canvases in his fifteen months at Arles alone. Van Gogh's letters to his brother Theo and artist friends (more than 750 survive) provide a unique insight into his creative thinking and theories on art. He was a well-read and intelligent man, familiar with the works of many artists through visits to museums and galleries. He completed versions of paintings by Rembrandt, Delacroix, Millet and others.

Van Gogh started painting in 1880 and spent the following five years, half of his life as an artist, in Holland, first drawing and then painting the miners, weavers and peasants of his native land. His early work was motivated by his concern for ordinary, working people. He wanted to say something about their way of life and expressed it in a style related to Millet and the current Dutch school. His most famous painting from this period is 'The Potato Eaters'. [6,68] Dark in colouring, it already has the vigorous painting style we associate with van Gogh. There is no sentimentality, just a direct response to what he saw.

[6,68] 'The Potato Eaters', 1885, by Vincent van Gogh, oil on canvas, 72 x 93 cm (Rijksmuseum Kröller-Möller, Otterlo, Belgium). The apparent mistakes in proportion and technique were unimportant to van Gogh. What he wanted to convey was simple people eating a meal they had honestly earned.

[6,69] 'Drawbridge with Carriage', 1888, by Vincent van Gogh, oil on canvas, 54 x 65 cm (Kröller-Möller Museum, Otterlo). The flat landscape and waterways near Arles reminded van Gogh of his native Holland. The influence of Japanese prints is apparent in the composition and broad areas of strong colour.

In 1886 he moved to Paris where his brother Theo worked as an art dealer. Van Gogh was overwhelmed with creative influences, including the Impressionists and Japanese colour prints which were popular at the time. His painting underwent radical change, most obviously in colour, but also in brushwork and composition.

The arguments and tensions between groups of artists with conflicting opinions led van Gogh to move out of Paris. He went to Arles where he hoped to find parallels to Japan in the sunshine and colour of the south of France. [6,69] He wanted to form an artists' co-operative like the Barbizon School, but of those he invited only Gauguin came. Their personalities and theories on art were quite different and it ended in a row after two months. Van Gogh suffered the first of his attacks and cut off part of his left ear.

Some of van Gogh's finest paintings come from this period in Arles. The 'Sunflowers', 'Bridges', landscapes, seascapes and portraits [6,70] all have the bright colours and descriptive brushmarks associated with van Gogh's mature style.

[6,70] 'Portrait of Joseph Roulin', 1888, by Vincent van Gogh, pencil on paper, 32 x 24.4 cm (John Paul Getty Museum, California). Van Gogh's vigorous drawing style includes dots, lines and gestural marks which express more than mere appearance. It is an outburst of activity based on intense observation.

[6,71] 'Cypresses and Two Figures', 1890, by Vincent van Gogh, oil on canvas, 92 x 73 cm (Rijksmuseum Kröller-Möller, Otterlo, Netherlands). One of a number of nocturnes by van Gogh; moonlight and starlight are expressed as moving forces, the tree snaking into the night almost splits the scene in two.

[6,72] 'The Salon in the Rue des Moulins', 1894, by Henri de Toulouse-Lautrec, oil on canvas, 111.5 x 132.5 cm (Musée Toulouse-Lautrec, Albi). Toulouse-Lautrec painted in diluted oil paint, sometimes on unprimed cardboard. Even his more finished works maintain the immediacy of a sketch.

In his last year he suffered more breakdowns and depressions, but continued to paint and draw prolifically. His style became even more vigorous, with swirling brushmarks that take on a life of their own. His painting of 'Cypresses and Two Figures' [6,71] shows how van Gogh creates a sense of movement in everything: even the road seems to flow. In a letter to Theo he explained how 'instead of trying to reproduce exactly what I have before my eyes, I use colour more arbitrarily, in order to express myself forcibly'. Van Gogh's sensitivity and passionate feelings became too much for him to cope with and he shot himself on 27 July 1890, dying two days later.

Although hardly known in his lifetime, his work quickly became influential with the young, avant-garde artists and sparked off a series of movements including Fauvism and Expressionism. Today his work is very popular — easy to enjoy, yet profound.

HENRI DE TOULOUSE-LAUTREC (1864–1901)

Painter, printmaker and poster designer, Toulouse-Lautrec was the son of an eccentric nobleman. A series of riding accidents stunted the growth of his legs and gave him a strange physical appearance. Despite this he led a rakish life in the cafés, bars and dancehalls of Paris which he recorded in his work. He met van Gogh at Cormon's school in 1886 and was familiar with

the work of the Impressionists and post-Impressionists. He particularly admired Degas's style and was also influenced by Japanese prints.

'The Salon in the Rue des Moulins' [6,72] highlights the expressive, graphic style and bold colour that Toulouse-Lautrec used in much of his work. He brought poster design to a new artistic level through a creative and innovative use of lithography which was a relatively new form of printmaking. The 'Jane Avril at the Jardin de Paris' poster [6,73] uses line and colour to great dramatic effect. The humour and tragedy in his work is often missed.

[6,73] 'Jane Avril at the Jardin de Paris', 1893, by Henri de Toulouse-Lautrec, poster, 130 x 95 cm (Musée Toulouse-Lautrec, Albi). In many ways modern graphic design begins with Toulouse-Lautrec. He was the first to see the potential in lithography for producing large, eye-catching posters. He also used lithography to produce editions of his work.

Vuillard worked with Bonnard from 1888 when they were both members of the Nabis movement. He painted, made prints and took photographs which he sometimes used as a starting point for paintings. His interest in pattern and flat colour comes from Gauguin whose work he admired. [6,75]

SYMBOLISM AND ART NOUVEAU

Symbolism was a loosely organised movement associated with the Symbolist poets and composers. It was a reaction to Realism and Impressionism and their representation of the visual and concrete world. The Symbolists sought to express mystical and spiritual ideas and thought that colour and line had inherent qualities that could create an emotional response in the viewer.

INTIMISTS

Many artists continued to paint in the Impressionist manner into the twentieth century. Of these Pierre Bonnard (1867–1947) and Édouard Vuillard (1868–1940) are sometimes called 'Intimists' because they portrayed scenes of domestic life in a close-up and intense way.

Bonnard's painting 'The Table' [6,74] displays the colour and detached observation of an Impressionist work, but the brushwork and treatment of space are different. There is often a static quality in Bonnard's work, as if time has frozen. He said he wanted 'to show all one sees upon entering a room'. His painting technique was flexible, following no formula. He relied on intuition to compose and complete his work.

There was a wide range of styles among Symbolists. Gauguin and his followers chose peasant scenes to express ideas of spirituality and mystery; Gustave Moreau (1826–98) painted exotic scenes of gem-like richness; Pierre Puvis de Chavannes (1824–98) produced pale, melancholy scenes; and Odilon Redon (1840–1916) painted dreams and fantasies. [6,76] Henri Rousseau (1844–1910), an untrained, naive or primitive artist, does not properly fit with the Symbolists, but there were many dream-like images in his work.

[6,74] 'The Table', by Pierre Bonnard, oil on canvas, 103 x 74 cm (Tate Gallery, London). Bonnard painted in an unconventional way, pinning pieces of canvas to the wall. He built up paintings from sketches and memory, selecting the parts he would frame and only adding final touches to the framed work.

[6,75] 'The Reader', 1896, by Édouard Vuillard, oil on canvas, 213 x 155 cm (Musée de la Ville de Paris). Figures and detail are almost lost in the strong pattern of this painting.

[6,76] 'The Cyclops', c. 1895, by Odilon Redon, oil on panel, 64 x 51 cm (Rijksmuseum Kröller-Möller, Otterlo). The encrusted surface and points of bright colour help create the unreality of this dream painting.

[6,78] 'Salomé', 1893, by Aubrey Beardsley, pen and ink on paper, 23 x 17 cm. Beardsley's illustrations for Oscar Wilde's book of the same title brought recognition while he was still only 21. The Salome theme was popular with the Symbolists for whom it represented the *femme fatale*, the woman who destroys men.

Outside France, Symbolism spread in various forms to many countries. Edvard Munch (1863–1944), a Norwegian painter, lithographer, etcher and woodblock printmaker, saw paintings by Gauguin while on a visit to Paris and responded to them in his own art. Illness, madness and death were recurring themes in his work, often relating to events from his own life. In his famous painting 'The Scream' [6,77] he tries to express in line and colour a state of extreme mental anguish, a neurotic's effort to let us see inside a troubled mind. Munch's prints, particularly his woodcuts, had a strong influence on young artists in Germany where he lived and worked for a number of years.

The English artist Aubrey Beardsley (1872–98) was part of the aesthetic movement and illustrated Oscar Wilde's *Salomé* [6,78] to great critical acclaim. He is a master of black and white, weaving line and pattern into works of great subtlety. His style incorporates elements of Symbolism and Art Nouveau, being both imaginative and decorative.

In Austria, Gustav Klimt (1862–1918) was the leader of the avant-garde artists in Vienna. He painted portraits and allegorical and mythological subjects and loved to paint beautiful women. His work combines realistic human figures with decorative backgrounds. Pattern and colour envelop the embracing couple in 'The Kiss'. [6,79]

The reflexive line and pattern of Art Nouveau lent itself to all the decorative arts — book printing, posters, printed fabrics, jewellery, furniture and interior design — and was popular all across Europe in the late nineteenth and early twentieth centuries.

CONCLUSION

The social, political and economic changes in the nineteenth century helped to bring about the greatest change in art since the Renaissance. Steel and glass, the new materials of the Industrial Revolution, created a whole new vocabulary for

[6,77] 'The Scream', 1893, by Edvard Munch, oil and tempera on cardboard, 91 x 73 cm (Nasjonalgalleriet, Oslo). Munch's expressive ability was a revelation to younger artists, particularly in Germany where he lived for a time. It helped to spark off the Expressionist movement.

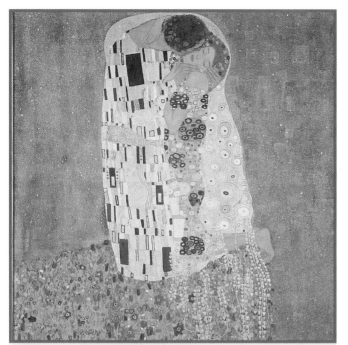

[6,79] 'The Kiss', c. 1907–8, by Gustav Klimt, watercolour and gouache on paper, mounted on wood, 180 x 180 cm (Österreichische Galerie, Vienna). 'The Kiss' is a wonderfully decorative work that combines Symbolist imagery with Art Nouveau decoration.

TWENTIETH CENTURY

The twentieth century witnessed a communications revolution, from high-speed manual delivery of newspapers and telegrams at the beginning of the century to the almost instant electronic delivery of words or images from all over the world at the end. This communications revolution led to an international dissemination of ideas and movements in society in general and also in the arts. New technology in building and manufacturing materials and improved techniques in mass production led to a huge change in design.

The two world wars had a decisive influence on European society. The First World War ended the Imperialist-Royalist control of Europe. The Fascist and Communist movements had huge international support in the period between the wars and art movements in the same period reached into almost every country in Europe. Following the Second World War, America — particularly New York — became a cultural centre to rival Paris and many of the postwar movements originated there.

The influence of primitive art, which we noted in the late nineteenth century, continued in the twentieth century as a source of inspiration to artists who were looking for alternative modes of expression to those of traditional forms.

ARCHITECTURE

The steel and glass construction we saw at the end of the nineteenth century was augmented by reinforced concrete early in the twentieth. This permitted a whole new range of forms which were gradually assimilated into architectural design. Before 1945 building in a modern style was confined to commercial and factory buildings and a few private buildings for intellectual clients. It was not until the need for large-scale rebuilding after the Second World War that modern architecture superseded traditional methods and designs.

In America, tall buildings constructed in steel and concrete with large windows — the forerunners of

architects which they had only begun to use. Sculpture was still figurative and had not yet made the transition into the new ways of looking at art. Painting, however, was transformed.

In contrast to the academies' and the Salon's grip on artistic taste and development at the beginning of the century, a position of total freedom emerged. Artists were now able to choose their own subject-matter: it did not have to fit into a recognised genre or tradition. 'Correct technique' no longer constrained artists. They could paint in any way they thought appropriate, applying paint impasto with a palette knife or diluting it so that it could be brushed or rubbed on quickly.

New materials were also available. Commercially prepared paints in tubes made their appearance about the mid-century and artists' suppliers provided pre-stretched and prepared canvases. All the material tasks that had been carried out by apprentices or the artists themselves were now done commercially.

A revival of interest in craftsmanship was a result of industrial mass production, widening the range of artists' activities. Ceramics, printmaking, graphic design and interior design were all now regarded as legitimate extensions of the artist's sphere of interest. In short, the basis for what we call modern art had evolved.

the modern skyscraper — were built in Chicago from the 1880s on. Frank Lloyd Wright's ideas on buildings which 'grew' out of the needs of the inhabitants and belonged to the surrounding landscape were very influential with young European architects.

DE STIJL

The Dutch painters, sculptors, poets, designers and architects who formed a group and published a journal called *De Stijl* (The Style) in 1917 were seeking principles of harmony and balance that could be applied to life and society, as well as to art and design. They developed an austere, abstract style which sought the expression of an ideal of universal harmony and therefore the escape from the use of individual or particular images and from the representation of natural objects.

GERRIT RIETVELD (1886–1964)

Gerrit Rietveld was the leading designer/architect of the *De Stijl* group. In the Schröder House [6,80] on the outskirts of Utrecht he used concrete and steel construction to produce a design closely related to the abstract paintings of Piet Mondrian, but developed in three dimensions. Rietveld's furniture design was also influential among the young Modernists.

THE BAUHAUS

Walter Gropius (1883–1969) founded the Bauhaus school of design in Weimar, Germany, in 1919 in an attempt to unify the arts and design under principles similar to those of the nineteenth-century English designer William Morris. In the 1920s the emphasis moved to design for mass production, in which the manufacturing process and the function of the object were the controlling factors in the design. [6,81] The phrase 'function before form' became one of the guiding principles of Bauhaus design.

In 1925 the school moved from Weimar to Dessau. Gropius, his staff and students designed the buildings which were to become the new Bauhaus. They look unremarkable today because the principles involved in the design of these buildings became the norm for the generations of architects that followed. The simple contrasts

[6,80] The Schröder House, Utrecht, 1924, by Gerrit Rietveld, steel and concrete construction. The projecting panels and balconies of the Schröder House were made possible by steel and concrete construction, still in its infancy in the 1920s.

[6,81] Bauhaus buildings, Dessau, Germany, 1915–26, by Walter Gropius. The simple lines and black and white colouring of the exterior of the Bauhaus buildings are the forerunners of many modern buildings. The workshops have a more industrial look, with glass fronts and small windowpanes to suggest mass production.

between solids and openings and the use of glass curtain walls outside the structure of the building are features of Bauhaus design. Mies van der Rohe was the last director of the Bauhaus from 1930 to 1933, when it was closed by the Nazis. He emigrated to the United States of America in 1938 where he taught and worked for the remainder of his life.

The Bauhaus school was enormously influential on twentieth-century art and design. [6,82] When it was closed in 1933 the staff and students emigrated all over the world, many of them becoming teachers in American universities where their design courses created a new foundation in American art and design.

[6,82] 'Tea Pot', c. 1924, by Marianne Brandt. The clean lines and simple forms of this tea pot are typical of Bauhaus designs for industry.

[6,84] Unité d'Habitation, Marseilles, 1947–52, by Le Corbusier. The Unité is a complete village with shops etc. reached from internal streets. The roof is a recreation area. The concrete finish is enlivened by primary colours in the areas surrounding the windows.

THE INTERNATIONAL STYLE

Most of the features of the International style have been noted in the *De Stijl* and Bauhaus buildings we have seen. The simple, asymmetrical arrangement of geometric forms, extensive glazing that often wraps around the corners of buildings and open-plan interiors are direct results of concrete, steel and glass construction.

LE CORBUSIER (CHARLES-ÉDOUARD JEANNERET) (1887–1965)

Le Corbusier was a French painter, writer, designer and one of the most influential architects of the twentieth century. In 1923 he published his beliefs in his book *Towards a New Architecture*. He wished to liberate buildings from their sites by raising them on stilts which were called 'pilotis'. This emphasised the core structure of the building and allowed outer walls and interior spaces to be divided in any way the architect chose. [6,83] He

[6,83] Villa Savoye, 1929, Poissy, France, by Le Corbusier. In his design Le Corbusier combined classical proportions with what he considered to be the best machine-made shapes. Trains, ships and man-made objects of all kinds influenced his designs.

used the golden section and human proportions to formulate the scale for the various parts of his buildings, referring to this system of proportions as 'the modular'. Le Corbusier said, 'architecture is the masterly, correct and magnificent play of masses brought together in light'; this denotes a sculptural and romantic view of buildings rather than a functional one.

The need for mass housing following the destruction of the Second World War gave Le Corbusier an opportunity to build several Unités d'Habitation. [6,84] These huge buildings, housing up to 2,000 people, have living space, shops and libraries which are reached from internal streets. They stand in parkland, providing vistas and recreational space for the inhabitants. A misinterpretation of these buildings has led to problems with large-scale housing in many cities of Europe.

LUDWIG MIES VAN DER ROHE (1886–1969)

Mies van der Rohe's solution to mass housing was quite different. [6,85] He was less interested in the play of light on masses; his buildings are steel and glass towers reflecting light from their shiny surfaces. These buildings are multi-functional. Their open-plan interiors can be divided into offices, apartments or other spaces depending on requirements.

[6,85] Commonwealth Promenade Apartments, Chicago, 1953–6, by Ludwig Mies van der Rohe. Mies's high-rise buildings show the steel frame and glass curtain wall in their purest form. The reflective surface of the glass provides the only relief in the repetition of the surface.

[6,87] The Pompidou Centre, Paris, 1977, by Renzo Piano and Richard Rogers. Buildings which were clearly not part of the International style were becoming more common in the 1970s. The Pompidou Centre wears its functional parts on the outside, colour coded for easy maintenance.

SPREAD OF INTERNATIONAL STYLE

The International style spread throughout the world during the 1950s and 1960s, with an increasing interest in free-form concrete construction. The Sydney Opera House, [6,86] designed by the Danish architect Jorn Utzon, used concrete shells to form the roof which was based on sail shapes.

[6,86] Sydney Opera House, 1959–73, by Jorn Utzon. Free-form concrete structures have been popular since the 1950s for covering large spaces like concert halls and sports arenas.

POST-MODERNISM

The steel and concrete structures of the Modern movement have been found to be uneconomical and unnecessary, except in the construction of very tall buildings. The purist forms of steel and glass construction lost their charm for late twentieth-century architects. The Pompidou Centre in Paris [6,87] was built inside out by traditional standards. All the services are exposed

on the exterior, leaving a completely uninterrupted interior exhibition space. The escalator projects from the front of the building, diagonally stepping across the exterior framework which looks like a scaffolding. This style of building, which makes an outward display of its functional elements, has been called 'boilerhouse architecture'.

The Neue Staatsgalerie in Stuttgart [6,88] was designed by the English architects James Stirling and Michael Wilford. It attempts a monumentality which is a move away from the functionalism of the Modernist movement and yet its colourful and playful elements prevent it from being pompous or overly serious. This balance between the function of a building and its attractiveness and symbolism is a concern for most modern architects.

[6,88] Neue Staatsgalerie, Stuttgart, 1984, by James Stirling and Michael Wilford. The architects took visual reference from the Altes Museum in Berlin, 1830, which was an important building in the museum culture which swept Europe in the 19th century, though this design does not copy the neo-classical formality of the earlier building.

[6,89] Youth Club, Möglingen, Germany, 1996, by Peter Hübner. The playful effect of a spacecraft landed in a wild meadow is combined with serious use of solar energy and environmental control within the building.

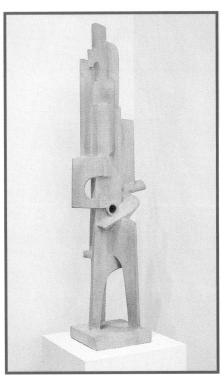

[6,90] 'Man with a Guitar', 1915, by Jacques Lipchitz, bronze, 97 x 27 x 18 cm (Museum of Modern Art, New York). Lipchitz is the most successful Cubist sculptor.

The German architect Peter Hübner designed a youth club at Möglingen in Germany in the shape of a flying saucer, [6,89] with the shape evolving from a brainstorming session held with the teenagers who were going to use the club. The steel-ribbed dome of the roof is supported by nine steel legs which look like a retractable undercarriage. They also carry the run-off water from the roof. The smaller dome tilted at an angle can be rotated to provide light or shade depending on the season.

This use of technology combined with environmental concerns is a growing area in architecture. Large and small buildings alike make use of solar energy and take account of the physical or historical environment in which they are constructed.

SCULPTURE

Sculpture was the last of the art forms to join the Modern movement after following, for a number of years, a step or two behind movements and ideas in painting. After the Second World War sculptors began to find modes of expression that led away from traditional models of what sculpture should be until, towards the end of the century, it became the most advanced art form, pressing out the frontiers of what a work of art is.

In the early part of the century Paris was still the centre of innovation, with German and Dutch avant-garde artists close behind. Artists from all over Europe came to train in Paris or the Bauhaus, which helped to spread modern ideas all over the world.

JACQUES LIPCHITZ (1891–1973)
Jacques Lipchitz was born in Lithuania and worked in France until 1941 when he went to the USA. In his early Cubist work he simplified forms and provided alternative views by the interplay of planes on the figure. [6,90] In the 1920s he developed a more abstract style, but he returned to the figure in his later work.

UMBERTO BOCCIONI (1882–1916)
Umberto Boccioni, an Italian, was the leading Futurist sculptor, as well as a painter and theorist. His views on sculpture were very advanced. He advocated the use of glass, electric motors and light, but his early death prevented him from developing these ideas. In his famous sculpture 'Unique Forms of Continuity in Space' [6,91] he tried to express the movement and unique emotional qualities which the Futurist believed to be inherent in natural shapes. The work certainly manages to express forces pent up being released in action.

CONSTANTIN BRANCUSI (1876–1957)
Constantin Brancusi was born in Romania, but worked mainly in Paris. He trained as an academic sculptor and gradually evolved a style of simplified forms. The highly polished bronze 'Bird in Space' [6,92] displays the clarity of line and form that is evident in much of his work. He

[6,91] 'Unique Forms of Continuity in Space', 1913, by Umberto Boccioni, cast bronze, 112 x 89 x 41 cm (Mattioli Collection, Milan). This figure emphasises lines of energy and movement rather than trying to represent the appearance of a walking person.

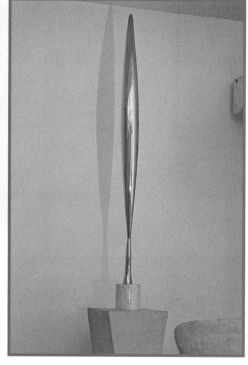

[6,92] 'Bird in Space', 1919, by Constantin Brancusi, standing on a column section, bronze, 137 cm tall (Musée Nationale d'Art Moderne, Paris). Brancusi's forms appear abstract, but their origins are usually found in nature.

CONSTRUCTIVISM

The move towards abstraction in sculpture came in a number of ways. The Constructivists in Russia produced the 'Realist manifesto' which suggested that art could be produced from non-traditional materials assembled together.

Constructivist ideas were influential in the Bauhaus and in many subsequent movements. The idea of making art by assembling objects was developed in the sculpture of the 1960s.

NAUM GABO (1890–1977)

Naum Gabo, one of the leading figures in the Constructivist movement, trained in engineering and physical sciences. He used metals, glass and plastics in his abstract constructions which sometimes had moving parts. [6,93] Gabo felt that art did not need to have any function: it was an end in itself. This kind of theory did not sit well with the Russian state in the 1920s, so he emigrated to Germany, England and finally America.

DADAISM

Dadaism, founded in Zurich in 1916, spread to Paris, Barcelona, New York, Austria, Belgium and the Netherlands in a few years. It has been one of the most influential movements in the twentieth century. It is really anti-art, or anti-establishment, protesting at the 'head-in-clouds' attitude of artists, dealers and critics in the face of war and social problems. Dadaists also poked fun at the idea of art as a precious or valuable thing. They

was a very accomplished craftsman who worked in a variety of materials, producing primitive-style woodcarvings and abstract 'endless columns' made of repeated units that could be extended to any height. Brancusi was one of the most influential figures in twentieth-century sculpture. In the words of Henry Moore, 'He made people "shape conscious" and opened eyes to the beauty and meaning of pure forms.'

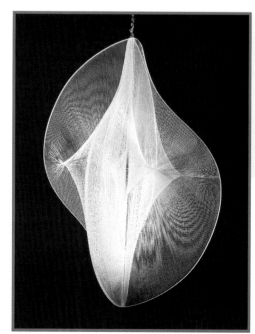

[6,93] 'Linear Construction in Space No. 2', by Naum Gabo, perspex with nylon monofilament, 114.9 cm high (Tate Gallery, London). Gabo created sculptures that appeared almost weightless. They occupy space in a way that was not previously thought of.

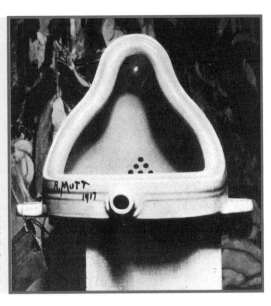

[6,94] 'The Fountain', copy 1966, original 1917, by Marcel Duchamp (1887–1968), sanitaryware and enamel paint, 30 cm tall (Philadelphia Museum of Art). Presenting found objects as art was meant to be a challenge to the art establishment who admired art for its value rather than its beauty or truth as a work of art.

exhibited found objects — a bottle rack, a urinal, an iron with tacks stuck to the smoothing surface — declaring that they were art. [6,94] Another aspect of Dadaism was the importance given to chance as an element in the creation of art. The encouragement of the absurd and the irrational led on to Surrealism and later Abstract Expressionism. Conceptual art was a logical progression from Dadaism, as was junk sculpture and Pop Art.

JEAN ARP (1887–1966)

Jean Arp, from France, was a Dadaist and Surrealist who painted, wrote poetry and sculpted in an abstract style which has its roots in nature but does not represent any real object. [6,95]

[6,95] 'Hybrid Fruit called Pagoda', 1935, by Jean Arp, bronze, 86 cm tall (Tate Gallery, London). One of Arp's earlier bronze sculptures, it is a deliberately ambiguous form based on nature.

FIGURATIVE SCULPTURE

Figurative sculpture continued in parallel with abstract work.

ALBERTO GIACOMETTI (1901–66)

The Swiss-born sculptor Alberto Giacometti evolved an individual style. After years of experimenting with Surrealism and Abstraction he worked from a model and from memory, attempting to render his experience of the existence of his subject. His 'Man Pointing' [6,96] shows the rough surface and long, slender form of much of his work. Even in his groups there is a sense of tension and isolation.

PABLO PICASSO (1881–1973)
(SEE ALSO UNDER PAINTING)

The Spaniard Pablo Picasso is better known as a painter, although he produced sculpture and ceramics throughout his life. He experimented widely with a range of styles and techniques. His early work was conventionally modelled and cast; but around 1914, when he was making collages in two dimensions, he began forming assemblies of found objects: wood, fabric and assorted scrap. He moved on to metal sculpture, often finding inspiration in the scrap items that he assembled. The 'Woman with Baby Carriage', [6,97] which is made from cake pans, terracotta, stove plate and a push chair, is witty and imaginative like much of his work. The 'Monkey and her Baby', [6,98] which is cast in bronze, also uses found elements in a creative way.

[6,96] 'Man Pointing', 1947, by Alberto Giacometti, bronze, 176.5 x 9.02 x 6.22 cm (Tate Gallery, London). Giacometti was Swiss-born but worked mostly in Paris where he evolved a very personal style in painting and sculpture.

[6,97] 'Woman with Baby Carriage', 1950, by Pablo Picasso, bronze, 79 x 57 x 26 in. approx, (assemblage of cake pans, terra-cotta, stove, plate and push chair). Picasso's use of found objects opened up a new avenue for creative sculptors.

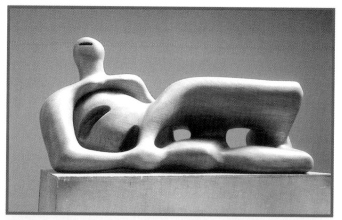

[6,99] 'Reclining Figure', 1945–6, by Henry Moore, elmwood, 191 cm long (Henry Moore Foundation). Moore's sympathy with his materials can clearly be seen in the way the grain of the wood forms part of the design of the sculpture.

Picasso did not exhibit much of his sculpture during his lifetime, but it has been gaining a reputation and may come to be more admired than his later painting.

HENRY MOORE (1898–1986)

The major English artist of the twentieth century, Henry Moore worked in wood, stone and bronze and also had a reputation for his drawings, particularly the studies he made of people in the bomb shelters during the Second World War. His work is always sensitive to his materials. When he worked in wood and stone, the grain and texture became part of the conception of the work.

[6,98] 'Monkey and her Baby', 1952, by Pablo Picasso, bronze, 53 cm tall (Musée Picasso, Paris). The toy car which makes up part of the baboon's head takes a moment to notice. Picasso's sharp observation saw possibilities in the most mundane objects.

The themes of a reclining figure and a mother and child recurred in his work throughout his life. [6,99] He used simplified forms to relate to natural objects like pebbles, bones and shells. Some of his work is more completely abstract, though the natural basis of the shapes is always evident.

AMERICAN INFLUENCE

After the Second World War New York became an artistic hothouse, having taken in many of the artists who fled the totalitarian regimes of pre-war Europe. English artists in particular looked to America for new modes of expression.

ANTHONY CARO (1921–)

Caro trained as an engineer before he studied sculpture in London. He was an assistant to Henry Moore for a few years, but his greatest influence was the American sculptor, David Smith (1906–65), whom he met in 1959. Following Smith's example, he created sculpture from prefabricated elements such as I-beams, metal tubing, steel plates and machine parts. These are welded together to create a movement or an atmosphere which he accentuates by painting the finished work in bold colours.

Caro is credited with being the first sculptor not to use a pedestal or base. The sculpture simply lies on the ground where the spectator can move around it, sharing the same space. It was from the tradition of heavy industry in England and America that this impulse to create art from industrial scrap evolved. The sculpture is not supposed to look like a machine; the industrial scrap is just the 'stuff' from which the work is made. [6,100]

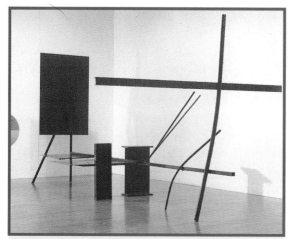

[6,100] 'Early One Morning', 1962, by Anthony Caro, acrylic sculpture on metal supports, 290 x 620 x 335 cm (Tate Gallery, London). Caro's sculptures are designed to sit on the ground where the viewer can interact more closely with the work.

[6,102] 'Il Opening of Umbrellas off Gorman Post Road', by Christo Javacheff. Christo's drawings and photographs record the progress of his temporary works, which are designed to make us reflect on our environment

CONCEPTUAL ART

The breaking of the boundaries of sculpture on a pedestal began a quick succession of expansions of the notion of what sculpture is. Minimalists tried to condense meaning into the simplest forms, usually geometric shapes which were part of a larger logic that the spectator might contemplate. In a way Minimalism was the first conceptual art where the idea was merely suggested by the object on exhibition and the spectator had to contemplate a meaning beyond it.

Conceptual art has been a major movement since the 1960s, taking many diverse forms, from performance and transitory events to sound and video recordings. Photographs or 'drawings' can be part of a record of the activity of the artist.

JOSEPH BEUYS (1921–86)

Joseph Beuys was a leader of the avant-garde. In the 1970s and 1980s much of his work took the form of lectures and performance. He became a cult figure, a sort of art guru, which allowed him to discuss his philosophy of art without any art objects to show. [6,101]

LAND ART

'Land art' was another way of going beyond the confines of gallery and conventional media. In the 1950s Christo Javacheff (1935–), a Bulgarian-born American artist, began using lengths of plastic or fabric to wrap objects like shopping trolleys and progressed to larger and larger forms until he was wrapping parts of the Australian coastline. Wrapping objects, Christo said, drew attention to the underlying forms. The 'Il Opening of Umbrellas off Gorman Post Road' [6,102], drew attention to the form of the landscape, and the effect of light and weather on the fabric of the umbrellas. Richard Long (1945–) is another land artist who records his 'drawings' on the landscape in photographs. He has walked barren landscape in many parts of the world where simple arrangements of the local materials recorded his journey. [6,103]

[6,103] 'A Circle in Ireland', 1975, by Richard Long, arrangement of stones in the Burren, Co. Clare. Long's landscape 'drawings' make a comment on the history and nature of the landscape he is exploring.

[6,101] 'Plight', 1958–85, by Joseph Beuys, environmental sculpture with felt, piano, blackboard and thermometer (Anthony d'Offay Gallery, London). Beuys's experience of being kept warm with fat and felt by Tartar tribesmen when he was shot down during World War II is often alluded to in his performances and installations.

[6,104] 'Model for a Sculpture', 1979–80, by Georg Baselitz (b. 1938), limewood, 199.4 x 199 cm. Baselitz and his fellow post-Modern Expressionists painted and sculpted in more traditional materials, borrowing style and technique from all phases of the history of art.

POST-MODERNISM

In the 1970s and 1980s reactions emerged to the Modernist movement in sculpture. The American Duane Hanson (1925–76) made casts from live models and dressed the resulting sculptures in real clothes and jewellery. His figures are often of the old and neglected. In Germany and Italy a new Expressionist movement used traditional materials and borrowed from historical styles to produce figurative sculpture. [6,104]

Late twentieth-century, three-dimensional work demonstrates the artist's attempt to come to terms with a changed environment. Social, economic, environmental and technological changes have created a background against which it is more difficult to be seen and heard, and artists have been working alternately with and against the change. There are now so many alternative modes of expression for the three-dimensional artist that it can be difficult to find one that is relevant to both the artist and the public. [6,105]

[6,105] 'Untitled' (Lover Boy), 1990, by Felix Gonzales Torres (1957–96), blue paper, endless copies, ideal height 19.1 x 73.7 x 58.6 cm (Andrea Rosen Gallery, New York). Spectators can take a sheet from the pile which is constantly replenished. Each page is open to any possibility. The blue colour is open to interpretation — blue for a boy, sky blue . . .

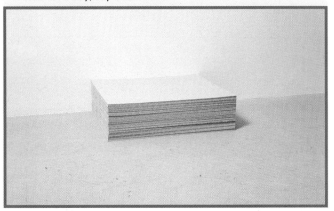

PAINTING BEFORE THE FIRST WORLD WAR

The pioneering work of Cézanne, van Gogh, Gauguin and the neo-Impressionists was seen in exhibitions and galleries in Europe and America in the first few years of the twentieth century. To the young artists who saw the work, it provided a new starting point from which to explore the possibilities of an art free from academic constraints. The years leading up to the First World War saw an explosion of new creative thinking, unparalleled since the Renaissance. The foundations had been kicked from under illusionist painting (where an impression of three dimensions is created on a two-dimensional surface). The art and culture of the world outside Europe and from before the Renaissance was seen to be as valid as the European painting tradition of the previous 300 years.

FAUVISM

The Fauves was a name given to a group of artists who first exhibited together in the Paris Salon d'Automne of 1905. The critic Vauxcelles, seeing a small bronze sculpture by Albert Marquet (1875–1947) in a Renaissance style in the same room as the brightly painted pictures, exclaimed 'Ah, Donatello au milieu des fauves' (Donatello among the wild beasts). It was neither a long-lived nor coherent association. There was no formal group or written manifesto, but simply a number of artists who had a feeling for colour as a mode of expression separate from reality. Pure colours could be used for emotional or decorative effects as in the work of van Gogh and Gauguin, or to describe space as in Cézanne's work.

The portrait of 'Madame Matisse: The Green Line' [6,106] by Matisse was one of the most controversial exhibits at the 1905 Salon. Not only the strange colouring but the deliberate crudeness of handling was criticised. It is an exercise in the use of colour for modelling. The warm tones of the face and dress contrast with the green background on the right-hand side and come forward in space from it, while the sharp yellow of the left side of the face also comes forward from the warm background on that side. Matisse shows that he can make a warm colour project from a cool background and at the same time

[6,106] 'Madame Matisse: The Green Line', 1905, by Henri Matisse, oil on canvas, 40.5 x 32.5 cm (Statens Museum, Copenhagen). The bold painting and colouring and the tight composition turn a simple portrait into a powerful work of art.

[6,107] 'The Pool of London', 1906, by André Derain, oil on canvas, 65.7 x 99 cm (Tate Gallery, London). Derain uses colour to emphasise shape and create space and drama in the composition rather than to describe what he saw.

make a cool colour project from a warm background. The green line down the middle of the face is the correct tone to connect the two different colours of the face.

André Derain (1880–1954), Raoul Dufy (1877–1953), Maurice Vlaminck (1876–1958), Braque and Rouault were among the major Fauves, most of whom went on to work in other styles later in their careers. Many of them began painting in a loose, divisionist style, but moved on to broader areas of colour in deliberately harsh contrasts.

Derain's 'The Pool of London' [6,107] is part of a series he painted along the Thames in London in powerful colours which are clearly divorced from reality. Fauve subjects were of the same type as those of the Impressionists — people and places of pictorial interest; they generally did not choose emotional or dramatic subject-matter.

HENRI MATISSE (1869–1954)
One of the major artists of the twentieth century and leader of the Fauves, Matisse soon moved on to develop a personal style that relied on pure colour and flat shape and pattern. 'La Danse' [6,108] of 1910 is reduced to areas of strong colour without brushwork or modelling. Sky, land and flesh are represented in single colours. The simplicity of line and shape was worked out in a series of preliminary sketches in which Matisse refined and simplified everything to a minimum.

This almost abstract style appears again in his later work; but during the 1920s he often used elements to express space and volume, though pattern and colour still predominate. Matisse said of his own work, 'What I dream of is an art of balance, of purity and serenity devoid of troubling or depressing subject-matter . . . like a mental soother, something like a good armchair in which to rest from physical fatigue.' This statement makes his work seem less serious and less carefully worked out than it really is. [6,109]

In his later years Matisse suffered from very poor health and was bedridden much of the time; but he continued to work, cutting out shapes in paper that had been painted in strong colours with gouache. 'The Creole Dancer' [6,110] is an amazingly joyful work for an old man in poor health. 'The paper cut-out allows me to draw in the colour,' he claimed, enabling him to produce work of simplicity and vigour as he had done all his life.

[6,108] 'La Danse', 1910, by Henri Matisse, oil on canvas, 258.5 x 390 cm (Hermitage, St Petersburg). Amazing vigour and rhythm are achieved in the primitive simplicity of this painting by Matisse.

[6,109] 'Odalisque Wearing Red Trousers', 1924, by Henri Matisse, oil on canvas (Orangerie, Paris). Matisse painted a series of Odalisques following visits to North Africa where the bright sunlight and colourful furnishings influenced his work.

[6,111] 'Five Women on the Street', 1913, by Ernst Ludwig Kirchner, oil on canvas, 120 x 90 cm (Museum Ludwig, Cologne). Kirchner often sets his figures in a vague background. The colours and shapes are used to focus our attention on the sharply drawn figures.

Matisse also produced sculptures, book illustrations and stage set designs for the ballet. He designed the complete decoration for the church of the Dominican convent in Vence, in the south of France, in gratitude for the care the nuns had taken of him during one of his illnesses. Priests' vestments, murals, stained glass and cross were all designed in his simple, calligraphic style.

EXPRESSIONISM

Expressionism is a term adopted to describe art that uses distortions and exaggerations in shape and/or colour to express the artist's emotions. It is used in this instance to refer particularly to a movement in German art which dominated from

[6,110] 'The Creole Dancer', 1950, by Henri Matisse, gouache collage, 210 x 120 cm (Musée Matisse, Nice). Matisse's later works use colour and shape in an abstract way in spite of the figurative elements.

about 1905 to 1930. The work of the post-Impressionists, the Norwegian Edvard Munch and the contemporary Fauves and Cubists contributed to a forceful and direct style, a style of protest and rebellion. The Expressionists experimented widely with media — many of them painted, sculpted, drew, made prints, wrote plays and music, as well as writing artistic criticism. It was the expression of ideas and emotions that counted, not artistic skill or external appearances.

DIE BRÜCKE

'Die Brücke' (The Bridge) was founded in Dresden in 1905 by a group of architectural students at the Dresden technical school. Ernst Ludwig Kirchner (1880–1938), Erich Heckel (1883–1970), Karl Schmidt-Rottluff (1884–1976) and Fritz Bleyl (1880–1966) were the founder members, while Emil Nolde (1867–1956), Max Pechstein (1881–1955) and Cornelius Kees van Dongen (1877–1968) had shorter associations with the group.

Ernst Ludwig Kirchner's 'Five Women on the Street' [6,111] shows how colour, brushwork and distortions of shape were used to create a harsh commentary on German city life. Besides painting in a forceful, almost violent style, the artists of Die Brücke also drew and made prints. Emil

[6,112] 'Prophet', 1912, by Emil Nolde, woodcut, 32 x 23 cm (National Gallery of Art, Washington DC). The artists of Die Brücke did much to popularise the print as an art form in the 20th century.

Nolde's woodcut 'Prophet' [6,112] makes use of the grain of the wood and rough, almost hacked cut marks to create the image. Crude but expressive handling of materials was a hallmark of their art. By 1913 the group was beginning to break up; their bridge to the future was short-lived.

DER BLAUE REITER

'Der Blaue Reiter' (The Blue Rider) was the title chosen for a yearbook which was being prepared by the Russian artist Vasily Kandinsky and the German Franz Marc during 1911. [6,113] When it was published it contained articles on art,

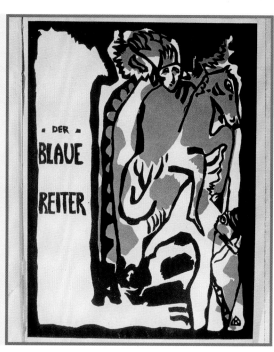

[6,113] 'Der Blaue Reiter', 1911, by Vasily Kandinsky, final design for the cover of the Almanac, ink and watercolour, 28 x 22 cm (Lenbachhaus, Munich). The Blaue Reiter Almanac had important essays on art and music and was illustrated with children's and primitive art as well as the work of contemporary French and German artists.

literature and music. They had a more analytical approach to art and wanted no divisions of the arts, as they felt the impulse to express emotions and ideas was beyond artificial boundaries. In one of his essays Kandinsky wrote, 'That is beautiful which is produced by internal necessity, which springs from the soul.' The artists who contributed to the *Blaue Reiter Almanac* organised two touring exhibitions which tried to show 'the variety of ways in which the artist's inner wishes manifest themselves'. International artists including Derain, Braque and Picasso were invited to exhibit with them and the work was seen in the major cities of Germany and in Moscow.

FRANZ MARC (1880–1916)

Franz Marc looked for a mystical relationship between colour and form in his paintings of animals. The 'Deer in the Forest II' [6,114] shows how he combined abstract shape and colour with simplified animal forms to create a world of harmony. The colour and movement of Futurist work had led him further away from realistic representation and his later paintings were abstract expressions of emotions and ideas revealed in titles like 'Struggling Forms'. He was called to military service in 1914 and died at Verdun in 1916.

OTHER ARTISTS

Other artists from the Blaue Reiter group, including Kandinsky, Paul Klee and Lyonel Feininger (1871–1956), went on to teach in the Bauhaus (see under Architecture), where artists of the avant-garde were valued for their intelligent and imaginative approach to problems of form and colour. We will look at them later.

GEORGES ROUAULT (1871–1958)

Georges Rouault was a French painter, graphic artist and designer who created a personal kind of Expressionism. He started as an apprentice in a stained glass workshop which influenced the strong outline surrounding fields of colour that we see in much of his work. He exhibited with the Fauves who were among his fellow students at the École des Beaux Arts in Paris, but his style developed along a different path.

[6,114] 'Deer in the Forest II', 1913–14, by Franz Marc, oil on canvas, 110.5 x 110 cm (Kunsthalle, Karlsruhe, Germany). The glowing colours and rhythmic geometry of Marc's work try to convey an ideal mystical world where all is in harmony.

[6,116] 'Cross Section 1920' (No. 68 in Ecce Homo) by Georg Grosz (British Museum, London). In the aftermath of World War I Germany was in turmoil. Grosz was a socialist and used his art to highlight social injustice.

Rouault was a religious man with a hatred of injustice and a strong feeling of sympathy for the downtrodden. His paintings of clowns, outcasts, prostitutes and judges as well as religious themes attempt to highlight the cruelty and hypocrisy of society. His 'Christ Mocked by Soldiers' [6,115] shows his mature style of impasto painting with strong outlines. The sombre mood is common in his work. Rouault was not only one of the major religious artists of the twentieth century, but he produced book illustrations, etchings, ceramics, designs for tapestry, stained glass and ballet sets.

CONCLUSION

Expressionism continued to expand outside Germany. The Austrians Egon Schiele (1890–1918) and Oskar Kokoschka (1886–1980) developed personal styles which expressed their emotional state in sometimes harsh and disturbing paintings. After the First World War Expressionism became a vehicle for protest against social injustice in Germany. Georg Grosz (1893–1959), Otto Dix (1891–1969) and Max Beckmann (1884–1950) were the leaders of the group which was banned by the Nazis as degenerate artists. [6,116]

CUBISM

The two leading artists of the Cubist movement, Pablo Picasso and Georges Braque (1882–1963), worked together from the time they were introduced in about 1907 to just before the First World War. In this short time they explored ideas and methods of creating art which were highly influential in the twentieth century. The initial influence was African art, particularly masks, and the later paintings of Cézanne.

[6,115] 'Christ Mocked by Soldiers', 1932, by Georges Rouault, oil on canvas, 92 x 72 cm (Museum of Modern Art, New York). Rouault's religious beliefs were central to his art. His concern about injustice was an important theme in his work.

[6,117] 'Les Demoiselles d'Avignon', 1907, by Pablo Picasso, oil on canvas, 244 x 234 cm (Museum of Modern Art, New York). The harsh drama of this painting prefigures Picasso's later style rather than the years of experiment in Cubism that followed it.

[6,118] 'Still Life with a Violin and a Pitcher', 1909–10, by Georges Braque, oil on canvas, 117 x 74 cm (Öffentliche Kunstsammlung, Basel, Switzerland). The muted colours of early Cubist paintings kept the focus on form. The sense of space might have been altered by the addition of colour.

Picasso's 'Les Demoiselles d'Avignon' [6,117] is often cited as the first Cubist painting. The influence of African masks is clear in the two faces on the right, while the faceted surface of the background has elements of Cézanne's approach. The female figures probably relate to Etruscan art, which was also an interest of Picasso's. With Braque, Picasso set about developing a new way of representing reality which did not depend on the European tradition of the single viewpoint or the illusion of a single moment in time.

The first phase of their explorations is called Analytical Cubism. They began with a limited palette of earth colours and also the colour blue which they eventually reduced to a range of warm greys. They tried to represent figures, landscape and still life as they might be seen from a number of different viewpoints, or as a person might notice different characteristics at different times. The Cubists did not follow a strict system but liked to encompass everything that might be useful in producing a work of art.

Braque's 'Still Life with a Violin and a Pitcher', [6,118] painted in 1909–10, can still be read quite easily. The violin, or its parts at least, and the pitcher can be found among the tightly painted planes of the surface. There is still a hint of conventional perspective in the description of space. Picasso's 'Daniel-Henry Kahnweiler', [6,119] painted later in 1910, went a step further. The two-dimensional surface of the canvas is hardly disturbed by the planes of Kahnweiler's face.

In the following year the paintings of both Braque and Picasso were almost completely abstract. A series of lines, marks and tones were applied in a painterly way to a flat surface.

Having achieved this freedom from the description of reality, Picasso and Braque moved on to the second phase of their development which has been called Synthetic Cubism. Both artists had been using materials such as sand, sawdust, plaster, metal filings and even ash mixed

[6,119] 'Daniel-Henry Kahnweiler', 1910, by Pablo Picasso, oil on canvas, 110 x 73 cm (Art Institute of Chicago). The image of the sitter is only just discernible. The interlocking planes of the surface have almost swallowed the subject.

[6,120] 'Collage 1913', by Pablo Picasso, collage, 45 x 48 cm (National Gallery of Ireland, Dublin). The word 'collage' comes from the French 'coller', to paste, which describes the process used to make many of the Cubist images of this time.

[6,122] 'Fantômas', 1915, by Juan Gris, oil on canvas, 60 x 73 cm (National Gallery of Art, Washington DC). The title 'Fantômas' is more than the name of the book on the table: it describes the way Gris has overlaid line, colour and texture to create illusions of transparent and changing objects.

with their paints to create surface texture. Then Braque added woodgrain effects and Picasso introduced letters and numbers. Eventually they began to stick objects to the surface of the paintings — tickets, pieces of newspaper, printed images — which were 'real objects' and not representations. Picasso's 'Collage 1913', [6,120] which includes part of a newspaper dated 1913, suggests angles of view and perspectives and then denies these perceptions by overlapping them with lines and shapes which suggest different viewpoints. Braque's 'Young Girl with Guitar' [6,121] from the same year includes parts of newspapers and woodgrain which have been painted in imitation of collage. There is frequently a light-hearted feel to some of these paintings, as if the artists were playing visual games with the viewer.

JUAN GRIS (1887–1927)

The Spanish painter Juan Gris was fully active with Picasso and Braque in this Synthetic phase of Cubism. He was the only member of the wider Cubist group to play such a close part in the development of the style. His painting 'Fantômas' [6,122] makes the reader question reality with its contradictions between line, shape, colour and texture. The subject-matter of the painting — objects that might be found on a café table — is typical of the Synthetic phase, but the sophisticated, illusionist handling sets it apart from Picasso and Braque.

[6,121] 'Young Girl with Guitar', 1913, by Georges Braque, oil on canvas, 130 x 74 cm (Musée National d'Art Moderne, Centre Georges Pompidou, Paris). Repeated images of face and guitar are contrasted with patches of woodgrain and newspaper headlines which disrupt any sense of three-dimensional illusion.

[6,123] 'Soldiers Playing at Cards', 1916, by Fernard Léger, oil on canvas, 130 x 193 cm (Kröller-Müller Rijksmuseum, Netherlands). Léger's interest in the shapes of industry and the human condition separate him from other Cubists who were not interested in subject-matter in painting.

[6,124] 'The Old Guitarist', 1903, by Pablo Picasso, oil on panel, 123 x 83 cm (Art Institute of Chicago). Painted in Barcelona, this sad figure symbolises the struggle of life.

[6,125] 'Two Women Running on the Beach', 1922, by Pablo Picasso, gouache on plywood, 32.5 x 41.1 cm (Musée Picasso, Paris). The bold sculptural qualities and classical dress of these figures are frequently used by Picasso in paintings, drawings and etchings from the 1920s to the end of his life.

FERNARD LÉGER (1881–1955)

Fernard Léger combined an interest in industry and machinery with Cubist ideas to produce paintings like 'Soldiers Playing at Cards' [6,123] in which the figures are created from metallic-looking cylinders and all the surfaces are fractured into geometric fragments. Léger's work frequently has a social message unlike the early work of Braque or Picasso. Man is often portrayed in his work as a component of industry or the war machine. The interaction of man with the urban and industrial environment was a recurring theme in his work.

PABLO PICASSO (1881–1973)

A child prodigy, son of an art teacher/painter, Picasso mastered painting and drawing skills as a child and graduated from art college while still a teenager. Born in Malaga, he attended college in Barcelona and Madrid, absorbing influences from old masters and modern painters. He was a member of the avant-garde in Barcelona before moving to Paris in 1904. This was his 'blue period' when he painted melancholy scenes concerning the difficulties of life for ordinary people. 'The Old Guitarist' [6,124] shows this style with hints of El Greco's elongated figures, the blue colouring adding to the sense of despair.

In Paris an interest in primitive art, particularly African masks, drew Picasso away from the European tradition of image making to the freedom of ritual art which lay in the realm of symbols and magic. This notion of the artist as maker of magic symbols occurs frequently throughout his career. We have seen the effect of African art and his meeting with Braque on his work, so we will now move to the end of the First World War when he went to Italy to design sets for Diaghilev's Ballet Russe, which was performing in Rome.

Picasso's contact with classical art added another element to his range of work. While he continued to paint and sculpt in the Synthetic Cubist style, he also made drawings, etchings and paintings in a modified classical style. 'Two Women Running on the Beach', [6,125] painted in 1922, provides an amazing contrast with 'Three Dancers' [6,126] with its Abstract, Surreal and Expressionist elements. These two styles existed alongside each other throughout Picasso's career and he chose whichever mode suited his needs at any particular moment.

The bombing of the town of Guernica by the Fascists during the Spanish Civil War prompted Picasso to paint 'Guernica', one of the greatest expressions of the horrors of war. [6,127] Considered by many to be his masterpiece, it combines symbols and allegories in an almost colourless composition of figures and shapes which describe the destruction and anguish of war.

[6,126] 'Three Dancers', 1952, by Pablo Picasso, oil on canvas, 215 x 142 cm (Tate Gallery, London). The primitive ritual painted in flat-coloured areas has a surreal and expressive power which frequently surfaces in Picasso's work.

[6,128] 'A Girl Running on the Balcony', 1912, by Giacomo Balla, oil on canvas, 128 x 128 cm (Galleria d'Arte Moderna, Milan). Futurist representations of dynamic action in their early paintings moved on to more abstract concepts in later work.

After the Second World War Picasso moved to the south of France where he continued to work, choosing the medium and technique he thought appropriate. 'If the subjects I have wanted to express have suggested different ways of expression, I haven't hesitated to adopt them,' he declared. He painted, sculpted, drew, etched and produced lino prints, illustrations and ceramics in great numbers until his death.

Cubist development ended after the First World War, but it proved to be an immensely adaptable source for many of the movements that followed, including Futurism and Abstract art.

FUTURISM

A Futurist manifesto was published by the Italian poet Filippo Marinetti in 1909 in which he declared that all the arts were to be harnessed to break with the past and glorify the modern world of industry, speed and violent action.

The artists Boccioni, Carlo Carrà (1881–1966), Luigi Russolo (1885–1947), Giacomo Balla (1871–1958) and Gino Severini (1883–1966) joined the movement and produced Futurist manifestos on painting and sculpture. Initially they used divisionist colour and technique to express action, but having seen early Cubist work on a group trip to Paris in 1911 they incorporated the crystalline surface of that style into paintings of the city environment and action. [6,128]

An exhibition of Futurist paintings which toured Europe in 1912 was highly influential in the development of European art. Several artists in France and Russia adopted the style and the Dadaists used the Futurists' approach to publicity and street protest. [6,129]

[6,127] 'Guernica', 1937, by Pablo Picasso, oil on canvas, 356 x 782 cm (Reina Sofia Museum, Madrid). This painting is an expression of the horror Picasso felt at the destruction of the Basque town of Guernica during the Spanish Civil War.

[6,129] 'Funeral of the Anarchist Galli', 1911–12, by Carlo Carrà, oil on canvas, 198.7 x 259.1 cm (Museum of Modern Art, New York). Galli's funeral turned into a riot. The flailing arms and legs are represented by repeated images which, with the colour, give a sensation of violent action.

INTERNATIONAL SCHOOL OF PARIS

The creative energy that was generated in Paris in the early years of the century attracted artists from all over the world, some of whom did not fit readily into any of the movements that were current in the city.

AMEDEO MODIGLIANI (1884–1920)

A painter, sculptor and draughtsman from Italy, Modigliani arrived in Paris in about 1906. He worked in a very narrow field of interest. His sculptures are all portraits or nudes. He was influenced by the Fauves, Cézanne and the sculptor Brancusi, but much of his elegant use of line and elongated features must refer back to his studies of Renaissance artists, particularly Botticelli. [6,130]

MARC CHAGALL (1889–1985)

Chagall arrived in Paris in about 1910 and mixed with the avant-garde artists and writers. The imagery in his work is based on Jewish folklore from his native Russia and from the Bible. His use of space and colour comes from contact with Cubism and the other advanced movements of the time, but his style is unique. Chagall worked in Germany and Russia and spent the years of the Second World War in America, where he had an important retrospective exhibition. He returned to France for the remainder of his life and produced paintings, book illustrations, stained glass and stage sets. [6,131]

ART BETWEEN THE WARS
THE DEVELOPMENT OF ABSTRACT ART

Abstract art is a term used to describe twentieth-century work in which the traditional European concept of art as imitation of nature has been abandoned. Abstract paintings do not represent any recognisable objects. Artists most frequently arrived at abstraction through one of two basic routes: the reduction of natural forms and appearances to extreme simplification; or the development of work from non-representational basic forms, like geometry.

Kandinsky is usually credited with having produced the first abstract picture around 1910 and Delaunay and other Cubists in Paris arrived at abstraction about 1913. At this time Malevich was producing suprematist compositions in Russia and in 1917 Mondrian and the *De Stijl* group produced abstractions in the Netherlands.

[6,130] 'Gypsy Woman with Baby', by Amedeo Modigliani, oil on canvas (National Gallery of Art, Washington DC). There is a sadness in much of Modigliani's work which probably reflects his problematic life.

[6,131] 'I and the Village', 1911, by Marc Chagall, oil on canvas, 192.5 x 151 cm (Museum of Modern Art, New York). Chagall's childhood memories are collected in dreamlike images independent of time and space.

[6,132] 'Composition No. 4', 1911, by Vasily Kandinsky, oil on canvas, 200 x 275 cm (Kunstammlung Norsheim West, Germany). Some traces of figures in landscape still exist in these early nonrepresentational paintings.

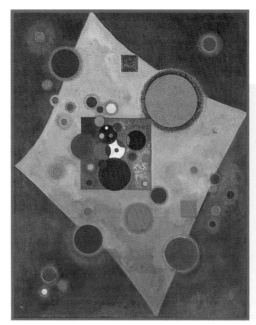

[6,133] 'Accent in Pink', 1926, by Vasily Kandinsky, oil on canvas, 101 x 81 cm (Musée National d'Art Moderne, Centre Georges Pompidou, Paris). Kandinsky often used dark grounds, which allowed him to emphasise light and colour. This is a painting completely free of subject-matter. The free-floating geometric shapes are nothing but themselves, harmonies in shape and colour.

VASILY KANDINSKY (1866–1944)

Born in Russia, Kandinsky was a painter, printmaker and art theorist. He gave up a legal career after seeing one of Monet's haystack paintings in an Impressionist exhibition in Moscow, which showed him that painting was about something more than subject-matter. He trained in Munich and encouraged an interest in French avant-garde painting in his fellow students. He was involved in the Blaue Reiter almanac and exhibitions and produced an essay on 'The Spiritual in Art' which provided a theoretical basis for abstract painting. He felt that art could be like music, free from the representation of reality, and he used musical terminology to describe his paintings, compositions, improvisations and impressions. [6,132]

By 1914 Kandinsky had evolved a completely abstract style in which line, colour and shape were used independently of each other and traces of subject-matter had almost disappeared. At the outbreak of the First World War he moved back to Russia and became involved in the reorganisation of art education in the new Bolshevik state after the war. But he soon found himself out of sympathy with the idea that artists should produce propaganda and designs for industry and not paintings. He returned to Germany in 1921 and took up a teaching post in the Bauhaus, where he taught the foundation course based on an investigation of form.

His painting during these years was more formalised than his earlier, largely colour, experiments. The pamphlet *Point and Line to Plane*, which he produced in 1926, suggests ways of making compositions, building on the tensions created within each form. His 'Accent in Pink' [6,133] from the same year shows how Kandinsky put this theory into practice. The influence of the younger Russian artist Malevich is evident, though Kandinsky's feeling for colour and paint takes the work beyond simple geometry.

When the Nazis closed the Bauhaus in 1933 Kandinsky went to live in France where the work of Miró and Arp had an impact on him. Some of his later paintings have creature-like images, but these are a result of the process of developing his abstract forms and not a return to image making.

PAUL KLEE (1879–1940)

Klee was not really an abstract artist, though many of his concerns were with the abstract qualities of art. He does not logically fit into any particular group since his interests and experiments in art were so wide-ranging. He was, for a time, involved with the Blaue Reiter group and he taught at the Bauhaus with Kandinsky, which is why he is included here.

Klee is one of the key figures of twentieth-century art. He spent years developing ideas and absorbing influences. 'I want to be as newborn, knowing absolutely nothing about Europe, ignoring facts and fashions, to be almost primitive,' he declared. He meant this in a spiritual way, having a sincere approach to art.

[6,134] 'Ceramic-Erotic-Religious' (The Vessels of Aphrodite), 1921, by Paul Klee, watercolour and oil on paper mounted on cardboard, 45 x 30.5 cm (Kunstmuseum, Bern, Switzerland). We can see some Cubist elements in this painting which explores line and form. The title often has little artistic significance in Klee's work.

[6,135] 'Death and Fire', 1940, by Paul Klee, oil on canvas, 46 x 44 cm. Klee's ill-health at the end of his life made him preoccupied with darker forces, but the childlike simplicity of his approach to art is retained.

He did not want to be caught up in current trends or fashions. As difficult as it seems, he did retain this honesty of approach throughout his life, which is why he is difficult to categorise.

Born in Switzerland, he trained in Munich and spent the years before the First World War travelling and meeting other artists, as well as painting and writing. His time in the Bauhaus was very important because his teaching made him formalise his ideas and record them. His books, *On Modern Art* and *Pedagogical Sketchbook*, were highly influential in art education in the twentieth century. The painting 'Ceramic-Erotic-Religious' [6,134] shows how this apparently light-hearted subject-matter can co-exist with more serious concerns of form and composition.

Klee was expelled from Germany by the Nazis in 1933 and spent his remaining years in Switzerland. His later work is darker, dealing with basic elements and the forces of nature. His compositions often have more than one focus. The elements are overlaid or arranged in an unconventional way which makes the viewer regard them as separate events or images though they are within the same frame. [6,135]

ROBERT DELAUNAY (1885–1941)

A French Cubist, Delaunay developed a series of paintings of the Eiffel Tower seen over the rooftops from a window. [6,136] As the series progressed, the light refractions on the window became the subject, and the tower and rooftops lost their significance. This prompted Delaunay to experiment further, and early studies of sun and moon developed into completely abstract disc paintings. This route from Cubism into abstraction was followed by several other Paris Cubists including Frantisek Kupka (1871–1957) and Francis Picabia (1879–1953).

[6,136] 'Window', 1912–13, by Robert Delaunay, oil on canvas, 111 x 90 cm (Musée National d'Art Moderne, Centre Georges Pompidou, Paris). Delaunay's studies of the Eiffel Tower seen over rooftops culminated in studies of the light itself reflected on the glass of the window.

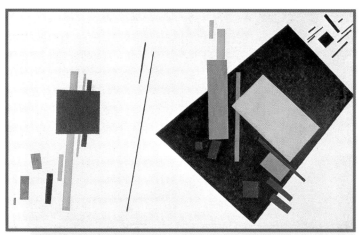

[6,137] 'Suprematist Composition', 1915, by Kasimir Malevich, oil on canvas (Stedelijk Museum, Amsterdam). Malevich hoped to suggest movement and depth of field through his arrangements of shapes and colours.

[6,138] 'Composition with Red, Yellow and Blue', 1921, by Piet Mondrian, oil on canvas, 103 x 100 cm (Tate Gallery, London). Mondrian's austere compositions in verticals and horizontals reduced harmonies to their most essential form.

KASIMIR MALEVICH (1878–1935)

Malevich was a Russian painter and designer who absorbed the lessons of Cubism and Futurism. He wrote a manifesto, *From Cubism to Suprematism*, published in 1915, in which he stated that representational art was a theft from nature and that paintings must be composed 'on the basis of weight, speed and the direction of movement'. The 'Suprematist Composition' of 1915 [6,137] illustrates this theory well. The colours and angles of the rectangles create a sense of space and movement.

About 1918 he produced a series of white-on-white paintings and concluded he could go no further in abstract painting. He was a very influential figure in Russian and German art. His theories were developed in the Bauhaus and had an effect on the development of architecture and industrial and graphic design.

PIET MONDRIAN (1872–1944)

A Dutch painter of great importance in the development of Abstract art, Mondrian had a conventional early career, becoming interested in contemporary art from about 1907. He moved to Paris in 1910 and painted in a Cubist style. His paintings of trees approach abstraction. He returned to the Netherlands during the First World War and continued to develop theories on Abstract art with Theo van Duesburg. He founded the periodical *De Stijl* in 1917 and became the leading exponent of a completely abstract style, based on verticals and horizontals, that he called

neo-Plasticism. He thought that modern art 'should find its expression in the abstraction of form and colour, that is to say, in the straight line and clearly defined primary colour'. On the strength of these theories he composed all his paintings in the following years of vertical and horizontal lines, with areas of primary colour and grey. [6,138]

He spent the years of the Second World War in London and New York, where the skyscrapers and jazz music made him transform his painting into some of his most lively compositions. [6,139] Mondrian's theories had an influence on architecture, the Bauhaus and on modern abstract painters.

DADAISM

Dadaism, which we have already seen under the heading of sculpture, was a complex international movement, essentially an attack on artistic and political traditions. Its very nature was anti-

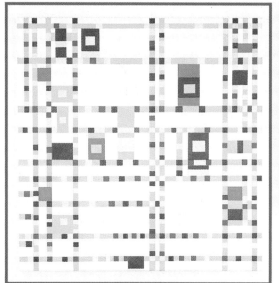

[6,139] 'Broadway Boogie Woogie', 1942–3, by Piet Mondrian, oil on canvas, 127 x 127 cm (Museum of Modern Art, New York). Skyscrapers and jazz were the inspiration for this abstract exercise in rhythm and colour.

painting, choosing instead collage which was often made of rubbish and photomontage and putting unlikely or ridiculous elements together into one image. Events were organised which combined the simultaneous reading of several poems, music made from noises and exhibitions of found objects. Dadaist performances often ended in noisy debate or fighting, which was in fact the kind of controversy they sought so as to draw attention to their theories on the need for change in art and society.

The French word Dada (hobby horse) was chosen at random from a dictionary as the name of the movement, partly for its nonsensical sound and also for its association with childhood freedom. Many artists were associated with Dadaism throughout Europe and the USA before it disbanded in the 1920s. Facts, reason and social order were shed in favour of imagination and randomness. This radical view of art and life was essential for the development of much of twentieth-century art — the Surrealism of the interwar period and the action painting, Pop Art, conceptual art and 'happenings' from the period after the Second World War. [6,140]

SURREALISM

Surrealism was a movement based on an alternative tradition to the Realist or classical styles that had come to the fore in the nineteenth century. It was an art of the imagination and of dreams. As a basis for their art, the Surrealists cited artists such as Bosch, Goya and Gauguin, primitive and naive art and twentieth-century manifestations such as cinema, detective novels and most especially the researches of Sigmund Freud as published in *The Interpretation of Dreams* in 1900. The Dadaist movement and some aspects of Cubism had also prompted an anti-rational approach to art.

There were two basic approaches to Surrealist painting. In one of these, 'automatism', the artist drew freely, automatically, allowing his or her hand to move over the work with a minimum of conscious control, using techniques like dribbling paint and making rubbings or scrapings, and then responding to these marks. Miró painted in this way. The other method was careful, realistic painting of scenes that made no rational sense. Dali and Magritte preferred this approach.

Surrealism was one of the most influential movements in the 1920s and 1930s. Large, dramatically publicised exhibitions, especially in London and New York in 1936, created an enormous impact. It provided an alternative to international abstract art which was often not as well received publicly.

JOAN MIRÓ (1893–1983)

Miró got his early training in his native Spain, but moved to Paris in 1919 where he spent much of his time. He experimented with Fauvism, Cubism and Dadaism before signing the Surrealist manifesto in 1924 and developing 'automatic' painting. 'The Birth of the World' [6,141] is in this style, combining a dribbled and rubbed

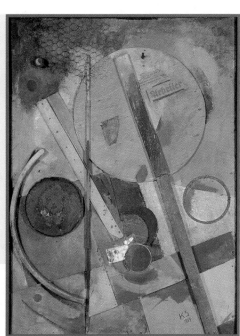

[6,140] 'Worker Picture', 1919, by Kurt Schwitters (1887–1948), collage, 125 x 91 cm (Statens Konstmuseum, Stockholm). Dadaist collages were often made by throwing odds and ends on the floor and then developing a composition from the chance or 'automatic' arrangement that was found.

[6,141] 'The Birth of the World', 1925, by Joan Miró, oil on canvas, 250.8 x 200 cm (Museum of Modern Art, New York). The title for this painting was provided by a poet friend of the artist who drew freely from his imagination to produce this and other 'dream' paintings.

[6,142] 'Uncertainty of the Poet', 1913, by Giorgio de Chirico, oil on canvas, 106 x 94 cm (Tate Gallery, London). The Metaphysical paintings of de Chirico with their disturbing dream imagery had a strong influence on Magritte and other Surrealists.

ground with 'figures' in black, white, red and yellow. Miró developed a series of private symbols of fertility and nature which he used in his paintings throughout his life. He produced a great range of abstract work in ceramics, sculpture, graphics, designs and painting with figurative suggestions which often have a playful atmosphere.

RENÉ MAGRITTE (1898–1967)

Born in Belgium, Magritte was a leading figure in the Surrealist movement. He was influenced by the work of Giorgio de Chirico (1888–1978) [6,142] and investigated the possibilities of illusion in painting. Each panel in 'On the Threshold of Liberty' [6,143] offers its own reality. Can we believe any of what we see? What

does it mean? Magritte poses these and other questions. The viewer is invited to play with the puzzle he creates — all is never what it seems. There are a number of recurring images in Magritte's paintings. A woman with a cloth over her face and a man in a bowler hat appear quite often, but they are never explained. The sense of mystery and illusion is strong in his work.

SALVADOR DALI (1904–89)

One of the best-known artists of the twentieth century through his self-publicity, Salvador Dali was born and trained in Spain. He developed a carefully executed realist style to produce his 'hand-painted dream photographs'. He painted nightmare pictures of his own neurotic fantasies, following the Surrealist belief in unflinching self-revelation. 'Soft Construction with Boiled Beans: Premonition of Civil War' [6,144] makes an interesting contrast with Picasso's 'Guernica'. Both artists were deeply affected by the Spanish Civil War though they supported opposite sides.

PAINTING SINCE THE SECOND WORLD WAR

Postwar Europe was going through a process of rebuilding. The harsh regimes that had suppressed modern painting were defeated; so it was expected that abstract and surreal art would develop anew. The major artists of the pre-war

[6,144] 'Soft Construction with Boiled Beans: Premonition of Civil War', 1936, by Salvador Dali, oil on canvas, 100 x 100 cm (Philadelphia Museum of Art). Dali's nightmare images are all the more horrible for the realism of the painting. The changes in scale and logic can be very disturbing.

[6,143] 'On the Threshold of Liberty' by René Magritte (Museum Boijmans van Beuningen, Rotterdam). Magritte's simplified rendering of surfaces offers a choice of realities to escape into. Will the gun go off if we choose the wrong one?

period continued to produce new and challenging work. Matisse, Magritte and others cast a long shadow over younger artists who struggled to find a mode of expression suited to the new age.

In the decade following the Second World War, New York became equal to Paris as a centre for avant-garde art. The European fine art tradition made it more difficult for artists in Paris to achieve the brashness and raw energy they saw in American paintings exhibited throughout Europe in the 1950s. Young English artists in particular began to look to New York as the new centre of development in modern art.

FIGURATIVE PAINTING

The tradition of figurative painting seems to continue through all phases of development in the history of art, and artists of talent and integrity are drawn to express their ideas through this mode of painting.

GRAHAM SUTHERLAND (1903–80)

In England Graham Sutherland developed an individual style with elements of Surrealism in landscape, portrait and religious painting. His beginnings as a graphic artist can be noted in the linear quality of his 'William Somerset Maugham' [6,145] which has overtones of caricature. His landscape paintings often evoke images of monsters in old rotten trees and other landscape elements, and use line and colour in a way more commonly seen in abstract art.

FRANCIS BACON (1909–92)

Francis Bacon became the most controversial painter in postwar Britain through his paintings of stunted and sinister figures in smudged and tortured paint, isolated in starkly coloured backgrounds. His 'Studies for a Crucifixion' and 'Popes' series highlight recurring themes in his work. The 1962 version of 'Three Studies for a Crucifixion' [6,146] shows an apparently dismembered body on a bed set in an ambiguous space, the smudged and vigorously applied paint of the figure contrasting with the plainness of the background. The viewer creates the gruesome scene in his or her own mind, based on the impact of the splashed paint and flowing line. Bacon faces us with our own fears and nightmares and our own mortality. [6,147]

ABSTRACT EXPRESSIONISM

Abstract Expressionism, sometimes called Free Abstraction, was the style more commonly practised by the younger artists following the war. It followed existentialist philosophy in believing that life must be spontaneous, and so representation or the ordered nature of geometric abstraction interfered with spontaneity. Abstract Expressionists wanted to speak directly through their media in a development of the automatism of the Surrealists. The gestural mark became an important element in their work and Oriental calligraphy was studied as a source of the kind of swift, expressive gesture they sought.

[6,145] 'William Somerset Maugham', 1949, by Graham Sutherland, oil on canvas, 137.2 x 63.5 cm (Tate Gallery, London). Sutherland painted a series of realistic portraits following the war which were a complete break from his surreal landscapes.

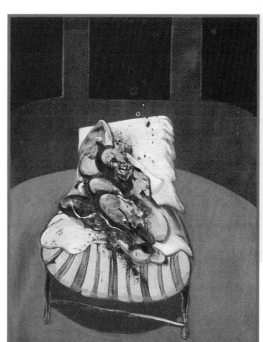

[6,146] 'Three Studies for a Crucifixion' (centre panel), 1962, by Francis Bacon, oil on canvas, 198.1 x 146.8 cm (Guggenheim Museum, New York). Bacon's handling of paint and surreal images make him one of the greatest 20th-century artists in Britain.

[6,147] 'Three Studies for a Crucifixion' (right panel), 1962, by Francis Bacon, oil on canvas, 198.1 x 146.8 cm (Guggenheim Museum, New York).

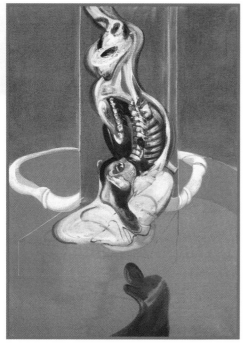

[6,149] 'Sacking and Red', 1954, by Alberto Burri, sacking, glue and plastic paint on canvas, 86 x 100 cm (Tate Gallery, London). Burri's experience as a wartime doctor is frequently seen in the blood and bandages imagery in his work.

HANS HARTUNG (1904–89) AND JACKSON POLLOCK (1912–56)

Hartung was a German-born French artist. He meditated before beginning his paintings so that he would be completely focused and his unconscious would suggest the marks and gestures he would make on the canvas. This method of working developed simultaneously in Europe and America, with the American 'action painter' Jackson Pollock taking the notion to its extreme. [6,148] Pollock was influenced by native American sand artists to place his canvas on the ground and walk around it, flicking and dripping paint, using sticks, brushes and other

tools and hand prints. A strange depth is developed in the resulting paintings, where line and colour become interchangeable. Painting in this way is as much a recording of an event as it is the creation of a work of art, and so it became a forerunner of some later conceptual art.

SURFACE QUALITIES

A natural development of the interest in the medium as part of the process of making art was the addition of textures into the surface. Artists in France, Spain and Italy experimented with surface qualities, scratching into thickened paint and adding materials to the work.

ALBERTO BURRI (1915–)

Burri, an Italian doctor during the Second World War, gave up medicine to become a full-time artist. His paintings incorporate sacking which is torn and patched, as well as areas of paint. He was one of the first artists to see the potential in waste material as an expressive element in art. [6,149]

JEAN DUBUFFET (1901–85)

Dubuffet was a French artist of unique vision. He took the non-art images of graffiti and the drawings of children and mental patients and used them as the graphic symbols in his own art. He also attempted to make it appear that the work had been carried out by someone completely untrained and 'that a weird logic had directed the painting of it'. He wanted to make a complete

[6,148] 'Cathedral', 1947, by Jackson Pollock, mixed media on canvas, enamel and aluminium paint, 179 x 89 cm (Dallas Museum of Art). Pollock's 'action paintings' were produced by dripping, splashing, flicking and applying paint directly from the tube. He used aluminium paint as well as artists' colours for its reflective and changing qualities. The paintings represent an outpouring of the artist's feelings directly onto the canvas.

[6,150] 'Body of a Woman', Château d'Etoupe, 1950, by Jean Dubuffet, oil on canvas, 114 x 87.5 cm (Allen Memorial Art Museum, Oberlin College, Ohio). Dubuffet sought the directness of completely untrained people in his art. The crude handling of materials was part of the force of the work.

break with good taste and beautiful technique. He referred to his own style as 'Art Brut'. [6,150] Dubuffet sometimes incorporated sand, plaster and other materials into the surface to increase the awkwardness of the task of creating the painting. He also created sculpture in scrap materials, continuing his explorations into no-art as an equally valid reality to art.

WILLEM DE KOONING (1904–97)

Born in Rotterdam, de Kooning mixed with a group of artists in Greenwich Village, developing his style into Abstract Expressionism in the 1950s. The paintings in his series of 'Women' [6,151] become increasingly violent and aggressive, executed in slashing brushstrokes and dramatic

[6,151] 'Woman II 1952', 1952–3, by Willem de Kooning, oil on canvas, 149.9 x 103.3 cm (Museum of Modern Art, New York). The wild freedom of de Kooning's painting almost smothers his subject-matter.

colours. For many, de Kooning represents the classic Abstract Expressionist, pouring his unconscious out onto the canvas in a series of dramatic symbols and expressive marks.

NEO-DADA

Neo-Dada is a term sometimes used to describe the work of a group of artists who objected to the purely aesthetic nature of Abstract Expressionism. Their work demonstrated the dominance of subject-matter or meaning over artistic gesture or process.

JASPER JOHNS (1930–)

The American artist Jasper Johns produced the painting 'Flag' which is part of a series of 'flags' and 'targets' painted from the mid-1950s on. [6,152] They are made by an elaborate process of soaking strips of rag or newspaper in encaustic paint (pigment in warm wax) and laying these out on cotton. Some areas are then painted in encaustic, leaving brushmarks. Johns's point was that this elaborate process was not noticed because of the strength of the subject of the painting. In other words, people were more affected by the *meaning* of a painting than they were by the *artistic process*, which is what Abstract Expressionism was about.

ROBERT RAUSCHENBERG (1925–)

The American Robert Rauschenberg made paintings which incorporated real objects: photographs, children's drawings, pieces of wallpaper. He combined these with brushmarks

[6,152] 'Flag', 1955, by Jasper Johns, encaustic, oil and collage on cotton, 107.3 x 153.8 cm (Museum of Modern Art, New York). Johns's paintings of 'flags' and 'targets' provide very simple, two-dimensional, abstract images which he creates by using elaborate, painterly methods.

[6,153] 'Small Rebus', 1956, by Robert Rauschenberg, combine painting, 88.9 x 116.8 cm (Museum of Contemporary Art, Los Angeles). A rebus is a word used by the psychiatrist Sigmund Freud for a dream which combines words and pictures.

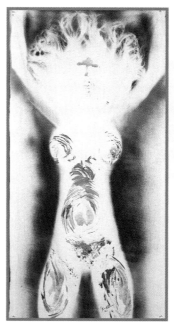

[6,154] 'Shroud' (Suaire), ANT-SU, 1962, by Yves Klein, mixed media and techniques, 138 x 75 cm (Statens Konstmusere, Stockholm). Klein's events where painted nudes were used to apply paint to canvas were the forerunners of a range of 'happenings' and conceptual art works from the 1960s on.

and blobs of paint. The assemblages represented 'the things that he had in mind' in the same way that the Abstract Expressionists described their inspiration. [6,153]

YVES KLEIN (1928–62)

In France, Yves Klein exhibited a bare white gallery and canvases painted in a smooth coat of Klein blue, and made paintings where nude bodies coated in paint were dragged or moved across the canvas. [6,154]

POP ART

Neo-Dadaism branched out into the 'happenings' of the 1960s and kinetic art as well as Pop and Op Art. It was the beginning of the process that took art beyond its traditional boundaries into film, video, photography and the written word. The answer to the question 'What is a work of art?' became open-ended.

Pop Art was a term coined by the English critic Lawrence Alloway to describe the range of art based on the images of popular culture and consumerism that flourished in England and the USA from the late 1950s to the 1970s. The collage 'Just what is it that makes today's homes so different, so appealing?' [6,155] was made by British painter Richard Hamilton (1922–) as a poster for the exhibition 'This is Tomorrow'. The picture acknowledges the strength and influence of advertising and cinema images on the

[6,155] 'Just what is it that makes today's homes so different, so appealing?', 1956, by Richard Hamilton, collage, 26 x 28.5 cm (Kunsthalle Tubingen, Germany). This send-up of commercial and media pressure on society was one of the first works of Pop Art.

consumer society and captures the intrusive nature of advertising on our daily lives. It uses the images of a body builder and a stripper amid the consumer goods and entertainment media of the late 1950s, pointing out the pressures on people to live out the advertiser's dream.

DAVID HOCKNEY (1937–)

Hockney, one of the best-known British painters and graphic artists of his generation, had early success with light-hearted paintings in the Pop Art style, though he does not accept the label himself. He spent much of his time in the 1960s in California, where the lifestyle encouraged him to produce his series of swimming pool paintings in a kind of hard-edge realism, more related to advertising design than to traditional painting. [6,156]

[6,156] 'Peter Getting out of Nick's Pool', 1966, by David Hockney, acrylic on canvas, 214 x 214 cm (Walker Art Gallery, Liverpool). Hockney's joy in the Californian lifestyle comes across in these quasi-realistic pool-side paintings.

[6,157] 'Marilyn', 1962, by Andy Warhol, silk screen on panels, 205 x 145 cm (Tate Gallery, London). One interpretation of the Marilyn series is that overexposure to media celebrity causes destruction. The cheaply reproduced, crudely printed images point out the distortions of the mass media.

ANDY WARHOL (C. 1928–87)

Andy Warhol produced paintings of rows of Campbell's soup cans, Coca-Cola bottles, Brillo boxes and faces of celebrities like Marilyn Monroe [6,157] and Elvis Presley. These were not carefully painted like Jasper Johns's 'flags', but screen printed with the colours badly registered. The point of reproducing these well-known products and people in large numbers was to point out the desensitising effect that familiarity through the media had on us. We could all recognise the Marilyn Monroe of movie promotions, but did she or anyone know who she really was any more?

Warhol and the other Pop Artists refused to differentiate between good and bad taste. They presented everything with equal conviction. His statement, 'In the future everybody will be world famous for fifteen minutes', predicts media hunger for new 'celebrities': lotto winners, accident victims, all will have their moment in the public eye because the media always need something new to feed on.

Other Pop Artists in the USA used comic book images and products of the consumer society as the subject-matter for their work which was often witty and gimmicky.

OP ART

Many of the illusions of Op Art — i.e. Optical Art, shortened to rhyme with Pop Art, of which it is a kind of offshoot — are based on images used in standard textbooks of perceptual psychology. They are usually painted with great precision to attain the correct retinal response.

VICTOR VASARELY (1908–97)

Born in Hungary, Vasarely moved to Paris in 1930 where he worked as a commercial artist until the 1940s. He then took up abstract painting. He was interested in creating hallucinatory impressions of space and movement, which he commercially printed in series as well as making one-off paintings. [6,158]

[6,158] Plate 2 from the Portfolio, 'Planetary Folklore', 1964, by Victor Vasarely, 62.7 x 60 cm (Museum of Modern Art, New York). The changing tone and colour within the grid pattern create a sense of depth and movement.

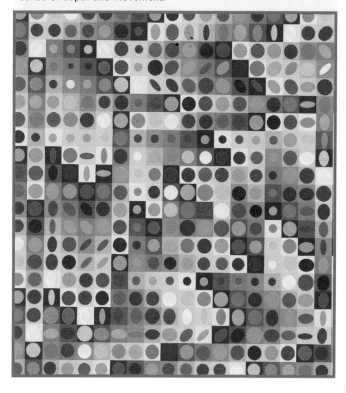

BRIDGET RILEY (1931–)

The leading English Op Artist, Bridget Riley is probably best known for her early black and white work which can create illusions of movement or vibration. [6,159] Her later work makes greater use of colour and relies less on purely retinal effects.

MINIMAL ART

Minimal Art, another movement which followed Abstract Expressionism, is sometime called 'post painterly abstraction', a more inclusive title. Its roots are in the geometric abstractions of Malevich and Mondrian and in the flag and target paintings of the contemporary Jasper Johns.

FRANK STELLA (1936–)

The American Frank Stella produced paintings by the simplest means, using household paint and brushes. He made compositions of the utmost simplicity, which were always the result of the external shape of the canvas and a simple mathematical division of it. [6,160]

His series of 'Black Paintings' which he exhibited in 1960 were followed by further stripe paintings in aluminium, copper and magenta paint. In the aluminium and copper paintings Stella used shaped supports to emphasise the fact that the pictures were objects themselves, not views of objects.

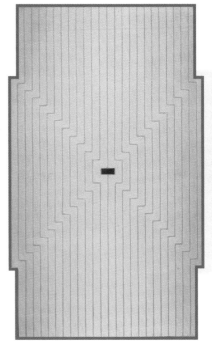

[6,160] 'Six Mile Bottom', 1960, by Frank Stella, aluminium paint on canvas, 300 x 182 cm (Tate Gallery, London). Stella made his paintings working from the outside in, painting each stripe freehand and leaving a small strip of canvas between each stripe. Technique did not matter to him, so small errors or changes in thickness of paint are left as part of the work.

ENGLAND

Minimal Art did not have a great impact outside the USA but some English artists worked with simple geometric forms, though a sense of perspective and depth is often present. Jeremy Moon's painting 'Blue Rose' [6,161] is an example of this modern abstract style which was the approved style into the 1970s.

POST-MODERNISM

Post-Modernism is an umbrella term used to describe the proliferation of styles, techniques and ideas which followed the abstraction of the 1970s. Some theorists would now deny a linear progression in late twentieth-century art history, preferring the notion of a multiplicity of attitudes and approaches all vying for attention. This freedom of approach has allowed artists to look anywhere for inspiration.

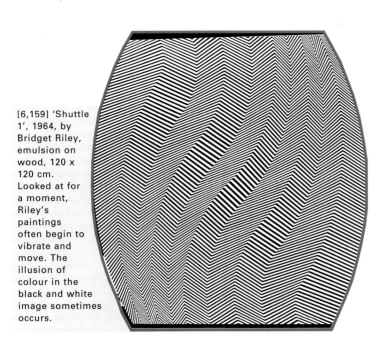

[6,159] 'Shuttle 1', 1964, by Bridget Riley, emulsion on wood, 120 x 120 cm. Looked at for a moment, Riley's paintings often begin to vibrate and move. The illusion of colour in the black and white image sometimes occurs.

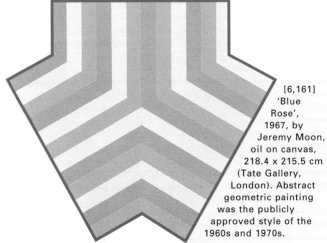

[6,161] 'Blue Rose', 1967, by Jeremy Moon, oil on canvas, 218.4 x 215.5 cm (Tate Gallery, London). Abstract geometric painting was the publicly approved style of the 1960s and 1970s.

[6,162] 'Grab des Unbekannten Malers', 1982, by Anslem Kiefer.

[6,163] 'Head', 1981, by Francesco Clemente, watercolour, 61 x 45.7 cm (Victoria and Albert Museum, London). Clemente uses a neo-Expressionist style to create paintings about everyday experiences.

NEO-EXPRESSIONISM

Neo-Expressionism emerged simultaneously in Italy, Germany, France, Britain, America, Denmark, Holland and Belgium during the late 1970s. It was also known as 'bad painting', which describes the crude workmanship often deliberately employed by the artists.

ANSELM KIEFER (1945–)

Kiefer, a German neo-Expressionist and pupil of Beuys, focused on the Nazi period to pose questions about German identity and nationhood. His paintings often include references to mythology and use symbols of transformation, like the straw in 'Grab des Unbekannten Malers' [6,162] which refers to the tale of Rumpelstiltskin who transformed straw into gold. For Kiefer this seems to be a metaphor for the artistic process.

FRANCESCO CLEMENTE (1952–) AND SANDRO CHIA (1946–)

The Italians Francesco Clemente and Sandro Chia returned to the traditional media of painting and sculpture and also borrowed images and ideas from various historical styles which they often combined randomly in their work. Clemente's work is mostly autobiographical. [6,163] He based his choice of medium and format on where the work was going to be exhibited. Chia's work is more a social commentary.

BORROWED IMAGES

Borrowed images also turn up in other forms of artistic expression. The American artist Barbra Kruger (1945–) uses photographically produced words and images to focus on feminist issues and the power of the commodity culture. [6,164] The

English performance artists Gilbert and George also use photographic images of themselves combined with background colours and images to create icons of twentieth-century living. [6,165] Their work crosses the boundaries of sculpture, performance and image making in a way that was more frequently seen in the 1980s and 1990s. The written word also appears as art object or art message. [6,166] Documents and slogans have been exhibited as works of art in a way that would have been incomprehensible at the beginning of the century.

[6,164] 'Your Gaze Hits the Side of my Face', 1981, by Barbra Kruger, photograph, 139.7 x 106.1 cm. Photographic images are frequently used by artists as an alternative way of presenting realities to traditional painting and drawing.

[6,165] 'We', 1983, by Gilbert and George, 242 x 202 cm, photopiece (Anthony d'Offay Gallery, London). Gilbert and George's work crosses all traditional boundaries of what a work of art is. They are the subject of their own performances and photographically produced images.

[6,166] 'The Great Bear', 1992, by Simon Patterson (b. 1967), lithograph print, 109 x 136.8 x 5 cm (Lisson Gallery, London). The placenames of London's underground are replaced with lists of football and television stars, comedians and philosophers to produce a map of society and its values.

[6,167] 'Untitled Installation', 1991, by Robert Gober (b. 1954), wood, wax, leather, fabric and human hair, 38.7 x 41.9 x 116.3 cm. Installations can be 'site-specific' or adaptable. In his multi-media works Gober points to the 'images of duplicity' with which we are often confronted.

CONCLUSION

The rate of change developed rapidly in the twentieth century. There was a revolution in transport and in communications, and art as part of communications also underwent revolutionary change. Art has always been a means by which society struggles for meaning, and in the twentieth century artists also struggled to find appropriate means to express the concerns of contemporary life. Art moved out of the galleries and museums and then back in again, in various phases of its development. Abstract and conceptual art were totally new forms which developed into the dominant forms of avant-garde art by the close of the century. [6,167] The art object gave way to the art idea, though the object did not lose its significance in the work of many artists.

IRISH ART

CHAPTER 7

PRE-CHRISTIAN IRELAND

THE STONE AGE: 7000–2000 B.C.

The first people to come to Ireland were hunter-fishers, who arrived in the north-east of the country about 7000 B.C. Little is known of these people, as only the limited archaeological remains of flint weapons and tools have been found. No artistic evidence has survived from this time.

By 3700 B.C. newcomers had brought a knowledge of agriculture from Eastern Europe through Britain. These farmers arrived on the east coast but soon spread westwards across the midlands. They brought seed and domestic animals with them and made polished stone axes to clear some of the forest which then covered the country.

[7,2] Reconstruction of court cairn, c. 3000 B.C.

This race was named Megalithic, after the large stones they used in the building of tombs. These tombs were of several types. The simplest were dolmens [7,1] which had two to seven large stones for legs, supporting one or two massive capstones. Court cairns were a more complex construction. [7,2] These had a rectangular burial chamber, sometimes divided with jambs and sills, which was entered through a semi-circular forecourt. There were several variations on this basic structure.

PASSAGE GRAVES

The most impressive tombs built by Megalithic man were passage graves. These were large tombs with side chambers around the perimeter of the main chamber, which was reached by a long passage of stones roofed with slabs or with a

[7,1] Dolmen, Kilcooley, Co. Donegal, c. 3000 B.C.

corbelled roof. This tomb and passage were covered with a huge mound of earth and stones, retained at the base by a kerb of large stones placed end to end.

Passage graves are the Megalithic tombs most interesting to the artist as they display the earliest known forms of art in Ireland. They are generally found on hilltops and are frequently grouped together in what are called passage grave cemeteries. There are well over 200 known passage graves in the country.

The Boyne valley is home to the best-known passage graves, which are grouped together in a big curving bend of the river. Knowth, Dowth and Newgrange are the largest tombs in the group. Situated on hilltops, each is visible from the top of the others. There are many small satellite tombs around them.

Newgrange is the single most impressive Megalithic tomb in Ireland, probably in Western Europe. [7,3] It was excavated in 1967 and then reinforced and partly reconstructed to give visitors an idea of how it might have looked when it was first built. A tall, white wall of quartz stones, bigger than a man's fist, reflects the light and can be seen for quite a distance. This wall stands on the largest kerbstones (3–4 metres long at the front of the tomb and 1.2 metres high). Many of these kerbstones were decorated by chip carving with a flint point driven by a atone hammer. It must have been slow, difficult work.

[7,4] Entrance at Newgrange showing entrance stone and roof box. The roof box over the doorway at Newgrange allows the sunlight to shine down the passageway into the central chamber at sunrise on the shortest day of the year, marking the Winter Solstice, the end of the old and the beginning of the new year.

The most famous of these ninety-seven stones is the one at the entrance which is richly carved with spirals and lozenges (diamond shapes). [7,4] A triple spiral appears on the left-hand side of this stone. Between this triple spiral and the end of the stone are three lozenges. A groove left of centre at the top of the stone marks the doorway. Right of the groove on the larger part of the stone are two double spirals, below which are two curves that follow through from the triple spiral. Near the end of the stone, spirals and curves give way to lozenges and zig-zag shapes. Kerbstone 52 [7,5] on the diametrically opposite side of the mound is also fully carved but does not have the same harmonious treatment as the entrance stone. Several other stones bear some carving but none so far discovered is as elaborate as the two mentioned.

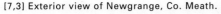

[7,3] Exterior view of Newgrange, Co. Meath.

[7,5] Kerbstone 52, Newgrange.

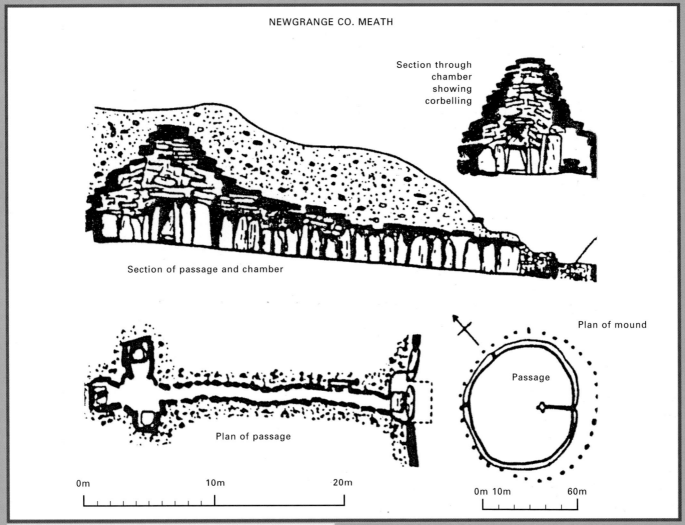

NEWGRANGE CO. MEATH

Section through chamber showing corbelling

Section of passage and chamber

Plan of passage

Plan of mound

Passage

0m   10m   20m

0m 10m   60m

[7,6] Plan and sections of Newgrange.

Outside the mound, which is 11–13 metres tall and 79–85 metres in diameter, there is a ring of standing stones of the same date as the tomb or later. It is an incomplete circle, with the largest stones near the entrance to the tomb. The significance of this circle remains a mystery.

Between the first and second roof slabs over the door is a box opening built in stone. The upper lintel stone of this opening is carved quite deeply with triangles that create a raised linear pattern of Xs separated by vertical lines. Through this small box on 21 December each year (the shortest day of the year) the rising sun shines down along the 18.7 metres long passage and across the chamber to the basin stone in the north recess of the tomb. This fact was only discovered after the excavation and repair of the tomb. Who knows what further secrets the designs and arrangements of stones still hold?

Inside the tomb the passage is constructed of standing stones capped with large stones near the entrance, then gradually raised by corbelling (flat stones are laid in a circle, each layer overlapping and oversailing the one below until they meet and can be capped by a single stone at the centre). Of the forty-three stones that make up the walls of the passage, fifteen are decorated and all have been dressed (the rough parts and corners removed by carving). Most of these carved stones have only small areas of decoration, mainly spirals, double spirals and chevrons (zig-zag lines one above the other in rows).

The central chamber, which is 3.6 metres from floor to capstone, has three side chambers which contain basin stones. [7,6] The central chamber and side chambers are made up of eighteen standing stones. All of those in the side chambers are decorated. Even the edges of some of the stones in the roof are decorated. The corbelled roof of this chamber was well constructed. It has stood for over 4,000 years, holding up the tons of earth and stone which make up the mound above it. During excavations, enough bone and ash for about five burials was found around the basin stones along with small chalk and steatite 'marbles' 2–3 cm in diameter. Hammer and baetyl-shaped pendants, a bone disc bead and bone chisel were also found. These are typical of objects found in passage grave burials. There was probably much more to be found but the tomb has been open to visitors for hundreds of years and it is, therefore, remarkable that so much has survived.

During excavations channels carved in the upper surfaces of the roof stones were discovered. These channels carried rainwater off into the mound and away from the tomb, and their success can be measured by the fact that the tomb is still remarkably dry inside.

Some items at Knowth deserve special notice. A decorated stone found near the entrance to one of the tombs has a semi-circle of radiating lines lightly carved, a maze-like circular pattern and other circular and rectangular patterns. [7,7] The overall effect is of a sundial or astronomer's instrument and is rather intriguing. There is also a basin stone which is carved into an open bowl shape and is decorated on the outside surface with a circle containing a pattern of curves and curved lines which follow the curve of the basin — quite a sophisticated piece for this early date. [7,8]

[7,7] Decorated stone found near the entrance to the second tomb at Knowth. This stone, which looks so much like a modern sundial, may have been used to calculate the movements of planets and record the seasons.

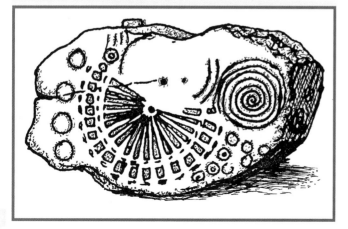

[7,8] Basin stone from niche at Knowth. This decorated basin stone may have held the ashes from cremations.

Megalithic art is almost exclusively abstract, consisting of spirals, circles, dots within circles, curves, zig-zags, lozenges and wavy parallel and radiating lines. The carving is well executed in many examples, but can be rough and crude. The designs are largely a mystery, with the symbolism lost in the mists of time. [7,9]

CONCLUSION

Other than the tombs and carvings, little has been found of Stone Age man's work. What pottery has been found is often of poor quality, though sometimes attractively decorated. [7,10] Other

[7,9] Designs used in Stone Age carving.

[7,10] Stone Age pottery.

[7,11] Stone axe heads.

[7,12] Stone beads and pendants.

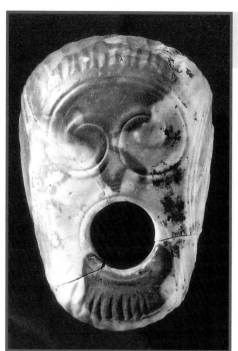

[7,13] Ceremonial macehead from eastern tomb at Knowth.

THE BRONZE AGE: 2000–500 B.C.

The arrival of the Bronze Age in Ireland seems to have been a gradual process. The people of the western part of the country, west Cork, Kerry, Limerick, Clare, Mayo and Donegal, retained many features of Megalithic culture while a new cultural group gained prominence in the east, north and midlands.

STONE CARVING

The western people continued to bury their dead in communal, wedge-shaped gallery graves, some of which may even have been built during the Bronze Age. These tombs were unadorned, but large standing stones have been found in Cos. Cork, Kerry and Donegal which are decorated with dots inside concentric circles, cup marks, cups inside circles, radial lines and maze-like patterns. A good example of this type of rock-scribing was found on a stone at Derrynablaha, Co. Kerry. [7,14] Parallels with these inscribed stones have been found in northern Spain. They are the only form of stone carving dating from the Bronze Age, though circles with no carving on the stones are comparatively common.

artifacts include stone axe heads and beads. [7,11], [7,12], [7,13] Little is known of the people's way of life. Their houses, of which only a few foundations have been found, were small, simple, round structures, probably with conical thatched roofs. They grew grains (seeds were found in the mound at Newgrange) and probably kept domestic animals, but we know nothing of their social structures or language.

[7,14] Stone with Bronze Age carving, Derrynablaha, Co. Kerry.

[7,16] Sun disc from Tedavent, Co. Monaghan.

METALWORK

As the name of the era suggests, it was the new metalwork technology practised most effectively by the Beaker people in the north-eastern part of the country that caught the attention and imagination of those with artistic talents. [7,15] Axe heads and Halberd blades decorated with incised geometric designs seem to have been exported to Britain, Germany and Denmark, suggesting that the Beaker people may have originated in, and maintained commercial contacts with, these areas.

When large-scale mining stripped Ireland of nearly all its superficial ore deposits in the nineteenth century, evidence was found of prehistoric mining by the Bronze Age people of

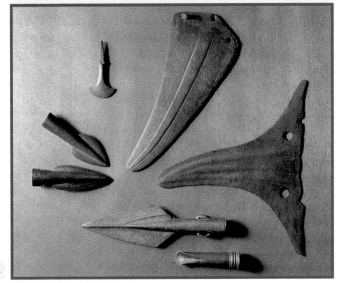

[7,15] Bronze Age metalwork. This selection of tools and weapons gives some idea of the skilled craftsmanship of Bronze Age people.

Ireland at nearly all the copper deposits. The Vale of Avoca had good quantities of copper and another important ore, gold. Gold was probably used to trade for tin from Cornwall, which, when mixed with native copper, produced the alloy, bronze. This richness in copper and gold gave Ireland a great trading advantage, of which the Irish seem to have made full use, as Irish bronze and gold objects are found in many parts of Western Europe.

The earliest form of gold ornaments found in Ireland are the so-called 'sun discs'. These were made from thin, flat gold sheets with simple geometric decoration, usually a cross beaten up from the back by use of the 'repoussé' technique, and were punched with two holes which probably allowed the discs to be attached to clothes or leather belts. A particularly fine pair was discovered at Tedavent, Co. Monaghan. [7,16]

The lunula [7,17] is the most commonly found gold object from the early Bronze Age. Crescent-shaped and made of flat gold sheet, lunulae were often plain but were sometimes decorated with simple geometric designs — parallel lines, zig-zags, hatched triangles and lozenges — which was incised into the surface, quite close in style to designs found on bronze axe heads. These lunulae were probably neck ornaments.

The Beaker people of the early Bronze Age also made beautiful pottery, food vessels which they put in their simple graves to give sustenance to the dead on their journey to the spirit world. [7,18] The style of decoration resembles that used

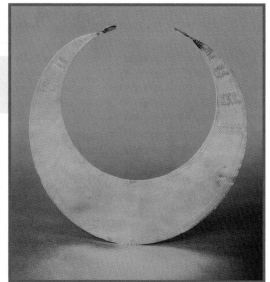

[7,17] Gold lunula from Mangerton, Co. Kerry.

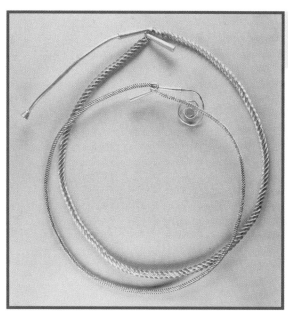

[7,19] Long torc found at Tara, Co. Meath.

[7,18] Bronze Age pottery.

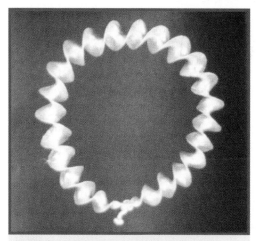

[7,20] Gold ribbon torc found near Belfast.

on bronze and gold objects of the same time, with surfaces textured with incised lines and dots, combined with raised lines and curves.

About 1400 B.C. a change seems to have come about in the country. Pottery was no longer included in burials and a different type of object was made. Trade then seems to have moved to the Scandinavian countries, probably because of the disturbed political climate in the Mediterranean. This period of development is called the 'Bishopsland Phase'. A new type of jewellery was produced. Bracelets, neck collars and earrings were all made of twisted gold. This type of work originated in Scandinavian countries where they were originally made of bronze. The twisting action required to make these objects gave them the name torc.

Irish torcs are made from a square, sectioned gold bar with v-shaped grooves taken out of each flat side, creating an x-shaped section which was then twisted. There are many examples of this

type of work in Ireland. A particularly fine, long torc was found at Tara. [7,19] It has a beautiful catch with a gold coil for decoration.

The ribbon torc seems to have been an Irish innovation. It was made from a flat tape of gold which was carefully twisted into a delicate spiral. A particularly good example of this type of torc was found near Belfast. [7,20] The ends of this ribbon were worked into rods finishing in knobs which locked together to close the neck ornament. These ribbon torcs seem to have been an important part of Irish gold manufacture for several hundred years.

Other types of gold jewellery were also made at this time. A pair of armbands found at Derrinaboy, Co. Offaly, shows that the 'repoussé' technique was still in use. [7,21]

195

[7,21] Armbands with repoussé decoration, Derrinaboy, Co. Offaly.

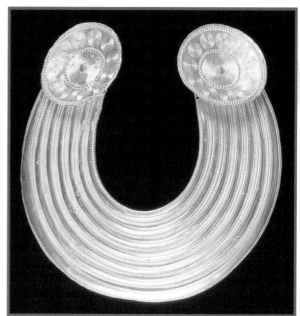

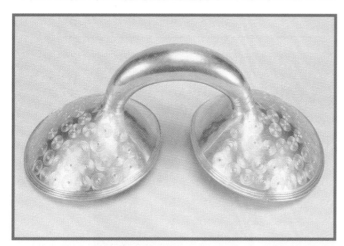

[7,22] Gold fibula found at Clones, Co. Monaghan.

A final phase of development, called the Dowris phase, occurred in the eighth to the sixth century B.C., Ireland's first 'Golden Age'. More gold artifacts have been found in treasure hoards in the counties around the Shannon estuary than in the rest of Western Europe. Items which were made in bronze in other countries were made in gold in Ireland. A good example of this is the fibula, a type of dress fastener with a cup-shaped disc at both ends connected by a heavy, gold bow. These came in a large variety of sizes, decorated and undecorated. Fibulae were made in bronze in most other countries. A beautiful example of a fibula was found in Clones, Co. Monaghan. [7,22] It has a large open cup, the back of which is decorated with rows of small concentric circles. The connection of the bow with the cup is decorated with incised triangles and bands of lines followed by another band of triangles.

Gorgets, semi-circular collars with a gold disc at each end, are perhaps the most beautifully made gold objects of the Bronze Age. There are several fine examples in the National Museum, the most famous of which is the Gleninsheen Gorget. [7,23] The crescent-shaped body of the collar is decorated with rows of 'repoussé' which are alternately smooth and cord patterned. The discs at each end have an outer row of bead pattern with a tiny cord pattern on both sides of it. This is followed by a row of finely incised concentric circles, another row of bead and string, rows of concentric circles, and finally a smooth cone standing up in the centre. The whole effect is dazzling. The circles and string patterns catch the light beautifully, creating a feeling of movement and dancing light.

Lock rings seem to be a uniquely Irish invention. They may have been hair ornaments. Structurally, they are the most advanced work of Irish goldsmiths during the Bronze Age. They are made of two cones of concentric gold wire rings, soldered end to end with one open side. When the openings of the rings were turned out of line, a plait could be held in place down the centre. Some of the gold wire of which these rings were made was very fine, sometimes five strands to the millimetre. The fine wire surface of the lock rings catches light in a very effective way. [7,24]

Late Bronze Age bronze objects that have come to light are also of a fine quality. Shields of sheet bronze have been found. One from Lough Gur, Co. Limerick, looks like a much enlarged version

[7,24] Lock rings.

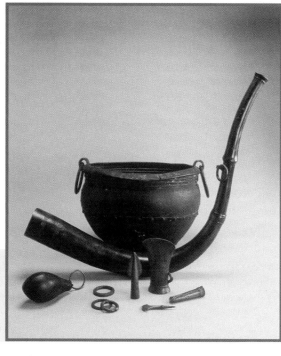

[7,25] Late Bronze Age objects. Cauldrons, trumpets and other tools and weapons.

The decorative elements of Bronze Age art are not closely related to Stone Age decorations. The spiral which will be seen again in the Iron Age was not an element in the Bronze Age. European influence seems to have provided much of the basic inspiration which was then elaborated upon by Irish craftsmen, with geometry as the basis for all decoration.

THE IRON AGE: 500 B.C.–A.D. 400

Iron work began in the Middle East about 1300 B.C. and gradually spread westwards over the following centuries. The Celtic peoples of Europe were using iron before the seventh century B.C. Knowledge of iron work arrived in Britain with the Hallstatt Celts by the sixth century B.C. Some vague influences of this immigration into England were found in Irish bronze weapons, but nothing substantial is known.

The establishment of iron as the superior metal for weapon and tool making must have destroyed the Irish export industry in bronze. There is evidence that Irish society had reached a low ebb by the fourth century B.C. with only subsistence farming being carried out.

In Switzerland in about 400 B.C. a new powerful group developed. The La Tène Celts were named after the site near Lake Neuchâtel where large quantities of their products were found. Luxury goods imported from Mediterranean countries brought these people in contact with classical art, which they adapted into a sinuous, abstract style of their own. By 300 B.C. some La Tène Celts were in Ireland. [7,26] It is unlikely that they met with much resistance from the poor native population.

of the end rings on the Gleninsheen Gorget. These shields were probably decorative as the bronze was too thin to stop a heavy blow.

Bronze trumpets of various sizes and types have also been found, all well made and finely finished. [7,25] It is not certain whether these trumpets sounded battle calls or were played for entertainment. Fine examples were found at Derrynane, Co. Kerry.

CONCLUSION

By the end of the Bronze Age, Ireland seems to have been divided into northern and southern communities as opposed to the east–west division of the early Bronze Age. This north–south division seems to have carried on into the Iron Age and into historic time.

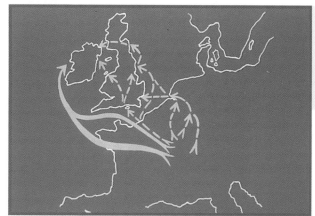

[7,26] Map of Europe showing spread of La Tène Celts.

These Celtic invaders seem to have been a warlike people because most of the artifacts found from the first few hundred years of their occupation were weapons or the neck collars known to have been worn by Celtic warriors who fought the Romans in Europe. [7,27]

It was probably these same conflicts with the Romans and the Germanic people of Europe that drove the Celts to the extreme west of Europe. The fact that they were left in peace here for the next 1,000 years allowed a distinctly Celtic society to develop, unparalleled elsewhere in the world.

BUILDING (ARCHITECTURE)

Much of our knowledge of the Stone and Bronze Ages is based on the tombs and burial rites of the time. Little is known of the burial rites or tombs of the Iron Age, but habitation sites and ring forts in earth and stone are common throughout the country. Some forts were built for defence, others for rituals and most of the smaller ones were simply homesteads. Ring forts were still in use in Ireland after the Norman invasion in the twelfth century. [7,28]

Crannógs (artificial islands built in shallow lakes) were a less common form of dwelling, but because they were man-made and less accessible they have often yielded many artifacts on excavation.

[7,28] Staigue Fort, Co. Kerry: an example of a ring fort.

SCULPTURE

A strange collection of sculptural objects in stone survives from the Iron Age. There are large boulders decorated with La Tène designs and a few small figure carvings, probably idols.

Large dressed stones have been found at Turoe, Co. Galway, [7,29] Castlestrange, Co. Roscommon, Killycluggin, Co. Cavan and Derry Keirghan, Co. Antrim. It is only possible to guess at the purpose of these stones. They may have been boundary markers or ritual sites. However, the style is La Tène and they are carved from native stone, which shows that by 50 B.C. craftsmen of some skill working in the La Tène style were resident in Ireland. Most of the stones are decorated with lines carved into the surface but the Turoe Stone is sculpted in low relief to a depth of about 3 cm.

[7,29] Turoe Stone, Co. Galway.

[7,27] Early Iron Age objects. This group of horse trappings, tools, weapons and ornaments is from the early Iron Age.

[7,29](a) Schematic drawing of carving on Turoe Stone.

[7,30] Triple head, Cornleck, Co. Cavan.

The pattern on the Turoe Stone takes the form of abstract leaf and vine shapes, trumpet ends and spirals, all flowing in a casual symmetry. [7,29](a) The design is in four segments. Two semi-circles take up most of the stone and between these are two smaller triangles of pattern which connect over the top of the stone. A triskele (three radiating trumpet curves) appears in one of the triangular segments. This flowing pattern takes up the domed top of the stone. A band of brick pattern forms a border between the top and the plain end of the stone.

A triple head from Cornleck, Co. Cavan, [7,30] a figure from Co. Armagh [7,31] and small stone figures from Boa Island, Co. Fermanagh [7,32] form another aspect of Iron Age stone carving. They are crude but vigorous carvings and may be idols or totem figures.

METALWORK

While iron was the preferred metal for tools and weapons, bronze was still used for decorative objects and domestic utensils. Gold was used for jewellery and status symbols. The techniques of repoussé and lines incised with tracers (chisel-type tools in a variety of shapes) were refined and developed.

A number of scabbard plates dating from the third to the first century B.C. were found in rivers and lakes in the north of Ireland, suggesting some sort

[7,31] Tandragee Idol, Co. Armagh (replica).

[7,32] Double figure, Boa Island, Co. Fermanagh.

199

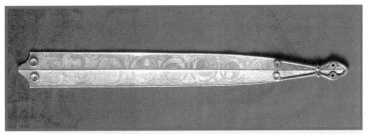

[7,33] Lisnacrogher Scabbard.

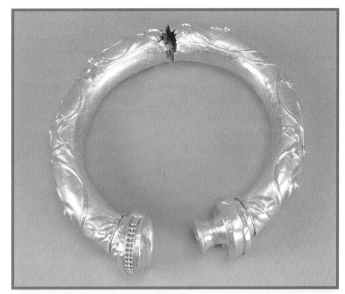

[7,35] Broighter Collar.

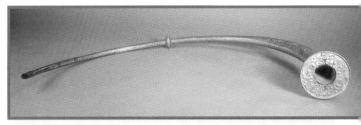

[7,36] Loughnashade Trumpet, showing bell end.

of ritual, maybe associated with the death of warriors. One scabbard plate found at Lisnacrogher Crannóg, Co. Antrim, has La Tène decorations on its flat surface which is carved with tracers in a flowing pattern of curves, spirals and trumpet ends. [7,33] The combination of line and texture swings left and right down the length of the scabbard plate, never becoming mechanical or merely repetitive. A cruder version of this style of scabbard plate was found near Coleraine in the River Bann; it may be a copy of an imported scabbard by a native craftsman. A sword hilt in the shape of a human figure found in the sea at Ballyshannon, Co. Donegal, is of a type common in Britain and France, and is probably an import. [7,34] It dates from the first century B.C.

The Broighter Collar, found in Co. Derry and dating from the first century B.C., is the finest piece made in this early (Insular La Tène) style so far discovered. [7,35] Leaf, spiral and trumpet end patterns are raised in high relief by the repoussé technique against a background of incised curves. The gold sheet was then formed into tubes and curved to form a collar. Separate spiral bosses are pinned to the surface to form part of the design. Drum-shaped terminals form a catch which was probably matched by another pair, now missing.

The last phase of the Iron Age, referred to as Ultimate La Tène, overlaps with the early Christian era. Designs become lighter and more symmetrical. The leaf shapes of Insular La Tène give way to more geometric shapes. The pelta (a linked pair of symmetrical spirals) is introduced from Roman work, bird heads appear and enamelling makes its first appearance.

The Loughnashade Trumpet, found in Co. Armagh and dating from the first century A.D., is made of two tubes of bronze sheet joined with a knob. [7,36] The decorated disc at the mouth of the trumpet has a four-part repeat pattern raised by the repoussé technique. Its design includes the pelta motif.

The Petrie Crown, dating from the first century A.D., an incomplete bronze decoration, has been called a crown, a tomb ornament and part of horse trappings. [7,37] It consists of a band of linked semi-circles decorated with spiral curves which have crested bird heads at their inner ends. The band is perforated along its top and bottom edges and could have been sewn on to cloth or leather. Fixed to the front of this band are two discs with central bosses, decorated with red

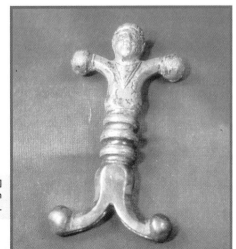

[7,34]
Ballyshannon
Sword Hilt.

[7,37] Petrie Crown.

enamel and a ring of pellets. A fine design has been incised into the surface of the discs. On the upper half of both discs spiral curves end in bird heads with eye sockets which once contained enamel. The lower parts of the discs are quite different, one having curves extending out from two triskeles, the other having a small cross in a circle contained in a crescent shape. The final part of the crown is a cone decorated with curves ending in crested bird heads, with sockets for enamel eyes.

CONCLUSION
The main elements of Irish Celtic art had been developed before the spread of Christianity to our shores. The combination of geometry and repetition, enlivened by animal and plant forms and other non-geometric elements, made a harmonious style full of little surprises.

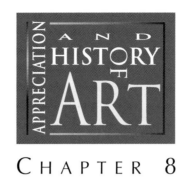

CHAPTER 8

THE CHRISTIAN CELTIC PERIOD

EARLY CHRISTIAN IRELAND: FIFTH AND SIXTH CENTURIES

Even before the arrival of St Patrick's mission to 'the believers in Christ in Ireland' in 432, there was evidence of small groups of Christians in the south-west of the country. Ogham writing (a crude transcription of Roman writing) is found on pillars in this area, mainly Christian burial markers.

When Pope Celestine sent St Patrick to Ireland with books and religious objects, mainly in the Roman style, he was accompanied by craftsmen who could continue this work. In Patrick's lifetime most of Ireland was converted to Christianity without martyrs or conflict with the pagan priesthood. Although the Christian community was formed into a series of bishoprics on the Roman model, Roman influence faded after the fall of their Empire. By about 500 the Roman system was superseded by a peculiarly Irish monastic system.

MONASTERIES (ARCHITECTURE)

St Enda founded a hermetic monastery on the Aran Islands and seems to have started the impetus for the development of the monastic system. It closely mirrored an Irish society that, instead of towns, had interlinked family homesteads under chieftains and petty kings. The new monastic system followed this order. The abbots of senior monasteries controlled several sub-monasteries, sometimes spread widely over the country and later overseas. These new powerful abbots often took over the title of bishop in their own area. Abbotships were passed on to members of the same family, following the Irish tradition of chieftains.

Monastic settlements were generally small in size and simple in structure — usually an enclosure of wood, earth or stone with huts and small chapels or oratories within. Most of these early settlements expanded or were built over in later years, but many examples remain. Among these is the well-preserved Skellig Michael, off the Kerry coast. [8,1] The stone huts and oratories were built by the corbelling technique, which had been used over 2,000 years earlier at Newgrange. Inishmurray, Co. Sligo, Illauntannig, Co. Kerry, Inishkeel, Co. Donegal and Nendrum, Co. Down, remain good examples of early monastic enclosures. These follow the model of secular

[8,1] Monastery on Skellig Michael, off Kerry coast, 6th–10th century.

[8,2] Gallarus Oratory, Co. Kerry.

Irish settlements of the Iron Age, some of which continued in use into the 1600s.

The plainness and simplicity of these monastic structures can be explained by the 'fierce asceticism' practised by the early monks. The life of St Columba written by Adamnan at the end of the seventh century gives an insight into the lives of the early monasteries, 'a mixture of pastoral work and copying sacred texts — a tenderness of heart'. The writings of St Columbanus in Gaul show the high quality of Irish letters and education at the time.

The buildings that survive from this time are primitive and quite small, though some of the corbelled oratories are thirty feet in diameter and eighteen feet high. The group of buildings on Skellig Michael off the Kerry coast, dating from anywhere from the sixth to the tenth century, displays both the round, beehive type and the rectangular, corbelled building found in the south-west and west of the country. Nearby, on the mainland, Gallarus Oratory is the most complete example of a rectangular, stone church built by the corbelling technique. [8,2] Made of small, carefully selected stones, its walls and roof curve inward, forming one continuous surface from ground to ridge. The doorway has inclined jambs with a plain lintel on top. The tiny east window has a rounded top made from two carved stones, not a true arch. Dates for the building of Gallarus vary from the seventh to the twelfth century.

An account of St Brigid's church at Kildare in the seventh century describes painted, wooden panels and coloured hangings. This, and probably the majority of early churches, was wooden, and so there are no physical remains; however, we can get some idea of how these churches might have looked from illustrations in the Book of Kells, shrines made in the shape of churches and the tops of High Crosses (for example, Muirideach's Cross at Monasterboice, Co. Louth: see [8,48], [8,49]). They appear to have been supported by a massive wooden frame with shingled or thatched roofs and walls of planks or of wattle and daub. Other evidence of how these wooden churches looked is a number of stone churches built in the same shape. The reconstructed church of St Macdara, Co. Galway copies wooden construction down to shingles carved in stone. [8,3] The antae which form extensions of the side walls projecting beyond the gable are relics of the corner posts of wooden buildings.

[8,3] Church of St Macdara, Co. Galway. This church was closely modelled on timber buildings which were common in the Early Christian period. The finials on the tops of the gables imitate the crossed ends of the barge-boards of a wooden roof.

[8,4] Ogham script.

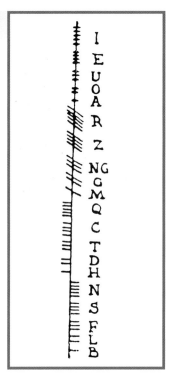

[8,5] Reask Pillar, Co. Kerry.

STONE CARVING

Stone slabs with incised decoration are often found near early monastic sites (some being said to mark the grave of the founder). The majority of these monuments are situated in the south-west and west of the country and sometimes have Ogham, Irish or Latin inscriptions. [8,4] The decoration can include Greek, Latin or Maltese crosses, sometimes in a circle, the Chi-Rho monogram, swastikas, simple knots, fretwork, spirals and curves. The Pillar at Reask, Co. Kerry, has a Maltese Cross in a circle with Celtic spirals below it and the letters DME inscribed on the left side (probably standing for the Latin 'Domine', meaning 'Lord'). [8,5]

Other slabs gradually developed into what is called the Celtic High Cross. The earlier stages of this development are to be found in the north-west of Ireland. Slabs at Dunvillaun and Inishkea North have interlace designs forming a cross on one side and a simple crucifix on the other. A slab at Fahan Mura shows a further development; a low relief ribbon interlace forms a cross on both sides with a figure on each side of the cross shaft on the west face. [8,6]

The Cross at Carndonagh, Co. Donegal, is carved on all sides into a simple, slightly uneven, cross shape. [8,7] One face has an interlace pattern all over, with the sides carved with figures and interlace. The second face has a ribbon interlace which forms a cross on the upper portion, with two groups of birds in triskeles under the arms. The shaft bears a large figure surrounded by four small ones (crucifixion with lance and sponge bearer and two angels, as on the Athlone Crucifixion Plaque: see [8,37]), with three more figures below. There are two small pillars beside the cross, carved on all sides. Subjects include David playing a harp, Jonah and the whale, ecclesiastics with bell and crosier — themes which recur on later crosses.

[8,6] Fahan Mura Slab.

[8,7] Carndonagh Cross, Co. Donegal.

[8,9] Capital from the Cathach — letter Q.

MANUSCRIPTS

It is known that St Patrick brought books and scribes with him on his mission to Ireland. These books were Latin texts of the Gospels and Psalms. Even the earliest Irish manuscripts bear decorations, so it seems likely that these also were decorated books. The Eastern influence (carpet pages, interlacing) is more difficult to explain. It may partly have come indirectly through Italy and Gaul (present-day France), but there is also evidence of direct contacts between Ireland and the monasteries of the Eastern Mediterranean which would help to explain the strength of Eastern influence in later Irish art. [8,8]

[8,8] Decorated page from a French manuscript of the 8th century. The Greek letters hanging from the cross show an Eastern Mediterranean influence.

St Columba (521–97) is credited with writing the Cathach, a mutilated sixth-century Psalter (copy of the Psalms), the oldest Irish manuscript known. The Battle of Cúil Dremhne in 561 was fought for possession of the book which was in dispute with St Finnian. Though Columba's side won, he banished himself to Iona in shame at the slaughter caused. Later the O'Donnells (Columba's clansmen) carried it into battle with them for protection; so the Cathach 'battler' got its name.

Each psalm begins with a capital letter executed in pen and embellished with red and yellow. [8,9] The majority of capitals are surrounded with red dotting, a technique probably of Coptic origin and not used elsewhere in Europe at the time. [8,10]

The letters are in majuscule: rounded capital letters with few letters ascending or descending above or below two ruled lines. Small leaf shapes are used to connect parts of the letters, with a few ending in animal heads. Interlace is not used, but all the elements of Ultimate La Tène design are present.

St Columbanus (c. 543–615) was an Irish missionary monk who established monasteries at Luxeuil in France, St Gall in Switzerland and Bobbio in Italy, where he died. The Ambrosian Library in Milan contains early manuscripts of Irish origin from Bobbio. These books are of

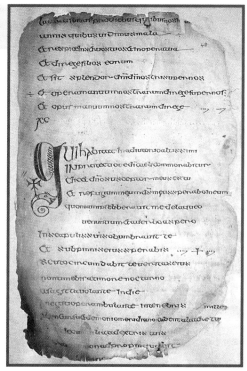

[8,10] Capital from the Cathach.

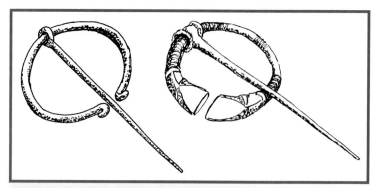

[8,11] Drawings of simple penannular brooches, 6th century.

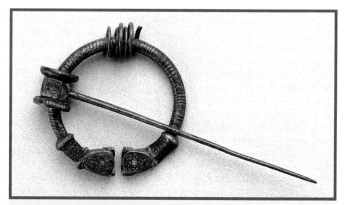

[8,12] Ballinderry Brooch, 6th century.

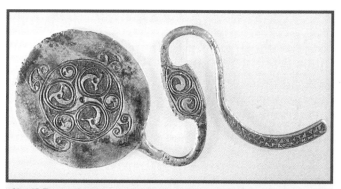

[8,13] Enamelled bronze latchet brooch with bird head design, 6th century.

better quality than the Cathach, using more colours and with fully decorated pages, with interlacing in the Coptic style. From these we can get some idea of the real quality of Irish manuscripts of the sixth century.

METALWORK

Many new designs and ideas were introduced into Ireland through metalwork. The influence of Rome brought new objects and methods of decoration from Gaul and Britain. Among the new objects were hand pins, penannular brooches, latchets and hanging bowls.

Of these, the penannular brooches might best show the kind of development that took place. [8,11] Beginning as simple, wire dress fasteners, the ends beside the opening of the ring of penannular brooches were bent back and the pin was fixed to the ring by a simple loop at its end. Later pins were cast in bronze or silver. The ends of the ring were cast in the shape of animal heads and the loop of the pin was widened to take decoration.

A brooch from Ballinderry Crannóg is a beautiful example of this style. [8,12] Later brooches became even more elaborate as we shall see.

New techniques emerged, probably through trade with Europe. Gold, wire filigree is found on a few small pieces dating back to the sixth century. A small, bird-shaped button was found in Lagore Crannóg, [8,13] where millefiori glass was also discovered in an enameller's workshop.

New designs which first appeared on High Crosses and in books also made their way into metalwork. The Ardakillin Brooch [8,14] has ribbon interlace as part of its design; the high relief patterns at each end have much in common with capitals from the Cathach.

[8,14] Ardakillin Brooch, 3rd–5th century. Note the similarity to the decorated capital of the Cathach. [8,9]

[8,15] Filigree bird from Lagore Crannóg, 6th century.

[8,16] Reconstruction of Kells.

These new designs and techniques were added to the repertoire of metalwork, casting and decoration which was already in use in Ireland, creating a great range of possibilities for the designer-craftsman. [8,15]

CONCLUSION

The Christian mission to Ireland brought with it new ideas which were incorporated into all the crafts. Further opportunities were created by the introduction of decorated books and the demand for beautiful metalwork and stone carving in the new, rapidly expanding monasteries. During the fifth and sixth centuries, technical skills and the repertoire of designs gradually increased to the point where all the elements needed for the explosion of creativity that happened in the seventh and eighth centuries were gathered together in the workshops of the larger monasteries.

HIGH CHRISTIAN IRELAND: SEVENTH AND EIGHTH CENTURIES

There was a huge growth in Irish monasteries during the seventh and eighth centuries, a period known as High Christian Ireland. The hermitages and places of retirement from the world developed into centres of learning and craftwork. Irish missionary activity in Britain and Europe allowed for a rich exchange of ideas, with Irish

monasteries emerging as the universities of Europe. Accounts of the day describe great monastic cities at Glendalough, Clonmacnoise, Kells and many other centres. [8,16]

MONASTERIES

There were few changes architecturally during this period. Churches were still plain buildings with flat-headed doorways and little decorative carving. Carved, wooden ridge-boards may have been a feature — there is evidence of this from house-shaped shrines of the day. When monasteries expanded, more small buildings were added, with enlarged enclosures surrounding them. High Crosses became a focal point. Accounts from Britain describe Irish missionary monks erecting large, wooden crosses and preaching before them. A schematic drawing from the Book of Mulling shows a circular enclosure with crosses outside: four at the cardinal points of the compass and four between these.

STONE CARVING

The decorated slabs and pillars of the sixth century developed in the seventh and eighth centuries in two ways. First, grave slabs became more decorative and were laid flat on the ground. Early Christian grave slabs from the sixth to the tenth century are found in many places, with fine examples in Clonmacnoise, Co. Offaly, [8,17] and Inis Cealteara, Co. Clare. The other line of development was standing crosses. By the eighth century the first, fully formed High Crosses had developed, featuring wheel head and pyramid-shaped base and cap. In south Kilkenny and south Tipperary a group of crosses can be found at Ahenny, Kilkieran, Killamery and Kilree. The closeness of their style to metalwork has often been commented upon.

[8,17] Decorated grave slab from Clonmacnoise, Co. Offaly, 7th–8th century.

[8,19] South Cross at Ahenny, Co. Tipperary — west face.

The Ahenny Crosses are the best examples of the group. The shafts, rings and arms of both crosses are covered in panels of curves, knotting, fretwork and spirals of very fine quality. There are bosses at the centre and, where the ring crosses the shafts and arms, these bosses have echoes in the studs used to hide rivets in metalwork. The North Cross, 3.5 metres high, has a tall base and a step at the bottom of the cross. [8,18] All four sides of the base are carved with human and animal figures. The west side has a funeral procession with a monk carrying a processional

[8,18] North Cross at Ahenny, Co. Tipperary — west face, including base.

cross with wheel head. This may be evidence of the roots of the High Cross in wood and metal crosses. The base of the South Cross, 3.35 metres high, is smaller and very weathered. [8,19] Each side is divided into two panels. The subjects include Adam and Eve, Daniel in the lion's den and various figure and animal scenes which are difficult to decipher.

Both crosses at Ahenny are outlined in a boldly carved rope border and are topped with conical caps which are not found elsewhere.

The Cross of Moone in Co. Kildare is a very different cross to these finely carved pieces. [8,20] Over 5 metres tall, its height is emphasised by the narrowness of the shaft and the smallness of the wheel head. It is set on a tall base which is carved in low relief with a series of illustrations of stories from the Old and New Testaments. [8,21] These stories demonstrate God's help given to his faithful followers throughout the ages. Many of the themes also carry other meanings, or allusions to prophecies from the Old Testament and to events in the life of Christ.

Françoise Henry suggests that the panels on the base should be read in sequence, starting on the top of the east side and moving clockwise round the cross. It begins with Adam and Eve under a stylised tree around which coils a serpent, 'Man's fall from grace'. Next is the sacrifice of Isaac, a

[8,20] Cross of Moone, Co. Kildare — west face.

[8,22] Cross of Moone, Co. Kildare — Flight into Egypt panel, south side of base.

[8,21] Cross of Moone, Co. Kildare — east base.

prefiguration of the crucifixion; then Daniel in the lion's den, also a prefiguration of the crucifixion and redemption. At the centre of the wheel head on this, the east side, is Christ in majesty, with huge hands outstretched in benediction.

The south side shows the three children (three Hebrews) in the furnace under a protecting angel. Below this are the flight into Egypt and an almost abstract portrayal of the miracle of the loaves and fishes, with five simple discs representing the loaves. [8,22]

The west side has the crucifixion in the top panel and the twelve apostles in the lower; they are represented as little armless rectangles with huge heads and conical feet in three rows. These little figures together make a strong geometric composition of subtle proportions and varied details.

The north side shows a bird giving bread to Saints Paul and Anthony the Hermit. This is an allusion to the Eucharist. The temptation of St Anthony by two bird-headed creatures fills the middle panel, with a many-headed monster at the bottom.

Most of the shaft and arms is decorated with panels of spirals and other abstract decorations, but the west face has five little square panels with animals in them, the significance of which is not clear.

The Cross of Moone is an important transition from the earlier cross type with mainly abstract decoration to the later figurative crosses. The themes developed on it recur on many crosses. Its style of carving still leans towards the abstract treatment current in all the crafts during the eighth century. Its panels are tightly filled, with hardly a centimetre of inactive space in the whole design.

MANUSCRIPTS

The Book of Durrow, now found in Trinity College Dublin, was associated with the Columban monastery of Durrow for centuries. [8,23] It is a

[8,23] St Mark, symbol page from the Book of Durrow.

[8,25] Opening words of St Mark's Gospel, Book of Durrow. Interlace and zoomorphs decorate the capital letters at the opening of each Gospel.

Gospel book which brings together many of the influences that were flowing into Ireland in the mid-seventh century. The 'carpet' page, a Coptic influence, is first seen here. [8,24] Interlace is also introduced and a wider range of colours — red, yellow, green and a colour which is now brown.

Each Gospel begins with an Evangelist's symbol — man for Matthew, lion for Mark, calf for Luke and eagle for John. The next page is a 'carpet' page, followed by the initial page. [8,25] The first letter of the text is enlarged and decorated, with the following letters surrounded by dots. Yellow is used to fill in some capital letters. Parallels with metalwork can be noted in the rectangular body of St Matthew, [8,26] which looks like millefiori decoration, and in details of the carpet pages. The St Matthew figure also has parallels in the figures on the Carndonagh Cross. There is a sense of space in the design of all the pages of the Book of Durrow. Open vellum balances intensely decorated areas. Animal interlace of a very high quality appears on one page. Other motifs include spirals, triskeles, ribbon plaits and circular knots in the carpet pages and the borders around the Evangelists.

[8,24] Carpet page from the beginning of St John's Gospel, Book of Durrow. This page has examples of the beautiful animal interlace found in the book.

[8,26] St Matthew, symbol page from the Book of Durrow. The cross-fertilisation of ideas between crafts can be seen in the similarity between this manuscript figure and figures from High Crosses. The decoration of the cloak also has echoes in millefiori enamel decoration in metalwork.

[8,27] Carpet page, with cross, precedes Gospel of St Matthew, from the Book of Lindisfarne.

The origins of manuscripts are very hard to pin down with certainty. So much traffic took place between Ireland, Britain (particularly Northumbria) and Irish monasteries on the continent that it is hard to tell if a book was written in Ireland or in an Irish monastery abroad. Styles are so close that they would have to be looked at together.

The Lichfield Gospels and the Book of Lindisfarne [8,27] in England and the St Gall Gospels in Switzerland are large, sumptuously decorated codices in the Irish or closely related style. They have portraits of the Evangelists, carpet pages and decorated initials with a wider range of colours and a greater use of animal interlace (probably a Saxon influence).

As well as these large books there are a number of small, pocket-sized Gospel books similarly but not so beautifully decorated. These include the Book of Mulling and the Book of Dimma (both in Trinity College Dublin), the Book of MacRegol of Birr (Bodleian Library, Oxford) and the Stowe Missal (Royal Irish Academy).

METALWORK

The metalwork of the seventh and eighth centuries is of a very high quality — it is easily the most elegant and technically refined work of any country in Europe during the early Middle Ages. It might help to examine some of the techniques and elements of design before we look at the objects themselves.

ENAMELLING
Various techniques were used in enamelling:

- Cloisonné: Areas of design were surrounded with silver, gold or bronze wire and filled with enamel.
- Champlevé: An old Celtic technique, in which areas of surface were carved away or beaten hollow and the spaces created were filled with enamel.
- Millefiori: Rods of coloured glass were heated and drawn together in a molten state and stretched into a long, thin rod from which thin sections were cut off and applied to enamelled surfaces. The sections can look like flowers, hence the name, millefiori, meaning thousand flowers.

STUDS
Studs were cast in clay moulds. Some had a wire grille fitted into the mould and then filled with coloured glass-enamel. Other studs were cast with a hollow pattern which was filled with a second colour. [8,28]

FILIGREE
Filigree consisted of fine gold wires which were twisted together into a fine rope. Sometimes wires of different sizes were twisted together to create a more glittering effect. The filigree was bent into shape and soldered to a background.

[8,28] Detail from the rim of the Ardagh Chalice including cloisonné enamel studs, filigree panel and engraved lettering.

211

[8,29] Detail from the Moylough Belt Shrine showing champlevé enamel, die-stamped gold foil and glass studs.

CHIP CARVING

Chip carving was a technique of carving metal in high relief, creating sharp outlines.

CASTING

A variety of methods and techniques were used in casting. Clay and bone moulds created both plain and decorated objects. Chip carving was sometimes imitated in cast objects.

ENGRAVING

Engraving involved cutting a design into a metal surface with a sharp pointed tool.

DIE STAMPING

Die stamping involved 'stamping' a thin sheet of metal, usually gold or silver, with a design which had been carved or cast on a block of wood or metal. [8,29]

TURNING

In turning, a metal sheet was pressed onto a former, rotating on a lathe, and gradually shaped into a bowl or cone shape as required.

AMBER

Amber, which is fossilised resin, was cut to shape and used like enamel studs as a contrast to areas of filigree or chip carving.

The elements used in designs on seventh- and eighth-century objects came from many sources. Spirals, curves and adaptations of them are Celtic in origin and had been in use in Ireland for a long time. Interlace, plaits and frets seem to have originated in the Middle East. In Irish art they are not merely geometric but are developed into flowing, intricate patterns. Animal forms were most likely of Saxon origin, but were adapted into much more lively creatures than their Saxon forebears. Many of the techniques used and the objects made were Roman in origin.

The predominance of these influences might suggest that Irish art was second-hand or copied, but an originality and flair was used which combined these elements into a unique and subtly balanced art.

Penannular brooches continued to develop with larger, decorated areas covering half the ring and closing the circle. This type of brooch is called 'pseudopenannular'. Large numbers of penannular and pseudopenannular brooches ranging from 7 cm to 13 cm in diameter are known from the seventh and eighth centuries; of these the Tara brooch, made of gilt bronze, is the finest.

The front side of the Tara Brooch is divided by raised borders in which gold filigree in animal and geometric patterns is held. [8,30] Glass and amber studs punctuate the surface. A chain is attached to the ring by an intriguing series of animal heads with interlocked jaws. This link also contains two tiny human faces made of moulded glass. The reverse side of the brooch has sections cast in high relief and two flat silvered copper plates with fine spiral patterns engraved in them. [8,31] Glass and amber studs are also used on the back. Fantastic animals seem to be the theme of the Tara Brooch; they appear in the filigree sections, in the castings on the back, at several places on the perimeter and on the pin and chain connection.

The Ardagh Chalice has many similarities to the Tara Brooch. [8,32] It is made of a silver bowl connected to a conical foot by a gilt bronze collar. It is 17.8 cm high and 19.5 cm in diameter. It was found with other objects in a hoard at Ardagh, Co. Limerick.

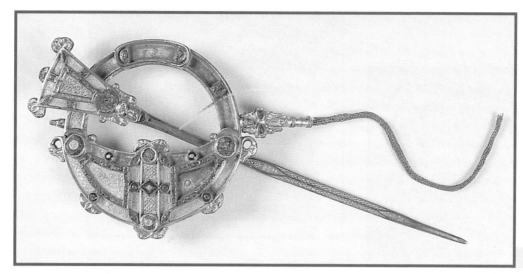

[8,30] Front of Tara Brooch.

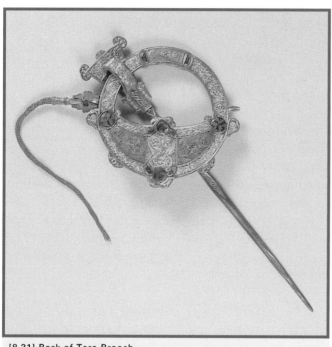

[8,31] Back of Tara Brooch.

The decoration of the chalice is a masterpiece of subtlety and refinement, with an almost perfect balance between areas of sumptuous decoration and the plain silver of the bowl and foot. A band of decoration just below the rim is made of panels of gold filigree punctuated with glass studs. The names of the Apostles are lightly engraved in a band of dots just below. The handles [8,33] and the plaques which attach them to the bowl are decorated with gold filigree, red and blue cloisonné enamelling and glass studs. Two medallions in the shape of a Greek Cross in a circle are on the bowl of the chalice. The collar joining the bowl to the base is decorated in high relief in the chip carving style, in spiral and interlace patterns. A rim around the conical foot is decorated with filigree panels punctuated by squares of blue glass.

[8,32] Ardagh Chalice.

[8,33] Ardagh Chalice — detail of handle and escutcheon.

213

[8,34] Ardagh Chalice — detail of the crystal and decoration underneath the base of the chalice.

[8,36] Emly Shrine: silver/gold/cloisonné/enamel/gilding as bronze applied to yew wood, 92 mm (h) x 105 mm (l) x 41 mm (w).

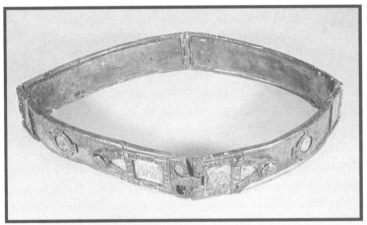

[8,35] Moylough Belt Shrine.

The Emly Shrine is a house-shaped, portable reliquary made of yew wood and decorated with silver, gold, enamels and gilt bronze. [8,36] The whole surface is covered in a step pattern of silver inlay, except for medallions in two shades of green and yellow cloisonné enamels. Animal heads form the ends of the ridge pole.

The Athlone Crucifixion Plaque, probably a book cover, is made of cast bronze which was once gilt. [8,37] The two figures and two angels surrounding the Christ figure are decorated in spirals and bands of interlace. Christ's robes are also richly decorated, leaving the large oval face of Christ as the only undecorated area. The plaque has echoes of the Carndonagh Cross and the Book of Durrow.

The Derrynaflan Paten, the only paten of its kind which has so far come to light, was found in 1980 buried in a bank at the Monastery of Daoire na Flan in Co. Tipperary. [8,38] It was discovered

Underneath, at the centre of the foot, [8,34] is a large glass crystal surrounded by three bands of decoration: the inner, animal interlace in gold filigree; the middle, a chip carved spiral decoration punctuated by small glass studs with gold granulations; the outer, an abstract interlace pattern in the chip carved style.

The Moylough Belt Shrine, c. 700, is a bronze, belt-shaped case in four segments, made to house the belt of an unknown saint. [8,35] The main area of decoration is around the buckle, with plates of silver die-stamped with spirals and triskeles forming the centres of bands of champlevé enamel, with studs of the types already seen on the Tara Brooch and Ardagh Chalice. Millefiori is also used in the buckle area and in the rectangular or round plaques fixed to other sections of the belt shrine. Animal and bird heads form part of the decoration.

[8,37] Athlone Crucifixion Plaque.

[8,38]
Derrynaflan
Paten.

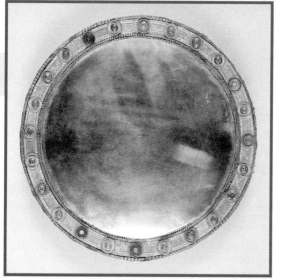

[8,40] Lough Kinale Book Shrine.

under a bronze cauldron with a chalice and other objects, of which we will see more later. It is 35 cm in diameter and made of over 300 components. The beaten silver dish has a gilt, bronze rim which is decorated with gold filigree panels and enamel studs.

The designs in the filigree panels relate closely to those on the Ardagh Chalice, as do the enamel studs. The quality of the decorative elements is very high. Animal, human and abstract designs are used in the filigree. The small studs which hide the rivets are set in small cups which contain fine filigree and granulated decorations. The die-stamped, gold panels on the side of the rim are decorated with interlace and scroll patterns. The panels on the foot are similar but not as finely made. [8,39]

The finding of this paten shows that work of the quality of the Ardagh Chalice and Tara Brooch was not a rarity in Ireland during the eighth century. It adds to our understanding of the richness and quality of craftwork of the period.

The Lough Kinale Book Shrine was found in a lake in Co. Longford in 1986. [8,40] It is made of

[8,39] Derrynaflan Paten — detail of filigree panels and enamel studs.

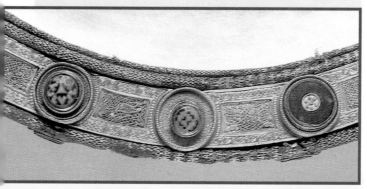

metal plates pinned to a wooden box. The front of the box has a cross design on it with large bosses at the ends of the arms and at the centre. These bosses are decorated with scroll patterns and have a coloured stud, inlaid with a metal grille in the centre. There is open-work decoration in the circles between the arms of the cross and around the border of the lid. An unusual piece, relating in design to carpet pages from near contemporary manuscripts (Lindisfarne Gospels and Book of Kells), it is the earliest, most complete and most unaltered book shrine to have been found to date.

CONCLUSION

The seventh and eighth centuries were a high point in Irish art and learning, when Ireland was the repository of scholarship for a Europe which was experiencing the Dark Ages. It is extraordinary that the finest craftsmanship and scholarship of the age should come from such an unstructured society. Work of extraordinary technical skill and subtle design characterises the period.

THE VIKING INVASIONS: NINTH AND TENTH CENTURIES

In 795 Viking raids on the coasts of Ireland and Britain began. By 801 Iona, chief city monastery of the Columban order, had been burnt and suffered so much in following years that the order moved its organisation to Kells, Co. Meath, where a new monastic city was built. In 830 Turgesius

[8,41] Map showing monasteries of 9th and 10th centuries.

However, a further movement of Vikings from Norway and Denmark renewed the instability, and Ireland resumed its conflict with the foreigners. This raiding and plundering caused many monasteries to be abandoned; the monks, with whatever books and valuables they could save, were scattered. Many of them found their way to Europe where they were welcomed into the newly developing courts. Irish scholars taught in all the major universities there.

However, the influence of the Vikings was not always negative: trading centres were established; it was a period of great productivity in metalwork; new building techniques in cut stone were developed; High Crosses were made larger and new styles evolved.

MONASTERIES

The growth of monasteries in previous centuries continued in the ninth and tenth centuries. The monastic city of Armagh, seat of the successor of Patrick, may have had as many as 4,000 inhabitants during this time. Accounts from the Annals record the murder of large numbers at the hands of the Vikings at several monasteries. Building in stone became more common, probably in reaction to Viking burnings. The layout seems to have remained largely unaltered, with churches and houses inside a rath of earth and wattles or stone, and further groups of huts outside the walls for laity, students and craftspeople. [8,42]

sailed from Norway with a great fleet to assume sovereignty over all the foreigners in Ireland. He landed in the north and established bases in Lough Neagh and Lough Ree. He then moved south and founded a stronghold at Dublin, where he became master of the earliest Viking state recorded in the history of Western Europe. Further Viking strongholds were gradually established at Limerick, Wexford and Waterford, all on estuaries with good harbours.

From these centres the plunder of Ireland was undertaken in earnest. When monasteries were raided, the buildings were burnt, the books destroyed, monks put to the sword or forced to flee. Valuables made of gold or silver were kept or melted into coins. Gilt objects or pieces with enamelling were often divided up and remade into jewellery for Viking women. Many a reliquary or book cover was torn apart, its precious relic or book destroyed and the metal case divided among the pagan pirates. [8,41]

Between 875 and 915 a period of comparative peace prevailed. The Viking onslaught had moved on to Europe and the Irish Vikings were more interested in trading than raiding. This period is referred to as 'the forty-year recess'. Much renewal and rebuilding was undertaken in Ireland at this time and a great vigour returned to all the crafts.

[8,42] Clonmacnoise, Co. Offaly.

[8,43] Trinity Church, Glendalough, Co. Wicklow, showing the chancel extending out from the nave.

The buildings themselves changed little from the eighth century — they remained plain rectangular edifices with antae and flat-headed doorways. Some, like the cathedral at Glendalough, were quite large. A new development which can be seen in the Reefert and Trinity churches at Glendalough was the separation of the chancel at the eastern end by a round arch. [8,43] The antae have also disappeared from these churches. Another church without antae at Aghowle, Co. Wicklow, has a plain moulding carved in high relief around its flat-headed doorway. The door frames on Reefert Church and the Round Tower at Monasterboice have two plain bands in low relief around them. Windows with a triangular head are a feature of a number of buildings and towers from this period.

ROUND TOWERS

Round towers seem to have been first built during the 'forty years recess'. [8,44] The Annals record them as 'cloictigh', bell houses, though this does not seem to have been their only function. They were places of refuge in times of trouble and stores for books and precious objects of all kinds. The burning of Slane Cloicteach in 948 is described in the Annals of the Four Masters. Its 'relics and distinguished persons together with Caineachair, Lector of Slane, and the Crosier of the Patron Saint, and a bell were burnt by the Foreigners'. Stone hooks for hanging book satchels or relic boxes have been found in the walls of a number of round towers.

The surviving towers are between 30 and 40 metres high, 5 metres in diameter, with walls tapering in from about 1 metre thick at the base.

The roofs are conical and made of cut stone. Inside there were between five and seven wooden floors, reached by ladders, with one window in each storey facing different directions. The top floor normally had four narrow windows facing north, south, east and west. Windows could be flat, triangular or round-headed; doorways were either rectangular or more commonly round-headed. The door of the tower normally faced the west doorway of the principal church of the monastery. The greatest danger to round towers was fire; if they took light the structure acted as a chimney, drawing the fire up through the building.

STONE CARVING

During the ninth and tenth centuries many developments took place in the style and decoration of High Crosses, which were still the chief outlet of the stone carver. Larger crosses were made and figure carving gradually replaced decorative patterns on most surfaces of the crosses. Illustrations of themes from the Old and New Testaments and occasionally the lives of saints became the main function of the High Cross. They were sermons or prayers in stone. A style of realism developed in the carving of human figures which was a foretaste of Romanesque carving in Europe. A common influence may have been Carolingian ivories which were in wide circulation at the time.

[8,44] Round Tower at Glendalough, Co. Wicklow.

Most of the scenes illustrate themes which demonstrate God's help to his faithful followers, though there are usually several layers of meaning and symbolism attributed to each scene. For example, Abraham's sacrifice of his son Isaac may indicate the forgiveness of God; Isaac carrying the wood for his own sacrifice can be seen as a prefiguration of the crucifixion, or the foretelling of the sacrament of the Eucharist.

High Crosses may have been painted, as European medieval carvings, similar in style, certainly were. Backgrounds were darkened to make figures or decoration stand out, or whole surfaces were painted in colour in the style of book illustrations. The fact that a number of crosses are made of stones of different colour strengthens this theory.

Dating crosses with accuracy is a problem, as only a few have decipherable inscriptions or details of style that would anchor them in time. Of the ninth-century crosses, two carved in granite at Castledermot, Co. Kildare, are certainly the most naive if not the earliest. [8,45] In style they are like the Cross of Moone, but are not so tall or imposing. Both crosses are outlined in a low border and divided into almost square panels. The arrangement of scenes is a new departure from crosses of the previous century: the figure scenes are on the base, shaft and arms, with only a few panels of decorative pattern remaining.

The crucifixion is portrayed on the west side of the South Cross at Castledermot, at the intersection of the shaft and arms. This intersection is surrounded by scenes from the Old and New Testaments: Adam and Eve, the arrest of Christ, David playing his harp and the sacrifice of Abraham among them. The animal scene on the base is obscure in meaning. The carving is in quite high relief and a greater degree of realism is apparent in the figure scenes which are tightly composed within the panels.

A group of crosses at Kells in Co. Meath shows an influence from the island of Iona. The Columban order moved their mother house to Kells when Iona was overrun by the Vikings. The Tower Cross, or the Cross of Saints Patrick and Columba as it is called after its inscription, may have been erected to commemorate the founding of the monastery in 802. [8,46] There are many parallels between the design of the cross and the Book of Kells, which was kept at the monastery. The

[8,45] South Cross at Castledermot, Co. Kildare — west face. This is the earliest cross which shows the arrangement of panels that became the norm in the 9th and 10th centuries.

[8,46] Tower Cross (Cross of Saints Patrick and Columba) at Kells, Co. Meath. The lively figures and lack of panel boundaries show an influence of the Iona style in this cross.

design is not broken into outlined panels. Groups of figures and interlace patterns meet without boundaries and scenes combine events. Adam and Eve and Cain killing Abel share the same space on the east face of the cross. The figures are almost comical in their busy, animated portrayal of Bible stories. The theme of salvation through the sacrifice of Christ, in spite of the fall from grace of Adam and Eve, is again the central theme, played out in scenes layered with symbolism.

The Market Cross and a broken cross at Kells are larger and more imposing than the Tower Cross. The figures are carved in high relief, almost in the round in some places. The processions of men and animals around their bases have yet to be deciphered.

An incomplete cross at Kells [8,47] shows how the sculptors first blocked out the shape, leaving the blank panels projecting from the surface to be carved into later. The crosses seem to have been erected in a rough state and carved at the site.

Muirideach's Cross at Monasterboice is 5.5 metres tall. [8,48] Its shaft is 75 cm wide and quite thick. While not the tallest, it is the weightiest of all the High Crosses and probably artistically and technically the finest. Except for the cap and base, it was carved out of one piece of stone. [8,49]

[8,48] Muirideach's Cross, Monasterboice, Co. Louth — east face.

[8,49] Muirideach's Cross, Monasterboice, Co. Louth — west face.

[8,47] Unfinished cross, Kells, Co. Meath.

The base is divided into panels and carved in low relief. Some panels are decoration, others are the animal and horsemen scenes found on other bases. The east face is made up of panels with large groups of figures: at the bottom Adam and Eve, with Cain killing Abel; the second panel, David and Goliath, along with Saul and Jonathan;

the third, Moses striking the rock, and a crowd of figures; the top panel on the shaft is the adoration of the Magi. Spread right across the arms of the cross is a scene from the Last Judgment, with the saved on Christ's right and the damned on his left. Above Christ's head are two angels lifting a soul up to heaven, while below his feet is the weighing of souls. On the bottom of the west face two cats lie curled up. In the background there is an inscription: 'Or do Muirideach las ndernad í chrossa' (Pray for Muirideach who caused this cross to be erected). [8,50] Above this there are three panels on the shaft: the arrest of Christ; doubting Thomas; and Christ giving the keys to St Peter and the new law to St Paul. Across the arms is the crucifixion and scenes from the Passion. Just below the cap is a panel with Moses between Aaron and Hur.

The theme of the cross is that of redemption, the same as most earlier ones, but the carving is much more detailed. One can get an idea of the dress, utensils and hair styles of the day by a study of the figures on the cross.

The Cross of the Scriptures at Clonmacnoise is stylistically very similar to Muirideach's Cross, with many themes in common; but it is physically much smaller and has peculiarly uplifted arms and decorative discs where the wheel crosses the arms and shaft. [8,51] The base was originally carved in high relief, but is now quite weathered. Horses, chariots and animals are depicted, as on many other bases.

[8,51] Cross of the Scriptures, Clonmacnoise, Co. Offaly — east face.

The ninth and tenth centuries were the great period of High Cross carving in Ireland. Many of the themes that appeared later in Romanesque carving in Europe first appeared on Irish High Crosses. The style of realism that developed in the figure carvings on crosses in the midlands did not transfer into other crafts to any great extent, though some echoes can be found in the Book of Kells. Abstract ornament, on the other hand, was still common to all crafts, with panels from crosses corresponding to panels on metalwork and in manuscript borders.

MANUSCRIPTS

Books were probably the greatest casualties of the Viking invasions. Of no use to the illiterate invaders, they were thrown onto fires or into the sea, or simply cast aside and allowed to rot. The Library of St Gall contains more books of Irish origin than there are in the museums and libraries of Ireland, which shows how Irish manuscripts were taken abroad by monks and scribes leaving the country for the refuge of monasteries in Europe.

The Book of Kells is the outstanding Irish manuscript. Work on the book began on Iona. It was then brought to Kells when the monks transferred there after 802 and may have been completed there in the scriptorium. It is a large codex, designed to decorate the altar on ceremonial occasions.

[8,50] Muirideach's Cross, Monasterboice, Co. Louth — bottom shaft west: arrest of Christ, cats and inscription.

Now measuring 33 by 24 cm it was probably 38 by 25 cm before it was trimmed by a thirteenth-century binder, who also cut off some decorations. Although originally it may have had 350 folios, it now contains only 340. The last four chapters of St John's Gospel and the first few pages of the manuscript are missing. Two pages which should have been decorated are blank and others are unfinished. The book is written on thick vellum in formal majuscule script. It is not always easily legible, with words not properly separated and many copyists' errors and spelling mistakes. The language is an Irish mixed Latin, not pure Vulgate.

None of these imperfections takes from the grand scale on which the book was laid out, or from the vigour and imagination of its decoration. Several scribes probably set to work on the book simultaneously, under the direction of the master scribe or abbot. There is certainly evidence of many hands at work, from stumbling apprentices to some of the most brilliant illuminators in the world.

The colours used in the decorated pages of the Book of Kells are red, yellow, blue, purple and green, with black and brown used for line and to darken backgrounds. The red is made from red lead and the yellow from a mineral called 'orpiment' which was mixed with egg white. The green comes from copper. These colours with the black and brown were available locally, but the blue and purple were probably imported. The purple was made from Mediterranean plants and the blue from a semi-precious stone called lapis lazuli found in Asia Minor. These colours were applied with reed or quill pens and a variety of palette knife blades.

Françoise Henry identifies four main artists. One she calls 'the Goldsmith' because of the relationship between his work and fine metal-work. He is responsible for the Chi-Rho (Christ's Monogram) page, [8,52] the cruciform, eight-circle, carpet page and the initial pages of the Gospels, except the Quoniam of St Luke. His work is boldly outlined in black with internal spirals, plaits, interlaces and coils in a variety of colours. The human figure often appears as part of the ornament distorted into circles, with legs or

arms forming an interlace and heads appearing at the ends of coils. Some of the work is so fine it is hard to appreciate with the naked eye, but there is never a slip.

'The Portraitist', the second artist, is responsible for two pictures of Evangelists, [8,53] one of Christ teaching, probably two of the Evangelist symbols in frames at the beginning of each Gospel and the Quoniam in St Luke. He uses the same elements of decoration as the Goldsmith, plus vegetal scrolls. Symmetry is one of the features of this artist's work, with elements balanced throughout the composition. The human figure in a stylised form is the main theme of these works, with decoration as a secondary though important component.

'The Illustrator' is responsible for the most dramatic work in the Book of Kells. His figures are more animated and his colours are striking in his use of strong contrasts to great effect. His contribution includes the arrest of Christ, Virgin and Child, [8,54] symbols of the Evangelists in St John and the 'Tunc Crucifixerant' page.

The fourth major contributor painted the 'Nativitas Christi' page and a page of the Canons, but his main contribution was in the small

[8.53] Book of Kells, Portrait of St John.

[8,54] Book of Kells, Virgin and Child.

capitals, the animals between the lines, the border of the Genealogy [8,55] and other incidental decorations. His treatment is humorous and observant. The little animals play among the text and give much of the unique atmosphere to the book.

The Book of Kells is the finest known Irish manuscript. The grandeur of its scale and layout is not found in other books. It makes use of a full range of colour and all the elements of design then known in Ireland.

A few other examples of ninth- and tenth-century manuscripts survive in museums and libraries around Europe, but none on the scale or of the quality of the Book of Kells. The Book of Armagh gives us some idea of how a more everyday copy of the Gospels looked. [8,56] The 'minuscule' text has decorated capitals, but no colour is used, even on the pages with the symbols of the Evangelists. A verse in the margin of a Priscian grammar book, written in the Armagh style and now in the Library of St Gall, reads:

'Fierce and wild is the wind tonight;
On such a night as this I take my ease;
Fierce Northmen only course the quiet seas.'

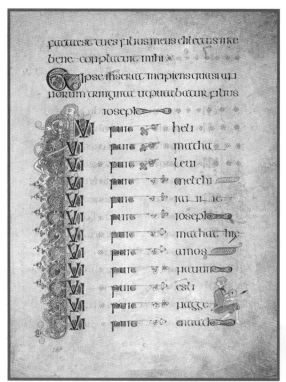

[8,55] Book of Kells, Genealogy of Christ.

[8,56] Book of Armagh, beginning of St Luke's Gospel.

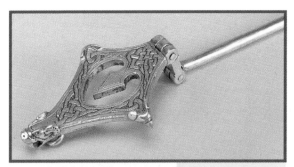

[8,58] Kite brooch.

[8,59] Thistle brooch.

METALWORK

The metalwork of the ninth century continued the High Christian style, but with less use of enamel and a degeneration of the fine detailed work into looser simpler forms. Precious materials like silver, gold and amber were widely used. The skill level of craftsmen was still high and objects were well constructed and carefully finished, but there was a loss of creative ingenuity and repetition becomes more common.

In the tenth century the influence of the Vikings was beginning to be felt, with an Irish form of the Viking jelling style of decoration appearing alongside Irish motifs.

The design of brooches changed considerably during the ninth and tenth centuries. The Roscrea Brooch, cast in silver and decorated with gold filigree and amber, is much broader and simpler in its design than the Tara Brooch. [8,57] Animal interlace forms a border around spiral-patterned filigree panels, and a border of semi-circular panels strengthens the outline of the pin and ring. Cast-silver brooches in a variety of shapes became more common as trade with the Vikings increased. The laws of the time dictated the size and value of brooches worn by people of different status. Kite brooches [8,58] and thistle brooches [8,59] were new types developed during this period.

The Derrynaflan Chalice, found in the same hoard as the Paten mentioned earlier, is the finest piece of ninth-century metalwork yet discovered. [8,60] Made of silver, it is decorated with gold filigree

[8,57] Roscrea Brooch.

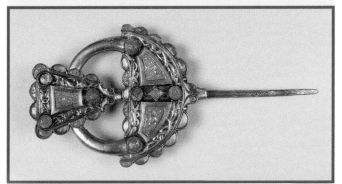

[8,60] Derrynaflan Chalice.

223

[8,61] Derrynaflan Chalice — detail of filigree animal.

and amber and is quite close in design to the Roscrea Brooch. Bird and animal shapes are the main elements in the filigree, which is less intricately wrought than that on the Ardagh Chalice. [8,61]

The layout of the decoration is similar to that on the Ardagh Chalice. It consists of a band of filigree and amber studs below the rim, handles with large decorated escutcheons, gold and amber at the joining of the bowl and the foot, and a ring of decoration around the rim of the foot. The whole chalice is a beautiful harmony of warm gold and amber and cool silver.

Examples of other metal artifacts of the ninth and tenth centuries include crosiers, book boxes and bell shrines. Although none of them is in very good condition, they indicate the range of objects made by craftsmen of the time. Skills and techniques had not fallen away since the eighth century, but the taste for intricate design seems to have changed in favour of bolder work, maybe more suited to the taste of Vikings who were now important trading partners.

CONCLUSION

The period of the Viking invasions brought great change to Ireland. A society which had lived in comparative isolation for nearly 1,000 years was violently opened up to new values and ideas. The notion of an island of saints and scholars was dealt a death blow. Irish book painting as a recognisable style vanished in a few generations, and though stone carving and metalwork were to have a revival in the Romanesque era, the style was heavily overlaid with Viking and European influence. The unique combination of Celtic society and Christianity that had proved to be so creative was at an end.

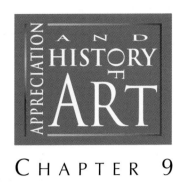

CHAPTER 9

THE MEDIEVAL PERIOD

Many complex influences led to the massive changes that occurred in Ireland during the Romanesque period. The Vikings, though their raiding was stopped after the Battle of Clontarf in 1014, continued to be a major influence in all spheres of Irish life. Their style of decoration was incorporated into Irish work and their social and ecclesiastical organisation on the European model was a constant reminder to the Irish of the uniqueness of their own social and ecclesiastical order.

The huge loss of books and religious goods during the Viking raids had to be made up; so Irish monks were sent to Britain and the continent to buy books and to be trained in European universities. This led to the importation of ideas from the mainstream of European education, as well as new books and learning.

The practice of going on pilgrimage to Europe and the Holy Land brought Irish kings and ecclesiastics into contact with the new style of building and social order now sweeping Europe.

Reforms within the Irish Church sparked off by monks educated on the continent reinforced all the other influences and also brought European orders of monks to Ireland, who built monasteries in the European style and ran them by more strict and disciplined rules than the Irish monasteries.

Irish kings were influenced by the feudal system and began to see themselves as rulers of people and land rather than leaders of family-based *tuatha*, or kingdoms. They saw the endowment of monasteries or the introduction of monks from Europe as ways of adding to their prestige and influence.

MONASTERIES (ARCHITECTURE)

Recovery from the Viking invasions was a slow process. The eleventh century was taken up with rebuilding and enlarging. Separated by an arch from the nave, the chancels that were introduced in the tenth century were added to many churches during this rebuilding period. Indeed any newly built churches included a chancel. The building of round towers continued. Some were incorporated into the structure of the churches, as at St Kevin's Kitchen at Glendalough and Temple Finghin at Clonmacnoise. [9,1] By the beginning of the twelfth century chancel arches, round-headed doors and windows with decorations were being incorporated into church building.

[9,1] Temple Finghin, Clonmacnoise, Co. Offaly.

[9,2] Cormac's Chapel, Cashel, Co. Tipperary — from south-east.

Most Irish monasteries kept the traditional layout, with buildings placed at random and spread over a wide area, as at Clonmacnoise. A move towards centralisation in education and ecclesiastical power turned important centres like Armagh and Kells into planned towns.

CORMAC'S CHAPEL

Any study of twelfth-century Irish architecture revolves around Cormac's Chapel at Cashel, Co. Tipperary, which was a major architectural influence. [9,2] Opinion is divided between those who believe all Romanesque decoration stems from there and those who believe it was just one major influence in the development of Irish Romanesque.

Built between 1127 and 1134 under the patronage of Cormac McCarthy, King of Desmond, on a site donated to the Church by the High King, Murtough O'Brien, Cormac's Chapel was the seat of the new archdiocese which was intent on bringing reform to the Irish Church. The chapel is a symbol of this reform, displaying influences of English and European design. The exterior, viewed from the east, has a Germanic appearance, with its steep roof and square towers. A French influence dominates the blank arcades on the exterior and interior walls, and the doorways and groin-vaulted chancel echo the English style. Only its small size and simple nave and chancel form seem Irish.

The doorways on the north and south walls of the nave each have a tympanum. The tympanum of the north door, with its six orders of arches decorated by chevrons, zig-zags and pellets, is the highlight of the exterior. [9,3] The hood moulding has a grotesque human head for a keystone. Above the door is a large gable-pediment divided into panels by a raised border of chevrons. Rosettes carved in high relief are placed in the panels.

The decoration inside is lavish. [9,4] Traces of paint indicate that much of the carving and plasterwork was originally painted. The chancel arch has four rows of decoration. Every second stone in one arch is carved with a realistic head,

[9,3] Cormac's Chapel, Cashel, Co. Tipperary — north doorway, tympanum.

226

[9,4] Cormac's Chapel, Cashel, Co. Tipperary — interior, showing chancel arch.

[9,6] Detail of capitals and arch mouldings at Clonfert Cathedral, Co. Galway.

and these continue down between columns to the ground. More of these heads with high cheekbones and long noses appear in other parts of the chapel.

Cormac's Chapel is the first building in Ireland which can properly be called architecture. It was designed as a unit, inside and out, in structure and decoration. Its influence appears everywhere, but its revolutionary barrel and groin-vaulted construction was lost on the Irish, who merely borrowed parts of its decoration for use in their own buildings.

SPREADING OF ROMANESQUE INFLUENCE

There are numerous churches with gables over their doorways in imitation of the north door of Cormac's Chapel, the most elaborate of which is Clonfert Cathedral, Co. Galway. [9,5]

[9,5] Doorway and decorative gable at Clonfert Cathedral, Co. Galway.

The doorway of the church has five receding orders of arches on pillars which are wrapped in decorative carving, with chevrons, lozenges, circles with pellets, elongated rosettes and other plant forms as part of the design. The capitals are made of grotesque and comical animal heads. [9,6] The decoration on the arches is carved almost in the round. On the second row animal heads hold a moulding in their jaws. Other arches combine circles with plant forms. Immediately above the arch is a blank arcade with a high-relief human head in each arch. The remainder of the gable is divided into triangles with a head in every second one. An inside arch of grey limestone was added in the Middle Ages which does not match the rich, brown sandstone of the original work. The overall effect is very strong due to the depth of carving and the richness of detail.

Beautifully carved chancel arches and round-headed doorways can be seen on many Romanesque churches. The Nuns' Church at Clonmacnoise combines geometric and animal forms in the richly carved doorway, while the chancel arch follows a purely geometric design. [9,7] Irish sculptors combined European and Viking influences and adapted them into a style that was still characteristically Irish.

Interlace, animal forms and geometry formed the basis of most design, though carving was much bolder and repetition of designs and patterns more common than it had been in earlier work.

227

[9,7] Close-up of doorway with 12th-century chancel visible in background, Nuns' Church, Clonmacnoise, Co. Offaly.

[9,9] Mellifont Abbey, Co. Louth, the lavabo and a section of the cloister arcade.

MELLIFONT

In 1142 St Malachy of Armagh formed a Cistercian community at Mellifont, Co. Louth. He brought the Cistercians from Clairvaux in France to help with the reformation of the Irish Church. The Cistercian rule was a complete contrast to the Irish. Everything was ordered, from the daily activities of each monk and brother to the

[9,8] Plan of Cistercian Abbey.

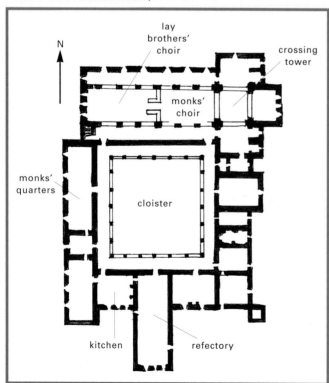

standard plan for the layout of monasteries. [9,8] The buildings were organised around an open square cloister, with the church on the north side and the living and working areas on the other three sides. The scale of the building was also quite different. Mellifont was almost 56 metres long compared with Cormac's Chapel at just 14 (a large church by traditional standards). Mellifont also had aisles and transepts, which were unknown in Irish buildings. Little of the original building survives at Mellifont, but a small section of the cloister arcade has been rebuilt. Its capitals relate closely to contemporary English work. A later lavabo (washhouse) built in late Romanesque style is more complete and has some fine stonework. [9,9]

By the time Mellifont was completed in 1157 it had eight daughter houses. This demonstrates the enthusiasm with which the new order was accepted in Ireland.

SCULPTURE

During the Romanesque period in Europe sculpture formed a decorative element to architecture. In Ireland the opposite was true. Most buildings were small and plain without many architectural qualities, but the decoration was of a very high standard. The decorative carving just discussed under the heading of architecture could just as easily be called sculpture. Many of the design elements — geometric and animal interlace, high-relief carving and plant forms — recur in the carving found on High Crosses.

[9,10] Drumcliff Cross, Co. Sligo.

Of the earlier crosses a cross at Drumcliff, Co. Sligo, is the most complete. [9,10] It has many of the features of the tenth-century crosses — wheel head and tall base — but it is not divided into panels. The cross is carved from two blocks of pale sandstone. A bead moulding surrounds the decoration on the face, leaving a plain border around the outline of the cross. The east and west faces have a mixture of interlace designs and figure scenes. A lion in high relief is superimposed midway up the shaft on the west face and a monster is in the same position on the east. More traditional scenes such as Cain killing Abel and Adam and Eve are also included. The interlace relates closely to contemporary metalwork and manuscript designs.

There is a gap of almost 200 years between the great period of High Cross carving in Ireland in the ninth and tenth centuries and the final phase in the development of the Irish High Cross.

Romanesque crosses at Tuam, Roscrea and Cashel are badly weathered and damaged. They appear to have had large high-relief figures and areas of interlace design. In Co. Clare a number of crosses survive, the latest and most unusual of which is the Dysart O'Dea Cross. [9,11] This cross has no traditional wheel head, though sockets in the ends of the arms may have held some further decoration. The figure of the crucified Christ wears a long robe in the style of some contemporary European sculptures. A bishop below Christ's feet has a socket at waist level, from which an arm carved from a separate stone once projected. Other surfaces of the cross are carved in low relief with patterns and a few figure scenes. Viking influence can be noted in the design of the interlace patterns of snakes and animals which relate closely to designs in metalwork.

There is a beautifully carved doorway in the nearby church at Dysart O'Dea, which has a row of heads in one of its arches. [9,12] A wonderful mixture of human and animal heads is carved in high relief. The pillars at each side of the door have interlace and geometric patterns; some of the capitals have faces carved on them.

Irish Romanesque sculpture, whether on doorways and arches or carved High Crosses, combined influences from England and Europe with the earlier Celtic tradition. Interlace patterns were modified through Viking influence into

[9,11] High Cross at Dysart O'Dea, Co. Clare.

[9,12] Romanesque doorway at Dysart O'Dea, Co. Clare.

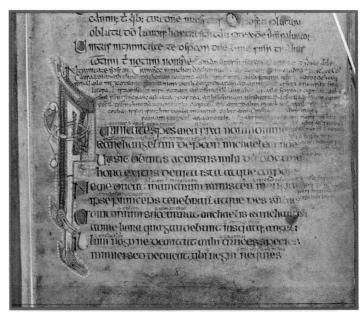

[9,13] Capital letter from Liber Hymnorum, 11th century (Trinity College Dublin).

battles between fantastic creatures. Geometric patterns often seen on doorways and chancel arches had their origins in English carving and the high-relief figures found on crosses and doorways relate to sculpture from France and Italy. All these influences were brought together in this final phase of truly Irish sculpture, in which Celtic roots were still clearly visible and provided the harmonising element in the style.

MANUSCRIPTS

Some interesting books survived the Romanesque period. Although a few books with decorative capitals do survive, most are interesting for their texts and associations rather than their decoration. A book of hymns in Irish and Latin written in the eleventh century is kept in the library of Trinity College Dublin. [9,13] The colours in this Liber Hymnorum were originally bright yellow, red, green and purple, but were dulled by the poor condition of the book. Leaf scrolls and other vegetal shapes have been added to the older repertoire of animals and interlace. The text is written in Irish majuscule.

Written in the twelfth century, the Psalter of Cormac betrays some continental influence which would have been introduced through the

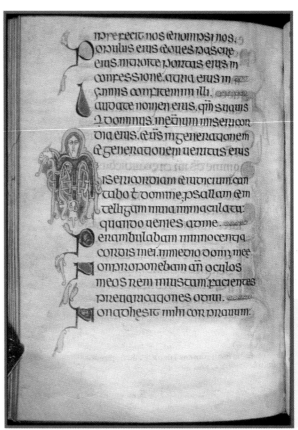

[9,14] Capital letter page from Psalter of Cormac, 12th century (British Library, London).

Cistercian monasteries. [9,14] The script is more regular and some background areas within the letters are coloured. Blue, purple, yellow and green are used against red backgrounds in the capital letters which begin the Psalms. Decorated capitals and small animals appear throughout the text in a scheme which comes closer in quality to the Book of Kells than any other manuscript.

The few decorated books that survive from the Romanesque period mark the end of the true Irish manuscript. All that followed were written in Britain or Europe or were copies of European styles. Only rarely in the following centuries did the Irish decorated capital make an appearance in a manuscript.

METALWORK

Most surviving examples of eleventh- and twelfth-century metalwork are reliquaries which have probably survived because of their importance to the Church as objects of veneration. Many of them were kept by their hereditary custodians until the last century. Little else survives. Brooches, which were such a feature in earlier centuries, may have gone out of fashion. Although few examples of any quality survive, we know of the existence of chalices and decorated drinking horns from accounts in the Annals.

A number of pieces from the Romanesque period were inscribed with the names of the craftsmen who made them and the bishops or patrons who commissioned them. Cuduilig Ó Inmainen and his sons made St Patrick's Bell Shrine in their workshop in Armagh. [9,15] It includes finely cast panels in the Urnes style: a Scandinavian version of Irish animal interlace, combining snakes and ribbon-bodied animals in a thin linear style. Most of St Patrick's Bell Shrine is complete except for a few semi-precious stones which were added to

[9,16] Lismore Crosier, crook showing crest and enamel studs (National Museum of Ireland, Dublin).

the box in later medieval times. The handle cover at the top of the box includes an open-work bronze cast of two interlaced birds.

Other bell shrines, book boxes and crosiers survive, encased in elaborate metalwork. The Lismore Crosier has a row of interlaced dogs and monsters on its crest. [9,16] The panels between the enamel studs once contained filigree, none of which remains. The whole crosier is clothed in bronze plaques held together by three cast-bronze knobs which are decorated in plant and animal interlace. Other crosiers of this type survive, decorated in a variety of styles and techniques. [9,17] All seem to have had a little box at the outer end of the crook, probably to hold the precious relic of the saint.

Crosiers in other shapes also existed. The National Museum houses a Tau crosier with a fine top consisting of a cast with two animal heads and an ivory crosier with a spiral crook found at Aghadoe in Co. Kerry, showing Jonah emerging from the whale.

The Shrine of St Lachtín's Arm is a well-preserved example of a type of relic once fairly common all over Europe. [9,18] It is 40 cm tall and is made of bronze plaques held in place on the wooden core by cast rings. The hand is a separate cast. The

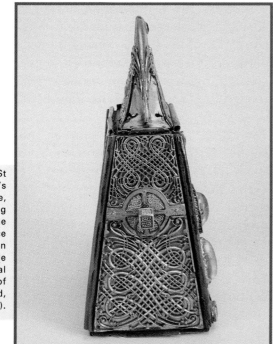

[9,15] St Patrick's Bell Shrine, showing the interlace panels on the side (National Museum of Ireland, Dublin).

[9,17] Crosier of the Abbots of Clonmacnoise. The ribbon of silver inlay on the crook of the crosier is in a version of the Scandinavian Ringerike style, where the lines of the pattern cut through each other rather than passing over and under.

[9,18] Shrine of St Lachtín's Arm. The panels on this shrine are decorated in silver and niello. Niello is a paste of sulphur and silver which makes a strong black line when inserted in a groove cut in a bronze background. It is frequently used to create a contrast with silver.

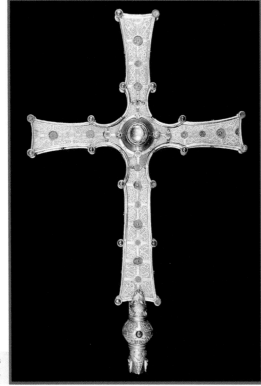

[9,19] Cross of Cong.

plaques are inlaid with silver and niello in a ribbon decoration of thread-like animals with open jaws. The hand has some panels of filigree, silver nails and a gilt silver palm decorated with foliage and tendrils. The bands which held the shrine together are decorated with interlace, and some glass studs survive around the base.

The Cross of Cong was made to display a fragment of the true cross taken from a larger fragment which was brought in 1119 from Rome to Ireland. [9,19] Made of bronze plaques mounted on an oak cross (76 cm tall), the surface is covered in a network of ornament. The cross is outlined by a tubular, silver edging, punctuated with glass studs on the front and enamel discs on the back. Rows of mounts, which once held glass or enamel studs, divide the front of the cross into panels. The centre of the cross has a semi-conical mount holding a rock crystal, behind which the cross fragment was displayed. Each panel on the front is filled with gilt bronze animal interlace, in the Urnes style. Four very skilfully cast, gilt bronze, open-work plaques, again in the Urnes style, make up the back of the cross. A pair of animal heads with blue glass eyes forms the mounting which joins the shaft to the cross. The animals, clamping the cross in their jaws, have scaly heads with mustachios and eyebrows of niello and silver.

House-shaped shrines with interesting cast figures can also be dated to the eleventh and twelfth centuries. The Lemanaghan Shrine (St Machan's Shrine) has a large cross on the front similar to the Lough Kinale Book Shrine, but the spaces between the arms contain strange little bare-chested figures, cast in bronze, which may be related to European crucifix figures. [9,20]

The Breac Maodhóg, another house-shaped shrine, also has cast figures in a very different style. [9,21] Closer to those from the Book of Kells, their hair and robes are formalised into patterns. The figures are quite individual and probably represent saints or biblical figures, but no definite identification has been made.

The metalwork of the eleventh and twelfth centuries was not refined and subtle like eighth-century work. It relied more on visual impact and

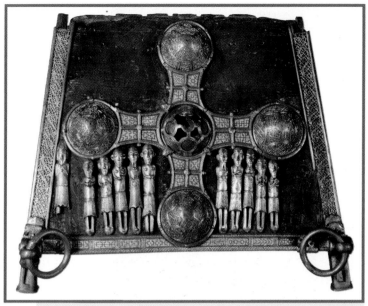

[9,20] The Lemanaghan Shrine (St Machan's Shrine).

colourful effects, though some pieces are very finely wrought. This period marks the last fling of the Irish metalworker using a uniquely Irish style.

THE END OF AN ERA

The European system of Church and state law and order arrived with the Cistercians and other European monks. Many of the Irish liked the new system and joined the European orders in great numbers in the twelfth century. This had immediate consequences for the arts in Ireland which were closely connected with an old Celtic Church now in rapid decline.

The increase in English and continental design which we have seen particularly in architecture followed the preference for plain churches and religious goods among the European orders. Many of the Irish accepted these changes and abandoned the fabulous decoration of their ancestors.

[9,21] The Breac Maodhóg house-shaped shrine.

THE ANGLO-NORMAN PERIOD: 1169–c. 1600

The first Norman knights arrived in Ireland in 1169 and in the following years brought radical change to the Irish way of life. The political, social and cultural fabric of the country changed. Initially the Normans built castles, cathedrals and churches in a completely English style, but as their power weakened, due to the Black Death of 1348–50 and isolation from England, an Irish style reasserted itself, particularly in the west of Ireland.

ARCHITECTURE

While some building continued under the patronage of Irish chieftains, most of the large construction was undertaken by the Normans.

RELIGIOUS ARCHITECTURE
CHRIST CHURCH CATHEDRAL

Work on the choir of Christ Church Cathedral began in the late Romanesque style (it has since been rebuilt, but the shape of the original can be worked out from the crypt below) and the transepts were finished in the transitional style by 1200. [9,22] The south transept [9,23] retains some of the original work, showing chevrons on the arches and capitals with human and animal ornament. [9,24] The north side of the nave is also original, in the 'Early English' Gothic style. The arcade between the nave and the aisle is supported on clusters of eight pillars. Above the

[9,22] Christ Church Cathedral, Dublin. Flying buttresses were hardly seen outside Dublin as most rural churches had wooden roofs and did not need the extra support.

[9,23] Elevation of the south transept, Christ Church Cathedral, Dublin.

[9,25] Nave of St Patrick's Cathedral, Dublin.

arcade a string course divides the wall horizontally in half. Resting on the string course the triforium and clerestory windows are united under one large pointed arch. Grimacing faces peer out of the leaf decoration of the capitals of the pillars. The stone, style and craftsmen were all imported from the Bristol area of England. Building was completed around 1240.

St Patrick's Cathedral

Like Christ Church, St Patrick's Cathedral is cruciform in shape. [9,25] It is the largest of the Irish cathedrals, almost 100 metres long. Although it has been greatly altered by renovation, the north side of the nave is original.

It has a three-stage elevation like Christ Church, but the triforium and clerestory windows are separated, leaving more blank wall space which creates a heavier effect. There is not so much decorative carving, but there is a good stone rib vault and the building is spacious and uniformly designed.

These two buildings are the finest thirteenth-century work in the country and the only ones to have got the full Gothic treatment of three-stage elevations, ambulatories (walking places) in the choir and stone rib vaults. In the rest of the country, true structural Gothic was not often used. It was more frequently a decorative element used in doors, windows and arcades. Almost all Irish churches had wooden roofs, with vaulting used only in small areas.

Other Cathedrals

Outside Dublin, cathedrals were not so elaborate, but some fine work does exist. St Canice's in Kilkenny is well restored and in use. [9,26] Begun in 1210 and finished after 1270, it is unusual in

[9,24] Capital with human head, Christ Church Cathedral, Dublin.

[9,26] St Canice's Cathedral, Kilkenny, built 13th century.

[9,26](a) St Canice's Cathedral, Kilkenny — looking east down the nave.

[9,28] Composite pillars and arch supporting the crossing tower at Cashel Cathedral.

that almost all the work dates from the thirteenth century, most other buildings having extensions or renovations from a variety of dates.

A Norman building, St Canice's has details in common with Christ Church in Dublin. It is a cruciform structure with a crossing tower. The choir is lit by lancets grouped in threes. The nave is aisled [9,26](a) and the transepts have two chapels to the east. It is well proportioned, with wide pointed arches supported by composite pillars and lit by quatrefoil (four-leafed) windows. The quatrefoil theme is repeated on the finely carved west doorway. [9,27]

The Irish chiefs were also patrons of Gothic building. Cashel Cathedral is probably their grandest effort. [9,29] Built over a considerable number of years, it is slightly later in date than St Canice's

and has an unusually long choir and a very short nave, probably due to a lack of funds. The vaulted crossing, supporting a tower, is the largest in the country at 10 square metres.

FRANCISCAN FRIARIES

The Franciscan order had been in Ireland from the early thirteenth century. During the fifteenth century it expanded enormously, creating a need for new buildings. Franciscan friaries differ from Cistercian monasteries in a number of ways. [9,29] The churches are usually long, narrow, nave and chancel buildings, with a tall, slender

[9,27] West doorway, St Canice's Cathedral, Kilkenny. Quatrefoil design appears on windows and doors at St Canice's.

[9,29] Kilconnell Franciscan Friary, Co. Galway.

[9,30] Quin Abbey, Co. Clare — west door, crossing arch and east window. This view down the length of the church at Quin shows the doorway with its rows of simple moulding and the switch line tracery of the east window.

[9,31] Lancet windows, Athassel Priory, Co. Tipperary.

[9,32] East window (5-part lancet window), Dominican Priory, Kilmallock, Co. Limerick.

tower over the screen wall which separates the nave from the chancel. A transept is often built on the south side of the nave. The cloister is normally on the north side of the church, with the ambulatory included in the ground floor of the domestic buildings. (The cloister ambulatory in Cistercian monasteries was normally a lean-to, separate from the structure of the surrounding buildings.)

Though Franciscan friaries are generally plain, in line with the simplicity of the order's teachings, there are some well-carved doorways, windows and cloister arcades. The abbey at Quin in Co. Clare displays some good examples of this clearly cut stone work. [9,30]

TRACERY
The design and construction of buildings changed very little during the Anglo-Norman period, and so it is through the decorative work that we get some idea of the development of design in this period.

The stone framework which often forms a decorative element on windows is called 'tracery'. From simple beginnings it developed into the major decorative element in Irish medieval buildings. Early windows, called 'lancet windows', were simple, narrow openings with a round or pointed head. [9,31] Later, groups of three or five lancets separated only by narrow pillars, called 'mullions', were placed together under a large arch. A fine example of this type of window can be found in the eastern gable of the Dominican Priory at Kilmallock, Co. Limerick, dating from about 1291. [9,32]

The next phase of development was switch line or intersected line tracery in which the mullions appear to cross through each other at the top of the window. The Franciscan Friary at Askeaton, Co. Limerick, has windows with switch line tracery dating from about 1302. [9,33]

Small, thorn-like points projecting from the mullions are called 'cusps'. Cusped tracery can be seen on many fourteenth-century windows and the style extends into the fifteenth century. [9,34]

[9,33] Franciscan Friary at Askeaton, Co. Limerick — east window, switch line tracery.

[9,35] Black Abbey, Kilkenny — window in south transept with trefoil and quatrefoil tracery. The stained glass is more modern.

[9,34] Window, cusped tracery, Rosserk Friary, Co. Mayo.

Examples of flamboyant (flame-like) tracery can be seen at Kilcooley Abbey in Co. Tipperary, close to Holy Cross Abbey, which has some of the finest Gothic carving in Ireland. [9,36]

These represent some of the basic types of tracery which were largely borrowed from English and continental models. It is likely that at least some of these windows contained stained glass, but no examples have survived the turbulent times that followed.

[9,36] Kilcooley Abbey, Co. Tipperary — flamboyant tracery.

The large window in the south transept of the Black Abbey in Kilkenny has trefoil (three-leafed) and quatrefoil (four-leafed) divisions. [9,35] We have already seen quatrefoil decoration on St Canice's Cathedral, also in Kilkenny.

[9,37] Carrickfergus Castle, Co. Antrim.

Secular Architecture

As the Normans took territory from the native Irish, they built strongholds at strategic places to help defend it. At first these were structures of earth banks and wood called a 'motte and bailey', but substantial castles with turreted curtain walls and a strong keep soon followed. Carrickfergus Castle, Co. Antrim, [9,37] is a well-preserved example of this type, versions of which were built at Dublin, Limerick and Trim, Co. Meath.

In the fifteenth century smaller tower houses were built to defend the Pale around Dublin, and these were copied by the native Irish chieftains in the south and west of the country where more than 2,000 were built. Larger castles were also built by the McCarthys at Bunratty, Co. Clare and by the MacNamaras at Cahir, Co. Tipperary. [9,38]

[9,38] Cahir Castle, Co. Tipperary.

[9,39] Rothe House, Kilkenny.

The earliest surviving examples of unfortified houses date from the sixteenth century. Rothe House in Kilkenny is an example of a street house. [9,39] The ground floor is a series of arches, with the central one leading through to a courtyard behind the house. Among its interesting features is an aerial window which projects from the front of the building, allowing a view of the street.

Ormond Castle at Carrick-on-Suir, Co. Tipperary, is a sixteenth-century mansion, built during the reign of Elizabeth I of England. [9,40] Her monogram appears in the plasterwork of the main reception rooms. The plain front of the house is broken by a central projecting porch and window, and three gables. The simple mullioned windows have an undecorated drip moulding overhead. The building is a unique survivor of a type of architecture otherwise absent in Ireland.

[9,40] Ormond Castle, Carrick-on-Suir, Co. Tipperary.

By the sixteenth century Ireland had become an architectural backwater. At a time when the High Renaissance was under way in Europe, people in Ireland were still building in a scaled-down version of the Gothic style.

SCULPTURE

We have already seen that decorative carving on architecture was practised to quite a high standard during the Anglo-Norman period, but figure carving was beginning to develop separately on tombs and carved wooden statues.

The Normans began a fashion for stone tomb chests, with carved panels, topped with the figure of the deceased carved in the round. Examples survive in many Norman churches. A number of tombs in the Kilkenny area are related in style and may have been carved by the O'Tunney family. The tomb of Piers Fitz Óg Butler in Kilcooley Abbey in Co. Tipperary is in this style. [9,41] Squat, robed figures on the side of the chest represent saints and biblical figures. Their hair and robes are arranged in symmetrical patterns. The figure of a knight on the tomb lid is carved in the round.

In the west of Ireland chest tombs were installed in niches with elaborate tracery over them. Robed figures in high relief, one of them Christ displaying his wounds, appear on the side of the chest at the tomb in the Dominican Friary at Straide, Co. Mayo. [9,42] The beautiful tracery in the arch above is among the finest in the country.

Carved figures also appear on the cloister arcade at Jerpoint Abbey, Co. Kilkenny. Monks, knights and ladies are in a style similar to the tomb figures from the Kilkenny area. These stone sculp-

[9,42] Tomb in the Dominican Friary at Straide, Co. Mayo.

[9,43] Figures from cloister arcade at Jerpoint Abbey, Co. Kilkenny.

tures relate to European models, though there are some resemblances to earlier manuscript figures. [9,43]

Some examples of wood carving from the late medieval period still exist. The twenty-three misericord stalls in Limerick Cathedral are carved with mythical creatures from the medieval bestiaries. [9,44] The black oak is beautifully carved in a vigorous style full of movement and texture.

Two figures in painted wood from Fethard in Co. Tipperary are housed in the National Museum. God the Father in a tall crown and coloured robes

[9,41] Tomb of Piers Fitz Óg Butler, Kilcooley Abbey, Co. Tipperary.

[9,44] Misericords from Limerick Cathedral.

[9,46] Page from De Burgo Genealogy.

sits with an impassive expression, in dramatic contrast to a figure of the scourged Christ, [9,45] his body spattered with blood, his hands tied and a huge crown of thorns resting on his head. The bright red robe contrasts with the pale body and downcast face. The polychromed wood carving in the Gothic style indicates that these figures may have been carved in Spain.

MANUSCRIPTS

Few decorated manuscripts from the medieval period can be identified as having been made in Ireland. The De Burgo Genealogy, a history of the Burke family, has a European style of script and decoration, though it was clearly written in Ireland. [9,46] It is interesting to see the knight on horseback clad in chain mail, carrying his long lance as he might have appeared in the sixteenth century — old-fashioned by European standards.

[9,45] Figure of scourged Christ from Fethard, Co. Tipperary (National Museum of Ireland, Dublin).

METALWORK

Much of the metalwork that survives from the medieval period was made by Irish craftsmen for Irish patrons, but the style and design of the work were based on European models. Almost nothing of the Celtic tradition remains. Older objects like bookboxes were sometimes reworked, with European-style decoration replacing Christian Celtic work which would now be considered superior but was not highly regarded by the medieval Irish clergy.

Fourteenth-century decoration adorns the Domhnach Airgid Book Shrine, carried out by John O Bardan for John O Carbry, Abbot of Clones, according to the inscription on the front. [9,47] A silver-gilt figure of the crucified Christ has the central place, with figure panels displaying images of the Virgin, saints and angels surrounding him. A fragment of the true cross is displayed behind a crystal above the head of Christ and an enamelled crest of the Passion sits above this. The style of the figures relates to European manuscript design and sculpture, rather than any Irish tradition. Some plates of seventh-century engraved interlace are incorporated into the sides and top of the box.

Bishop Cornelius O'Dea of Limerick commissioned Tomas O'Carryd to make him a crosier [9,48] and mitre in 1418. These two objects have, uniquely, been kept in the possession of the Bishops of Limerick to the present day. The

[9,47] The Domhnach Airgid Book Shrine, front (National Museum of Ireland, Dublin).

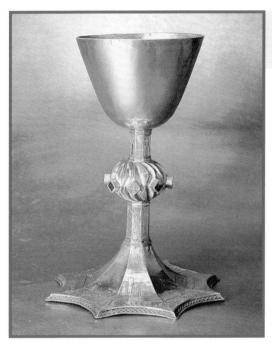

[9,50] De Burgo O'Malley Chalice.

[9,48] O'Dea Crosier, Treasury, Limerick Cathedral.

[9,49] Ballylongford Processional Cross.

crosier is in a style unrelated to earlier Irish examples. The crook, which holds a miniature Annunciation scene, is heavily outlined in plant forms. The base of the crook has two rows of images of saints and clerics topped with canopies. These look like the canopied niches designed to hold sculptures on contemporary churches. The crook is connected to the shaft of the crosier by a studded boss, similar in design to the boss which connects the Ballylongford Processional Cross to its shaft. [9,49] The stem of the De Burgo O'Malley Chalice has a boss which is close in style to the two already mentioned. [9,50] Although carefully crafted by Irish hands, these objects were all of European design.

CONCLUSION

It is debatable that the pressure of influences from Europe would have brought about the end of the Christian Celtic tradition even without the invasion of the Normans. Whether or not that is so, European styles had completely taken over in all the crafts by the sixteenth century. England had become a Protestant kingdom and sent out orders for the dissolution of monasteries in Ireland. This marked the end of Church patronage, which had provided the main source of commissions for Irish craftsmen. The Catholic Normans and Irish struggled to retain power and independence from England, but their days were numbered.

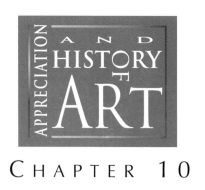

CHAPTER 10

SEVENTEENTH AND EIGHTEENTH CENTURIES

SEVENTEENTH CENTURY

The seventeenth century saw the final defeat of the Catholic Irish and Anglo-Normans by the English Crown. Ten thousand Irish soldiers and officers, 'The Wild Geese', left after their final defeat at Limerick in 1691. Lands confiscated from the Catholic landowners were given to English, Scottish and Welsh settlers, and the Catholic peasants were banished to Connaught under the Penal Laws.

It is hardly surprising that with all this warfare and strife little of architectural or artistic importance occurred until later in the century.

ARCHITECTURE

Most seventeenth-century buildings had some fortification though there was a tendency to include larger windows and create more spacious living quarters. In 1643 a large extension was built on to the O'Brien Castle at Lemaneagh on the edge of the Burren in Co. Clare. [10,1] The window frames (called mullions) are of stone and the roof had high pointed gables and tall chimney stacks. Battlements and defensive positions were an important part of the structure.

This robust style was common in the large houses built in the period, but the classical style was

[10,1] Lemaneagh Castle, Co. Clare.

beginning to appear, influenced by Dutch and English models. Beaulieu, Co. Louth, built around 1660, makes a startling contrast to Lemaneagh. [10,2] Built solely as a domestic abode, no provision for defence was made in the construction of this house. The hipped roof with dormer windows rests on a large eaves cornice in red brick. Brick is also used for the string course which creates a horizontal line around the building, in contrast to the vertical shapes of the doors and windows which have brick surrounds. The classical elements are in the proportion of the house and in the sculptured pediments over doors which are supported on pilasters (pilasters are pillars which project only slightly from the wall surface). It is difficult to realise that this elegant house is almost contemporary with Lemaneagh.

[10,2] Beaulieu, Co. Louth.

[10,4] The O'Connor Donn Monument, Sligo Abbey.

Sir William Robinson (d. 1712) is the first architect known to have designed a specific building in Ireland. His design for the Royal Hospital in Kilmainham, Dublin, is based on 'Hôtel des Invalides' in Paris and includes numerous classical elements. [10,3] A loggia, which is an open row of arches, faces onto the square around which the hospital was built. Externally the length of each range of the building is broken by projecting the last three bays (window or door openings) and the middle five bays a small distance forward. There is an entrance arch and pediment in the middle section of each façade. Corinthian pilasters, which run the full height of the building, and a tower overhead stand on the north side where the main entrance is situated.

The beautifully unified design of the Royal Hospital is well balanced and proportioned throughout. It was the first large-scale classical building in the country.

[10,3] Royal Hospital, Kilmainham, Dublin, designed by Sir William Robinson.

SCULPTURE

Religious sculpture was forbidden by the Penal Laws. Therefore only decorative sculpture or memorials remain from the seventeenth century. Much of the work was imported or carried out by English sculptors working in Ireland.

Carved around 1624, the O'Conor Don Monument, found in Sligo Abbey, is an Irish copy of a style of monument produced by English sculptors. [10,4] It was probably painted originally, as the English versions were. O'Connor and his wife kneel in separate niches facing each other. Classical decorations and family crests provide the surrounding ornamentation. Under the hood, on the highest parts of the monument, a small crucifix and angels are found.

Classical vine and leaf patterns, cherubs and urns along with coats of arms (family and royal crests) became the standard elements in late seventeenth-century decorative carving in stone and wood. Some fine examples of the wood-carver's craft survive in the Royal Hospital at Kilmainham, boldly carved in high relief. [10,5]

PAINTING

Almost nothing is known of painting in Ireland before the seventeenth century. Houses seem to have been hung with tapestries rather than paintings. The first paintings made in Ireland

[10,5]
Overdoor,
Royal
Hospital,
Kilmainham,
Dublin.

[10,7] Portrait of
'Caryll, 3rd
Viscount
Molyneaux of
Maryborough', c.
1700, by Garret
Morphey, oil on
canvas, 75 x 61 cm
(National Gallery of
Ireland, Dublin).

[10,6]
Portrait of
'Maura Rua
O'Brien', c.
1640,
unknown
artist, oil on
canvas,
81.25 x 66
cm (Private
collection).

flesh tones have a life-like quality which is an improvement on the less skilful portrait of Maura Rua we have just seen.

It is fairly clear that Irish landowners were not interested in the aesthetic qualities of art, but wanted portraits of their important family members or views of their houses and lands as prestige objects.

CONCLUSION

The seventeenth century saw the raw beginnings of a resurgence in the arts in Ireland. All styles were imported from England and the continent, particularly Holland. The unstable political situation in the country, however, did not allow for the leisure and refinement that was necessary to appreciate the new art forms which were being introduced.

EIGHTEENTH CENTURY: IRISH GEORGIAN PERIOD

There was a great effort in the eighteenth century to bring order and prosperity to the newly pacified country. The Protestant Parliament met in Dublin and succeeded in getting some trading advantages for the country, though real power still lay in Westminster. The Dublin Society was founded in 1731 to improve 'Husbandry, Manufacture and Other Useful Arts'. It sponsored research and awarded premiums to encourage industry and crafts. The Wide Streets Commission was set up in 1757 to regulate building in Dublin.

were by foreigners, Dutch artists in the main, who were employed by the new landowners to paint portraits or topographical pictures showing their houses and estates.

A portrait of Maura Rua O'Brien by an unknown artist shows a stiff and formalised style. [10,6] The subject's clothes and jewellery, and the large house at Lemaneagh already mentioned, show that native Irish leaders could still live in some splendour up to the mid-seventeenth century. The painting is not very skilfully done and has a naive quality which is typical of early Irish paintings.

Garret Morphey (1650–1716) was one of the first native artists of quality. He painted in a Dutch style and may have been trained by Gaspar Smits who worked in Dublin for many years. Morphey mainly painted portraits of Jacobite leaders. The armour-clad 'Caryll, 3rd Viscount Molyneaux of Maryborough' is one of these. [10,7] Hair, lace and armour are all well rendered and the warm

This was the age of the Grand Tour, when the wealthy made a tour of the sights of Europe, with particular emphasis on seeing the great works of art and architecture from classical and Renaissance times. Rome was one of the great centres of this tourist industry.

Irish patrons began to demand work in the European style, a need that was quickly filled by foreign artists first but then also by Irishmen trained in Europe and later in the Dublin Society's schools.

ARCHITECTURE
PALLADIANISM

The movement towards a more classical design in architecture in the seventeenth century evolved into the 'Palladian' style in the early eighteenth. This was modelled on the work of the sixteenth-century Italian architect Andrea Palladio, who based his designs on observations and measurements of Roman ruins. He published *Four Books of Architecture* which became the standard reference work for architects in the following century. Eighteenth-century architects also looked to the designs of the English architect Inigo Jones (1573–1652) for guidance.

SIR EDWARD LOVETT PEARCE (1699–1733)

Sir Edward Lovett Pearce introduced the Palladian style to Ireland. He spent only seven years here before his death, but in that time designed many major buildings.

Bellamont Forest, Co. Cavan, is a Palladian villa designed by Pearce. [10,8] Two storeys stand over the basement and the villa is five bays wide. The stonework on the basement is rusticated — deep joints and roughened surfaces emphasise the outlines of the cut stone. A string course separating the main floor from the top storey gives a horizontal contrast to the vertical shapes of the openings.

The main entrance is emphasised by a pediment supported on Doric columns. Without this projecting portico, which is a feature of many of Pearce's buildings, the villa would have the appearance of a simple box. Parliament House in Dublin (now the Bank of Ireland, College Green) also has a fine portico.

[10,8] Bellamont Forest, Co. Cavan, designed by Sir Edward Lovett Pearce.

[10,9] Parliament House (now Bank of Ireland, College Green), Dublin, designed by Sir Edward Lovett Pearce.

The Parliament House was the first large-scale Palladian building in Britain or Ireland and was designed to house both the Commons and Lords of the Irish Parliament. [10,9] An open colonnade surrounds the forecourt. The ends facing the street have round-headed arches with pediments overhead. Inside only the House of Lords retains its original shape and decoration. [10,10] This was the first large-scale building in Dublin and it provided a focus for the rebuilding of the city which followed.

Pearce was also involved in the design of Castletown House, Co. Kildare, which was built for William Conolly, Speaker of the House of Commons. It is one of the largest of about two dozen Irish country palaces built between 1716 and 1745.

RICHARD CASSELS (CASTLE) (D. 1751)

After Pearce's death, Richard Cassels took over his practice. He continued to work in the same style, designing large country houses like Russborough, Co. Wicklow, which may be his finest achievement.

The central block of Russborough is a villa, like Bellamont, joined to two wings by curved colonnades. [10,11] From the wings, long straight walls stretch out to end pavilions. Large Baroque entrance arches topped with little belfries are set in the centre of each wall, allowing access to the courtyards behind. The whole front of Russborough stretches well over 200 metres long. It is the best-preserved Georgian country mansion in its external architecture and its interior decoration and furniture. Cassels also designed the Rotunda Hospital and Leinster House in Dublin.

GEORGIAN TOWN HOUSES

After the death of Cassels, no single talent dominated for about twenty years. The building of fashionable city residences by the nobility and wealthy blossomed into a scheme for the development and planning of the whole city. Luke Gardiner (Lord Mountjoy), and Nathaniel Clements began this development from about

[10,11] Russborough House, Co. Wicklow, designed by Richard Cassels. Irish country palaces were working farms as well as luxurious homes. The west wing, on the left of the house, included stables; the east wing housed kitchens and workrooms.

[10,12] Georgian doorway in Dublin.

1720 on. The Ensor, Darley and Semple families were responsible for much of the work as speculators, architects and builders.

The Gardiner family laid out streets on the north side of Dublin, centred on Mountjoy and Rutland (now Parnell) Squares. The Fitzwilliams laid out the south side, centred on Merrion and Fitzwilliam Squares. [10,12] It is this phase of building that gave Dublin so much of its character.

The Wide Streets Commission, set up in 1757, oversaw the opening up of the city centre and the connection of the north and south sides of the city from Sackville Street (now O'Connell Street) to

[10,10] House of Lords, Parliament House, Dublin — interior.

[10,13] Georgian houses in Merrion Square, Dublin.

[10,15] Casino at Marino, Dublin, designed by Sir William Chambers.

D'Olier and Westmoreland Streets by a new bridge (O'Connell Bridge). This bridge was designed by the architect James Gandon, of whom we will see more later. Some of these streets were designed with matching shop fronts, an innovation which did not reach London until later. Sadly, little remains of the original designs. More ambitious plans for complete street elevations with centrepieces and end houses never materialised, probably due to lack of funds. [10,13]

Planned Georgian streets were built in other cities in Ireland. The Mall in Cork and Newtown Pery in Limerick [10,14] are among the larger developments outside Dublin. Pery Square has a fine block of houses with rusticated basements and first floors. End houses are part of the design.

Georgian street houses are generally plain on the outside except for wrought-iron balconies and doors with pillars and fanlights. The decoration inside was often lavish, with decorative plasterwork, fireplaces and woodwork.

[10,14] Pery Square, Limerick.

NEO-CLASSICAL
The neo-classical style came to Ireland through the work of several English architects.

SIR WILLIAM CHAMBERS (1723–96)
Sir William Chambers was the most prominent of the neo-classical architects. He never came to Ireland but had his designs carried out by architects working in this country. He designed the Chapel and Theatre (Examination Hall) of Trinity College Dublin.

A town house in Rutland (Parnell) Square, now the Sir Hugh Lane Municipal Gallery, was Chambers's first commission in Ireland. This was designed for Lord Charlemont, as was the Casino at Marino in Dublin, a country villa.

Carefully and completely designed, the Casino was conceived as an architectural gem rather than a functional building. [10,15] In plan it is the shape of a Greek cross inside a Doric colonnade. It is raised on a podium which is stepped on the east and west. The building is deceptively large, having a second storey almost hidden in the decorative entablature above the colonnade. The entire decoration follows classical models from Greece or Rome. Urns, swags and geometric patterns decorate friezes and pediments. The decorative carvings are of high quality, made by Simon Vierpyl. The building is elegant and well proportioned from every angle, with the functional parts disguised. The chimney pots are in the shape of urns and the downpipes are inside the pillars.

247

[10,16] James Malton painting of the Blue Coat School (King's Hospital), Dublin, designed by Thomas Ivory (National Gallery of Ireland, Dublin). Malton's painting of Ivory's design for the Blue Coat School includes the large central tower which was never built.

THOMAS IVORY (1732–86)

Thomas Ivory was one of the few native Irish architects to receive any public commissions. He was architectural drawing master of the Dublin Society's schools from about 1759.

In 1772 Ivory won a design competition for a new building for the Blue Coat School (King's Hospital) in Blackhall Place, Dublin, now owned by the Law Society of Ireland. [10,16] A central block, still in the Palladian style, is joined to two neo-classical wings by curved connecting walls. The façades of the wings have blank niches, windows without mouldings and swags set in the walls. To draw the elements together a balustrade runs the full width of the building along the bottom of the windows and across the top of the connecting walls. The towers have a Baroque look and are slim in comparison with the bulk of the buildings.

A contemporary watercolour by James Malton shows a central tower which was in Ivory's design but never built. It would have given the building an added elegance which is somewhat lacking in the present version.

JAMES GANDON (1743–1823)

Born in London, James Gandon trained in the offices of Sir William Chambers. He came to Dublin in 1781 to build the Custom House and stayed on to design many of the more prestigious buildings in eighteenth-century Dublin.

[10,17] The Custom House, Dublin, designed by James Gandon.

The Custom House has a two-storey front, with an attic storey and dome to create a focus at the centre of the building. [10,17] The entrance features a pediment supported on a colonnade, and columns are also used on the central block and at the slightly projecting ends to create a more interesting surface. A row of arches built in rusticated stone completes the ground floor, and the windows above them have little pediments on top. Interest is created at roof level by balustrades and skyline sculptures. This long, low building was designed to be reflected in the river, giving it apparent additional height.

The Four Courts is a larger building consisting of a central block, which is dominated by a grand dome, and two wings. [10,18] The massive columned drum is capped with a shallow copper dome. The façade has a large pedimented portico, with Corinthian pillars rising over two floors. Niches in the first floor are deeply recessed. The west wing is a modification of an earlier building which Gandon matched on the east. Between the central block and the wings are two courtyards which are fronted by arcaded screens with impressive triumphal arches in the centre. Large

[10,18] The Four Courts, Dublin, designed by James Gandon.

sculptural crests surmount these arches. Sculptures are used again on the roofline of the central building; these were produced by Edward Smyth of Dublin who carved most of the sculptures on Gandon's buildings.

CONCLUSION

There was a strong revival in architecture in Ireland in the eighteenth century, even though most of the important architects came from England or the continent. The revival was only of benefit to a small wealthy minority but it did bring architecture in Ireland back on a par with contemporary work in England.

SCULPTURE

Much of the sculpture from the eighteenth century is architectural decoration or sculpted monuments without figures. As the century progressed there was a greater demand for portrait busts and decorative figure sculpture. The Dublin Society schools which were set up in the 1740s trained young Irish students in drawing and design, and apprenticed them to sculptors working in Ireland.

JOHN VAN NOST THE YOUNGER (C. 1712–80)

John van Nost the Younger was an English sculptor of Dutch ancestry to whom a number of Irish students were apprenticed. He carved in a classical style and produced a number of fine tombs and monuments, as well as portrait busts of many of the founding members of the Dublin Society. His statues of Justice and Mars on the gateway to the Upper Castle Yard, Dublin Castle, are his only public sculptures to survive. [10,19]

CHRISTOPHER HEWETSON (C. 1739–94)

A number of the students of the Dublin Society schools apprenticed to van Nost turned out to be good sculptors, but they found it difficult to make a living in Ireland. Of these, Christopher Hewetson emigrated to Rome where he was well regarded and ran a successful studio. The sculpture 'A Memorial to Provost Baldwin' in Trinity College Dublin, gives some idea of his skill as a sculptor. [10,20] It is a fine, sensitively rendered piece, technically well made, with a high degree of realism. It is interesting to note that a student could receive training to the highest international standards in Ireland during the late eighteenth century.

EDWARD SMYTH (1749–1812)

Simon Vierpyl came to Ireland to make the carvings for the Casino at Marino and stayed to produce sculptures for the Royal Exchange (now City Hall) and other buildings. Edward Smyth was apprenticed to him and became the best-known sculptor in eighteenth-century Dublin, due to his work on Gandon's buildings. His faces on the keystones of the Custom House, personifying the rivers of Ireland and the Atlantic Ocean, show his bold style at its best. [10,21] They are carved in high relief and are classically proportioned, based on Greek and Roman models. The hair or head-dress is adorned with plant and animal forms which symbolise the rivers depicted in each keystone. There are fourteen heads in all, representing the Foyle, the Erne, the Liffey, the

[10,20] Memorial to Provost Baldwin, by Christopher Hewetson (Trinity College Dublin).

[10,19] Justice from the Upper Castle Yard Gate, Dublin Castle, by John van Nost the Younger.

249

Boyne, the Nore, the Blackwater, the Atlantic, the Bann, the Shannon, the Lee, the Lagan, the Suir, the Barrow and the Slaney. Smyth also carved figures and tombs. A life-size statue of Charles Lucas which stands in City Hall, Dublin, shows a quality and refinement lost on his outdoor sculptures through time and weathering.

PAINTING

In the eighteenth century Irish painting joined the mainstream of European art. Foreign artists came and worked in Ireland in the early years, introducing European styles to the country. Wealthy patrons who had been on the Grand Tour wanted work comparable to what they had seen in Europe. The Dublin Society schools employed masters trained in Europe to pass on continental methods to their Irish students. In the latter part of the century artists trained in Ireland were able to make a living in Britain and Europe and were considered the equal of artists trained abroad.

CHARLES JERVAS (1675–1739)

Charles Jervas was an Irish gentleman painter who studied in Rome and lived and worked mainly in London with occasional visits to Dublin. He moved in literary circles and knew both Alexander Pope and Jonathan Swift. The main body of his work consisted of well-designed

[10,22] Portrait of 'Jane Seymour Conway', c. 1720, by Charles Jervas, oil on canvas, 92 x 168 cm (National Gallery of Ireland, Dublin).

portraits. His brushwork was fluent and his rendering of fine fabrics was admirable.

He painted several portraits of Swift, of which 'The Dean in his Study' is the most famous. His portrait of 'Jane Seymour Conway' shows Jervas at his best. [10,22] The figure, bathed in silvery light, is elegantly posed and relaxed. Jervas was made principal painter to the King, which gives some idea of his contemporary standing in England.

THOMAS FRYE (1710–62)

Thomas Frye was Irish-born, but spent most of his working life in England. He painted in oils, pastels, miniatures and mezzotint (a form of engraving with tiny dots which gave prints a finer quality than line engraving). Frye is probably best known for his mezzotints of single, imaginary figures, dramatically lit in chiaroscuro. Frye also painted many fine portraits which capture a very natural likeness of the sitter. The portrait of 'Sir Charles Kemeys-Tynte' [10,23] shows his accomplished painting style in which colours and textures are beautifully handled.

THE 'DUBLIN GROUP'

The 'Dublin Group' of mezzotint engravers — Richard Houston, James McArdell, John Brooks, James Watson and others — became the most sought after in London from about 1750 to 1775. They copied the old masters and also made prints of contemporary work. McArdell's engravings of Joshua Reynolds's work are beautifully made.

THE DUBLIN SOCIETY SCHOOLS

The founding of the Dublin Society art schools in the mid-1740s was a very important event in the course of Irish art. The schools provided training

[10,21] Faces of the Rivers of Ireland — keystones from the Custom House, Dublin, by Edward Smyth.

[10,23] Portrait of 'Sir Charles Kemeys-Tynte', 1739, by Thomas Frye, oil on canvas, 127 x 102 cm (National Gallery of Ireland, Dublin).

not only for aspiring painters and sculptors, but also for silversmiths, furniture-makers, stucco-dores, potters, glass-makers and all the crafts. This common training accounts for what comes close to an Irish style in the craftwork of the later eighteenth century. Designs were stronger and more vigorous than other European work, with an emphasis on animals, birds and figures not found outside Ireland.

ROBERT WEST (D. 1770)
Robert West was the master of figure drawing in the Dublin Society schools. He got his training in Paris and so brought a French flavour to his students' work. He put an emphasis on working in pastels, to which he brought a French delicacy of colour.

JAMES MANNIN (D. 1779)
James Mannin was a French artist who worked in Dublin and was appointed master of design and landscape drawing in the Dublin Society schools.

THOMAS IVORY (1732–86)
Thomas Ivory was appointed master of architec-tural drawing about 1759, and through his

[10,24] 'Self-Portrait with Robert West', 1758, by Matthew William Peters, black and white chalk on paper (National Portrait Gallery, London).

students is responsible for the good quality of the minor country houses in the late eighteenth and early nineteenth centuries.

MATTHEW WILLIAM PETERS (1741–1814)
A pupil of West, Matthew William Peters's 'Self-Portrait with Robert West' [10,24] shows the quality of the students' work at the schools. This black-and-white chalk drawing was done while Peters was a sixteen-year-old pupil. Peters went on to make a career as a painter of portraits and subject pictures. 'The Gamesters' (Dublin Castle) is a good example of his lively use of colour.

HUGH DOUGLAS HAMILTON (C. 1739–1808)
Another student of West, Hugh Douglas Hamilton was considered one of the best pastel artists in Britain or Ireland in the eighteenth century. There was hardly a member of fashionable society in Dublin or London who did not sit for one of his 26 by 20 cm oval portraits, which were always lively and expressive, with hair, skin and eyes well rendered. He also painted portraits in oils. [10,25]

Hamilton moved to Italy from 1778 to 1791, where he was one of the most successful foreign artists in Rome. He was influenced by the English sculptor, John Flaxman, and the classical Italian sculptor, Antonio Canova, to try more ambitious work. His pastel picture 'Henry Tresham and Canova Looking at Canova's Cupid and Psyche' is

[10,25] 'A Portrait of a Young Gentleman in Rome', by Hugh Douglas Hamilton, oil on canvas, 94 x 66 cm (National Gallery of Ireland, Dublin).

[10,26] 'Cupid and Psyche in the Nuptial Bower', 1800, by Hugh Douglas Hamilton (National Gallery of Ireland, Dublin).

a masterpiece of the medium. Back in Ireland he exhibited his own 'Cupid and Psyche in the Nuptial Bower', [10,26] a typically classical piece.

LANDSCAPE

The Dublin Society schools were very advanced in having a landscape drawing master and the students who painted landscape were in the vanguard of the landscape painters of Europe.

GEORGE BARRET (1732–84)

Another student of the Dublin Society schools, George Barret spent the early years of his career painting in Wicklow and the Dargle valley on the

[10,27] 'A View of Powerscourt Waterfall', by George Barret, oil on canvas, 100 x 127 cm (National Gallery of Ireland, Dublin).

advice of his friend, Edmund Burke, whose essay 'On the Sublime and Beautiful' was very influential in its day. His painting 'A View of Powerscourt Waterfall' [10,27] is a good example of his early work.

In 1763 he travelled to London and was greatly impressed by the Welsh mountain landscape he passed through on his way. He spent several summers painting in north Wales. Some of his best work is from this time. Barret also painted in Scotland and the Lake District as well as painting imaginary Romantic landscapes. His 'Stormy Landscape' in the National Gallery of Ireland shows his vision of the sublime landscape, full of drama and excitement.

LONDON

Towards the end of the eighteenth century most of the best Irish artists went to London to make their living.

NATHANIEL HONE THE ELDER (1718–84)

Nathaniel Hone began his career as a miniature painter in Dublin. He moved to London in his twenties and began painting portraits in oils in the 1760s. He made a living as a fashionable painter, particularly of children. He painted several fine portraits of his own children. [10,28]

Hone was one of the founder members of the Royal Academy in 1768, but quarrelled with the Academy mainly due to his dislike of the working methods of Joshua Reynolds, whom he satirised in his painting 'The Conjuror'. [10,29] In this painting Reynolds is shown waving his wand over prints of the old masters from which he is going to

[10,28] 'The Piping Boy' (Hone's son, Camillus), 1769, by Nathaniel Hone the Elder, oil on canvas, 36 x 31 cm (National Gallery of Ireland, Dublin).

[10,29] 'The Conjuror', 1775, by Nathaniel Hone the Elder, oil on canvas, 145 x 173 cm (National Gallery of Ireland, Dublin).

conjure up his own composition. Hone despised this direct borrowing of old master compositions and avoided it in his own work.

His preference for Dutch art, particularly Rembrandt, is seen in Hone's use of light and shadow and the rendering of textures. Note the use of fur in 'The Conjuror'. Nathaniel the Elder was the first in a line of members of the Hone family who went on to pursue a career as an artist.

JAMES BARRY (1741–1806)

Like Barret, James Barry was a protégé of Edmund Burke. He studied in Italy from 1765 to 1771 and spent the rest of his life in London. From his earliest days he was imaginative and a little controversial. He showed a picture of 'St Patrick

Baptising the King of Cashel' at the Dublin Society in 1763, years before Irish subjects were considered suitable. In London he became Professor of Painting at the Royal Academy, but was dismissed in 1795 for verbally attacking fellow members of the Academy.

Barry tried to remain true to neo-classical ideals by devoting his time to subject pictures instead of the more lucrative portrait commissions he might have had. His fine 'A Self-Portrait' [10,30] shows him sitting at the feet of the statue 'Hercules crushing the snake of envy' while holding his own painting 'The Cyclops and the Satyrs' in his hand. This is one of his best works. In some of his other works his ambition and high ideals exceeded his talent. His 'Adam and Eve' [10,31] is lifeless, with stone-like figures in cumbersome poses.

CONCLUSION

The role of the Dublin Society schools was extremely important in the eighteenth century. They brought Irish artists to a standard acceptable all over Europe and Irish art back into the main-stream of European developments in painting, from which it had been separated for hundreds of years.

THE APPLIED ARTS

In the earlier part of the eighteenth century most Irish craftwork followed the English style, but was usually a few years behind the fashion. After 1750 a number of coincidences combined to create a vibrant and original crafts industry in Ireland.

[10,30] 'A Self-Portrait', 1804, by James Barry, oil on canvas, 76.2 x 63 cm (National Gallery of Ireland, Dublin).

[10,31] 'Adam and Eve', by James Barry (National Gallery of Ireland, Dublin).

253

Some trade restrictions between Ireland and England were lifted and artisans who had received training and encouragement from the Dublin Society schools were available to produce craftwork for the newly wealthy middle class.

PLASTERWORK

While plasterwork is found in seventeenth-century buildings and even a few examples from the Middle Ages survive, the first important stucco (from the Italian for plaster) work was produced for the much more elaborate eighteenth-century houses.

The Francini brothers worked in Ireland in the 1730s and 1740s. They were Italians and introduced full-size human figures and a great wealth of high-relief festoons, garlands and 'putti'. The saloon at Carton, Co. Kildare, is a marvellous example of their work, which can also be seen at Riverstown House, Co. Cork, Castletown, Co. Kildare, 85 St Stephen's Green, Dublin, and many other places. [10,32]

In the 1750s an Irish stuccodore called Robert West — not to be confused with the master of the same name in the Dublin Society school — produced some lively and elaborate plasterwork. In 20 Lower Dominick Street, Dublin, a house which he built for himself, some of his finest work

[10,33] Plasterwork in the stairway of 20 Lower Dominick Street, Dublin, by Robert West.

can be seen. [10,33] The ceiling of the staircase is decorated with birds, heads, musical instruments and cornucopias, all interconnected by scrolls.

Michael Stapleton was another great Irish stuccodore working a little later than West, in the neo-classical style. His work was more formalised and in lower relief. The stairway of Belvedere House in Great Denmark Street, Dublin, is a fine example of what Stapleton could do. [10,34]

The English decorators, Robert Adam and James Wyatt, supplied designs for the interiors of many houses in the neo-classical period, Slane Castle, Co. Meath, Curraghmore, Co. Waterford and Westport, Co. Mayo, among them.

[10,34] Plasterwork in the stairway of Belvedere House, Great Denmark Street, Dublin, by Michael Stapleton.

[10,32] Section of plasterwork from saloon at Carton House, Co. Kildare, by the Francini brothers.

[10,35] Silver dish ring, c. 1780, Dublin.

[10,37] Carved mahogany table, c. 1735, with paw-shaped feet.

SILVERWORK

Workshops were established in Dublin, Cork and Limerick, where silverwork in the late Rococo style was produced. Repoussé, chasing and open-work were features of this style. Designs included country scenes, flowers, birds and masks. Dish rings, [10,35] three-legged sugar bowls and helmet-shaped cream jugs were particularly Irish designs. [10,36]

FURNITURE

Mahogany traded from the West Indies became the most commonly used wood for furniture-making and Irish carvers developed a style to suit it. Chairs, cabinets and particularly side tables were heavily carved with foliage, animals and masks. Legs were often finished in big, hairy paws. [10,37]

GLASS

Trade restrictions were dropped after 1780 and a new tax was put on English glass. The Irish glass industry, therefore, went through a very product-ive period. There were glass factories in Dublin, Belfast, Cork and Waterford, all producing thick, deeply cut glasswork. The large serving dish with turnover rim and deeply cut design is typical of Irish work of the period. [10,38]

OTHER CRAFTS

Delftware, book-binding and linen-printing industries also flourished, producing work of the highest quality equal to the best in Europe.

[10,36] Silver pierced dish cover, 1780s, Dublin.

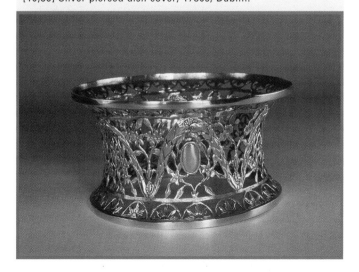

[10,38] 18th-century cut glass selection.

[10,38(a)] 18th-century silverware.

CONCLUSION

Towards the end of the century, the neo-classical Adam style took over in all the crafts, ending the short, creative fling of the native craftsmen; work became more restrained and repetitive.

CONCLUSION

In the eighteenth century Irish art rejoined the mainstream of European development. The influx of outside influences during the first half of the century was taken on board by Irish artists and craftsmen, and through the guidance of the Dublin Society schools an Irish style developed for a time. Painters, sculptors, architects and craftsmen were well trained and confident, in any company, in their own ability. It is true that the wealth generated in the period of the Irish Parliament benefited only a privileged few who were able to afford a life of luxury and refinement, but many of the artists and craftsmen were Irish and are worthy of our respect and admiration for what they achieved.

At the close of the century, Ireland was again in political turmoil. The 1798 Rebellion and the threat of war in Europe brought the period of comparative independence to an end with the Act of Union and the closing of the Irish Parliament.

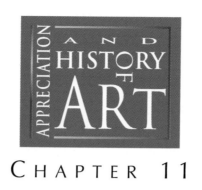

CHAPTER 11

NINETEENTH AND TWENTIETH CENTURIES

NINETEENTH CENTURY

As a result of the Act of Union of 1800, Ireland lost its Parliament and all the social and economic status that went with it. This made it difficult for artists to get commissions, and so many were forced to make their living abroad. On the other hand, the increased British presence led to a building boom. Army and police barracks, poorhouses, courthouses and administrative buildings were erected. Although the architecture was not generally very beautiful, some good work has survived.

Some peculiar contradictions dominated nineteenth-century society. Traders exploited the poor to make large profits even through the Famine years, and then used these profits to buy sentimental or romantic paintings and sculptures.

[11,1] General Post Office, Dublin, designed by Francis Johnston.

Styles continued largely in the classical mode. Accuracy of drawing and careful finish were still the norm well into the century. It was only towards the end of the century that painters began to question subjects and techniques.

ARCHITECTURE

The nineteenth century was one of the most extraordinarily productive periods of building in the country's history. It is impossible to give more than an outline of the work carried out at this time. Styles followed English developments, although they were generally introduced to Ireland a few years after their arrival in England. In the early part of the century architects followed the classical and Gothic styles, depending on the taste of the client.

CLASSICAL STYLE

Used for most public buildings, the classical style varied from a continuation of eighteenth-century fashions to a more severe style based on Greek models.

FRANCIS JOHNSTON (1760–1829)

Francis Johnston was the chief public architect of his day. He designed the General Post Office in Dublin, with its large portico supported on Ionic columns. [11,1] The rusticated stone on the ground floor and the balustrade and skyline sculptures at roof level add interest and a sense of scale to this large functional building. It typifies the nineteenth-century use of classical elements in the design of public buildings in Ireland.

Johnston, who began as an apprentice to Thomas Cooley, designed buildings like Townley Hall in Co. Louth and St George's Church in Hardwicke Street, Dublin, in the classical style, while at the same time the Chapel Royal in Dublin Castle was being built in the Gothic style to his design.

Nelson's Pillar, which used to stand in O'Connell Street in Dublin, was also the work of Johnston.

GOTHIC STYLE

A version of the medieval English perpendicular style was used in the design of Gothic buildings in the early nineteenth century. Some houses and most of the Church of Ireland churches which were built in the first half of the century were in this style. They were mainly rectangular in plan, having pointed windows with switch line tracery. The external decoration included buttresses with pinnacles on top and battlements along the walls and on the towers. [11,2] Churches of this type can be found in almost every town in Ireland.

The Pain brothers (James and George Richard), who came to Ireland to work on Lough Cutra Castle in Co. Galway, built up a practice designing churches in the Munster area. They also castellated a number of houses, among them Dromoland Castle in Co. Clare [11,3] and the picturesque Blackrock Castle on the estuary at Cork. The Pains designed a number of Catholic churches in the classical style, of which Millstreet Parish Church, Co. Cork, is an example.

[11,2] Monkstown Parish Church, Co. Dublin, designed by John Semple (active 1820–31).

[11,3] Dromoland Castle, Co. Clare, designed by the Pain brothers.

In the 1840s both classical and Gothic styles underwent significant changes. An increased interest in the study of archaeology and architectural history led to the availability of more accurate information on particular styles.

CLASSICAL (VICTORIAN) STYLE

A style based on Italian Renaissance villas was used as an alternative to the classical. It had more texture, using rusticated stone on basements and quoins (cornerstones). String courses and cornices were more sculpted, and small, arcaded towers called belvederes were sometimes used. William Deane Butler (active 1830–49) designed Amiens Street (Connolly) Station in this style. [11,4] Kingsbridge (Heuston) Station by the English architect, Sancton Wood, is similar in style.

Towards the end of the century architects mixed styles to create a more dramatic effect that was almost Baroque in the use of decoration.

[11,4] Connolly Station, Dublin, designed by William Deane Butler.

THOMAS DREW (1838–1910)

Thomas Drew designed the Ulster Bank in College Green, Dublin, [11,5] which combines a number of classical elements into a very decorative façade. The original building, which could only be called Victorian in design, had an iron and glass roof that was flanked by tall chimneys.

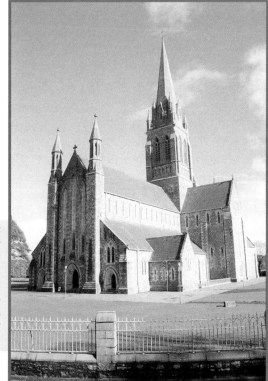

[11,6] St Mary's Cathedral, Killarney, Co. Kerry, designed by Augustus Welby Pugin.

GOTHIC REVIVAL
AUGUSTUS WELBY PUGIN (1812–52)

The designs and writings of the English architect Augustus Welby Pugin were very influential in the second half of the nineteenth century. He idealised the society of the Middle Ages when the great Gothic cathedrals of England and France were built, and he recommended the early 'decorated style' as the ideal for church building.

Pugin had two basic tenets in design: first, that buildings should have no features that were not necessary for convenience, construction or propriety; second, that ornamentation existed only to enrich essential construction. Traditional medieval decoration in wood or stone was approved.

His Irish churches were austere in design. St Mary's Cathedral in Killarney, Co. Kerry, [11,6] one of the best examples of Gothic revival in Ireland, is large but simple. Pugin also designed the Loreto Convent in Gorey, Co. Wexford, and St Mark's Church and the cathedral in Enniscorthy, Co. Wexford.

J.J. McCARTHY (1817–82)

J.J. McCarthy was very much influenced by Pugin. He completed the cathedral at Armagh and the spire and tower at Maynooth. The chapel in All Hallows College, Dublin, is a good example of his work on large buildings and the Church of St Agatha, Glenflesk, Co. Kerry, displays the theories of the Gothic revival applied to a small church. [11,7]

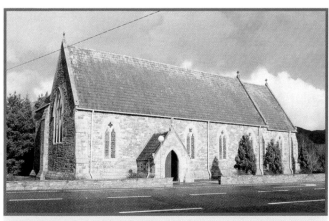

[11,7] Church of St Agatha, Glenflesk, Co. Kerry, designed by J.J. McCarthy.

[11,8] Staircase hall of the Museum Building, Trinity College Dublin, designed by Benjamin Woodward.

BENJAMIN WOODWARD (1816–61)

A partner in the Cork firm of Sir Thomas Deane and Son, Benjamin Woodward spent his early years with the firm working on Queen's College, Cork (UCC). A well-designed building in simplified Gothic style, it is built around three sides of a square, with the south side left open for light.

Woodward's best building, the Museum Building (School of Engineering) at Trinity College Dublin, [11,8] is a departure from the Gothic style. A variation on the Lombardy Romanesque style, stones of different colour were used in the construction to produce a decorative pattern. An original feature of this building is that the masons, the O'Shea brothers from Cork, who carved the decorations were given a free hand to sculpt what they liked within the constraints of the structure and produced some marvellous work. This notion of allowing freedom to craftsmen was based on the writings of John Ruskin, the English author and critic, who was a key influence on Woodward. The carvings on the bases of the pillars of the Kildare Street Club, also by Woodward, were made by the Harrisons, another family of masons.

CONCLUSION

The end of the century saw great changes — particularly in industrial buildings — in the new building materials available such as mass-produced and moulded bricks, iron, glass and concrete. Craftsmanship began to disappear with the increase in mass production and machinery.

SCULPTURE

The classical style continued in sculpture almost to the end of the century. The Greek revival led to the use of Greek draperies and props in many works, even portraits. There were a good many commissions for public monuments, often decided by competition. Although there was some commissioning of religious works for churches after Catholic Emancipation in 1829, most were imported from Italy or executed by poor-quality Dublin workshops.

JOHN HENRY FOLEY (1818–74)

John Henry Foley trained under John Smyth in the Dublin Society schools and then went to London in 1834 where he soon made a name for himself. He won public commissions in Ireland, England and India, and did a variety of other work, including portraits and subject sculptures.

A number of his outstanding public works survive in Dublin, including the statues of Goldsmith, Burke and Grattan outside Trinity College, and the seated figure of Sir Benjamin Lee Guinness outside St Patrick's Cathedral. In his largest Irish piece, the O'Connell monument in O'Connell Street, [11,9] the female figure representing Erin is the centrepiece of the frieze on the base. She holds the Act of Catholic Emancipation in one hand and points to O'Connell, overhead, with her other. A group representative of professions and all classes of Irishmen read the Act. The group is beautifully designed, with the modelling varying from low relief in some of the background figures to a full three-dimensional treatment for the outer figures. Each figure in the well-composed group is given an individual character. Monuments by Foley outside Dublin include one to Lord Rosse in Birr, Co. Offaly.

[11,9] O'Connell monument, Dublin, by John Henry Foley.

Foley's most important work in England was his contribution to the Albert Memorial. He carved the figure of Albert and the beautiful group representing Asia.

JOHN HOGAN (1800–58)

John Hogan lived and worked in Rome from 1824 to 1848 before returning to his native Cork where he had received his early training. He got some public commissions including the Father Mathew statue in Cork, [11,10] the Daniel O'Connell monument in Limerick and the O'Connell and Drummond group in City Hall, Dublin. He also

[11,10] Fr Mathew statue, Cork, by John Hogan.

made a fine, life-size portrait of William Crawford in marble, now kept in the Crawford Municipal Gallery in Cork, as is his 'Drunken Faun', a classical study in plaster, from his early years in Rome. Hogan was one of the few talented Irish sculptors to get religious commissions. His 'Dead Christ' in the Carmelite Church in Dublin shows the quality of his work in the neo-classical style.

PAINTING

In the early part of the nineteenth century, style and technique continued much as they had in the eighteenth. Most artists got their initial training in Ireland and then went to England to continue training and, hopefully, to make a living. Artists painted in the neo-classical or Romantic styles, drawing carefully and finishing with blended brushstrokes. Subject-matter in some pictures was quite sentimental, a trend that also existed in English literature of the period. Watercolour became more popular, not only as a sketching medium, but for finished painting as well.

JAMES ARTHUR O'CONNOR (1792–1841)

James Arthur O'Connor was the son of an engraver and print seller in Dublin, whose collection of prints of Dutch landscape may have influenced the young O'Connor. He used dramatic light and shadow in paintings that usually showed man as insignificant in the face of nature. His 'Poachers' and 'Thunderstorm: The Frightened Wagoner' [11,11] highlight his 'Romantic' view of nature. The work of Claude

[11,11] 'Thunderstorm: The Frightened Wagoner', 1832, by James Arthur O'Connor, oil on canvas, 65 x 76 cm (National Gallery of Ireland, Dublin).

[11,12] 'The Last Circuit of Pilgrims at Clonmacnoise', 1838, by George Petrie, pencil and watercolour on paper, 67.2 x 98 cm (National Gallery of Ireland, Dublin).

[11,13] 'The Toy-Seller', 1835, by William Mulready (National Gallery of Ireland, Dublin).

Lorrain, which was very fashionable in England and Ireland in the nineteenth century, strongly influenced his style. The rendering of textures in trees, sky and water and the strong colouring all give effect to the dramatic atmosphere in the paintings.

GEORGE PETRIE (1790–1866)

George Petrie was famous as an antiquarian. His watercolours and drawings complement his researches into the early history of Irish art and architecture. This interest is apparent in his 'The Last Circuit of Pilgrims at Clonmacnoise', [11,12] which also demonstrates good technical detail, a high quality of drawing and an ability to use watercolours well. This was the same Petrie who discovered the late Iron Age object called the Petrie Crown.

WILLIAM MULREADY (1786–1863)

Born in Ennis, Co. Clare, William Mulready's family moved to England when he was five years old. He is, therefore, essentially an English artist, although he did exhibit at the Royal Hibernian Academy (RHA) and was made an honorary member in 1860. He was a teacher, illustrator and landscape painter, but particularly a genre painter. His painting of the human figure is sensitively and accurately done, with wonderfully observed details of expression and movement. Some of his best work includes children, like his 'The Toy-Seller'. [11,13]

DANIEL MACLISE (1806–70)

Daniel Maclise was born in Cork and got his early training in the Cork School of Art. He financed his own further education in London and Paris by selling portraits and landscapes. By the 1830s he was an established painter, working on large detailed canvases and subject pictures such as 'The Falconer', which hangs in the Crawford Municipal Gallery, Cork. In the 1850s he painted part of the mural decorations in the House of Lords, London, 'Wellington and Blucher on the Field of Waterloo' and 'The Death of Nelson'. His 'The Marriage of Aoife and Strongbow' [11,14] is similar in scale to the murals and shows Maclise's ability at figure drawing and large-scale composition.

FREDERICK BURTON (1816–1900)

Born in Corofin, Co. Clare, Frederick Burton was a very accomplished draughtsman and watercolourist. He worked with Petrie and was influenced by him. His painting of the 'Aran

[11,14] 'The Marriage of Aoife and Strongbow', 1854, by Daniel Maclise, oil on canvas, 309 x 505 cm (National Gallery of Ireland, Dublin).

[11,15] 'The Meeting on the Turret Stairs', 1864, by Frederick Burton, watercolour on paper, 95.5 x 60.8 cm (National Gallery of Ireland, Dublin). This painting illustrates a scene from the Danish saga of Helelill and Hilderbrand. Subjects from the romantic past were popular in Victorian society.

[11,16] 'Feeding Pigeons', c. 1860, by Nathaniel Hone the Younger, oil on canvas, 46 x 37 cm (National Gallery of Ireland, Dublin).

Fisherman's Drowned Child' was made after an experience on a trip to the Aran Islands with Petrie. He was an art historian and, like many of his era, was very interested in the medieval period. His painting 'The Meeting on the Turret Stairs' [11,15] shows his medieval interest and his incredibly rich use of watercolours. His choice of brilliant colour and subjects from ancient legends betrays the influence of the contemporary pre-Raphaelite movement in England on Burton.

CONTINENTAL INFLUENCE

From about 1850 onwards, Irish artists began to find their way into continental academies of art, particularly in Antwerp and Paris, the latter of which had superseded Rome as the art centre of the western world. New approaches to painting were developing in the French academies and in the artist colonies that sprang up in the small towns around the Forest of Fontainebleau, south of Paris. Subjects changed from the formal classical and Romantic themes to scenes from the daily lives of ordinary people and pieces of ordinary landscape. Techniques also changed. Brushwork became looser and paint was applied thickly, allowing artists to work more quickly and expressively.

NATHANIEL HONE THE YOUNGER (1831–1917)

Nathaniel Hone the Younger was a grand-nephew of the older Hone. He took up painting only at the age of twenty-two, after a short career as an engineer. He had independent means and so was free to develop his work as he liked, not having to rely on commissions for income.

After some initial training in Paris, he moved to the town of Barbizon and worked among the famous French plein-air artists of the day, including Millet and Harpignies. Corot was a strong influence on his work. He spent twenty years in the area, except for painting and sketching trips. He returned to Ireland in 1875 and spent the remainder of his life painting, farming and teaching at the RHA, where he was a major influence on young Irish artists.

Hone sold fewer than 100 paintings in his life. The remaining 550 oils and 900 watercolours were left to the National Gallery of Ireland. His early work in France is often of woodland, with light playing among trees. His painting 'Feeding Pigeons' [11,16] shows his subtle use of colour and light. In his later work in Ireland the sky often predominates, in both landscape and seascape. His 'Pastures at Malahide' [11,17] shows his use of the changing moods of the Irish landscape in

[11,17] 'Pastures at Malahide', c. 1907, by Nathaniel Hone the Younger, oil on canvas, 82 x 124 cm (National Gallery of Ireland, Dublin).

[11,19] 'Scene in the Phoenix Park', 1890s, by Walter Osborne, oil on canvas, 71 x 91 cm (National Gallery of Ireland, Dublin).

the quick, vigorous brushwork and subtle colours. Hone also painted boats, seascapes and farming activities. His watercolour sketches are loosely painted in bold, watery strokes, capturing the essential tone and colour of a fleeting moment in a changing landscape. [11,18]

WALTER OSBORNE (1859–1903)

Walter Osborne began his studies at the RHA and then went to Antwerp for further training, followed by painting trips in England, Holland, France and Spain. He spent a year painting in Brittany. His 'Apple-Gathering Quimperlé' dates from this time and shows the influence of the plein-air style on his work in the small brush-strokes and subtle representation of light and colour. Osborne made a living in Dublin by painting fine portraits, such as 'Nathaniel Hone, Artist', and street scenes of the lives of ordinary people in the Coombe. In the 1890s his work became more Impressionistic. 'Scene in the Phoenix Park', [11,19] painted more freely and colourfully than his earlier work, is a beautiful study of dappled light falling on a group of people.

JOHN BUTLER YEATS (1839–1922)

John Butler Yeats began his career as an architect. He took up painting in 1867 and went to study in London, where he worked for a number of years. However, little of this work survives. On his return to Dublin he made a living as a portrait painter. His sitters included many of the great Irishmen of the day, whose characters he captured perfectly. He painted in an English style, influenced at second hand by the French movements. The use of paint and light in his portraits is well handled. The paintings of 'John O'Leary, Fenian', 'William Butler Yeats, Poet' and 'Lily Yeats' [11,20] are among his finest.

SARAH PURSER (1848–1943)

Born in Dún Laoghaire, Sarah Purser went to the Metropolitan School of Art, Dublin and then to France for further study. She made a good living as a portrait painter in Ireland and England, but her best work is more informal and freely painted. 'Le Petit Déjeuner' and 'A Lady Holding a Rattle' [11,21] show the freer treatment reserved for her more personal work. She was a founder member of 'An Túr Gloine', a group of artists who wanted to foster stained glass design in Ireland.

[11,18] 'Dinghies on a Normandy Beach', c.1860, by Nathaniel Hone the Younger, pencil and watercolour on paper, 19.7 x 28.4 cm (National Gallery of Ireland, Dublin).

[11,20] 'Lily Yeats', 1901, by John Butler Yeats, oil on canvas, 91 x 71 cm (National Gallery of Ireland, Dublin).

[11,22] 'La Jeune Bretonne', 1890, by Roderic O'Conor, oil on canvas, 65 x 50 cm (National Gallery of Ireland, Dublin).

[11,21] 'A Lady Holding a Rattle', 1885, by Sarah Purser, oil on canvas, 41 x 31 cm (National Gallery of Ireland, Dublin).

brushwork and bright colours. He also painted landscapes. 'The Farm at Lezaver, Finistère' [11,23] displays a painting technique close to van Gogh's, with bright colours laid on in stripes which follow the contours of the objects portrayed. This use of strong contour lines in bold, complementary colours develops further in his work in the late nineteenth century. In the early twentieth century, O'Conor moved to Paris and began painting interiors and nudes in more muted colours, basing his themes and approach on the old masters.

[11,23] 'The Farm at Lezaver, Finistère', 1894, by Roderic O'Conor, oil on canvas, 72 x 93 cm (National Gallery of Ireland, Dublin).

RODERIC O'CONOR (1860–1940)

Roderic O'Conor was born in Roscommon and first went to art school in Dublin. He later studied in Antwerp and then Paris. His training was quite normal for the time, but he took an early interest in the latest styles of painting in France. He was impressed by the work of van Gogh and Gauguin.

O'Conor painted in Brittany during the late 1880s and 1890s, with some of his finest work dating from this period. 'La Jeune Bretonne' [11,22] shows an Impressionist treatment with loose

THE APPLIED ARTS

We have already referred to architectural carving and the quality of the work of the artisan craftsman under the heading of architecture above. Some fine stonework was carried out on banks, churches and public buildings during the nineteenth century. The large variety of work produced by memorial carvers can be seen in the elaborate imitation High Crosses found in almost every graveyard in the country.

PLASTERWORK

Plasterwork was still of high quality in the earlier part of the century. The interior of Ballyfin, Co. Laois, [11,24] is a good example of this work, often more elaborate than that of the late eighteenth century. However, as the century progressed, mass production took over from the craftworker in plaster.

OTHER CRAFTS

Glass, silver, furniture and porcelain were still of high quality well into the century. Irish themes were popular, with shamrocks, round towers, wolfhounds, etc. being incorporated into designs. [11,25] Work became increasingly ornate before going into decline in the face of mass production.

STAINED GLASS

As a result of the building boom there was a high demand for stained glass in the nineteenth century. Michael O'Connor and his studio produced some fine windows in England and Ireland. He won the gold medal in the stained glass section of the Great Exhibition of 1862 in London. His east window in St James's Church, St James's Street, Dublin, [11,26] shows the high

[11,25] Selection of 19th-century glass and silver.

quality achieved by some Victorian stained glass studios. More frequently work was of poor quality, with an over-emphasis on pictorial effects rather than the beauty that can be obtained by the play of light through the rich colours of high-quality glass.

CONCLUSION

The arts became a more important element in society during the Victorian era. An educated person was expected to be familiar with the major artists and styles of architecture of the past. Wealthy individuals and organisations collected art and commissioned buildings to enhance their social status. Many of the great collections of the world were enlarged by nineteenth-century

[11,24] Plasterwork at Ballyfin, Co. Laois.

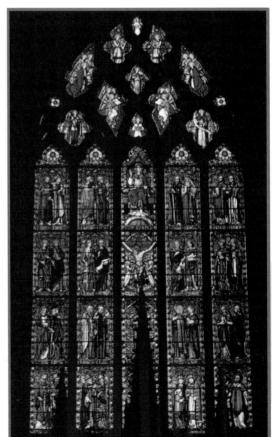

[11,26] East window, St James's Church, St James's Street, Dublin, 1859, by Michael O'Connor.

purchases of artifacts from all over the world, the collections of our own National Gallery and National Museum among them.

The expansion of the market for works of art and design led to the foundation of schools of art and design outside Dublin. However, graduates found it difficult to make a living in Ireland and many were forced to make their careers abroad.

There were huge social gaps in Irish society, with the privileged few living like princes. A new, expanding middle class was housed in the new suburbs of red-brick houses that sprang up around the larger towns and cities, while the rural poor still lived at subsistence level in thatched cottages unchanged since medieval times. It suited the well-off to romanticise the life of the poor as one of rustic simplicity and charm rather than hunger and desperation.

TWENTIETH CENTURY

In the early part of the twentieth century the literary movement and increased national awareness had a great effect on the arts. Designers looked to Ireland's pre-Norman past for their references. The War of Independence and the Civil War that followed disrupted these early movements, leaving the country without a sense of artistic direction.

The modern movements in the arts in Europe were slow to penetrate into the conservative backwater that Ireland had become. Younger artists working in modern styles were not accepted at the Royal Hibernian Academy and so they set up the Irish Exhibition of Living Art in 1943 to put their work on public view. In the following decades awareness of modern art and design increased. The ROSC exhibition, begun in 1967 and held at intervals until the 1980s, brought the work of contemporary international artists into the country, creating a response in Irish artists and the public. There was an enormous growth in the number and quality of art and design colleges from the early 1970s on, which put Irish art and design in the healthiest condition it has been in for generations.

ARCHITECTURE

In the early part of the century architects continued to turn to the past to find a style in which to dress their buildings. Various forms of the classical style prevailed in the design of public buildings and Gothic remained in use for churches. Hiberno-Romanesque architecture also became fashionable for church building. It was seen as an Irish style which would fit in with the literary revival and the crafts movement.

EDWARDIAN STYLE

In a conscious effort to create impressive buildings, architects used Georgian models as a basis for their designs. This Edwardian style continued well into the century.

Aston Webb (1849–1930) and T.M. Deane (1852–1933) were architectural partners who designed the new Government Buildings in Merrion Street, Dublin, in 1904. They copied the projecting end bays with recessed columns from the Custom House, but theirs is a much more square building. Webb also designed the College of Science building in Merrion Street.

R.M. Butler (1872–1943) won the 1912 competition for the design of the new University College Dublin building in Earlsfort Terrace, now the National Concert Hall. [11,27] The influence of the Custom House appears again in the end bays with recessed columns, but the building is much more solid, without the variety of openings and skyline sculptures of the Custom House. Butler designed an interesting church at Newport, Co. Mayo, based loosely on the Hiberno-Romanesque style.

[11,27] National Concert Hall, Earlsfort Terrace, Dublin, designed by R.M. Butler.

[11,28] Stormont Parliament House, designed by Sir Arnold Thornley.

[11,29] Doorway, Honan Chapel, Cork, designed by James F. McMullen.

Jones and Kelly won the 1923 design competition for Cork City Hall with a building in the Edwardian style.

In Belfast, Sir Alfred Brumwell Thomas designed the City Hall, which was completed in 1906. It is a fussy design with decorative towers and a large central dome. The impressive new Parliament House at Stormont, [11,28] placed at the end of a long avenue, was designed by Sir Arnold Thornley.

Church building in the classical style continued quite late into the century. Ralph Byrne designed the cathedrals at Mullingar (c. 1936) and Cavan (c. 1942) in a Renaissance style. Also in a Renaissance style is the Church of St Thomas in Seán McDermott Street, Dublin, designed by F.G. Hicks (c. 1932). Indicative of the movement towards more economical building materials during the 1930s, it is built of brick and has a lovely arcaded front with a wheel window over.

HIBERNO-ROMANESQUE REVIVAL

Around the turn of the century the literary and crafts movements, which were strongly influenced by nationalist feelings, found a parallel in architecture in the revival of the Hiberno-Romanesque style. Teampall Einde, the small parish church at Spiddal, Co. Galway, designed by W.A. Scott (1871–1921), was built to fit the needs of the local community and to harmonise with its surroundings. It depends for its effect on its simplicity and sculptural form.

The Honan Chapel in Cork, [11,29] designed by James F. McMullen (c. 1916), uses the design of the west front from St Cronan's, Roscrea, as the basis for its west doorway. Inside, the windows and Stations of the Cross were designed by Sarah Purser and Harry Clarke.

Many other examples of Hiberno-Romanesque style can be found around the country, even occasionally in secular buildings. The Carnegie Library in Limerick, now the City Gallery, has round-headed windows and doorways with geometric mouldings. It was designed by George Sheridan (c. 1906).

During the War of Independence and the Civil War, very little building took place and immediately afterwards rebuilding took up most of the energies of architects and builders.

MODERN MOVEMENT

A new type of architecture began to develop in Europe in the early twentieth century. It did not look to the past for its forms but to the new building materials which were becoming available. Iron and glass construction were already in use in the nineteenth century for railway stations, glasshouses, factories and bridges. Reinforced concrete, invented in France towards the end of the century, completed the elements needed for new building forms.

At first buildings constructed in these materials were regarded as engineering works, but a group of young architects in Europe formulated new architectural theories using the new materials to make buildings whose function and structure

[11,30] Dublin Airport (1941 part), designed by Desmond FitzGerald.

[11,32] Bank of Ireland, Baggot Street, Dublin, designed by Michael Scott.

were the basis for design. The Bauhaus design school was the chief instigator of the new 'truth to materials' approach to architecture.

Steel and concrete structures made their first appearance in Ireland in the 1930s in domestic architecture. Robinson and Keefe's 'Sunshine' homes at Dollymount, Dublin, are an early example (c. 1932). Larger work was also undertaken in hospitals, factories and cinemas. The original terminal building at Dublin Airport, [11,30] designed by Desmond FitzGerald and completed in 1941, is a fine example of steel, concrete and glass construction. The flexibility of the materials is used to advantage in the curved building. No decoration is used and all the parts are structural.

Michael Scott of the Scott, Tallon and Walker partnership has been designing buildings in modern materials since the 1930s. He designed a number of buildings for CIÉ, a factory at Inchicore, the bus garage at Donnybrook and the large Busáras in Store Street, Dublin. [11,31] Completed in 1953, it is considered Ireland's first

[11,31] Busáras, Store Street, Dublin, designed by Michael Scott.

major modern building. The building has stone, brick and mosaic finishes which have weathered well, maintaining its modern appearance.

The influence of Mies van der Rohe in the creation of buildings without walls can be seen in Liberty Hall, Dublin, which was built in 1965 to the design of Desmond R. O'Kelly. Mies van der Rohe's influence can also be seen in County Hall, Cork, built in 1968 to the design of P.L. McSweeney, and in the P.J. Carroll factory at Dundalk, 1972, designed by Ronald Tallon of Scott, Tallon and Walker. The Carroll's building allows its complete structure to be seen through the dark glass walls. Michael Scott's Bank of Ireland building in Baggot Street, Dublin [11,32] is in a similar style, made to fit the urban streetscape by placing the large multi-storey part of the building behind a courtyard keeping it back from the street front.

Another bank building set back from the street is Sam Stephenson's Central Bank in Dame Street, Dublin. [11,33] It was the source of some controversy when it was first built. The structure of the building is unusual. It is suspended from two internal towers by steel rods which run down the outside of the building, almost like string around a parcel.

Trinity College Dublin and University College Dublin have been the centres of some new and exciting building in the second half of the century. The Library at Trinity College [11,34] was designed by Paul Koralek, the winner of the 1960 design competition. The unfaced, reinforced

269

[11,33] Central Bank, Dame Street, Dublin, designed by Sam Stephenson.

[11,34] New Library Building, Trinity College Dublin, designed by Paul Koralek.

concrete structure creates a very different atmosphere to the steel and glass structures looked at earlier.

A competition for the layout design of the arts block and administration buildings was held for the new University College Dublin complex at Belfield. A Polish architect, Andrzej Wejchert, won and set a high standard of design on the campus.

At Trinity the restoration of the Dining Hall was completed in 1987 after it had been destroyed by fire. The architects, de Blacam and Meagher, restored the building with great care and added an atrium, designed to harmonise with the old

building. This tendency to redesign and refurbish existing structures for modern use holds out some hope for maintaining the character of Irish towns and cities.

A building boom in the final decades of the twentieth century led to disputes among designers, developers and environmentalists concerning quality and quantity. Shopping centres, office blocks, apartments and a variety of public and private buildings appeared in a short number of years. All kinds of solutions to the problems of fitting in with existing structures and honesty of design have been tried. The Stephen's Green Shopping Centre in Dublin [11,35] uses features from Victorian markets and borrows elements from the front of the Gaiety Theatre which faces the long side of the shopping centre. The success or otherwise of the design has been debated and opinion remains divided.

Renewal in Dublin city centre has produced some interesting new buildings along the quays and in Temple Bar, where planning regulates not only the ground plans but the full three-dimensional environment. Buildings in the area include the award-winning Arthouse Multi-Media Centre, [11,36] a purpose-built media exhibition, installation and performance space. The curved façade is broken by an irregular pattern of window and door openings which reflects the use of the internal spaces.

Significant and architecturally interesting buildings were constructed in almost every part of the country in the 1980s and 1990s.

[11,35] Stephen's Green Shopping Centre, Dublin.

[11,36] Arthouse Multi-Media Centre, Temple Bar, Dublin.

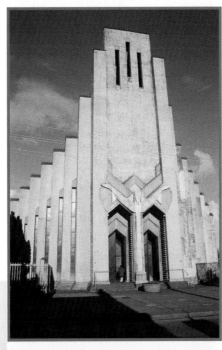

[11,37] Christ the King Church, Cork, designed by Barry Byrne: exterior and interior.

[11,38] Church of St Aengus, Burt, Co. Donegal, designed by Liam McCormick.

Modern design has become more common in Irish church architecture only since the Second Vatican Council in the 1960s. There has been much experimentation with circles and polygons to find ways of grouping the congregation around the altar. Roofs are often a strong feature of the design. The partnership of F.M. Corr and McCormick has been influential in church design. The Church of St Aengus at Burt in Co. Donegal, [11,38] designed by Liam McCormick in 1967, uses a circular plan with an off-centre tower throwing light on the altar.

SCULPTURE

Sculpture was a conservative branch of art up to the mid-century. The old craft of the stone carver gradually declined as modern materials became more commonly used.

OLIVER SHEPPARD (1865–1941)

Oliver Sheppard trained in the Metropolitan School in Dublin, then in London and Paris. He was influenced by the Art Nouveau movement which combined well with the Celtic revival in Ireland, both movements being interested in craft and design. He carved portrait busts and carried out architectural work, including the carvings on the College of Science in Merrion Street. The bronze figures commemorating the 1798 Rebellion in Wexford and Enniscorthy and the 1916 memorial figure of Cúchulainn in the GPO in Dublin are among his best public work. [11,39]

MODERN CHURCH ARCHITECTURE

One of the most remarkable early modern buildings in the country is the Church of Christ the King in Cork, [11,37] designed c. 1928 by Barry Byrne, an Irish-American from Chicago. The absence of divisions inside allows a large congregation an uninterrupted view of the altar. The large Christ figure which dominates the entrance was designed by the American sculptor, John Storrs.

[11,39] 'The Death of Cúchulainn', by Oliver Sheppard.

[11,41] 'Christ the King' monument, Dún Laoghaire, Co. Dublin, by Andrew O'Connor.

ALBERT POWER (1883–1945)

A student of John Hughes and Sheppard, Albert Power assisted them in their work on the College of Science. He carved the façade sculpture on Mullingar Cathedral, but his small informal pieces are more lively and interesting. His 'Connemara Trout' in green marble and Icarus in white marble are both well carved, full of movement. He also carved portrait busts of W.B. Yeats and James Stephens. In the bronze figure of Pádraic Ó Conaire in Eyre Square, Galway, [11,40] Power tried to combine intimacy with a public monument.

ANDREW O'CONNOR (1874–1941)

Andrew O'Connor was born in America of Irish parents. When he came to Europe for further study he became a friend of Rodin in France, who greatly influenced his work. He settled in Ireland. The Hugh Lane Municipal Gallery in Dublin houses a model of the doors he designed for the Church of St Bartholomew in New York and an equestrian statue of Lafayette. Bronze statues of Commodore Barry and Abraham Lincoln stand in the American Ambassador's Residence in Phoenix Park and a statue of O'Connell in the National Bank in Dame Street. The controversial bronze triple-cross monument to 'Christ the King' [11,41] in Dún Laoghaire was originally a memorial to the dead of the First World War.

SÉAMUS MURPHY (1907–75)

A Cork-born sculptor, Séamus Murphy trained as a stone carver and was the last to make the transition between carving and sculpture. He was inspired by early Irish Christian and Romanesque carving and worked in strong, simplified forms. He made portraits of some important national figures including Michael Collins. Murphy designed the Church of the Assumption in Blackpool, Cork and also carved the statues and tympanum over the main door. [11,42]

SCULPTURE SINCE 1950

It is only in comparatively recent times that Irish sculpture has taken up the challenge of the modern movements. Commissions were scarce

[11,40] Pádraic Ó Conaire, Eyre Square, Galway, by Albert Power.

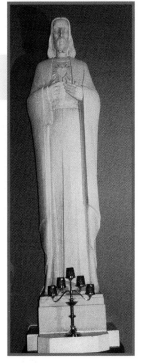

[11,42] 'The Sacred Heart', by Séamus Murphy, Church of the Assumption, Blackpool, Cork.

[11,43] 'The Children of Lir', Garden of Remembrance, Parnell Square, Dublin, by Oisín Kelly.

[11,44] 'Women of Belfast' by F.E. McWilliam (Hugh Lane Municipal Gallery, Dublin).

and understanding of anything other than realism very limited. It was only when some enlightened architects incorporated sculpture into the design of modern churches in the 1960s that a revival began.

OISÍN KELLY (1915–81)

Oisín Kelly worked in a variety of media and executed work both large and small. The carved wooden screen in the church at Knockanure, Co. Kerry, which shows great sensitivity to materials and working methods, is a fine example of his large wood carving. 'St Peter' in the church at Milford, Co. Donegal, and the skyline crucifixion on the Church of the Redeemer in Dundalk, Co. Louth, are in bronze. The large 'The Children of Lir' sculpture in the Garden of Remembrance in Parnell Square, Dublin, [11,43] is one of the most dramatic public monuments of his time.

F.E. MCWILLIAM (1909–92)

Born in Co. Down, F.E. McWilliam lived and worked in London. His work developed through various phases, including abstracts and surrealistic images in a variety of materials. He produced figurative work during the 1970s and 1980s. The statue of 'Princess Macha' outside Altnagelvin Hospital in Derry is one of his more imposing public works in Ireland. His 'Women of Belfast' [11,44] is a series of bronze female figures thrown by a bomb blast. Executed in an Expressionist style, they were made in response to the Troubles.

ABSTRACT AND ENVIRONMENTAL SCULPTURE

The work of the following artists is mostly abstract.

GERDA FRÖMEL (1931–75)

Gerda Frömel worked in both stone and steel. Her 'Alabaster Interlocking Shapes II' (1970) (Bank of Ireland Collection) are so beautifully finished that they almost 'demand' to be touched. The 'Steel Mobile' [11,45] outside Carroll's factory in Dundalk is one of the most impressive large sculptures in the country. The reflections and movements from the pool it stands in and from the moving steel sails are mirrored in the dark glass of the factory façade.

273

[11,45] 'Steel Mobile', by Gerda Frömel.

[11,47] Steel sculpture, 1978, outside Bank of Ireland, Baggot Street, Dublin, by John Burke.

MICHAEL BULFIN (1939–)

Michael Bulfin has produced some large painted metal sculpture, a good example of which stands outside the Bank of Ireland in Dublin and creates a relationship to the building, its bright colour contrasting with the dark glass. [11,46]

JOHN BURKE (1946–)

Working in Cork, John Burke is another artist who produces large steel sculptures. Visual rhythms and movement are often part of the work he creates from scrap. He has a large sculpture outside the Bank of Ireland in Dublin. [11,47] A founder member of the annual national Sculpture and Drawing Exhibition, SADE, which started in 1982, John Burke has been an important influence on younger sculptors.

[11,48] 'Apparatus No. 7, Sweeney's Monument', by Tom Fitzgerald (Hugh Lane Municipal Gallery, Dublin).

TOM FITZGERALD (1939–)

Tom Fitzgerald works in a variety of media, creating assemblages in a range of colours and textures from leather, wood, stone, lead, rope, steel and man-made objects. There are often magical overtones in his work and a sense of mysterious purpose in the parts. 'Apparatus No. 7, Sweeney's Monument' in the Hugh Lane Municipal Gallery, Dublin, [11,48] is an example of his work.

MICHAEL WARREN (1950–)

Michael Warren's work in stone, wood and steel sometimes seems to surround rather than occupy space. His 'Articulation of Void I' and 'Escultura Blanca' in painted steel show this attempt to enfold space. More recent work has been in wood, carefully jointed and hand finished. 'After-Image' is an example of this type of work, as is the large sculpture outside the new Dublin Civic Offices at Wood Quay. [11,49]

[11,46] Metal sculpture, by Michael Bulfin, outside Bank of Ireland, Baggot Street, Dublin.

[11,49] Sculpture outside new Civic Offices, Wood Quay, Dublin, by Michael Warren.

[11,51] 'The Ram', by Deborah Brown, papier mâché and twine.

BRIAN KING (1942–)

Brian King has produced works in painted metal and creates environmental sculptures. His yellow abstract in the courtyard in front of the new building at University College Galway is a focal point in the area. His 'Celtic Knot' (Bank of Ireland Collection) seems to deny the inflexible nature of steel. He has also been working with conceptual art. 'Sea Holes' [11,50] is an example of this type of work. He also created works which combine geometric forms, cubes and pyramids, with natural objects such as stones.

WOMEN SCULPTORS

Separated from their contemporary males, not for any sexist reasons but for what they have in common artistically, these women sculptors seem to share a continuing sense of exploration with materials and subject-matter, and have independently found similar truths in their work.

[11,50] 'Sea Holes', by Brian King.

DEBORAH BROWN (1927–)

Deborah Brown was born in Belfast and trained in Dublin. She began as a painter and then, through collage, developed an interest in three-dimensional abstract reliefs in wire and papier mâché sculptures. She went on to work with fibreglass and then turned to more figurative work of people and animals in the environment, created in wire and papier mâché. 'Sheep on the Road' and 'The Ram' [11,51] are examples of these studies in behaviour.

EILÍS O'CONNELL (1953–)

Most of the early work of Eilís O'Connell was in steel. Then, through drawing, she explored new materials using paper with natural materials made into it, or stone and wood, sometimes combined with steel. Her 'Tallaght Sculpture' made in painted steel is based on segments of circles, a recurring theme in her work. The 'Wind Column' erected near Derry to commemorate Amelia Earhart's flight across the Atlantic is designed to make noise by the action of the wind. Other work like the wall sculpture 'Chachi's Farm' combines painted steel, handmade paper, cord and feathers.

Large public commissions at home and abroad have led O'Connell to explore other materials. The 'Secret Station', The Gateway, Cardiff, [11,52] is in painted bronze, steel and fibre optics, and has steam generators within. The combination of traditional and modern methods

275

[11,52] 'Secret Station', The Gateway, Cardiff, 1992-3, by Eilis O'Connell, bronze, steel and fibre optics, 11 x 11 x 10 metres.

[11,54] 'Stack', 1989, by Kathy Prendergast, cloth, string, paint and wood, 270 x 260 x 70 cm (Irish Museum of Modern Art).

[11,53] 'Sharp Back', by Eilis O'Connell, stainless steel, woven cotton, 256 x 61 x 62.5 cm (Irish Museum of Medium Art).

feeling or atmosphere for the viewer to experience. More recent work like 'Stack' [11,54] explores soft forms, colour and texture.

FIGURATIVE SCULPTURE

A number of artists base their work on human or animal forms, generally working with a greater degree of realism than other modern sculptors.

EDWARD DELANEY (1930-)

Edward Delaney produced many public monuments in Dublin during the 1960s and 1970s. The Thomas Davis memorial in College Green and the Wolfe Tone memorial and 'Famine Group' in Stephen's Green [11,55] are examples of his work in bronze. The figures are boldly

and materials and the contrast between man-made and natural forms are recurring aspects of her work. 'Sharp Back' [11,53] uses steel cable, woven like traditional basketwork. Smaller exhibition pieces explore a variety of forms and materials. The cycles of life and natural forces are themes repeated in her work.

KATHY PRENDERGAST (1958-)

Kathy Prendergast has constructed environmental pieces as well as more conventional sculpture. She uses a great variety of materials in her work, such as plastered bandage, resin, steel and wire in her 'Waiting', 1980 (Hugh Lane Municipal Gallery). Prendergast typically tries to create

[11,55] 'Famine Group', Stephen's Green, Dublin by Edward Delaney.

[11,55](a) Famine memorial, Co. Mayo, by John Behan.

[11,56] Photograph of performance by Nigel Rolfe.

textured and occupy their space forcefully. The shining, stainless-steel abstract work, made in the 1980s, is in stark contrast with the earlier sculptures.

JOHN BEHAN (1938–)

John Behan spent a number of years working on sculptures based on the Táin. The figure of the bull as a symbol of strength and power occurs frequently in his work. His sculptures are made both by welding pieces together and by casting. He was one of the first involved with the Dublin Art Foundry in 1970. His 'Flight of Doves', 1981, is typical of his energetic response to natural forms created in bronze. The Famine memorial in Co. Mayo [11,55](a) is an impressive piece, using combined techniques and images which evoke the flight from a land of death and despair.

PERFORMANCE ART

Included under the heading of sculpture because it is a three-dimensional activity, in performance art the artist-performer becomes the work of art — a sort of living sculpture — or performs the action which is the work of art. There is usually no end product. The act itself is the art work.

NIGEL ROLFE (1950–)

Nigel Rolfe, born on the Isle of Wight, creates environments of flour, sand, paint, clay and sometimes food, in which he performs in the manner pioneered by Yves Klein. His performance is a kind of controlled ritual in which duration is an important element. [11,56] Rolfe describes the physical part of his work as ground drawings

which can take up to twelve hours to create. He then uses his body in slow, deliberate movements to erase the drawing. This can take from thirty to forty-five minutes to perform.

INSTALLATIONS

Installations by artists can take on various qualities, but they are generally temporary and site-specific.

JOHN AIKEN (1950–)

John Aiken has created installations in moulded sand, chalk lines and other materials. The initial phase of the work is a written proposal which describes the artist's intentions. The 'Sand Installation' [11,57] created for the Project Arts Centre in Dublin in 1981 was worked on by Aiken over five days 'to develop a number of sand structures which use the space, alter the space, make demands on visitors to the space'. The work, which had no title, was seen as part of a development of ideas by the artist on his observations of 'objects, environment, landscape and architecture'.

[11,57] 'Sand Installation' by John Aiken.

277

CONCEPTUAL ART

Conceptual art is the art of ideas, which can come in the form of written proposals, statements, photographs, maps, diagrams, recorded sound, video, etc. Most artists who work in this way make their work visually uninteresting to divert attention to the idea.

Some critics consider conceptual art to be the ultimate form of art; others would say that it has crossed the border into philosophy.

NOEL SHERIDAN (1936–)

Noel Sheridan produced 'Everybody Should Get Stones', [11,58] an installation of photographs and text which poses questions about the nature of art and how people relate to it. By putting ordinary stones into an art gallery and saying that they are now an art work, the artist wanted people to question the whole idea of how it is decided what an art work is. Who decides this — the artist, the public, the art establishment? The work also poses questions about how we use language in relation to works of art and what effect this has on our understanding of art.

PAINTING

There were few changes in painting in Ireland in the early part of the twentieth century. The emphasis on drawing continued on from the nineteenth century in the academies. Students often went to England or the continent for further training.

As the century progressed the literary movement, with its nationalist sentiments, inspired a number of artists to search for 'Irish subjects'. These were either realist landscapes of the west or subject pictures which romanticised the lives of the western people. Technically there was a freeing-out of brushwork and a more lively use of colour. The War of Independence, the Civil War and the founding of the new state brought little change in the development of Irish art, though moments of importance were painted by some artists.

Through the 1920s and 1930s the art scene was quite static, and it was not until the 1940s when Mainie Jellett and Evie Hone founded the Living Art Exhibition that influences from the continent again began to trickle in. Even then art education remained in the hands of academics and it was not until the 1970s that modern visual education theories became widespread.

In the 1960s, 1970s and 1980s the influence of modern art movements arrived in Ireland with increasing rapidity. The first ROSC exhibition was held in 1967 and was followed irregularly by other exhibitions until the 1980s. These brought the current works of major international artists into the country and provided a stimulus for many Irish artists.

EARLY TWENTIETH CENTURY

Early twentieth-century work in Ireland was generally conservative, with the major artists making the greater part of their living abroad.

SIR JOHN LAVERY (1856–1941)

John Lavery was born in Belfast. He studied in Glasgow and London, and then in Paris and Grez-sur-Loing. His work in Grez, in the plein-air style, is among his best.

He became a successful landscape and portrait painter in England and Dublin, and was appointed an official war artist during the 1914–18 war. Lavery's drawing skills and masterful handling of paint can be seen in the large painting of Lady Lavery, her daughter and granddaughter. [11,59]

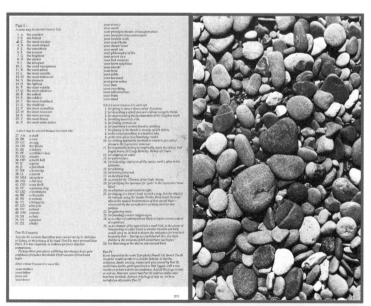

[11,58] 'Everybody Should Get Stones', by Noel Sheridan.

[11,59] 'Lady Lavery with her Daughter and Grand-Daughter', 1911, by John Lavery, oil on canvas, 344 x 274 cm (National Gallery of Ireland, Dublin).

[11,61] 'A Convent Garden', c. 1905, by William Leech, oil on canvas, 132 x 106 cm (National Gallery of Ireland, Dublin).

[11,60] 'The Vere Foster Family', c. 1905, by William Orpen, oil on canvas, 198 x 198 cm (National Gallery of Ireland, Dublin).

academic training in drawing nearly always shows through. This is highlighted in the figures in 'A Convent Garden'. [11,61] The vegetation in this painting displays vigorous brushwork in thick paint; the composition is also modern in its off-centre placement of the main figure.

INFLUENCE OF THE LITERARY MOVEMENT

As the century progressed the nationalist sentiments of the literary movement influenced a number of artists to seek an Irish type of subject. Some like George Russell (Æ, 1867–1935) found inspiration in mythology; others sought the 'real' people and landscape of Ireland. With this change of subject-matter, new techniques also developed. Brushwork and colour were influenced by Impressionism, though the academic approach to drawing and composition still formed the basis of art education.

JACK BUTLER YEATS (1871–1957)

Jack Butler Yeats was the son of John Butler Yeats and brother of the poet, W.B. Yeats. He was born in London, but spent much of his childhood in Co. Sligo with his grandparents. He went to art school in London and spent his early years as an illustrator of magazines, papers and books. The drawings are tightly composed and depend for their effect on strong line. An impish sense of humour often appears in his illustrations. From the 1890s into the early 1900s, Yeats painted

SIR WILLIAM ORPEN (1878–1931)

William Orpen studied at the Metropolitan School, Dublin, and the Slade School, London. He did not go to France. He was a successful society portrait painter and subject picture painter, and was also appointed war artist in the First World War. His work is based on great drawing ability which can be seen in the unusual group portrait 'The Vere Foster Family', [11,60] which Orpen considered to be his best work. 'Midday on the Beach' (1910) shows an Impressionist approach to light and colour.

WILLIAM J. LEECH (1881–1968)

William J. Leech studied at the Metropolitan School and the RHA under Osborne before going to Paris. He was influenced by the post-Impressionist work he saw in Paris, but his

[11,62] 'The Man from Inis Mór', c. 1905, by Jack B. Yeats, chalk and watercolour on board, 38 x 27.3 cm (National Gallery of Ireland, Dublin).

[11,64] 'Grief', 1951, by Jack B. Yeats, oil on canvas, 102 x 153 cm (National Gallery of Ireland, Dublin).

[11,65] 'A Connemara Landscape', c. 1913, by Paul Henry, oil on canvas, 69 x 84 cm (National Gallery of Ireland, Dublin).

watercolours of events from everyday life in England — characters and public events, races, markets and street scenes. 'The Man from Inis Mór', [11,62] is a watercolour painted in this early style while on a trip to Aran.

In the early 1900s Yeats moved to Ireland and began painting in oils. His subjects were still ordinary events. 'The Double Jockey Act', a circus scene from 1916, shows a typical moment of tension and action which Yeats liked to depict. By the 1920s Yeats had developed a more fluent painting style. 'The Liffey Swim' [11,63] shows the vigorous brushmarks and brighter colours of this stage of development.

Yeats began to paint more from memory than from direct observation in the 1930s. His mature painting style was developing with vigorous

brushmarks, thick paint and strong colours, all combined to create a sense of movement and transition. 'In Memory of Boucicault and Bianconi' (1937) displays this type of treatment. The theatrical group, in full costume, have alighted from the Bianconi car to play a scene against the blue background of Glencar waterfall. The painting encapsulates some of the formative influences from Yeats's Sligo youth.

His later work became expressionist and moody; strong blues dominate the colour schemes, with loose brushmarks producing dreamlike images. 'Men of Destiny' (1946) and 'Grief' [11,64] illustrate this final phase of his development.

PAUL HENRY (1876–1958)

Paul Henry was born in Belfast and studied in Paris. He spent much of his time from 1910 to 1919 painting near Achill. Through the imitation

[11,63] 'The Liffey Swim', 1923, by Jack B. Yeats, oil on canvas, 61 x 91 cm (National Gallery of Ireland, Dublin).

[11,66] 'Men of the West', c. 1917, Seán Keating, oil on canvas, 97 x 125 cm (Hugh Lane Municipal Gallery, Dublin).

of his work by so many lesser artists his paintings have become almost a caricature of western landscape. His 'A Connemara Landscape' [11,65] shows his typical composition of low horizon and large cloudy sky.

WILLIAM CONOR (1881–1968)

Born in Belfast, William Conor portrayed the people of that city going about their daily lives. 'The Jaunting Car' [11,67] is typical of his sensitive approach to his subject.

OTHER ARTISTS

Yeats may have come closest to expressing the Ireland of his day. A group of younger artists also went to the west to find the soul of the nation. Patrick Tuohy (1894–1930), Charles Lamb (1893–1964) and Seán Keating (1889–1977) [11,66] were all pupils of Orpen. They painted the people and landscape of the west of Ireland in a romantic way, making heroes of the ordinary people, as Millet had in France in the previous century.

STAINED GLASS ART

An Túr Gloine (The Tower of Glass) was founded in 1903 and Sarah Purser, the portrait painter, agreed to be its first manager, though she did not

design many windows herself. Dublin's Metropolitan School of Art opened a stained glass department under A.E. Child, an Englishman who had been trained in the studios of William Morris. He brought a high technical standard to the craft in Ireland.

MICHAEL HEALY (1873–1941)

Michael Healy was a member of An Túr Gloine from the beginning. His Italian training produced a very classical note in his work, which he gradually moved away from through greater technical innovation in his glass designs. His use of 'aciding', which reduces colour in the glass, had a strong effect on his later work. The figure of Judith [11,68] from a window in the Catholic church at Bridge-a-Crin, Co. Louth, shows his leanings towards the pre-Raphaelite style.

CATHERINE O'BRIEN (D. 1963)

Catherine O'Brien joined the studio straight out of art school and worked there until it closed with her death. Her clear draughtsmanship and simplicity of style can be seen in all her windows. [11,69]

WILHELMINA GEDDES (1888–1955)

Wilhelmina Geddes was born in Belfast. She joined An Túr Gloine around 1912 and worked there until 1925, when she set up her own studio in London. Her strong personal style can be seen in 'The Fate of the Children of Lir' [11,70] window in the Ulster Museum.

[11,68] 'The Agony, Judith and St Thomas', church at Bridge-a-Crin, Co. Louth, by Michael Healy.

[11,67] 'The Jaunting Car', c. 1933, by William Conor, oil on canvas, 70.5 x 90.5 cm (Ulster Museum, Belfast).

[11,69] 'Christ Welcoming a Soldier', by Catherine O'Brien, detail of the Supper at Emmaus. Window in Tullow Church of Ireland Church.

[11,71] 'Cartoon for the Crucifixion, Sacrifice of Isaac and Last Supper', Eton College Chapel, England by Evie Hone (National Gallery of Ireland, Dublin).

EVIE HONE (1894–1955)

Evie Hone joined An Túr Gloine after her training in France, and combined her love of Irish medieval carving and design with her figurative style. The huge 'Crucifixion, Sacrifice of Isaac and Last Supper' [11,71] window in Eton College Chapel, England, established her as one of the major stained glass artists in postwar Europe. Most of her work in Ireland is on a smaller scale. 'Christ with Jesuit Saints', [11,72] designed for a small chapel at the Jesuit seminary in Tullabeg, shows the rich colour and pattern of her design. The contrasts of warm and cool colours and the figure arrangements remind one of medieval glass.

HARRY CLARKE (1889–1931)

Harry Clarke inherited a church decoration and stained glass business from his father and did not become involved in the co-operative venture of An Túr Gloine. He was trained in the Dublin Metropolitan School under A.E. Child and quickly developed an original style in book illustration and stained glass. His work shows influences of both the exhibition of Symbolist paintings he saw while in London and the work of Aubrey Beardsley whom he admired.

In 1915 Clarke was commissioned to make the windows for the Honan Chapel in Cork, work that established him as a major stained glass artist. More commissions followed and he ran a busy

[11,70] 'The Fate of the Children of Lir', 1917, by Wilhelmina Geddes (Ulster Museum, Belfast).

[11,72] 'Christ with Jesuit Saints', by Evie Hone.

[11,73] 'The Sacred Heart' from the Church of St Agatha, Glenflesk, Co. Kerry, by Harry Clarke.

colours of good glass were realised and used to advantage. Pictorial effects took a back seat to the colours, patterns and light from the windows.

THE CUBIST INFLUENCE

The modern movements, which followed each other in quick succession in Europe during the early decades of the century, were hardly felt in Ireland. Mainie Jellett and Evie Hone went to Paris to study Cubist theories under the guidance of Albert Gleizes and André Lhote. Their first exhibitions of Cubist work in 1923 and 1924 were little understood, but they did create an awareness of new theories among younger artists. In 1943 Jellett and others founded the Irish Exhibition of Living Art to display work which was not given space at the Royal Hibernian Academy.

MAINIE JELLETT (1897–1944)

The early work of Mainie Jellett is semi-figurative, often inspired by religious themes. 'I Have Trodden the Winepress Alone' [11,76] shows her use of flat colour and shape, based on Cubist theory. Geometric shapes and combinations of curved and straight lines make up her compositions. The relative strengths of colours provide the only depth. Mainie Jellett was an important influence on Irish art through her teaching, lectures and the founding of the Living Art Exhibition.

stained glass studio for both secular and religious work, as well as illustrating books and other graphic work. [11,73] 'The Eve of St Agnes' [11,74] window which is now in the Hugh Lane Municipal Gallery is a technical and artistic tour de force based on Keats's poem of the same title. Clarke creates gem-like colours and elegant line drawings in leaded decorative frames. [11,75] He produced a large volume of work in his short life, in spite of repeated illness in his final years.

CONCLUSION

The artists of An Túr Gloine and Harry Clarke stand out from their contemporaries because of the quality and craftsmanship they brought to their work. The possibilities inherent in the

[11,74] 'The Eve of St Agnes', by Harry Clarke, (Hugh Lane Municipal Gallery, Dublin).

[11,75] 'Walpurgis Night' from Faust, 1924, by Harry Clarke.

[11,76] 'I Have Trodden the Winepress Alone', c. 1943, by Mainie Jellett, oil on canvas, 76 x 56 cm (National Gallery of Ireland, Dublin).

[11,78] 'Garden Green', c. 1962, by Norah McGuinness, oil on canvas, 102 x 71 cm (Hugh Lane Municipal Gallery, Dublin).

EVIE HONE (1894–1955)

Evie Hone, best known as a stained glass artist, also produced landscapes throughout most of her life. [11,77] The strong use of line in her work relates to the leading in stained glass, though, unlike the brilliance of her glass, her use of colour in painting is often muted.

NORAH McGUINNESS (1903–80)

Norah McGuinness trained at the Metropolitan School of Art and, on the advice of Jellett, with Lhote in Paris. She used multiple viewpoints and fragmentation in her early work which shows Cubist influence, but her style was never as geometric as Jellett's. 'Garden Green' [11,78] shows her emphasis of outline to give strength to

her work. This outlining continued through a more abstract phase, such as 'Patterns on the Featherbed Mountain' (1975), which McGuinness adopted later in life. The colours are cool and muted.

PAINTING SINCE 1950

Since the turn of the century theories on art and art education have changed radically, though these theories were slow to arrive in Ireland in the first place. The founding of the Living Art Exhibition in 1943 was an important development. It gave modern artists a platform to display their work. The introduction of the ROSC exhibitions beginning in 1967, which brought the work of contemporary international modern artists into Ireland, created an important reaction in Irish artists.

LOUIS LE BROCQUY (1916–)

Largely self-taught, Louis le Brocquy toured the galleries of Europe to gain an understanding of art. His early work shows Cubist influence but his interest in the human condition, particularly isolation, led him to seek new methods of expression. His 'Isolated Beings', painted in the 1950s, are half-seen images emerging from a white ground. In the 1960s he began to explore the Celtic notion of the head as the 'magic box' which contains the spirit. This led to a series of paintings of heads of literary and artistic figures whose features emerge in primary colours, sensuously painted, through a white background. [11,79]

[11,77] 'Landscape with a Tree', by Evie Hone (National Gallery of Ireland, Dublin).

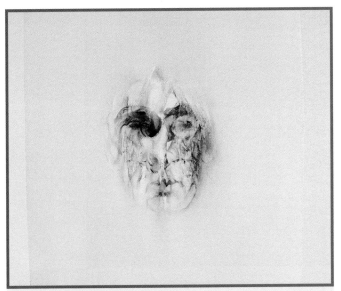

[11,79] 'Image of W.B. Yeats', 1989, by Louis le Brocquy, oil on canvas, 80 x 80 cm.

[11,81] 'Blue Still Life with Knife', by William Scott, oil on canvas, 122 x 198 cm (AIB Collection of Modern Irish Art).

Le Brocquy also works in other media. He has designed tapestries throughout his career, often based on themes from Celtic legend. His brush drawings in black ink which illustrate Thomas Kinsella's translation of the Táin [11,80] have immense strength and vigour. Le Brocquy's work is always sympathetic to the medium he is working in and often seems as much a result of the action of the materials as the action of the artist.

Like so many of our major artists over the centuries, le Brocquy lives outside the country, much of the time in France.

WILLIAM SCOTT (1913–)
Born in Scotland and educated in Belfast, William Scott also spent much of his life outside Ireland, in England. His still-life paintings have developed into abstract compositions over the years. 'Two and Two 1' (1963) is an example of Scott's

[11,80] 'The Raising of the Armies', brush drawings from the Táin, by Louis le Brocquy.

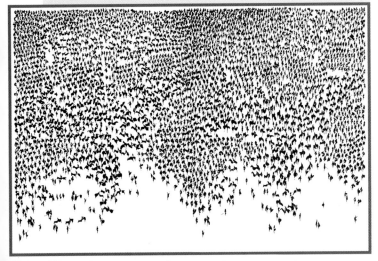

carefully balanced composition in a limited colour range with a subtle handling of paint. 'Blue Still Life with Knife' [11,81] shows how he simplifies his forms to their most basic shapes.

ABSTRACT WORK
A number of Irish artists have found their way into completely abstract work.

PATRICK SCOTT (1921–)
Patrick Scott trained and worked as an architect until 1960, though he was painting at the same time. From early realism he moved into abstract work, developing a technique of staining rather than painting canvas. His 'Large Solar Device' painted in the early 1960s shows this technique. Since then he has experimented with combinations of gold leaf, raw canvas and thinly painted areas in subtle abstract compositions. His 'Chinese Landscape' [11,82] is made in this way. Scott has also designed some fine tapestries in glowing colours which are in contrast to his canvases.

CECIL KING (1921–86)
Cecil King became an artist through collecting paintings. A meeting with the American artist, Barnett Newman, who was exhibiting in the ROSC 1970 exhibition, led to an interest in hard-edge painting. King's works are composed of simple geometric elements. Through colour and shape he creates the illusion of a third dimension in much of his work. 'Intrusion 2', [11,83] 'Pendulum' and 'Link 3' are all works by King that hang in the Municipal Gallery, Dublin.

285

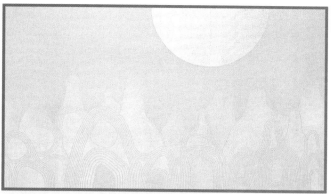

[11,82] 'Chinese Landscape' by Patrick Scott (Hugh Lane Municipal Gallery, Dublin).

[11,85] 'Harbour, Bangor', 1975, by Colin Middleton, oil on canvas, 90 x 90 cm (AIB Collection of Modern Irish Art).

[11,83] 'Intrusion 2', by Cecil King (Hugh Lane Municipal Gallery, Dublin).

TRADITIONAL SUBJECTS

In contrast with these abstract artists, a number of their contemporaries worked with more traditional subjects though treated in a modern way.

GERARD DILLON (1916–71)

Born and educated in Belfast, Gerard Dillon portrays the human figure with childlike simplicity of colour and drawing. 'Yellow Bungalow' (1957) (Ulster Museum) shows his imaginative

[11,84] 'Medical Students' 1949–50, by Gerard Dillon (Ulster Museum, Belfast).

use of distorted perspective and strong colour. His work often explores texture and different media including collage. His self-portrait in the National Gallery includes the Pierrot and the nude, two of his perennial themes, which reflect his interest in the human condition. The painting 'Medical Students' shows Dillon's 'naïve' treatment of domestic scenes. [11,84]

COLIN MIDDLETON (1910–83)

Born and trained in Belfast, Colin Middleton went through various developments of style, finally settling on a semi-abstract approach to landscape. In his 'Harbour, Bangor' [11,85] there is a tension between his geometric and emotional response to painting. Cool geometric planes are overlaid with golden wavy lines.

TONY O'MALLEY (1913–)

Born in Callan in Co. Kilkenny, Tony O'Malley took up painting during a long stay in hospital while suffering from TB. After his recovery he gave up his job in a bank and went to live in St Ives in Cornwall which was a thriving artists' colony in the years following the Second World War. During the 1970s he made several trips back to Ireland, staying for longer and longer periods and rediscovering the landscape of his ancestors. This landscape became the theme of many of his paintings, expressed in abstract symbols which try to portray the essence of a place. [11,86]

O'Malley sometimes works on board or even old scraps of wood where texture and surface can be developed by cutting lines and holes or by building layers of paint or paper, creating works which have an organic quality. His later paintings from the Bahamas retain this organic quality, glowing with tropical light and colour. [11,87]

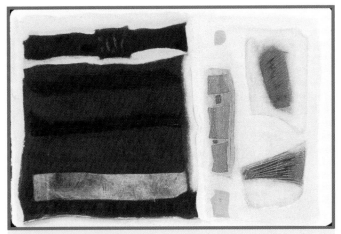

[11,86] 'The Old Place, Callan', by Tony O'Malley.

[11,88] 'Waiting to Go on the Canal', 1968, by Camille Souter (Hugh Lane Municipal Gallery, Dublin).

[11,87] 'Bird Lake, Paradise Island, Bahamas', 1986, by Tony O'Malley, acrylic on canvas.

CAMILLE SOUTER (1929–)

Camille Souter paints abstracts based on landscape. Her early work was influenced by American Abstract Expressionists and this feeling for gesture and paint comes through in all her work. The colours are often evocative of the Irish climate. 'Waiting to Go on the Canal' [11,88] shows how she can take anonymous pieces of landscape and create works of light and beauty, rich in colour and texture. Receding horizons and simple divisions of space are frequent elements in her work.

ANNE MADDEN (1932–)

Landscape was also the basis for Anne Madden's early work, painted impasto in oils. As her work developed, she used multiple canvases. 'Sixpartite, 1967 Red Mountain Sequence', which is in Trinity College Dublin, is one of these paintings. In the 1984 ROSC exhibition she exhibited a series of works in graphite and paint called 'Openings'. These create ambiguous

spaces which seek to reconcile opposites, inside/outside, light/dark, day/night, male/female. 'Fata Morgana 1995 (Odyssey) II' [11,89] develops a similar theme, combining geometry with painterly marks.

BARRIE COOKE (1931–)

American-born, Barrie Cooke came to live in Ireland in 1951. Much of his work is based on nature and its 'cycles'. He spent a number of years making bone boxes — perspex boxes containing arrangements of real or artificial bones. The 'Portrait of the Lough Derg Pike, Life-size with Relics' [11,90] combines fluid painting of the great fish with real objects. This fluid painting style has been used to produce works in which animal and plant forms flow together in a natural harmony. 'Red Stag' which he exhibited in the 1988 ROSC exhibition is in this style.

[11,89] 'Fata Morgana 1995 (Odyssey) II', 1995, by Anne Madden, oil on canvas 173 x 171 cm.

287

[11,90] 'Portrait of the Lough Derg Pike, Life-size with Relics', by Barrie Cooke (Crawford Municipal Gallery, Cork).

[11,92] 'Woman with a Pierre Soulages', 1972, by Robert Ballagh.

REALISM AND SURREALISM

Since the 1960s various forms of realism and surrealism have followed from pop art and its offshoots. A number of Irish artists have developed their own style in this area.

EDWARD McGUIRE (1932–86)

Edward McGuire is best known for his realist portraits, often of literary people. While there is a surface likeness of the sitter, there is often a mystery in the eyes or in the surrealist backgrounds. His 'Portrait of Seamus Heaney' [11,91] offers such a puzzle to the viewer.

ROBERT BALLAGH (1943–)

Robert Ballagh began as a Pop Artist and gradually, through flat interpretation of master paintings like Goya's 'The Third of May 1808' and paintings of people looking at pictures from the ROSC 1972 exhibition, i.e. 'Woman with a Pierre Soulages', [11,92] he moved towards photo realism in the late 1970s. 'The Conversation' (1977), which shows Ballagh talking to Vermeer, was the beginning of a series of paintings about his own life and environment. To enhance our knowledge of the sitter, Ballagh also paints portraits with carefully chosen backgrounds. [11,93] His work includes printmaking and designing postage stamps and paper currency.

MARTIN GALE (1949–)

Martin Gale began by painting surrealist pictures and an element of unreality still clings to his photo realist work. A sense of tension or unease permeates his paintings of moments from everyday life. 'Bus Stop' (1981) and 'Waking Up' [11,94] show his meticulously detailed 'large colour-photograph' approach in which brushwork and texture are secondary to the created image.

[11,91] 'Portrait of Seamus Heaney', 1974, by Edward McGuire (Ulster Museum, Belfast).

[11,93] 'Homage to Bernadette Greevy', 1978, by Robert Ballagh.

[11,94] 'Waking Up', 1986, by Martin Gale, oil on canvas, 122 x 152 cm (AIB Collection of Modern Irish Art).

OTHER ARTISTS

There are almost as many techniques, choices of subject-matter and methods of working practised today as there are artists. The following is a sample of people finding their own means of expressing their vision.

BRIAN BOURKE (1936–)

Brian Bourke has found inspiration in a variety of subjects and media. 'Knock-a-Lough Summer' is an example of his landscape painting. He has painted, drawn and etched a series on 'Don Quixote' and has done a number of self-portraits. He also paints commissioned portraits and works in sculpture. It is as much the process of painting, drawing or sculpting as the subject that motivates Bourke — the vigorous lines, the treatment of materials and a feeling of exploration of subject and medium. [11,95]

[11,96] 'Alcool de Serpent sur Table', 1981, by Michael Farrell (Hugh Lane Municipal Gallery, Dublin).

MICHAEL FARRELL (1940–)

Michael Farrell has worked in a variety of styles. His abstract 'Pressé' series in the early 1970s and 'Orange Squash' (1972) broke the boundaries between painting and sculpture. He then returned to figurative work in his 'Miss O'Murphy' series. 'Alcool de Serpent sur Table' [11,96] shows further development, combining hard edge with gestural painting, and abstraction with realism.

CHARLES HARPER (1942–)

Charles Harper paints in a variety of media, often within a geometric grid pattern. The human figure and condition is at the core of his work. 'Cradle' [11,97] combines geometric shapes with figurative elements all painted in strong colours. The action of painting or drawing and the handling of the materials are always part of the work, which contrasts with the mathematical background.

THE HUMAN FIGURE

Many artists use the human figure as the central image in their work, often as a means of expressing views on life.

[11,95] 'Sweeney Falls to Captivity', 1988, by Brian Bourke, oil on canvas, 122 x 152 cm.

[11,97] 'Cradle', 1982, by Charles Harper, acrylic on canvas, 142 x 155 cm.

289

[11,98]
'Woman/Waterlilies',
1979, by Pauline
Bewick.

[11,99] 'The Coming of Lugh the Il-Dána', 1979, by Jim Fitzpatrick.

PAULINE BEWICK (1935–)

Pauline Bewick paints in watercolours, sometimes combined with pen line. Her work often expresses a sense of being a part of nature. 'Woman/Waterlilies' [11,98] expresses this feeling strongly. Other work simply illustrates events from her life.

JIM FITZPATRICK (1945–)

An interest in Celtic mythology has led Jim Fitzpatrick to produce paintings and prints which illustrate legends in a style that combines Celtic pattern with the type of drawing used in American superhero comics. [11,99] His print publications include *The Book of Conquests*, *The Silver Arm* and *The Son of Suns*.

MICHAEL ASHUR (1950–)

Michael Ashur paints pictures based on complex geometric forms, aglow with films of delicate colour. Many of his works have titles which link them to solar bodies and outer space. 'Great Nebula (Orion) No. 2' [11,100] is typical of this series. 'Time Crystal Disintegration' shows a range of modern painting techniques. Spray and airbrush work predominate.

POST-MODERNISM

The notion that, to be modern, art had to be abstract and experimental was no longer accepted by the late twentieth century. Artists felt free to work in any medium or in any way that seemed appropriate to their needs, which explains the range of styles and techniques practised by artists in the 1980s and 1990s, some of which we have already seen.

[11,100] 'Great Nebula (Orion) No. 2', 1974, by Michael Ashur.

[11,101] 'Fading Dreams', 1990, by Willie Doherty,

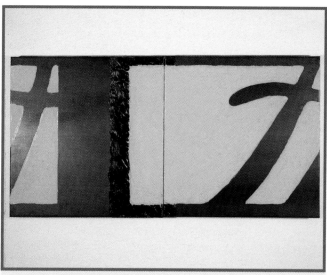

[11,103] 'Seein', 1995, by John Cronin.

[11,102] 'Fear Haunts the Soul', 1990, by Mick Cullen, 50 x 70 cm lithograph (Fenderesky Gallery).

WILLIE DOHERTY (1959–)

To evoke thoughts in his audience Willie Doherty combines photographs with written statements. The statements are almost always ambiguous, setting off chains of related ideas when combined with the patterns, textures and images of the photographs. [11,101]

MICK CULLEN (1946–)

Mick Cullen paints in an expressionist style that follows movements in Germany and Italy. The strong colouring and vigorous brush drawing create images of movement tinged with violence. 'Fear Haunts the Soul', [11,102] a lithograph, leaves the viewer to create the significance for the rapidly drawn combination of figurative and abstract marks.

JOHN CRONIN (1966–)

John Cronin emphasises painterly technique at a time when some critics say painting is a dead medium. The 'Serein' series painted in oils and dry pigment on steel panels contrasts oil painting and colour with the sculptural metal surface in an effort to resolve problems between the artistic process and modern technology. [11,103]

This conflict between art and technology is further explored in his series '[sic] an error in quoted matter' in which the artist destroys an oil painting after it has been scanned into a computer and printed by the ink jet process to a size of 244 x 122 cm. Cronin's work asks fundamental questions about the nature of painting in the technological age.

CONCLUSION

In spite of a very slow start Irish art managed in the twentieth century to catch up with developments in Europe. Young Irish artists in the 1960s and 1970s had to struggle to break out of a backward-looking education system and create the groundwork which allowed artists in the 1990s to be a part of contemporary movements in art throughout Europe. The arts in the late twentieth century are better supported by state and commercial institutions than they have ever been. Irish artists are well known internationally and their work is represented in collections world-wide.

INDEX

A Wear, 21, 22
Abstract art, 173–8
Abstract Expressionism, 161, 179–80
abstract painting, Irish, 285–6
Academie Royale de Peinture et de Sculpture, 98
'Accent in Pink' (Kandinsky), 174
'Acis and Galatea' (Poussin), 101
Act of Union, 257
action painting, 177, 180
Adam, Robert, 112–13, 254
'Adam and Eve' (Barry), 253
Adam style, 256
Adamnan, 203
'Adoration of the Lamb' (van Eyck), 65–6
'Adoration of the Magi' (da Vinci), 76, *77*
advertising design, 20
African art, 171
'Age of Bronze' (Rodin), 129, *130*
Aghadoe Crosier, 231
Aghowle, Co. Wicklow, 217
'Agony, Judith and St Thomas, The' (Healy), 281
Ahenny High Crosses, 207, 208
Aicher, Otl, 19
Aiken, John, 277
Albert, Archduke, 102
Albert Memorial, 261
Alberti, Leon Battista, 52–3, 55
'Alcool de Serpent Sur Table' (Farrell), 289
All Hallows College, Dublin, 259
'Allegory of the Incarnation, An' (Tiepolo), *115*
Alloway, Lawrence, 182
Altnagelvin Hospital, Derry, 273
'Ambassadors, The' (Holbein), *89*
amber, 212
Ambrosian Library, Milan, 205
Amiens Cathedral, 39, 40
Amiens Street (Connolly) Station, 258
Analytical Cubism, 169
Andre, Ellen, 145
Angelico, Fra, 61–2
Anglo-Norman period, 233–41
Annals of the Four Masters, 217
'Annunciation, The' (Fra Angelico), 61
'Annunciation' (Martini), 47–8
'Apollo Fountain' (Flotner), 75
'Apparatus No. 7, Sweeney's Monument' (Fitzgerald), 274
applied arts, 253–6, 266. *see also* crafts
Aran Islands, 202, 262–3
architecture
    Baroque, 92–7
        England, 95–7
        France, 94–5, 98
    early Renaissance, 53–5
    and environment, 14–17
    Gothic, 37–41
    High Renaissance, 68–72
    Ireland
        Anglo-Norman period, 233–9
        High Christian, 207
        Iron Age, 198
        monasteries, 202–3
        nineteenth century, 257–60
        seventeenth century, 242–3
        tracery, 236–7
        twentieth century, 267–71
        Viking invasions, 216–17
    Rococo, 110–13
    Romanesque, 28–31, 225–8
    Romantic movement, 125–8
    twentieth century, 155–9
Ardagh Chalice, *211*, 212–14, 215, 224
Ardakillin Brooch, 206, *207*
Arena Chapel, Padua, 46–7, 63
Arezzo, 63
Armagh Cathedral, 259
'Armstrong in the Cafe de Madrid, Madrid' (Osborne), *4*
'Arnolfini Wedding' (van Eyck), 66
Arp, Jean, 161, 174
art, appreciation of, 3–13
art, history of
    eighteenth century, 110–23
    fifteenth century, 52–67
    medieval period, 27–51
    nineteenth century, 124–55
    seventeenth century, 92–110
    sixteenth century, 68–91
    twentieth century, 155–86
Art Brut, 180–81
art galleries, 9–10
Art Nouveau, 126, 127–8, 133, 141, 153–4, 271
Arthouse Multi-Media Centre, 270, *271*
arts and crafts movement, 126
Asam, Egid Quirin, 114
Ashur, Michael, 290
Askeaton Friary, Co. Limerick, 236, *237*
'Assumption of the Virgin, The' (Asam), 114
'Assumption of the Virgin, The' (Titian), 84
Atelier Suisse, 138, 143, 148
Athassel Priory, Co. Tipperary, *236*
Athlone Crucifixion Plaque, 204, 214
'Attempted Martyrdom of Ss Cosmos and Damian' (Fra Angelico), 61–2
automatism, 177
Autun Cathedral, 31, 32–3, 42

Bacon, Francis, 160, 179
'Baldassare Castiglione', portrait of (Raphael), 82–3
Balla, Giacomo, 172
Ballagh, Robert, 288
Ballet Russe, 171
Ballinderry Brooch, 206
Ballyfin, Co. Laois, 266
Ballylongford Processional Cross, 241
Ballyshannon Sword Hilt, 200
'Balzac' (Rodin), 130
Bamberg Rider, 43
'Ban the Bomb' (Carey), *11*
Bank of Ireland, Baggot Street, 245, 269, 274
Banqueting Hall, Whitechapel, 95, *96*
'Baptism of Christ, The' (della Francesca), 63
Baptistry, Florence, 55–6
Baptistry, Pisa, 44–5
'Bar at the Folies Bergère, A' (Manet), 140, *141*
Barberini family, 94
Barbizon School, 132, 136–7, 138, 146, 151,
    263
Baroque design, 92–110
  architecture, 92–7
  painting
    Italy, 99–100
  sculpture, 97–8
Barret, George, 252
Barronini, Francesco, 94
Barry, Charles, 126
Barry, Commodore, 272
Barry, James, 253
Barye, Antoine-Louis, 128
Baselitz, Georg, 164
'Bathers at La Grenouillère' (Monet), *142*
'Battle of San Romano' (Uccello), 60–61
Baudelaire, Charles, 139, 140
Bauhaus Design School, 17, 156, 160, 167, 174,
    175, 176, 269
Bavaria, 114
Bayeux Tapestry, 35, *36*
Bazille, Frédéric, 142, 143
Beaker people, 194–5
Beardsley, Aubrey, 154, 282
Beaulieu, Co. Louth, 242, *243*
Beck, Jason, 11
Beckmann, Max, 168
Behan, John, 277
Belfast, 255, 268
Belfast Waterfront Hall, *17*
Belfield, Dublin, 269, 270
Belgium, 127
Bellamont Forest, Co. Cavan, 245, 246
Bellini, Giovanni, 58, 59, 64–5, 83, 86
Bellini, Jacopo, 59, 64
Belvedere House, Dublin, 254
Benedictine order, 27
Benetton poster, *4*

Bernard, Émile, 150
Bernini, Gian Lorenzo, 96
  architecture, 93–4
  sculpture, 97–8
Berry, Duc de, 48–9, 49
Beuys, Joseph, 163
Bewick, Pauline, 290
'Bird Diving over an Iris' (Hiroshige), *142*
'Bird in Space' (Brancusi), 159–60
'Bird Lake Paradise Island, Bahamas' (O'Malley),
    287
'Birth of Christ' (Pisano), 44, *45*
Birr, Co. Offaly, 260
'Birth of the World, The' (Miro), 177–8
'Birth of Venus, The' (Botticelli), 62
Black Abbey, Kilkenny, 237
'Black Paintings, The' (Goya), 122–3
Blackrock Castle, Co. Cork, 258
Blake, William, 125, 130–31
Blanche of Castile, Queen, 50
Blasket Centre, Dunquin, 15
'Blaue Reiter, Der,' 167, 174
Blenheim Palace, Oxfordshire, 97
Bleyl, Fritz, 166
Blue Coat School, Dublin, 248
'Blue Rose' (Moon), 184
'Blue Still Life with Knife' (Scott), 285
Boa Island figures, 199
Bobbio monastery, 205–6
Boccioni, Umberto, 159, 160, 172
'Body of a Woman' (Dubuffet), *181*
Bonaparte, Napoleon, 124, 127
Bonnard, Pierre, 153
Book of Armagh, 222, *223*
Book of Dimma, 211
Book of Durrow, 209–10, 214
Book of Kells, 203, 215, 218–19, 220–22, 232
Book of Lindisfarne, 211
Book of MacRegol of Birr, 211
Book of Mulling, 207, 211
book-binding, 255
Borghese family, 94
borrowed images, 185–6
Bosch, Hieronymus, 89, 177
Botticelli, Sandro, 62, 173
Boucher, François, 117, 118
Boudin, Eugène, 143
Bourke, Brian, 289
Bramante, Donato, 68–9, 78
Brancacci Chapel, Florence, 59–60
Brancusi, Constantin, 159–60, 173
brand identity, 19–20
Brandt, Marianne, 157
Braque, Georges, 165, 167, 168–70, 171
Breac Maodhóg, 232, *233*
Bridge-a-Crin church, Co. Louth, 281
'Broadway Boogie Woogie' (Mondrian), *176*

Broighter Collar, 200
Bronze Age, 193–7
Bronzino, Agnolo, 83
Brooks, John, 250
Brueghel, Pieter, the Elder, 89–90
Brunel, Isambard Kingdom, 125
Brunelleschi, Filippo, 52–3, 54–5, 56
Buffrand, G.G., 111
Bulfin, Michael, 274
Bunratty Castle, Co. Clare, 238
Burgos Cathedral, 40
Burgundy, Duke, 65
'Burial at Ornans' (Courbet), 139
'Burial of Count Orgaz' (El Greco), 90
Burke, Edmund, 252, 253, 260
Burke, John, 274
Burlington, Lord, 112
Burri, Alberto, 180
Burton, Frederick, 262–3
Bury Bible, 34–5
Busaras, Store Street, 269
Butler, Piers Fitz Og, tomb of, 239
Butler, R.M., 267
Butler, William Deane, 258
Byrne, Barry, 271
Byrne, Ralph, 268
Byzantine Empire, 34–5

'Cabinet de la Pendule,' Versailles, 110, 111
Cahir Castle, Co. Tipperary, 238
'Camera degli Sposi,'Palazzo Ducale, Mantua, 63–4
camera obscura, 108
camerawork
  in cinema, 12
Campidoglio, Rome, 69, 70
Campin, Robert, 66
Canaletto, 115–16
Canova, Antonio, 113, 251
Caracci, Annibale, 99–100, 120
Caravaggio, 100–101, 102
'Cardplayers in a Sunlit Room' (de Hooch), 109
Carey, Ellen, 11
Carlyle, Thomas, 134
Carndonagh High Cross, 204, 205, 210, 214
Caro, Anthony, 162–3
Carpeaux, Jean-Baptiste, 129
Carra, Carlo, 172, 173
Carrickfergus Castle, Co. Antrim, 238
Carton, Co. Kildare, 254
Carucci, Jacopo (Pontormo), 83
'Caryll, 3rd Viscount Molyneaux of Maryborough' (Morphey), 244
Casa Battlo, Barcelona, 127, 128
Cashel, Co. Tipperary, 225–7
  Cathedral, 235
  High Cross, 229
Casino, Marino, 247, 249

Cassels, Richard, 246
Castle Howard, Yorkshire, 97
'Castle of Bentheim, The' (Ruisdael), 109, 110
Castledermot, Co. Kildare, 218
Castlestrange, Co. Roscommon, 198
Castletown, Co. Kildare, 254
Castletown House, Co. Kildare, 246
Cathach, the, 205–6, 206, 207
'Cathedral at Rouen: Harmony in Blue and Gold' (Monet), 144
'Cathedral' (Pollock), 180
Catholic Emancipation, 260
'Cattle on a Riverbank' (Aubigny), 137
Cavan Cathedral, 268
Céide Fields Interpretative Centre, 16
Cellini, Benvenuto, 74
Celtic revival, 271, 279
Celts, 197–201
Central Bank, Dublin, 269, 270
'Ceramic-Erotic-Religious' (Klee), 175
Cézanne, Paul, 5–9, 142, 146, 148–9, 150, 164, 168, 173
Chagall, Marc, 173
Chambers, Sir William, 247, 248
Chambord, Château of, Loir-et-Cher, 71
Champs-Elysées, Paris, 127
'Chapeau de Paille' (Rubens), 103
Charlemont, Lord, 247
'Charles Coote, 1st Earl of Bellamont' (Reynolds), 120
Charles I, King of England, 103, 104
'Charles I of England Out Hunting' (van Dyck), 103–4
Charles IV, King of Spain, 121
'Charles IV and His Family' (Goya), 121–2
Charles V, King of France, 48
Charles VI, King of France, 49
Chartres Cathedral, 37–9
  sculpture, 42–3
  stained glass, 50
Chavannes, Pierre Puvis de, 153
'Cheat with the Ace of Diamonds, The' (de la Tour), 102
Chia, Sandro, 185
Child, A.E., 281, 282
'Children of Lir, The' (Kelly), 273
'Chinese Landscape' (Scott), 285, 286
Chiswick House, London, 112
Christ Church Cathedral, Dublin, 233–4, 235
'Christ Mocked by Soldiers' (Rouault), 168
'Christ Preaching the Forgiveness of Sins' (Rembrandt), 107
'Christ the King Monument' (O'Connor), 272
'Christ Welcoming a Soldier' (Catherine O'Brien), 282
'Christ with Jesuit Saints' (Evie Hone), 282

Christianity
  Romanesque design, 27–36
Church of Christ the King, Cork, 271
Church of St Aengus, Burt, 271
Church of St Agatha, Glenflesk, 259
CIE buildings, 269
Cimabue, 45, 46
cinema, 11–13
'Circle in Ireland, A' (Long), 163
'Circus, The' (Seurat), 148
Cistercians, 228, 232, 235, 236
City Hall, Belfast, 268
City Hall, Cork, 268
City Hall, Dublin, 249, 250, 261
City Hall, Munster, 41
Civil War, 267, 278
Claesz, Pieter, 3, 109
Clarke, Harry, 282–3
Classical style architecture, 257–8
Classical (Victorian) style architecture, 258–9
Claude Lorrain, 102, 112, 115, 131, 137, 261–2
Clemente, Francesco, 185
Clements, Nathaniel, 246
Clifton Suspension Bridge (Brunel), 125, 126
Clones fibula, 196
Clonfert Cathedral, Co. Galway, 227
Clonmacnoise, Co. Offaly, 207, 208, 216, 220,
    225, 226, 227, 228, 262
Clonmacnoise Crosier, 232
'Cloud Study' (Constable), 132
Cluniac order, 27, 30–31
Cluny Abbey, 32
Cluny III, church of, 30–31
Coeur, Jacques, 41
Colbert, Jean Baptiste, 98
'Collage 1913' (Picasso), 170
College of Science, Dublin, 272
Collins, Michael, 272
Cologne Cathedral, 40, 42
'Colossus, The' (Goya), 122–3
colour, in film, 12
Columba, St, 203, 205
Columbanus, St, 203, 205
'Coming of Lugh the Il-Dana, The' (Fitzpatrick), 290
Commonwealth Promenade Apartments, Chicago
    (van der Rohe), 158
communications technology, 18–19
'Composition No. 4' (Kandinsky), 174
composition sketches, 5
'Composition with Red, Yellow and Blue'
    (Mondrian), 176
Conceptual Art, 161, 163, 177, 278
'Conjuror, The' (Hone), 252–3
'Connemara Landscape, A' (Henry), 280
Conolly, William, 246
Conor, William, 281
Constable, John, 131–2, 144

Constructivism, 160
'Convent Garden, A' (Leech), 279
Cooke, Barrie, 287
Cooley, Thomas, 258
Copyright Act, 1735, 119
Coram, Captain, 119
Corbusier, Le, 157
Cork, 247, 255
Cormac's Chapel, Cashel, 225–7, 228
Cornaleck triple head, 199
Corot, Jean Baptiste Camille, 137, 146, 263
Corr and McCormick, 271
Correggio, Antonio Allegri da, 83
'Corsage Noir, Le' (Morisot), 147
'Costanza Buonarelli' (Bernini), 97–8
County Hall, Cork, 269
Courbet, Gustave, 138–9
Couture, Thomas, 140
Coysevox, Antoine, 98
'Cradle' (Harper), 289
crafts
  Gothic, 49–50
  Ireland
    eighteenth century, 253–6
    nineteenth century, 266
    Romanesque, 35
Cranach, Lucas, 87
crannógs, 198
Crawford, William, 261
'Creole Dancer, The' (Matisse), 165, 166
Cronin, John, 291
'Cross in the Mountains, The' (Friedrich), 125
Cross of Cong, 232
Cross of the Scriptures, Clonmacnoise, 220
'Cross Section 1920' (Grosz), 168
'Crucifixion, Sacrifice of Isaac and Last Supper'
    (Evie Hone), 282
Crusades, 27
Crying Game, The, 12
Cubism, 148, 149, 159, 166, 168–72, 174, 175,
    176, 177
  Ireland, 283–4
Cullen, Michael, 291
'Cupid and Psyche' (Canova), 113
'Cupid and Psyche in the Nuptial Bower'
    (Hamilton), 252
Curraghmore, Co. Waterford, 254
Custom House, Dublin, 248, 249–50, 267
'Cyclops, The' (Redon), 154
'Cypresses and Two Figures' (van Gogh), 152

Dadaism, 160–61, 172, 176–7
Dali, Salvador, 177, 178
'Danae' (Titian), 84
'Daniel-Henry Kahnweiler' (Picasso), 169
'Danse, La' (Carpeaux), 129
'Danse, La' (Matisse), 165

Dante, 36, 46–7
Darley family, 246
Daubigny, Charles, 137
Daumier, Honore, 137–8
David, Jacques Louis, 118–19, 124
'David' (Donatello), 57
'David' (Michelangelo), 73
'David' (Verrocchio), *58*
Davis, Thomas, 276
'Day Dream' (Rossetti), *134*
de Blacam and Meagher, 270
De Burgo Genealogy, 240
De Burgo O'Malley Chalice, 241
de Chirico, Giorgio, 178
de Hooch, Pieter, 109
de Huy, Renier, 35
de Kooning, Willem, 181
de la Pena, N. V. Diaz, 137
de la Tour, Georges, 102
De Stijl, 156, 173, 176
Deane, Sir Thomas, 260
Deane, T.M., 267
Deane and Woodward, 126
'Death and Fire' (Klee), *175*
'Death of Cuchulainn, The' (Shepard), 271, *272*
'Death of Marat, The' (David), 119
'Death of Sardanapalus, The' (Delacroix), 124, *125*
'Deer in the Forest II' (Marc), 167, *168*
Degas, Edgar, 135, 140, 141, 142, 145, 152
'Dejeuner sur l'Herbe' (Manet), 140
Delacroix, Eugène, 121, 123, 124, 125, 128, 131, 134–5, 136, 148, 151
Delaney, Edward, 276–7
Delaroche, Paul, 138
Delaunay, Robert, 173, 175
delftware, 255
della Francesca, Piero, 63
della Porta (architect), 93
'Demoiselles d'Avignon, Les' (Picasso), 169
'Departure of the Volunteers in 1792' (Rude), 128, *129*
'Deposition of Christ, The' (Giotto), 46–7
'Deposition' (Pontormo), *83*
'Deposition' (van der Weyden), 66, 67
Derain, André, 165, 167
Derrinaboy armbands, 195, *196*
Derrynablaha, Co. Kerry, 193, *194*
Derrynaflan Chalice, 223–4
Derrynaflan Paten, 214–15
Derrynane, Co. Kerry, 197
Desboutin, Marcel, 145
design, appreciation of, 13–24
'Detail of Still Life' (Claesz), *109*
di Buoninsegna, Duccio, 46
'Diana Getting out of her Bath' (Boucher), 117
Die Brucke, 166–7

Dillon, Gerard, 286
'Dinghies on a Normandy Beach' (Hone the Younger), 264
direction, in film, 12
divisionism, 148
Dix, Otto, 168
'Doge Leonardo Loredan, The, portrait of (Bellini 64), *65*
Doge's Palace, Venice, 41
Doherty, Willie, 291
Domhnach Airgid Book Shrine, 240, *241*
'Domine Quo Vadis' (Carracci), 99, *100*
Dominican convent, Vence, 166
Dominick Street, Dublin, 254
Donatello, 52, 56–7, 63
'Drawbridge with Carriage' (van Gogh), *151*
drawing, 58–9
Drew, Thomas, 259
Dreyfuss, Henry, 18
Dromoland Castle, Co. Clare, 258
Drumcliff High Cross, 229
Dublin, 255
    Georgian architecture, 245–9
Dublin Airport, 269
Dublin Castle, 249
Dublin Civic Offices, Wood Quay, 274, *275*
Dublin Group, 250
Dublin Society, 244–5, 249, 250
    art schools, 250–52, 253, 256, 260
Dubuffet, Jean, 180–81
Dufy, Raoul, 165
Dupré, Jules, 137
Durand-Ruel, 143, 147
Durer, Albrecht, 64, 86–7
Durham Cathedral, 31
Dysart O'Dea High Cross, 229

'Early One Morning' (Caro), 162, *163*
Early Renaissance, 52–67
    architecture, 53–5
    painting, 58–67
    sculpture, 55–7
Ecole des Beaux Arts, Paris, 129, 145, 148, 167
'Ecstasy of St Teresa' (Bernini), 97
editing, film, 13
Edwardian style architecture, 267–8
Eiffel Tower, 127, 175
El Greco, 90–91, 171
Elizabeth I, Queen, 238
Emly Shrine, 214
enamelling, 211
Enda, St, 202
England
    architecture, 72
    Baroque, 95–6
    Gothic architecture, 40
    High Renaissance, 88–9

minimalism, 184
Rococo
  architecture, 112–13
  painting, 119–21
  sculpture, 114
Romantic movement
  architecture, 125–7
  painting, 130–34
Enniscorthy, Co. Wexford, 259, 271
Ensor family, 246
environment
  and architecture, 14–17, 159
ergonomics, 18, 23
'Et in Arcadia Ego' (Poussin), 101
Etruscan art, 169
Eugenie, Empress, 129
'Eve of St Agnes, The' (Clarke), 283
Evelyn, John, 98
'Everybody Should Get Stones' (Sheridan), 278
examination, of art, 4–9
exhibition, visiting, 9–10
'Experiment with an Air Pump' (Wright), 121
Expressionism, 152, 164, 166, 168, 273

'Fading Dreams' (Doherty), 291
Fahan Mura stone slab, 204
'Famine Group' (Delaney), 276–7
'Famine memorial' (Behan), 277
'Fantômas' (Gris), 170
'Farm at Lezaver, Finistère' (O'Conor), 265
Farnese, Cardinal Odoardo, 99
Farrell, Michael, 289
'Fascicolo di Medicina' (de Ketham), 58
fashion, 21–3
'Fata Morgana 1995 (Odyssey) II' (Madden), 287
'Fate of the Children of Lir' (Geddes), 281, 282
Father Mathew statue, Cork (Hogan), 261
Fauvism, 152, 164–6, 166, 173, 177
'Fear Haunts the Soul' (Cullen), 291
'Feast in the House of Levi, The,' 85–6
'Feeding Pigeons' (Hone the Younger), 263
Feininger, Lyonel, 167
'Fêtes Venitiennes, Les' (Watteau), 116
Fethard, Co. Tipperary, 239–40
fibulae, 196
Figurative painting, 179
Figurative sculpture, 161–2, 276–7
Finnian, St, 205
First World War, 128, 174
FitzGerald, Desmond, 269
Fitzgerald, Tom, 274
Fitzpatrick, Jim, 290
Fitzwilliam family, 246
'Five Women on the Street' (Kirchner), 166
'Flag' (Johns), 181
'Flamboyant' style, 40
Flanders, 92, 102–5

'Flatford Lock and Cottage Bridge, Suffolk'
  (Constable), 131
Flaxman, John, 114, 251
Flemish art, 58, 65, 66
  early Renaissance, 67
'Flood at Port Marly' (Sisley), 147
Florence, 53, 68
  architecture, 54–5
  early Renaissance, 52–7
  painting, 58–67
  sculpture, 55–7, 73
Florence Cathedral, 40, 54, 55–7, 57
Flötner, Pieter, 75
Foley, John Henry, 260–61
'Fontaine des Innocents' (Goujon), 75
Fontainebleau, 71, 72, 75, 263
'Fountain, The' (Duchamp), 161
Four Courts, Dublin, 248–9
'Four Horsemen of the Apocalypse, The' (Durer),
  86, 87
Foy, St, reliquary of, 28
Fragonard, Jean Honoré, 117, 146, 147
France
  architecture, 71
  Baroque
    architecture, 94–5, 98
    painting, 101–2
  Gothic architecture, 37–41
  Rococo
    architecture, 110–11
    painting, 116–19
    sculpture, 113–14
  Romantic movement
    architecture, 127
    painting, 134–54
Francini brothers, 254
Franciscans, 235–6
François I, King of France, 71, 75
Franco-Prussian War, 1870-71, 124, 143
Free Abstraction, 179–80
French Revolution, 110, 117, 118–19
fresco, 58, 59
Freud, Sigmund, 177, 182
Friedrich, Caspar David, 125, 134
Frömel, Gerda, 273
Frye, Thomas, 250
'Funeral of the Anarchist Galli' (Carra), 173
furniture, 255, 266
Futurism, 167, 172, 176

Gabo, Naum, 160
Gainsborough, Thomas, 120
Gale, Martin, 288
Galerie des Glaces, Versailles, 95
Gallarus Oratory, 203
Gandon, James, 247, 248–9, 249
'Garden of Earthly Delights, The' (Bosch), 89

Garden of Remembrance, Parnell Square, 273
Gardiner, Luke, Lord Mountjoy, 246
Gare du Nord, Paris, 127
Garnier, Charles, 127
'Gattamelata' (Donatello), 57
Gaudi, Antoni, 127–8
Gauguin, Paul, 147, 149–50, 151, 153, 154,
    164, 177, 265
Geddes, Wilhelmina, 281
General Post Office, Dublin, 257–8
genre painting, 106–9
Georgian period, 244–56
Gericault, Theodore, 125, 135–6
Germany, 97, 175, 176
  Expressionism, 168
  Gothic architecture, 40
  High Renaissance, 86–9
  Rococo, 111–12
  Romantic movement, 134
Gesù, Rome, 92–3
Ghent Altarpiece (van Eyck), 65–6
Ghiberti, Lorenzo, 56
Ghirlandaio, Domenico, 72
Giacometti, Alberto, 161
Giambologna, 74
Gilbert and George, 185, *186*
Gilroy McMahon, 16, 17
Giorgione, 65, 78, 83–4
Giotto di Bondone, 40, 46–7, 59, 63, 72
Giovanni, Bertoldo di, 72
'Girl Running on the Balcony, A' (Balla), 172
Gislebertus, 32–3
Glasgow, 128
glass, 206, 211, 255, 266
'Gleaners, The' (Millet), 138
Glendalough, Co. Wicklow, 207, 217, 225
Gleninsheen Gorget, 196
Gleyre, Charles, 142, 143, 147
Gober, Robert, 186
Goethe, 133
'Going to Work' (Millet), 138
Goldsmith, Oliver, 260
goldworking
  Bronze Age, 194–6
  early Christian, 206
  High Christian, 211–15
  Viking invasions, 223–4
Gonzaga, Duke Ludovico, 63–4
'Good and Evil Angels, The' (Blake), 131
     gorgets, 196
Gothic design, 36–51
  architecture, 37–41, 258
  crafts, 49–50
  painting, 45–9
  sculpture, 41–5
Gothic revival, 125–6
  architecture, 259–60

Goujon, Jean, 75
'Governess, The' (Chardin), 117–18
Government Buildings, Merrion Street, 267
Goya, Francisco de, 121–3, 125, 177
'Grab Des Unbekannten Malers' (Kiefer), 185
Grand Tour, 245, 250
graphic design, 19–21
Grattan, Henry, 260
grave slabs, 207
Gravelot (engraver), 120
'Great Bear, The' (Patterson), *186*
Great Exhibition, 1862, 266
'Great Nebula (Orion) No. 2' (Ashur), 290
Greek revival, 260
Green Building, Temple Bar, 16
'Grenouillère, La' (Renoir), *142*
'Grief' (Jack B. Yeats), 280
Gris, Juan, 170
Gropius, Walter, 156
Grosz, Georg, 168
Grunewald, Mathis, 87–8
'Guernica' (Picasso), 171, *172*, 178
Guinness, 19–20
Guinness, Sir Benjamin Lee, 260
'Gypsy Woman with Baby' (Modigliani), *173*

Hallstatt Celts, 197
Hals, Frans, 107–8
Hamilton, Hugh Douglas, 251–2
Hamilton, Richard, 182
Hanson, Duane, 164
'Harbour, Bangor' (Middleton), 286
Harper, Charles, 289
Harpigines, 263
Harrison family, 260
Hartung, Hans, 180
Haussmann, Baron, 127
Hawksmoor, Nicholas, 96
'Head' (Clemente), *185*
Healy, Michael, 281
Heckel, Erich, 166
Henry, Françoise, 208–9, 221
Henry, Paul, 280, 281
Henry VIII, King of England, 89
Henry VII's Chapel, Westminster Abbey, 40, *41*
Hewetson, Christopher, 249
Hiberno-Romanesque Revival, 268
Hicks, F.G., 268
High Crosses, 203, 204, 207–9
  Romanesque, 228–9
  Viking invasions, 217–20
High Gothic style, 39–40
High Renaissance, 68–91
  architecture, 68–72
  painting, 76–91
  sculpture, 72–6
Hildesheim Cathedral, 33

Hiroshige, Ando, 141, 142
'Hoar-Frost' (Pissarro), 146, *147*
Hockney, David, 182
Hogan, John, 261
Hogarth, William, 119, 122
Holbein, Hans, 88–9
'Holy Family' (Michelangelo), 78
'Holy Trinity, The' (Masaccio), 60
'Holy Women at the Sepulchre' (di
        Buoninsegna), 46
'Homage to Bernadette Greevy' (Ballagh), 288
Honan Chapel, Cork, 282
Hone, Evie, 282, 283, 284
Hone, Nathaniel, the Elder, 252–3
Hone, Nathaniel, the Younger, 263–4
Horta, Victor, 127, 128
Houdon, Jean-Antoine, 114
'House of the Hanged Man, The' (Cézanne), 148
Houses of Parliament, London, 126
Houston, Richard, 250
Hubner, Peter, 159
Hudson (painter), 120
Hugh, Abbot, 30–31
Hugo, Master, 34–5
Humanism, 52, 65
Hunt, William Holman, 133
'Hunters in the Snow' (Breughel), 90
'Hybrid Fruit called Pagoda' (Arp), *161*

'I and the Village' (Chagall), *173*
'I Have Trodden the Winepress Alone' (Jellett),
        284
Illauntannig, Co. Kerry, 202
'Impression of Morning Sunrise' (Monet), 143
Impressionism, 6, 132, 133, 139, 140, 142–7,
        152, 165, 265
'In the Meadow' (Renoir), 146
Industrial Revolution, 124, 125, 154
Ingres, Jean Auguste Dominique, 134–5
Inis Cealtra, Co. Clare, 207
Inishkeel, Co. Donegal, 202
Inishmurray, Co. Sligo, 202
Innocent X, Pope, 104
Innovation Shop, Brussels, 127
installations, 277
interior design, 23–4
International Gothic style, 48
International School of Paris, 173
International style, 157–8
Intimists, 153
Into the West, 11
'Intrusion 2' (King), 286
Iona, 215, 218
Ireland, history of
    early Christian, 202–15
    eighteenth century, 244–56
    High Christian, 207–15

medieval
    Anglo-Norman period, 233–41
        Romanesque, 225–33
    nineteenth century, 257–67
    pre-Christian, 189–201
    seventeenth century, 242–4
    twentieth century, 267–91
    Viking invasions, 215–24
Irish Exhibition of Living Art, 267
Iron Age, 197–201
Isabella, Infanta, 102
'Isenheim Altarpiece' (Grünewald), 88
Isolde's Tower Apartments, Essex Quay, 16, *17*
Italy
    Baroque
        architecture, 92–4
        painting, 99–100
        sculpture, 97–8
    Gothic architecture, 40
    High Renaissance, 68–71, 72–86
        painting, 76–86
    Quattrocentro, 52–7
    Rococo
        painting, 115–16
        sculpture, 113
Ivory, Thomas, 248, 251

Jacque, Charles-Émile, 137
James I, King of England, 103
'Jane Avril at the Jardin de Paris' (Toulouse-
        Lautrec), 152, *153*
'Jane Seymour Conway' (Jervas), 250
'Jaunting Car, The' (Conor), 281
Javacheff, Christo, *163*
Jellett, Mainie, 283, 284
Jerpoint Abbey, Co. Kilkenny, 239
Jervas, Charles, 250
'Jeune Bretonne, La' (O'Conor), 265
'Jewish Bride, The' (Rembrandt), 107
Johns, Jasper, 181, 183
Johnston, Francis, 257–8
Jones, Inigo, 95–7, 103
Jones and Kelly, 268
Jongkind, Johan Barthold, 143
Jordan, Neil, *12*
'Judith with the Head of Holofernes' (Mantegna),
        64
Julius II, Pope, 68, 73, 78, 82
'Juno Confiding Io to the Care of Argus' (Claude
        Lorrain), 102
'Just what is it that makes today's homes so
        different, so appealing?' (Hamilton), 182

Kandinsky, Vasily, 167, 174
Keating, Sean, 280, 281
Keirghan, Co. Armagh, 198
Kells, Co. Meath, *207*, 215, 218–19

Kelly, Oisin, 273
Kent, William, 112
Kiefer, Anslem, 185
Kilconnell Friary, Co. Galway, *235*
Kilcooley Abbey, Co. Tipperary, 237, 239
Kildare Street Club, Dublin, 260
Killcluggin, Co. Cavan, 198
Kilmallock Priory, Co. Limerick, *236*
kinetic art, 182
King, Brian, 275
King, Cecil, 285
King's College Chapel, Cambridge, 40
Kingsbridge (Heuston) Station, 258
Kirchner, Ernst Ludwig, 166
'Kiss, The' (Klimt), 154, *155*
'Kiss, The' (Rodin), 129, 130
'Kitchen Maid with Supper at Emmaus'
        (Velázquez), *105*
Klee, Paul, 167, 174–5
Klein, Yves, 182, 277
Klimt, Gustav, 154
Knowth, Co. Meath, 192, *193*
Kokoschka, Oskar, 168
Koralek, Paul, 269–70
Kruger, Barbra, 185
Kupka, Frantisek, 175

La Tène Celts, 197–201
Labrouste, 127
'L'absinthe' (Degas), 145
'Lady Holding a Rattle, A' (Purser), 264, *265*
'Lady Lavery with her Daughter and Grand-
        Daughter' (Lavery), 278, *279*
'Lady with the Unicorn,' 49
'Lady Writing a Letter' (Vermeer), 108
Lagore Filigree Bird, 206, *207*
Lamb, Charles, 281
Land Art, 163
Languedoc style, 32
'Last Circuit of Pilgrims at Clonmacnoise, The'
        (Petrie), 262
'Last Judgment, The' (Michelangelo), 80, 81
'Last Supper, The' (da Vinci), 77
'Last Supper' (Tintoretto), 85
'Laughing Cavalier, The' (Hals), 107, 108
Laurana, Luciano da, 53
Lavery, Sir John, 278
le Brocquy, Louis, 284–5
Le Nain brothers, 102
Le Nôtre, Andre, 95
Le Vau, Louis, 94–5
Lebrun, Charles, 95, 98
Leech, William J., 279
Léger, Fernand, 170, 171
Leinster House, Dublin, 246
Lemanaghan Shrine, 232, *233*
Lemaneagh Castle, Co. Clare, 242, 244

'L'enlèvement d'Europe' (Gauguin), *150*
lens art, 11–13
Leo X, Pope, 69, 73
Leroy, Louis, 143
Les Invalides, Paris, 95
Liber Hymnorum, 230
Liberty Hall, Dublin, 269
Lichfield Gospels, 211
'Liffey Swim, The' (Jack B. Yeats), 280
'Light of the World' (Hunt), 133, *134*
lighting, in film, 12
'Lily Yeats' (John B. Yeats), 264, *265*
Limbourg brothers, 48–9
Limerick, 247, 255
  crosier and mitre, 240–41
Limerick Cathedral, 239, *240*
Limoges, 35
Lincoln, Abraham, 272
Lindisfarne Gospels, 215
'Linear Construction in Space No. 2' (Gabo), *160*
linen-printing, 255
'Lion Hunt in Morocco' (Delacroix), *136*
Lipchitz, Jacques, 159
Lippi, Fra Filippo, 58
Lismore Crosier, 231
Lisnacrogher scabbard, 200
Literary Movement, 279–81
lithography, 153
'Little Gold Horse' tabernacle, 49
Living Art Exhibition, 283
lock rings, 196, *197*
Lombardy, 29
London, 116
  Irish artists in, 252–3
Long, Richard, 163
Longleat House, 72
Loreto Convent, Gorey, 259
Lough Cutra Castle, Co. Galway, 258
Lough Gur, Co. Limerick, 196–7
Lough Kinale Book Shrine, 215, 232
Loughnashade Trumpet, 200
Louis VI, King of France, 37
Louis XIV, King of France, 94, 98
Louis XV, King of France, 117
Louis XVI, King of France, 119
Louis-Philippe, Emperor, 124, 137
Louvre, 96
Lucas, Charles, 250
Lufthansa, 19
Luxeuil monastery, 205

McArdell, James, 250
McCarthy, Cormac, King of Desmond, 225
McCarthy, J.J., 259
McCormick, Liam, 271
McGuinness, Norah, 284
McKenna, Mary, 16

'Mackinnon Children, The' (Hogarth), *120*
Mackintosh, Charles Rennie, 128
Maclise, Daniel, 262
McSweeney, P.L., 269
McWilliam, F.E., 273
'Madame Matisse: The Green Line' (Matisse), 164–5
Madden, Anne, 287
'Madonna in Maestà' (Cimabue), 45, *46*
'Madonna of Burgomeister Meyer, The' (Holbein), 88
'Madonna of the Meadow' (Bellini), 64–5
'Madonna of the Meadow' (Raphael), *82*
'Madonna with the Long Neck' (Parmigianino), *83*
Magdeburg Cathedral, 43, *44*
Magritte, René, 177, 178, 179
'Maid Pouring Milk' (Vermeer), *108*
Maison des Peuples, Brussels, 127, *128*
Malevich, Kasimir, 173, 176
Mall, Cork, 247
Mallarmé, Stéphane, 150
Malton, James, 248
'Man from Inis Mor, The' (Jack B. Yeats), 280
'Man Pointing' (Giacometti), 161
'Man with a Guitar' (Lipchitz), *159*
Manet, Edouard, 123, 140, 142, 144, 145, 147
Mannerism, 68, 75, 77, 78, 99
  in Italy, 83
Mannin, James, 251
Mansart, Jules-Hardouin, 94–5
Mantegna, Andrea, 58, 63–4, 86
Mantua, 62, 102
manuscripts, 31, 34–5
  Anglo-Norman, 240
  early Christian, 205–6
  Gothic, 48–9
  High Christian, 209–11
  Romanesque, 230–31
  Viking invasions, 220–22
Marc, Franz, 167
Maréchal de Saxe, monument to (Pigalle), 114
'Mares and Foals in a River Landscape' (Stubbs), 121
'Marilyn' (Warhol), 183
Marinetti, Filippo, 172
Marlborough, Duke of, 97
Marque, Albert, 164
'Marriage of Aoife and Strongbow, The' (Maclise), 262
'Mars' (Sansovino), 74
'Martin van Nieuwenhove', portrait of (Memling), 67
Martini, Simone, 47–8
'Mary, Countess Howe' (Gainsborough), 120
Masaccio, 47, 52, 58, 59–60, 61, 66, 72
Mathew, Fr T., 261

Matisse, Henri, 164–6, 179
'Maura Rua O'Brien' (unknown artist), 244
Maynooth, Co. Kildare, 259
Mazzola, Francesco (Parmigianino), 83
'Medical Students, 1949-50' (Dillon), 286
McGuire, Edward, 288
Medici, Maria de, 103
Medici family, 52, 61, 62, 67, 83
Medici tomb, Florence (Michelangelo), 73
'Meeting on the Turret Stairs, The' (Burton), 263
megalithic tombs, 189–92
Meilander Madonna, Cologne, *42*
Mellifont, Co. Louth, 228
Memling, Hans, 67
'Memorial to Provost Baldwin' (Hewetson), 249
'Men of the West' (Keating), *280*
'Meninas, Las' (Velázquez), 104–5
metalwork
  Anglo-Norman, 240–41
  Bronze Age, 193–7
  early Christian, 206–7
  High Christian, 211–15
  Iron Age, 199–201
  Romanesque, 231–3
  techniques, 211–12
  Viking invasions, 223–4
Metropolitan School of Art, 271, 279, 281, 282
Michelangelo Buonarroti, 68, 69–70, 72–4, 76, 84, 90, 99, 129–30, 135
  painting, 78–80
Middleton, Colin, 286
Milan Cathedral, 40
Milford, Co. Donegal, 273
Millais, John Everett, 133
Millet, Jean François, 137, 138, 151, 263, 281
Millstreet Parish Church, Co. Cork, 258
'Milo of Crotona Attacked by a Lion' (Puget), 98
Minimal Art, 184
Minimalism, 163
Miro, Joan, 174, 177–8
'Model for a Sculpture' (Baselitz), *164*
Modernism, 128
  architecture, 268–71
Modigliani, Amedeo, 173
'Mona Lisa' (da Vinci), 77, 78
Monasterboice, Co. Louth, 203, 219–20
monasteries, 36, 202–3
  High Christian, 207
  Romanesque, 225–228
  Viking invasions, 216–17
Mondrian, Piet, 173, 176
Monet, Claude, 142, 143–5, 146, 147, 174
'Monkey and Her Baby' (Picasso), 161, *162*
Monkstown Parish Church, Co. Dublin, *258*
Monroe, Marilyn, 183
'Montagne Sainte-Victoire' (Cézanne), *6*, 6–9
Moon, Jeremy, 184

Moone High Cross, 208–9
Moore, Henry, 160, 162
Moreau, Gustave, 153
Morisot, Berthe, 140, 147
Morphey, Garret, 244
Morris, William, 126, 133, 156, 281
'Moulin de la Galette, Le' (Renoir), 146
Mountjoy, Lord, 246
Moylough Belt Shrine, *212*, 214
Muiriedach's Cross, Monasterboice, 203, 219–20
Mullingar Cathedral, 268, 272
Mulready, William, 262
Munch, Edvard, 154, 166
Munich Olympics, 1972, 19
Murillo, Bartolomé Esteban, 105
Murphy, Seamus, 272
Murray O'Laoire Associates, 16
Museum Building, TCD, 260
museums, 9–10
'Mystic Marriage of St Catherine' (Rubens), 102, *103*

'Nadar Elevating Photography to the Height of Art' (Daumier), *137*
Napoleon III, Emperor, 129, 140
Narni, Erasmo da, 57
National Concert Hall, Earlsfort Terrace, 267
National Gallery of Ireland, 10, 267
National Library, Paris, 127
National Museum of Ireland, 10, 267
National Sculpture and Drawing Exhibition (SADE), 274
'Nativity' (Campin), 66
Naumberg Cathedral, *42, 43,* 44
Nelson's Pillar, Dublin, 258
Nendrum, Co. Down, 202
Neo-classical style, 247–9
Neo-Dada, 181
Neo-Expressionism, 185
Neo-Impressionism, 147–52, 164
Neo-Plasticism, 176
Netherlands, The, 92, 176
  Baroque
    painting, 105–10
  High Renaissance
    painting, 89–90
Neue Staatsgalerie, Stuttgart, 158
Neumann, Balthasar, 111–12, 115
Newgrange, Co. Meath, 189–92, 202
Newman, Barnett, 285
Newport, Co. Mayo, 267
Newtown Pery, Limerick, 247
'Night Watch' (Rembrandt), 106
Nolde, Emil, 166
Notre Dame de Paris, 37, 39, 42
Notre-Dame-la-Grande, Poitiers, 35, 36
Nuns' Church, Clonmacnoise, 227, *228*

Ó Bardan, John, 240
Ó Carbry, John, Abbot of Clones, 240
Ó Conaire, Padraic, 272
'Oath of Horatii, The' (David), 118
O'Brien, Catherine, 281
O'Brien, Murtough, 225
O'Carryd, Thomas, 240–41
O'Connell, Daniel, 272
O'Connell, Eilís, 275
O'Connell Monument, Dublin, 260, *261*
O'Connell Monument, Limerick, 261
O'Connor, Andrew, 272
O'Connor, Ciaran, 15
O'Connor, James Arthur, 261–2
O'Connor, Michael, 266
O'Conor Don Monument, 243
O'Conor, Roderic, 265
'Odalisque Wearing Red Trousers' (Matisse), *166*
O'Dea, Cornelius, Bishop of Limerick, 240
O'Donnell family, 205
Office of Public Works, 15–16
Ogham script, 204
Ó Inmainen, Cuduilig, 231
O'Kelly, Desmond R., 269
'Old Guitarist, The' (Picasso), 171
'Old Place, Callan, The' (O'Malley), *287*
Olivetti, 17
'Olympia' (Manet), 140
O'Malley, Tony, 286–7
'On the Threshold of Liberty' (Magritte), 178
O'Neill, Marc, 21, 22
Op Art, 182, 183–4
'Opening of Umbrellas off Gorman Post Road, 11' (Javacheff), 163
'Ophelia' (Millais), 133
Oriental art, 140, 141, 150
Ormond Castle, Co. Tipperary, 238
Orpen, Sir William, 279, 281
Osborne, Walter, 4, 264
O'Shea brothers, 260
Ospedale degli Innocenti, Florence, 54
O'Sullivan, Gerard, 15
Otto II, statue of, 43, *44*

packaging design, 21
Padua, 57, 63
Pain brothers, 258
painting
  Baroque, 99–110
    France, 101–2
    Netherlands, 105–10
    Spain and Flanders, 102–5
  early Renaissance, 58–67
    Florence, 58–62
    outside Florence, 62–5
    outside Italy, 65–7

Gothic, 45–9
High Renaissance, 76–91
  Germany, 86–9
  Netherlands, 89–90
  Spain, 90–1
  Venice, 83–6
Ireland
  eighteenth century, 250–53
  landscape, 252
  nineteenth century, 261–5
  seventeenth century, 243–4
  twentieth century, 278–91
Rococo, 115–23
Romanesque, 34–5
Romantic movement, 130–55
  England, 130–4
  France, 134–54
  Germany, 134
  twentieth century
    before First World War, 164–8
    since Second World War, 178–86
    between the wars, 173–8
Palazzo Farnese, Rome, 99
Palazzo Labia, Venice, 115
Palazzo Publico, Siena, 41
Palazzo Rucellai, Florence, *53*, 55
Palladianism, 245–6
Palladio, Andrea, 69–70, 95, 112, 245
Pantheon, Paris, 111
'Paolina Borghese as Venus' (Canova), 113
paper making, 58–9
Paray-le-Monial, church of, 31
Paris Opera, 127, 129
Parliament House, Dublin, 245
Parliament House, Stormont, 268
Parma, 83
Parmigianino, 83
passage graves, 189–92
'Pastures at Malahide' (Hone the Younger),
  263–4
Patrick, St, 202, 205
Patterson, Simon, 186
Paxton, Joseph, 125
Pazzi Chapel, Santa Croce, Florence, 54, *55*
Pearce, Sir Edward Lovett, 245–6
Pechstein, Max, 166
Penal Laws, 242, 243
pennanular brooches, 212
performance art, 185–6, 277
Perrault (architect), 94
'Perseus' (Cellini), 74
Perugino, 80
Pery Square, Limerick, *247*
Peter Abelard, 36
'Peter getting out of Nick's Pool' (Hockney), *183*
Peters, Matthew William, 251
Petrie, George, 262

Petrie Crown, 200–201, 262
Philip II, King of Spain, 84, 89
Philip IV, King of Spain, 103
Philip the Bold, Duke of Burgundy, 44
Philips, 17
photography, 11
Piano, Renzo, *158*
Picabia, Francis, 175
Picasso, Pablo, 135, 167, 178
  painting, 168–70, 171–2
  sculpture, 161–2
Pietà (Michelangelo), 72
Pigalle, Jean Baptiste, 113–14
Pilon, Germain, 75
'Piping Boy, The' (Hone), 252
Pisa Cathedral and Leaning Tower, 28
Pisano, Andrea, 55–6
Pisano family, 44–5
Pissarro, Camille, 6, 138, 142, 143, 145, 146–8,
  150
P.J. Carroll factory, Dundalk, 269
'Planetary Folklore' (Vasarely), *183*
plasterwork, 254, 266
'Plight' (Beuys), *163*
pointillism, 146, 148
Pollaiuolo, Antonio, 57
Pollock, Jackson, 180
Pompadour, Madame de, 117
Pompidou Centre, Paris, 158
'Pont d'Argenteuil, Le' (Monet), *144*
Pontormo, 83
'Pool of London, The' (Derain), 165
Pop Art, 177, 182–3
Pope, Alexander, 250
'Pope Paul III', portrait of (Titian), 85
porcelain, 266
Porsche, Ferry, 19
'Portinari Altarpiece' (van der Goes), 67
'Portrait Bust of Louis XIV' (Coysevox), 98, *99*
'Portrait of a Young Gentleman in Rome, A'
  (Hamilton), *251*
'Portrait of a Young Lady, A' (Rembrandt), 106
'Portrait of Joseph Roulin' (van Gogh), *152*
'Portrait of Seamus Heaney' (Maguire), 288
'Portrait of the Lough Derg Pike, Life-size with
  Relics' (Cooke), 287, *288*
Post-Impressionism, 147, 152
Post-Modernism, 184, 290
  architecture, 158–9
  sculpture, 164
'Potato Eaters, The' (van Gogh), 151
Poulnabrone dolmen, Kilcooley, *189*
Poussin, Nicolas, 101, 115, 118, 148
Power, Albert, 272
Prendergast, Kathy, 276
Pre-Raphaelites, 126, 133–4, 263
Presley, Elvis, 183

Primaticcio (architect), 71, 72
'Primavera' (Botticelli), 62
'Prodigal Son Feasting, The' (Murillo), 105
product design, 17–19
'Prophet' (Nolde), 166–7
Proudhon, Pierre Joseph, 139
Psalter of Cormac, 230
Puget, Pierre, 98
Pugin, Augustus Welby, 126, 259
Purser, Sarah, 264, 281

Quattrocentro, 52–7
    painting, 58–67
Queen's College, Cork, 260
Queen's House, Greenwich, 95
Quin Abbey, Co. Clare, 236

'Raft of the Medusa, The' (Gericault), 135
'Rain, Steam and Speed — The Great Western
        Railway' (Turner), 133
'Raising of the Armies, The' (le Brocquy), 285
'Rake's Progress, The' (Hogarth), 119
'Ram, The' (Brown), 275
'Rape of the Sabine' (Giambologna), 74, 75
Raphael, 68, 76, 78, 80, 82–3, 84, 90, 99
'Rayonnant' style, 39–40
'Reader, The' (Vuillard), 137
Realism, 136–40, 177
    Irish, 288
Reask Pillar, 204
'Reclining Figure' (Moore), 162
Red House, Bexley Heath, 126, 127
Redon, Odilon, 153
Reformation, 92
Reims Cathedral, 39–40, 43
reliquaries, 35, 49
Rembrandt van Rijn, 106–8, 122, 151, 253
Renaissance. see Early Renaissance; High Renaissance
Renoir, Pierre Auguste, 135, 136, 142, 144, 146
repousse technique, 194, 195
'Rest on the Flight into Egypt' (Cranach), 87
'Resurrection of Christ, The' (della Francesca),
        63
Reynolds, Joshua, 120–21, 250, 252–3
Rietveld, Gerrit, 156
Riley, Bridget, 184
ring forts, 198
Riverstown House, Co. Cork, 254
Robinson, Sir William, 243
Robinson and Keefe, 269
Robinson and McIlvaine, 17
'Rocky Landscape near Aix' (Cezanne), 149
Rococo design
    architecture, 110–13
    painting, 115–23
    sculpture, 113–14

Rodin, Auguste, 129–30
Rogers, Richard, 158
Rolfe, Nigel, 277
Roman Empire, 202, 206
Romanesque design, 27–36, 225–33
    architecture, 28–31
    crafts, 35
    painting, 34–5
    sculpture, 31–4
Romantic movement, 124–55
    architecture, 125–8
    sculpture, 128–30
Rome, 68, 72–4
ROSC Exhibitions, 267, 278, 284, 285, 287, 288
Roscrea Brooch, 223
Roscrea High Cross, 229
Rosse, Lord, 260
Rossetti, Dante Gabriel, 133–4
Rosso (architect), 71, 72
Rothe House, Kilkenny, 238
Rotunda Hospital, Dublin, 246
Rouault, Georges, 165, 167–8
Roubiliac, 114
Rouen Cathedral, 40, 144
Round Towers, 217
Rousseau, Henri, 153
Rousseau, Theodore, 137
Royal Academy, 119, 120, 121, 132, 252, 253
Royal Crescent, Bath, 112
Royal Exchange, Dublin, 249, 250
Royal Hibernian Academy, 262, 263, 267, 279
Royal Hospital, Greenwich, 96
Royal Hospital, Kilmainham, 243, 244
Rubens, Peter Paul, 95, 102–3, 116, 135, 136
Rude, François, 128
Ruisdael, Jacob van, 109
Ruskin, John, 121, 126, 133, 260
Russborough, Co. Wicklow, 246
Russell, George (AE), 279
Russia, 172, 173, 174, 176

'S. Giorgio Maggiore, Venice' (Turner), 133
'Sacking and Red' (Burri), 180
'Sacred Heart, The' (Clarke), 283
'Sir Charles Kemeys-Tynte', portrait of (Frye),
        250, 251
St Andrea, Pistoia, 45
St Angelo, church of, Capua, 34
St Apollinare, church of, Ravenna, 28
St Barthélémy, church of, Liège, 35
St Bavo's Cathedral, Ghent, 65–6
St Brigid's church, Kildare, 203
St Canice's Cathedral, Kilkenny, 234–5, 237
St Carlo alle Quattro Fontane, Rome, 94
St Denis, church of, 37, 49
St Foy, church of, Conques, 28, 30
St Foy, reliquary, 35

'St Francis Receiving the Stigmata' (El Greco), 91
St Gall Gospels, 211
St Gall monastery, 205
  Library, 220, 222
'St George' (Donatello), 57
St George's Church, Hardwicke St, 258
St Giorgio Maggiore, Venice, 70–71
St James's Church, Dublin, 266
'St Jerome in his Study' (Dürer), 86, *87*
St Kevin's Kitchen, Glendalough, 225
St Lachtin's Arm, Shrine of, 231–2
St Macdara's Island, Co. Galway, 203
St Manchan's Shrine, 232, *233*
St Maria delle Grazie, Milan, 77
St Mark's Church, Enniscorthy, 259
St Martial, church of, Limoges, 30
St Martin, church of, Tours, 30
St Mary's Cathedral, Killarney, 259
St Patrick's Bell Shrine, 231
St Patrick's Cathedral, Dublin, 234, 260
St Paul's Cathedral, London, 96, 111
St Peter's, Rome, 69–70, 93–4
St Pierre, church of, Mouissac, 31–2
'St Rufina' (Zurbaran), 105
St Serin, church of, Toulouse, 30
St Stephen's Green, Dublin, 254
St Sulpice, Paris, 136
St Thomas's Church, Dublin, 268
St Valerie, reliquary of, 35
Sainte Chapelle, Paris, 49, 50
Salisbury Cathedral, 40
'Salomé' (Beardsley), 154
Salon, France, 134–6, 142, 143
Salon des Refusés, 140, 142
'Salon in the Rue des Moulins' (Toulouse-
    Lautrec), 152
'Salon of the Princess,' Hôtel de Soubise, 110–11
San Ambrogio, basilica of, Milan, 29
San Marco, Florence, 61–2
San Sepolcro
'Sand Installation' (Aiken), 277
Sansovino, Jacopo, 69, 74
Santa Maria del Fiore, Florence, 54, 55–7
Santa Maria Novella, Florence, 55, 60
Santiago de Compostella, Spain, 29–30, 34
scabbard plates, 199–200
'Scene in the Phoenix Park' (Osborne), 264
Schiele, Egon, 168
Schmidt-Rottluff, Karl, 166
School of Art, Glasgow, 128
'School of Athens' (Raphael), 82, 84
Schröder House, Utrecht (Rietveld), 156
Schwitters, Kurt, 176
Scott, Michael, 269
Scott, Patrick, 285
Scott, Tallon and Walker, 269
Scott, William, 285

'Scream, The' (Munch), 154
Scrovegni, Enrico, 46
sculpture, 15
  abstract and environmental, 273–6
  Baroque, 97–8
  early Renaissance, 55–7
  figurative, 276–7
  Gothic, 41–5
  High Renaissance
    Italy, 72–4
    outside Italy, 76
  Ireland
    Anglo-Norman, 239–40
    early Christian, 204
    eighteenth century, 249–50
    High Christian, 207–9
    Iron Age, 198–9
    twentieth century, 271–7
  nineteenth century, 260–61
  Rococo, 113–14
  Romanesque, 31–4, 228–30
  Romantic movement, 128–30
  seventeenth century, 243
  twentieth century, 159–64
  Viking invasions, 217–20
'Sea Holes' (King), 275
'Second of May 1808, The' (Goya), 122
Second Vatican Council, 271
Second World War, 155, 159, 162, 172, 173,
    176
'Secret Station' (O'Connell), 275–6
'Self-Portrait' (Barry), 253
'Self-Portrait' (Durer), 86
'Self-Portrait with Robert West' (Peters), 251
Semple, John, 258
Semple family, 246
'Serin' (Cronin), 291
Seurat, Georges, 136, 146, 148
Severini, Gino, 172
Sforza, Lodovico, Duke of Milan, 77
'Sharp Back' (O'Connell), 276
Sheppard, Oliver, 271
Sheridan, Noel, 278
shields, bronze, 196–7
'Ship Against the Mew-Stone at the Entrance to
    Plymouth Sound, A' (Turner), *132*
shrines, 212, 215, 224, 231–2, 240
'Shroud 1' (Klein), *182*
'Shuttle' (Riley), *184*
Siddal, Elizabeth, 134
Siena Cathedral, 44–5
silverwork, 255, 266
Sir Hugh Lane Municipal Gallery, Dublin, 247
Sisley, Alfred, 142, 143, 144, 147
Sistine Chapel, 73, 78–80, 84, 99, 130
'Six Mile Bottom' (Stella), *184*
Skellig Michael, 202, 203

Slane Castle, Co. Meath, 254
Sligo Abbey, 243
Slüter, Claus, 44, 45
'Small Rebus' (Rauschenberg), *182*
Smith, David, 162
Smits, Gaspar, 244
Smyth, Edward, 249–50
Smyth, John, 260
Smythson, Robert, 72
'Snow Storm: Hannibal Crossing the Alps'
        (Turner), 132
'Soft Construction with Boiled Beans:
        Premonition of Civil War' (Dali), 178
'Soldiers Playing at Cards' (Leger), *170, 171*
Soufflot, Jacques Germain, 111
sound, in film, 11–12
Souter, Camille, 287
Space Truckers, 12
Spain, 92, 97
   Art Nouveau, 127–8
   Baroque, 102–5
   Gothic architecture, 40
   High Renaissance, 90–91
   Rococo, 121–3
Spanish Civil War, 178
special effects, 12
Speyer Cathedral, Rheinland, 29
Squarcione, Francesco, 63
'Stack' (Prendergast), 276
'Stages of Life, The' (Friedrich), 134
Staigue Fort, Co. Kerry, *198*
stained glass, 264, 266, 281–3
   Gothic, 49–50
   technique, 50
stamp design, 21
Stapleton, Michael, 254
'Steel Mobile' (Frömel), 273, *274*
Steen, Jan, 109
Stella, Frank, 184
Stephens, James, 272
Stephen's Green Shopping Centre, 270
Stephenson, Sam, 269
'Still Life, A' (Claesz), *3*
'Still Life with a Violin and Pitcher' (Braque),
        169
'Still Life with Basket' (Cézanne), 149
Stirling, James, 158
Stone Age, 189–93
   stone carving, 193
   early Christian, 204
   High Christian, 207–9
   Viking invasions, 217–20
'Stonemason's Yard, The' (Canaletto), 116
Storrs, John, 271
Stowe Missal, 211
Straide Friary, Co. Mayo, 239
Strasbourg Cathedral, 43, *44*

'Stream in a Ravine' (Courbet), *139*
Strozzi family, 52
Stubbs, George, 121
'Study for the Death of Sardanapalus'
        (Delacroix), 136
'Study for the Libyan Sybil' (Michelangelo), 80
'Sudden Shower at Ohashi Bridge at Ataka'
        (Hiroshige), 141
Suger, Abbot, 37, 49
sun discs, 194
Sunlight Chambers, Essex Quay, 16
'Sunshine' Homes, Dollymount, 269
'Supper at Emmaus, The' (Caravaggio), 100, *101*
'Suprematist Composition' (Malevich), 176
surface qualities, 180–81
Surrealism, 161, 177–8, *179*
   Irish, 288
'Surrender of Breda, The' (Velázquez), 104–5
Sutherland, Graham, 179
Sutton Hoo burial, *27*
'Sweeney falls to Captivity' (Bourke), 289
Swift, Jonathan, 250
'Swing, The' (Fragonard), 117, *118*
Switzerland, 175
Sydney Opera House (Utzon), 158
Symbolism, 134, 153–4, 282
Synthetic Cubism, 169–70
Syon House, Middlesex, 112, *113*

'Table, The' (Bonnard), 153
'Tain, The' (Kinsella), 285
'Taking of Christ, The' (Caravaggio), 100
Tallon, Ronald, 269
Tandragee idol, 199
tapestries, 49
Tara, Co. Meath, 195
Tara Brooch, 212, *213*, 215, 223
Tassel House, Brussels, 127
'Tea Pot' (Brandt), *157*
Tedavnet, Co. Monaghan, 194
telephone, 18–19
Telford, Thomas, 125
'Tempest, The' (Giorgione), 84
Tempietto, S. Pietro in Montorio, Rome, 68–9
Temple Bar, Dublin, 16, 270
Temple Finhgin, Clonmacnoise, 225, *226*
'Third Class Carriage, The' (Daumier), *138*
Thomas, Sir Alfred Brumwell, 268
Thomas Aquinas, 36
Thornhill, Sir James, 119
Thornley, Sir Arnold, 268
'Three Dancers' (Picasso), 171, *172*
'Three Graces' (Pilon), 75
'Three Studies for a Crucifixion' (Bacon), 179,
        180
'Thunderstorm: The Frightened Wagoner'
        (O'Connor), 261

Thynne, Sir John, 72
Tiepolo, Giambattista, 112, 115
'Tiger Devouring a Gazelle' (Barye), 128, *129*
Tintoretto, 85, 90
Titian, 65, 84–5, 90, 103–4, 104–5, 140
Toledo, 90
'Tooth Hunting' (Goya), 122
torcs, 195
Torres, Felix Gonzales, 164
Toulouse-Lautrec, Henri de, 152
'Towards an Image of W.B. Yeats' (le Brocquy), *285*
Town Hall, Bruges, 41
Townley Hall, Co. Louth, 258
'Toy-Seller, The' (Mulready), 262
Trent, Council of, 92
Très Riches Heures, Les, 48–9
'Tribute Money, The' (Masaccio), 60
Trinity Church, Glendalough, 217
Trinity College Dublin, 247, 260, 269–70, *270*
'Triumph at the Name of Jesus' (Gaulli), *93*
Troyon, Constant, 137
trumpets, bronze, 197, 200
Tuam High Cross, 229
Tuohy, Patrick, 281
Túr Gloine, An, 264, 281–3
Turgesius, 216
'Turkish Bath, The' (Ingres), *135*
Turner, J.M.W., 125, 132–3, 144
Turoe Stone, 198–9
'Two Ballet Dancers in a Dressing Room' (Degas), 145
'Two Gentlemen and a Lady' (Watteau), *117*
'Two Men: Shadows on Yellow Background' (Beck), *11*
'Two Women Running on the Beach' (Picasso), 171

U2, 20
Uccello, Paolo, 58, 60–61
Ulster Bank, College Green, 259
'Uncertainty of the Poet' (de Chirico), *178*
uniforms, 22–3
'Unique Forms of Continuity in Space' (Boccioni), *160*
Unite d'Habitation, Marseilles (Le Corbusier), 157
United States, 179, 184
architecture, 155–6
sculpture, 162
universities, 36
University College Dublin, 269, 270
Earlsfort Terrace, 267
University Museum of Natural History, Oxford, 126
'Untitled Installation' (Gober), *186*
'Untitled' (Torres), *164*

Urbino, 53, 62, 63
Utzon, Jorn, 158

van der Goes, Hugo, 67
van der Rohe, Mies, Ludwig, 156, 157, 269
van der Weyden, Rogier, 66–7
Van Dongen, 166
van Duesburg, Theo, 176
van Dyck, Anthony, 103–4, 120
van Eyck, Jan, 65–6, 105
van Gogh, Vincent, 136, 138, 141, 144, 147, 149, 150–52, 164, 265
van Nost, John, the Younger, 249
Vanbrugh, Sir John, 96, 97
Vasarely, Victor, 183
Vasari, 52, 59, 68
Vauxcelles, 164
Vaux-le-Vicomte, France, 95
Velázquez, Diego, 104–5, 121, 140
Venice, 53, 58, 62, 115–16
architecture, 69–70
High Renaissance in, 83–6
painting, 64–5
'Venus and Anchises' (Carracci), 99
'Vere Foster Family, The' (Orpen), 279
Vermeer, Jan, 108, 109
Veronese, Paolo, 85–6
Verrocchio, Andrea del, 57, 58, 76
Versailles, 95, 110, *111*
Vézelay Abbey, 31, 32
video, 13
Vien (painter), 118
Vierpyl, Simon, 247
Vierzehnheiligen Abbey, 111, *112*
'View of Powerscourt Waterfall, A' (Barret), 252
'View of the Piazza San Marco' (Canaletto), 116
Vignola (architect), 93
Viking invasions, 215–24, 225
Villa Barbaro, Maser, 71
Villa Savoye, Poissy (Le Corbusier), *157*
'Village School, The' (Steen), 109
'Ville d'Avray' (Corot), *137*
Vinci, Leonardo da, 54, 57, 69, 80
painting, 76–8
'Virgin of the Rocks' (da Vinci), 77
'Vision after the Sermon, The' (Gauguin), 150
Vitruvius, 53, 95
Vlamink, Maurice, 165
Volkswagen, 19
Vollard (dealer), 149
Voltaire, 114
'Voltaire' (Houdon), 114
Vuillard, Édouard, 153

'Waiting to go on the Canal' (Souter), 287
'Waking Up' (Gale), 288, *289*
'Walpurgis Night' (Clarke), 283

War of Independence, 267, 278
Warhol, Andy, 183
Warren, Michael, 274
Washington, George, 114
Waterford, 255
Waterford crystal, *14*
'Water-lilies' (Monet), *145*
Watson, James, 250
Watteau, Jean Antoine, 116–17
'We' (Gilbert and George), 186
Webb, Aston, 267
Webb, Philip, 126, 127
Wejchert, Andrzej 270
West, Robert, 251, 254
Westminster Abbey, London, 40, 41
Westport, Co. Mayo, 254
Wexford, 271
Wide Streets Commission, Dublin, 245, 246–7
'Wild Geese,' 242
Wilde, Oscar, 154
Wilford, Michael, 158
'William Somerset Maugham' (Sutherland), 179
Wilson, Ian, *12*
Wilton Diptych, 48
Wilton House, 96
Wincklemann, 118
'Window' (Delaunay), *175*
Wolfe Tone, Theobald, 276
'Woman II 1952' (de Kooning), *181*
'Woman with a Pierre Soulages' (Ballagh), 288

'Woman with Baby Carriage' (Picasso), 161, *162*
'Woman/Waterlilies' (Bewick), 290
'Women in the Garden' (Monet), *143*
'Women of Belfast' (McWilliam), 273
'Women of Tahiti on the Beach' (Gauguin), 150
women sculptors, 275–6
Wood, John, the Younger, 112
Wood, Sancton, 258
Woodward, Benjamin, 260
work of art
  method of examining, 4–9
'Worker Picture' (Schwitters), *177*
Wren, Sir Christopher, 96
Wright, Frank Lloyd, 156
Wright, Joseph 'of Derby,' 121
Wurzburg, Prince Archbishop of, 112, 115
Wyatt, James, 254

Yeats, Jack B., 279–80, 281
Yeats, John B., 264, 279
Yeats, W.B., 272, 279, *285*
'Young Fisherboy of Schevenigen' (Hals), 107
'Young Girl with Guitar' (Braque), 170
'Your Gaze Hits the Side of my Face' (Kruger),
  185
Youth Club, Möglingen, 159

Zola, Émile, 140, 148
Zurbaran, Francisco de, 105

ACKNOWLEDGMENTS

Where possible museums and galleries are credited in the captions which accompany the illustrations. The following additional acknowledgments relate to copyright holders and suppliers of the illustrations used in the book.

© ADAGP, Paris & DACS, London 1998 Alberto Giacometti 6,96; © ADAGP, Paris & DACS, London 1998: Andre Derain 6,107; © ADAGP, Paris & DACS, London 1998: Constantin Brancusi 6,92; © ADAGP, Paris & DACS, London 1998: Edouard Vuillard 6,75; © ADAGP, Paris & DACS, London 1998: Fernand Leger 6,123; © ADAGP, Paris & DACS, London 1998: Georges Braque 6,118 6,121; © ADAGP, Paris & DACS, London 1998: Georges Rouault 6,115; © ADAGP, Paris & DACS, London 1998: Jean Dubuffet 6,150; © ADAGP, Paris & DACS, London 1998: Joan Miro 6,141; © ADAGP, Paris & DACS, London 1998: Marc Chagall 6,131; © ADAGP, Paris & DACS, London 1998: Marcel Duchamp 6,94 © ADAGP, Paris & DACS, London 1998: Pierre Bonnard 6,74; © ADAGP, Paris & DACS, London 1998: Rene Magritte 6,143; © ADAGP, Paris & DACS, London 1998: Victor Vasarely 6,158; © ADAGP, Paris & DACS, London 1998: Wassily Kandinsky 6,113 6,132 6,133; © ADAGP, Paris & DACS, London 1998: Yves Klein 6,154; A.F. Kersting Architectural Photographer 3,4 3,12 3,15 3,32 3,37 3,62 5,8 5,46 5,47 5,48 5,50 5,58; Aerofilms 8,42 9,30; Aidan O'Sullivan (Photos) 2,8 3,26 5,45 7,10 7,35 8,1 8,18 8,48 8,50 9,7 9,26 9,27 9,28 9,29 9,31 9,33 9,34 9, 9,36 9,41 9,45 9,50 10,32 11,1 11,2 11,5 11,6 11,7 11,9 11,10 11,24 11,29 11,31 11,35 11,37a 11,37b 11,38 11,42 11,43 11,49 11,73; AKG, London 3,18 3,46 3,47 4,83 6,68 6,113; An Post 2,18; © Andy Warhol Foundation for the Visual Arts, The, Inc./ARS, NY & DACS, London 1998: Andy Warhol 6,157; Angelo Hornak Photograph Library 5,9 5,10 5,11 6,5 6,7 6,10 6,85; Anne Madden 11,89; Anne Yeats and Michael Yeats 11,62 11,63 11,64; Anthony Caro Studios, London 6,100; Anthony d'Offay Gallery, London 6,165; Arcaid 6,6 6,8 6,9 6,80 6,81 6,83 6,84 6,86 6,87 6,88; © ARS NY &

DACS, London 1998: Jackson Pollock 6,148; © ARS NY: Emil Nolde 6,112; Art House, Multimedia Centre for the Arts, Dublin 11,36; Bank of Ireland 11,32 11,46 11,47; Barbara V. Mitchell 11,61; Board of Trinity College Dublin 8,23 8,24 8,25 8,26 8,52 8,53 8,54 8,55 8,56 9,13 9,47 10,20 11,8 11,34; Bórd Fáilte 9,22 9,39 9,40 10,9 10,11 10,12 10,13 10,14 11,39 11,40; Brian Bourke/Taylor Galleries 11,95; Brian King 11,50; Brian O'Halloran 8,16; Bridgeman Art Library, London/New York 1,5 3,1 3,2 3,20 3,25 3,64 4, 2 4,3 4,4 4,5 4,6 4,7 4,8 4,12 4,16 4,18 4,20 4,21 4, 4,29 4,33 4,36 4,42 4,44 4,47 4,48 4,49 4,50 4,51 4,54 4,55 4,56 4,57 5,48 4,63 4,65 4,66 4,67 4,69 4,71 4,72 4,73 4,77 4,79 4,80 4,84 4,86 4,90 4,91 5,6 5,7 5,12 5,13 5,14 5, 5,16 5,17 5,23 5,24 5,25 5,26 5,27 5,28 5,37 5,44 5,49 5,51 5,53 5,61 5,63 5,64 5,66 5,67 5,68 5,70 5,74 6,2 6,4a 6,4b 6,11 6,14 6,26 6,27 6,28 6,32 6,37 6,44 6,45 6,47 6,48 6,52 6,59 6,62 6,65 6,71 6,72 6,73 6,76 6,77 6,79 6,91 6,92 6,98 6,108 6,118 6,125 6,128 6,130 6,137 6,163; Additional credits on the following transparencies supplied by Bridgeman Art Library: 3,25 reproduced with special authorisation of the City of Bayeaux, 4,2 & 4,6: K and B News Foto, Florence, 4,3: Fratelli Fabbri, Milan, 4,44: Francesco Turio Bohm, 4,49: Ackermann and Johnson Ltd, London, 4,66, 4,67, 4,69 & 4,71: Vatican Museums and Galleries, 5,49 & 5,51: John Bethell, 6,26: Manchester City Art Galleries; British Library, The 8,27 9,14; Bridget Riley 6,159; Burri Foundation, Perugia 6,149; Caisse Nationale des Monuments Historiques et des Sites (Paris) 3,10; Camille Souter 11,88; Central Bank of Ireland 11,33; Charles Harper 11,97; Christie's Images, London 6,82 6,162; Christopher Hill Photographic 2,9; Clive Hicks Photo Library of Architecture 3,3 3,6 3,8 3,9 3,11 3,13 3,16: and Landscape 3,17 3,19 3,30 3,31 3,33 3,34 3,35 3,36 3,40 3,41 3,42 3,43 3,44 3,45 3,48 3,49 3,51 3,63; Collection of Andrea Rosen, New York/Peter Muscato 6,105; Collections 6,3; © DACS 1998: Carlo Carra 6,129; © DACS 1998: George Grosz 6,116; © DACS 1998: Giacomo